Moral Philosophy through the Ages

James Fieser
University of Tennessee at Martin

Mayfield Publishing Company
Mountain View, California
London • Toronto

To my twin daughters,
Emma and Michelle

Library of Congress Cataloging-in-Publication Data
Fieser, James.
  Moral philosophy through the ages / James Fieser.
    p. cm.
  Includes index.
  ISBN-13: 978-0-7674-1298-8
  ISBN-10: 0-7674-1298-2

  1. Ethics. I. Title.

BJ1012 .F499 2000
171'.09—dc21   00-028443

Manufactured in the United States of America
10   9   8   7   6   5   4

Mayfield Publishing Company
1280 Villa Street
Mountain View, CA 94041

Sponsoring editor, Kenneth King; production editor, Julianna Scott Fein; manuscript editor, Thomas L. Briggs; design manager, Violeta Díaz; text and cover designer, Linda Robertson; cover illustration, Claude Monet, *Boulevard des Capucines*. 1873. Oil on canvas. 31¾'' x 23¹³⁄₁₆''. The Nelson-Atkins Museum of Art, Kansas City, Missouri. Purchase: The Kenneth A. and Helen F. Spencer Foundation Acquisition Fund. Photography by Robert Newcombe (1/1998); manufacturing manager, Randy Hurst. The text was set in 10/12.5 Sabon by G&S Typesetters, Inc., and printed on acid-free 45# Highland Plus by Malloy Lithographing, Inc.

Preface

On Halloween night in 1997, an 11-year-old boy from Michigan named Nathan Abraham shot to death a young man outside a convenience store. Dressed in his Halloween costume at the time, Abraham fired a .22-caliber rifle from about 200 feet away. Abraham claimed that he was aiming at trees and accidentally hit his victim, but prosecutors were not convinced. Abraham apparently had had many run-ins with the police and had even bragged to his friends that he planned to shoot someone. Tried as an adult, Abraham became one of the youngest murder defendants in the United States. He was eventually found guilty of second-degree murder.

We are all disturbed by stories of violent juvenile crimes such as this, which are becoming all too frequent. They suggest that something has gone seriously wrong in our society, that we've lost our ability to instill a sense of moral responsibility in our children. Who is to blame for the problem? How can we fix it? Although we are not likely to find any quick and easy answers to these questions, we can nevertheless find some help by turning to moral philosophy. The subject of moral philosophy involves systematizing, defending, and recommending concepts of right and wrong behavior. As far back in civilization as we find writing, we find people struggling with ethical questions. At one point in Western civilization—about 600 BCE—philosophers began offering theories that clarified the source and content of our moral obligations. This book traces some of the major themes that have emerged in the history of Western moral philosophy, from the earliest days to the present.

Moral philosophers offer a range of theories to explain the nature and content of our moral obligations. Some theories—commonly called *metaethical* theories—try to explain where morality comes from and what psychologically takes place when we make moral judgments. Does society create morality? Is morality a fixed and objective feature of the cosmos? Am I doing anything more than expressing my feelings when I make moral judgments? Metaethical theories attempt to address these questions. Other theories—commonly called *normative* theories—try to tell us exactly what our moral obligations are. According to some of these theories, there is a specific list of foundational duties that we need to follow. Other theories maintain that a single principle encapsulates our obligations, such as that we should maximize the greatest good for the greatest number of people. Still others maintain that our obligations are grounded in a group of virtuous habits that we develop, such as courage, temperance, justice, and wisdom.

The variety and complexity of both metaethical and normative ethical theories is sometimes daunting. If we study and come to understand one theory, we are likely to find that the very next theory criticizes the prior theory. And this new theory, in turn, is attacked by the next theory. So, not only are the theories themselves challenging, but we face a new challenge in trying to see how these competing theories illuminate the nature and content of our moral obligations. In writing this book, I've taken measures to make the reader's philosophical exploration of ethics easier—or at least less overwhelming—than it otherwise might be. I've minimized the use of technical vocabulary. I've also tied each of the chapters to matters of practical moral concern. The opening of each chapter discusses some concrete ethical issue, such as suicide, capital punishment, or abortion, which helps establish the importance of the chapter's topic and often serves as a consistent example for discussion throughout the chapter.

When discussing the various ethical theories, I didn't attempt to evaluate them all from the vantage point of a single tradition, such as the utilitarian tradition. To do so would be cumbersome and risk forcing theories into molds they don't fit. Instead, I present the various theories in a positive light, defend them against key criticisms if possible, revise them if necessary, and find some central feature of the theory that illuminates the nature of morality. In the final chapter, I integrate as many of these theories as possible into a single coherent system, which I call an *ethical supertheory*. I also argue that each ethical theory can have value in our common moral lives by helping us visualize our moral obligations.

There are many possible topics and figures that an ethics book might cover, and it's impossible for any single text to adequately touch upon everything of value. The issues selected here are restricted to the Western philosophical tradition that began in ancient Greece and developed in the countries of western Europe and, later, in America. They are also the issues that philosophers today commonly find interesting. Although scholars of moral philosophy today will certainly have their own lists of favorite issues, the ones presented here should have a common appeal.

Introductory books in ethics are typically structured in one of two ways. Some are arranged topically and focus on major themes and issues, such as cultural relativism, virtue, or duty. Although it is interesting to discuss morality from a topical standpoint, the drawback to this approach is that writers often sacrifice historical context and sometimes even present theories that no traditional philosopher actually ever proposed. Other ethics textbooks are structured historically and present a continuous chronological sequence of theories, beginning in ancient Greece and ending in present times. Although this approach preserves historical context, many historically-oriented ethics books are tedious to read and give us too many details about a philosopher's theory.

This book takes a middle ground between the topical and historical approaches. The chapters are topically arranged, but they preserve the flow of history in two ways. First, each chapter explains the historical development of the topic under consideration. Many ethical topics have very ancient origins, and by highlighting their history we can better grasp how moral philosophers fall into specific traditions. Second, most chapters focus on a specific famous philosopher who championed a particular tradition, such as Aristotle, Locke, or Kant, and the chapters are chronologically ordered based on when these key philosophers lived. Although chronologically ordered, the chapters in this book are conceptually self-contained, which allows them to be read in any order. To achieve the full benefit of their historical sequence, though, they should be read in the order presented. Many of the sections and subsections in the chapters are also conceptually self-contained discussions. So, a reader who skips some sections will not necessarily be at a loss to understand the remaining sections.

I would like to thank those who reviewed the manuscript: John R. Danley, Southern Illinois University, Edwardsville; Paul Newberry, California State University, Bakersfield; Curtis H. Peters, Indiana University Southeast; and Michael F. Wagner, University of San Diego. I also wish to thank friends and colleagues who have generously offered advice on this book's contents. Alphabetically, they are John Danley, Ken King, Norman Lillegard, Matthew McCormick, James Otteson, Gregory Pence, Louis Pojman, and Laura Roberts.

Study Questions

1. What is "metaethics," and what are the main questions that metaethical theories try to answer?
2. What is "normative ethics," and what are the main questions that normative theories try to answer?

Contents

1

Cultural Relativism

Introduction

In the early twentieth century, journalist Robert L. Ripley traveled around the world gathering stories of strange rituals, which he published in his popular newspaper column "Believe It or Not." Our fascination with bizarre practices of other cultures is no less prominent today. Some foreign practices amuse us, such as that of Japanese men who tattoo their entire bodies. Others make us squeamish, such as a Latin American culinary practice of eating handfuls of live bugs in tortillas. Still other foreign cultural practices, however, make us morally indignant. One of these is female genital mutilation (FGM), which is common in East African countries and parts of the Near East. This practice involves removing portions of a young girl's genitals, including her clitoris and labia. Social scientists estimate that over 100 million women alive today have had this operation performed. An article published by UNICEF describes the situation for one 6-year-old girl and her sympathetic aunt:

> The lights are dim and the voices quiet. Tension fills the room where Nafisa, a six-year-old Sudanese girl, lies on a bed in the corner. Her aunt, 25-year-old Zeinab, watches protectively as her niece undergoes the procedure now known as female genital mutilation (FGM), formerly called female circumcision. In this procedure, performed without anaesthesia, a girl's external sexual organs are partially or totally cut away. Zeinab does not approve. For the past year she has been trying to persuade her mother and sister to spare Nafisa from the procedure. She lost the battle with her family, but she will stay at her niece's side. She watches Nafisa lying quietly, brave and confused, and remembers her own experience. Zeinab underwent the procedure twice. At six years old she had the more moderate form of FGM, called Sunni, in which the covering of the clitoris is removed. When she was 15 the older women of her family insisted she have the Pharaonic form, which involves removal of the entire clitoris and the labia and stitching together of the vulva, leaving just a small hole for elimination of urine and menstrual blood. Zeinab still remembers the pain, the face of the women performing the procedure, the sound of her flesh being cut. She also remembers bleeding and being sick for weeks.

The purpose of FGM is to reduce sexual drive and thus assure a woman's virginity prior to marriage and her fidelity after marriage. FGM is performed as a rite of passage, sometimes involuntarily, in unsterile conditions and without the aid of painkillers and antibiotics. Ironically, older women of the community, who themselves underwent it in their youth, perform the procedure. Although this practice is cultural rather than religious, it occurs predominantly in Muslim countries.

In North America, we find FGM grossly immoral, and there is widespread public outcry against cultures that endorse this practice. However, East African defenders of the practice charge that American culture has degenerated to the point that promiscuity, infidelity, and childbirth outside of marriage are acceptable behaviors. By guarding against such sexual misconduct, their culture, so they claim, remains on morally higher ground. From a philosophical perspective, these foreign practices directly challenge our traditionally held moral views, and they make us wonder whether their morality or immorality reduces to mere social convention.

For centuries, moral philosophers have reflected on the philosophical problems raised by clashing social values. The key question is whether moral values exist independently of human social creations. **Cultural relativism** is the view that societies create their own traditions, pass them along from one generation to another, and continually reinforce them through rewards and punishments. In this view, morality is a distinctly human invention, so it makes no sense to look for a foundation of morality outside of human social approval. This is true for the East African practice of female genital mutilation, as well as for the American condemnation of the practice. This isn't simply an issue of anthropological curiosity concerning how different people and cultures view morality. Instead, it is an issue of whether *my* and *your* specific moral obligations are grounded in nothing other than cultural approval.

Cultural relativism is a component of a broader moral theory called **moral relativism**, which holds more generally that moral values are *human* inventions. This broader theory includes both (1) **individual relativism**—namely, that each person creates his or her own moral standards—and (2) cultural relativism—namely, that social cultures create moral standards. We will focus here on the theory of cultural relativism, looking at its historical development and the key arguments against it.

Classic Cultural Relativism

The issue of cultural relativism was one of the first hotly debated issues in Western moral philosophy, and the views of early cultural relativists remain even today largely unchanged.

Xenophanes and the Greek Skeptics   One of the earliest accounts of cultural relativism was offered by the ancient Greek philosopher **Xenophanes** (570–475 BCE). Although his writings are lost to us, enough quotations from his works survive that we can gain a general view of his position. Xenophanes focuses specifically on the culturally relative nature of *religious* beliefs, rather than ethical beliefs per se. In two fragments, he explains how different ethnic groups depict their deities differently:

> Ethiopians say that their gods are flat-nosed and dark, Thracians that theirs are blue-eyed and red-haired.

> If oxen and horses and lions had hands and were able to draw with their hands and do the same things as men, horses would draw the shapes of gods to look like horses and oxen to look like ox, and each would make the gods' bodies have the same shape as they themselves had.

In the first of these passages, Xenophanes notes that different ethnic groups portray the gods with physical attributes that are unique to their own people. In the second passage, he speculates that if animals could draw they would make the gods look like animals. Xenophanes' point is that our own cultural experiences shape the things that we say about the gods, and our religious views aren't really objective descriptions of the gods themselves.

Although Xenophanes' comments are confined to views of gods, it isn't much of a stretch to extend this reasoning to ethical issues and see that morality is also culturally relative. Greek historians after Xenophanes fueled the discussion of cultural relativism in both religion and ethics by providing graphic examples of differing cultural practices in various civilizations of the day. After surveying the traditions of different regions, the Greek historian Heroditus (484–425 BCE) concluded, "Everyone without exception believes his own native customs, and the religion he was brought up in, to be the best." Heroditus's point is that, not only do we all adopt the religious and ethical value systems of our respective cultures, but we typically go a step further and denounce foreign value systems as inferior to our own.

The next big step in the development of cultural relativism was made by ancient Greek philosophers of the skeptical tradition, who were directly influenced by Xenophanes. Once again, we only have sketchy information about the earliest philosophers in this tradition. The founder was a charismatic and original moral philosopher named **Pyrrho** (c. 365–275 BCE), who had several loyal followers but who wrote nothing himself. In one of his few surviving statements, Pyrrho argues that in moral matters we cannot determine whether anything is truly good or bad, and so we must suspend judgment.

As the skeptical tradition continued, followers of Pyrrho developed this line of reasoning, and eventually the views of the skeptics were systematically written down by Greek philosopher **Sextus Empiricus** (fl. 200 CE). Sextus presents the definitive statement of cultural relativism. Drawing on anthropological data compiled by earlier Greek historians, Sextus gives example after example of moral standards that differ from one society or culture to another. These include attitudes about homosexuality, incest, cannibalism, human sacrifice, the killing of the elderly, infanticide, theft, and consumption of animal flesh.

Sextus believes that this **social diversity** in and of itself is a good reason to adopt cultural relativism. The differing cultural attitudes are quite extreme, and

Sextus clearly wants to shock us into thinking seriously about this diversity. Here is his account of differing attitudes concerning the treatment of corpses:

> Some wrap the dead up completely and then cover them with earth, thinking that it is impious to expose them to the sun; but the Egyptians take out their entrails and embalm them and keep them above ground with themselves. The fish-eating tribes of the Ethiopians cast them into the lakes, there to be devoured by the fish; the Hyrcanians expose them as prey to dogs, and some of the Indians to vultures. And they say that some of the Troglodytes take the corpse to a hill, and then after tying its head to its feet cast stones upon it amidst laughter, and when they have made a heap of stones over it they leave it there. And some of the barbarians slay and eat those who are over sixty years old, but bury in the earth those who die young. Some burn the dead; and of these some recover and preserve their bones, while others show no care but leave them scattered about. And they say that the Persians impale their dead and embalm them with niter, after which they wrap them round in bandages. (*Outlines of Pyrrhonism*, 3.24)

Sextus concludes that "the skeptic, seeing so great a diversity of usages, suspends judgment as to the natural existence of anything good or bad or (in general) fit or unfit to be done." That is, we should doubt the existence of an independent and universal standard of morality, and instead regard moral values as the result of cultural preferences.

Sextus and other Pyrrhonian skeptics have a particular goal in mind in advancing cultural relativism. That goal is personal tranquility. Suppose I believe that there exists a fixed and objective standard of truth; suppose further that this standard guides all my actions. Since I see myself on the side of moral truth, I become morally outraged by those who don't follow these moral standards. Ultimately, I make myself miserable through my extreme convictions. However, once I seriously reflect on the wide diversity of cultural practices that Sextus describes, I will be more inclined to see that my own cultural practices are rooted in social customs. I will then get off my moral high horse and be content to accept the moral diversity that I see in other cultures.

Later Defenders of Cultural Relativism   Christian philosophers of the Middle Ages harshly rejected the skepticism and cultural relativism of their Greek predecessors. According to most medieval Christian philosophers, moral values are eternal principles, mandated by God and binding on all humans. Although some "heathen" cultures might consistently engage in bizarre customs, such as ceremonial prostitution, medieval philosophers argued that these practices are immoral no matter how widespread they are. This Christian view of morals was finally challenged by skeptically minded Enlightenment philosophers, who were inspired by Sextus Empiricus's writings.

French philosopher **Michel Eyquem de Montaigne** (1533–1592) was among the first to resurrect the skeptical views of Sextus. Montaigne wholeheartedly endorsed Sextus's cultural relativism, which he articulates in an essay entitled "Of Custom, and That we should not Easily Change a Law Received" (1580). In this essay, Montaigne describes dozens of strange cultural practices from foreign countries, focusing especially on sexually-related practices. In one culture, unmarried women "may prostitute themselves to as many as they please," and when they get pregnant, they can lawfully abort their fetuses "in the sight of everyone." In another culture, male guests at weddings are invited to sleep with the bride even before the groom does, "and the greater number of them there is, the greater is her honor and the opinion of her ability and strength." Montaigne describes one culture in which gender roles are strangely reversed: Houses of prostitution contain young men "for the pleasure of women," and "wives go to war as well as the husbands."

In addition to sexually related practices, Montaigne lists others from almost every aspect of life:

> [There are societies] where they boil the bodies of their dead, and afterwards pound them to a pulp, which they mix with their wine, and drink it; where the most coveted burial is to be eaten by dogs . . . where they live in that rare and unsociable opinion of the mortality of the soul; . . . where women urinate standing and men squatting; where they send their blood in a token of friendship . . . where the children nurse for four years, and often twelve; . . . where they circumcise the women; . . . in another it is reputed a holy duty for a man to kill his father at a certain age; . . . where children of seven years old endured being whipped to death, without changing expression . . . (*Essays*, "Of Custom")

Montaigne concludes that custom has the power to shape every possible kind of cultural practice. Although we pretend that morality is a fixed feature of nature, morality, too, is formed through custom: "The laws of conscience, which we pretend to be derived from nature, proceed from custom." Montaigne argues further that peer pressure is so strong that we automatically approve of our society's customs: "As everyone has an inward veneration for the opinions and manners approved of and received among his own people, no one can, without very great reluctance, depart from them, or apply himself to them without approval."

Almost two centuries later, Scottish philosopher **David Hume** (1711–1776) reiterated Sextus's skeptical view of cultural relativism. Hume presents a fictitious dialog in which the leading character argues that many moral practices are accepted by some cultures, but condemned by others; these include homosexual pedophilia, adultery, infanticide, and euthanasia. The leading character in Hume's dialog boldly concludes that "fashion, vogue, custom, and law [are] the chief foundation of all moral determinations."

Cultural relativism received another boost from sociologists of the late nineteeth and early twentieth centuries. Perhaps the best example is American sociologist **William Graham Sumner** (1840–1910). In his classic work *Folkways* (1906), Sumner argues that the morality of a given society simply amounts to the folkways or traditions of that society. For Sumner, theories that try to ground morality in some absolute standard are misguided:

> In the folkways, whatever is, is right. . . . When we come to the folkways we are at the end of our analysis. . . . Therefore rights can never be "natural" or

"God-given," or absolute in any sense. The morality of a group at a time is the sum of the taboos and prescriptions in the folkways by which right conduct is defined. (*Folkways*, 1.31)

Sumner argues that there are no exceptions to this: A society's values concerning slavery, abortion, killing of the elderly, and cannibalism only reflect that society's traditional taboos and prescriptions.

One of the most articulate philosophical defenders of cultural relativism in recent years was Australian philosopher J. L. Mackie (1917–1981). Like his skeptical predecessors, Mackie believes that moral values vary from culture to culture. Also like his predecessors, he believes that there simply are no objective moral values, a view that he calls **moral skepticism**. For Mackie, this means that morality is something that we invent: "Morality is not to be discovered but to be made: we have to decide what moral views to adopt, what moral stands to take." From Xenophanes on through Mackie, the key points associated with the tradition of cultural relativism are these:

- *Cultural relativism:* Moral values are created by society.
- *Social diversity:* Moral values vary from culture to culture.
- *Moral skepticism:* There is no objective moral truth.

The Argument from Social Diversity

A running theme among cultural relativists is that values differ from society to society, and the best explanation for such variation is that societies simply create their own values. We can express this intuition more formally in the argument here:

1. Morally significant values differ from society to society.
2. These differing moral values are grounded either in objective moral standards or only in social custom.
3. It is difficult to explain how these differing moral values are grounded in objective moral standards.
4. Therefore, it is more reasonable to believe that these differing moral values are grounded in social custom.

To understand this argument we need to consider it premise by premise. Premise 1 advocates the view of social diversity, that is, the view that different cultures in fact have different moral values. Defenders of this claim—from Sextus to Mackie—believe that this is a matter of factual observation. We can directly see differences in values among various cultures. For example, Sumner argues that our observations will clearly reveal that even taboos against incest are "by no means universal or uniform, or attended by the same intensity of repugnance." Similarly, in our own day, we directly observe that many East African cultures favor the practice of female genital mutilation; by contrast, in North America, we plainly abhor the practice. If we make accurate observations, then we must accept the fact of social diversity for at least some morally significant values.

If we grant premise 1, we can next consider the other two premises of this argument. Premise 2 maintains that there are two contending ways of understanding where moral values come from. Values are grounded in either (1) an objective standard that is independent of human society or (2) social custom. Over the centuries, moral objectivists have proposed a variety of objective standards of morality. For example, some objectivists hold that moral standards are grounded in eternal truths, or in laws of nature, or in God's commands—in some more stable level of reality beyond mere human social custom. Premise 2 then, is at least a plausible way of seeing the possible foundations of moral standards: Either they are grounded in a more stable level of reality *beyond* social custom, or they are grounded *in* social custom.

Finally, premise 3 states that it is hard to see how moral standards are grounded in an objective reality if they change from culture to culture. Moral objectivists believe that our objectively grounded moral beliefs should shape our cultural practices. For example, we condemn stealing in our culture because some objective standard tells us that stealing is wrong. However, when we consider the wide variety of conflicting moral values in societies around the world, it does not seem reasonable that these all are grounded in a universal and objective standard. On face value, then, premise 3 also seems credible.

The conclusion that we draw, then, is that moral values are grounded in social custom, which—compared to moral objectivism—more reasonably explains the moral diversity that we see. Suppose, for example, that I believe that polygamy is immoral while my friend from Saudi Arabia believes that polygamy is morally permissible. The more reasonable explanation is that our respective cultures influence our individual beliefs, rather than the objectivist alternative that objectively informed beliefs influence our cultures. Cultural relativism, then, is the most reasonable explanation for why our moral beliefs mimic our culture. Although this argument seems plausible at face value, critics have pointed out some flaws. We will look at two criticisms.

Balfour's Criticism: Many Customs Are Simply Depraved Over the centuries, critics of cultural relativism have attacked the argument from social diversity on several grounds. One response is to challenge premise 3, which states that "it is difficult to explain how these differing moral values are grounded in objective moral standards." The entire argument from social diversity will topple if we can offer a cogent explanation as to how differing cultural values might be grounded in an objective reality.

In responding to Hume's statement of cultural relativism, eighteenth-century Scottish philosopher **James Balfour** (1705–1795) argued that, even if customs do vary over time and from place to place, there is still an underlying ideal moral standard that these cultures simply ignore. The whole batch of these cultures are simply corrupt, and these corrupt values only highlight true morality all the more:

Such an opinion leads to this unavoidable consequence, that whatever any set of men, or even any individual person, may think fit to do, however criminal in itself, must yet be deemed a virtue; because it is immediately agreeable to those who practise it.

But let us suppose that a whole nation should universally countenance a bad practice, this never would alter the nature of things, nor give sanction to vice. . . .

But so far are the depraved customs of the multitude, or even the practices of the great from being the just standard of morality, that virtue shines forth with the greater lustre from amidst bad practices; and even an universal corruption renders it the more conspicuous. (*Delineation*, 5)

Part of Balfour's attack is plausible—namely, his contention that the customs of the multitude may be depraved. Perhaps there exists an objective standard of morality, and our particular moral beliefs become distorted as we try to perceive objective standards through our diverse cultures. So, if I believe polygamy is immoral and my friend from Saudi Arabia believes it is moral, then at least one of us, and perhaps both of us, might have a distorted understanding of objective morality.

Even if this is so, we need to know *how to determine* which of our practices are depraved and which reflect true morality. Balfour's solution is that the true standard of morality "shines forth with the greater lustre from amid bad practices." For Balfour, the contrast between depraved practices and true morality is so pronounced that we all can intuitively see the difference. Unfortunately, Balfour's solution does not work. Certainly, Balfour genuinely believed that some moral values "shine forth" as more legitimate than others. But it probably never occurred to Balfour that the strength of his moral convictions might have been shaped by his eighteenth-century Scottish moral tradition, which was heavily influenced by Calvinistic religious beliefs. In a different culture, other moral values might "shine forth" to those people as more legitimate than those that Balfour holds to be true. In short, since our internal intuitions themselves may be products of our respective cultures, we can't safely appeal to these intuitions to determine which of our practices are depraved and which reflect true morality.

Objectivist moral philosophers have offered a variety of more stringent litmus tests to help distinguish between true morality and depraved values; these proposed tests include rationality, natural law, religious scripture, and human nature. Although these appear to be more rigorous than Balfour's test, they nevertheless all fall prey to the same problem that Balfour's did. That is, they all may be products of their respective cultures. A chemical test to determine the pH level of swimming pools will work the same around the world. A mathematical test to determine the structural integrity of bridge designs will also work the same around the world. But notions of rationality, natural law, scripture, and human nature are matters of debate and do not represent uniform standards. Ultimately, if we can't offer a uniform test to distinguish true morality from depraved values, then we should accept premise 3 in the argument from social diversity.

Rachels's Criticism: Some Key Values Do Not Vary   A second approach to attacking the argument from social diversity is to challenge premise 1, which holds that "many morally significant values differ from culture to culture." Some critics of relativism argue that there is less variation than relativists claim. Although many values do vary from culture to culture, they say, a large number of these so-called values are not truly moral in nature and would be better classified as "rules of prudence." That is, they involve personal lifestyle choices that, in spite of their strangeness, don't warrant moral condemnation by anyone. Many of the culturally relative practices noted by Sextus Empiricus fall into the prudence category, including men wearing "dresses":

> No man here would dress himself in a flowered robe reaching to the feet, although this dress, which with us is thought shameful, is held to be highly respectable by the Persians. And when, at the court of Dionysis the tyrant of Sicily, a dress of this description was offered to the philosophers Plato and Aristippus, Plato sent it away with the words "A man am I, and never could I don a woman's garb." . . . (*Outlines of Pyrrhonism*, 3.24)

Even Sextus's discussion of the differing cultural rituals surrounding corpses involves issues of prudence rather than morality. The same goes for many social customs that Montaigne lists.

Distinguishing between true morality and prudence takes away some of the force from premise 1 in the argument from social diversity. But some critics of relativism argue even further that, if we look hard enough, we will actually find basic moral values that are *the same* in all cultures. In Hume's "Dialogue" on cultural relativism, one character in the conversation who opposes relativism argues just this point:

> It appears, that there never was any quality recommended by any one, as a virtue or moral excellence, but on account of its being useful, or agreeable to a man himself, or to others. For what other reason can ever be assigned for praise or approbation? Or where would be the sense of extolling a good character or action, which, at the same time, is allowed to be good for nothing? All the differences, therefore, in morals, may be reduced to this one general foundation, and may be accounted for by the different views, which people take of these circumstances. ("A Dialogue")

In other words, although there might be some diversity with regard to *specific* types of conduct, there is one *general* moral standard that we find in all societies. This uniform moral standard involves the usefulness of right conduct and the pleasure that we immediately experience from such conduct. Consequently, underlying general moral standards don't vary from culture to culture.

In recent years, **James Rachels** has made a similar argument for three core common values: (1) caring for children, (2) truth telling, and (3) prohibitions against murder. For Rachels, these are all necessary conditions for the survival of a society since, if a society consistently violated any one of these, it would disintegrate. As to caring for children, all societies need to replenish their supply of educated and productive citizens; otherwise, in only a few generations, that society would die out. As to truth telling, the successful operation of industries, businesses, schools, and governments rests on the individuals involved trusting each other's word. For example, I would not buy groceries at my local store if I couldn't trust that the grocer would let me take home what I paid for. As to prohibitions against murder, if society allowed us to randomly kill other humans for sport or at whim, then everyone would head for the hills and stay as far from society as possible.

The list of common values doesn't need to stop with the three that Rachels mentions. Society would fall apart if there were no prohibition against stealing either privately held or publicly held property. Imagine what would happen, for example, if, to expand my garden, I simply annexed my neighbor's backyard or the street in front of my house. Society also must commit itself to enforcing its core values; otherwise, the values themselves would be empty words.

So, by distinguishing between issues of morality and prudence, and by identifying common social values, the critic of relativism successfully raises serious questions about the truth of premise 1. What at first seems to be an obvious truth for relativists—that moral values differ from culture to culture—now seems more like a hasty generalization. The critic's victory may not be absolute, though, especially when we consider sexual values such as those concerning pedophilia, incest, homosexuality, adultery, and polygamy. Most of us don't see these as issues of mere prudence; indeed, attitudes about these practices vary so widely that we can't link them with a core value. Nevertheless, enough damage is done to premise 1 that the sweeping conclusion of the argument from social diversity no longer follows. That is, it isn't necessarily more reasonable to believe that differing moral values are grounded in social customs.

Common Arguments against Cultural Relativism

Even if the argument from social diversity fails as a proof for cultural relativism, this isn't a decisive loss for the cultural relativist. The issue of cultural variability is not necessarily the central issue behind the cultural relativism/objectivism dispute. Even if all cultures throughout time consistently endorsed a particular value, such as that murder is wrong, cultural relativists could still argue that this value is grounded in societal traditions, not in objective standards. There may be common factors that prompt *all* societies to create and endorse similar values, such as a prohibition against murder. But this doesn't make these values any less social creations; moral values would still be grounded in social approval. So, we may distinguish between two ways of viewing cultural relativism:

- *Variable cultural relativism:* Moral values are grounded in social approval, and these values vary in different cultures.
- *Nonvariable cultural relativism:* Moral values are grounded in social approval, and these values do not necessarily vary in different cultures.

Nonvariable cultural relativism is a more modest approach to relativism since it grants in principle that moral values might be the same in different cultures. Although this sidesteps the objection that Rachels offered, even this more modest relativism has its critics. We will consider three objections.

Whether Cultural Relativists Deny All Moral Values   Critics of cultural relativism sometimes argue that denying an objective basis of morality amounts to rejecting all moral values. But this criticism confuses the cultural relativist's position with that of the **moral nihilist,** who holds that there are no moral values at all, but simply repressive social conventions that a truly free person will reject. The cultural relativist, by contrast, recognizes society's moral values, and even endorses them; he or she denies only that they are grounded in an objective realm.

To clarify the relativist's point, it is helpful to distinguish between issues of metaethics and issues of normative ethics. **Metaethics** investigates where morality comes from, and one of the key issues of metaethics concerns whether moral values exist in an objective realm that is external to human society. The relativist denies that moral values exist in a realm outside of human society. **Normative ethics,** by contrast, involves a quest for the best values and guiding principles of human conduct. Some leading normative values are the Ten Commandments of Judaism, the Confucian principle of reciprocity that we should avoid treating others in ways we wouldn't want to be treated ourselves, and the utilitarian position that we should pursue the greatest happiness for the greatest number of people. The cultural relativist will acknowledge the binding nature of some set of moral values such as these. Like everyone else, the relativist lives in a society, raises children, is appalled by crime, and hopes for a better future. There are many practical and emotional reasons to adopt and perpetuate normative moral standards. In short, it is only the more abstract metaethical issue of objectively existing values that the relativist questions. The relativist would argue that it is the normative that really matters in life, that makes us good citizens.

Whether Cultural Relativism Leads to Horrible Values   Critics of cultural relativism argue that, without the objective grounding of moral principles, societies would create many arbitrary and perhaps horrible values and simply give them the rubber stamp of "morality." But if societies ground values in fixed objective principles, these values will be good ones. The cultural relativist has three replies to this charge. First, even if we grant that there are objective moral principles, objectivists simply assume that these principles are fixed, unchanging, and essentially good. However, this is a position that must be argued for rather than merely assumed. The nineteenth-century German idealist philosopher G. W. F. Hegel (1770–1831) believed that the universe is a giant, continually evolving spirit. As this absolute spirit evolves over time, so, too, do human social values evolve on earth: They started out a bit rough but over time became better. Hegel may not have gotten the story of the universe right, but the cultural relativist will argue that, even if moral principles are objective, they are not necessarily unchanging, nonarbitrary, or even good.

Second, for the sake of argument, let's grant that there are objective moral principles that are unchanging. However, if we have no clear litmus test for recognizing them, then, in practice, we may create our value system independently of them. So, the mere existence of objective moral principles alone doesn't *guarantee* that we will formulate our social value systems in a certain way. The objectivist needs to bolster his or her views with additional theories about how we *recognize* these unchanging moral truths and how we *are motivated* to follow them. In our discussion of Balfour's criticism, we noted that this is difficult to do.

Third, cultural relativists don't necessarily hold that moral values are completely arbitrary creations of human society. Some aspects of human nature might influence the kinds of customs that we approve of. Sextus Empiricus and most other traditional philosophers argued that humans and animals alike are biologically programmed to find some things pleasing and other things painful. Skeptical philosophers also point to other factors in human nature that might influence how we develop social conventions, such as our natural sense of self-preservation, fear of death, and desire to live in peace. Even Mackie argues that we "create" morality in response to our natural drive to improve our well-being as active social creatures. Cultural relativists would still deny that moral values are permanently *fixed* through our natural drives; however, relativists don't typically deny altogether the influence of human nature.

Whether Cultural Relativism Rules Out Universal Judgments   Perhaps the strongest resistance to cultural relativism comes from our negative reactions to what we see as barbaric customs such as female genital mutilation. Regardless of how defenders of such practices view them in their homelands, we feel strongly that they are wrong. It isn't simply that they are wrong here in the United States; they are wrong *everywhere,* even in the cultures in which they are practiced the most. The cultural relativist doesn't seem justified in making this universal pronouncement if he or she denies the existence of an independent and objective moral realm.

In response, imagine that morality is a game we play that involves following specific rules created by society. Some of the rules have us arrive at a normative list of dos and don'ts; other rules involve punishments and rewards for those who break or abide by these dos and don'ts; still others govern the vocabulary we use when playing the morality game. For example, I'm allowed to call you a "good person" if you consistently perform the "dos." I am allowed to call you a "bad person" if you consistently violate the "don'ts." The rules also allow me to make universal pronouncements, such as "Female genital mutilation is wrong everywhere." Not only can I *say* this, but, according to the rules, I can also *mean* it, *argue* for it, feel anger toward those who perform this practice, and stipulate that defenders of this practice are simply wrong. All of these rules are consistent with the cultural relativist's view that morality is grounded in a combination of human nature and social convention.

The moral objectivist won't be satisfied with this game-based notion of universal pronouncement. Instead, objectivists such as Balfour will still argue that we need objective moral principles to give full force to universal pronouncements. The relativist can agree that there is in fact a greater metaethical strength to the objectivist's notion of universal pronouncement. However, the relativist will argue that nothing is gained with objectivism from the standpoint of universal pronouncements. The rules of the morality game remain the same for both the objectivist and the cultural relativist, and both are entitled to make universal pronouncements according to the rules.

Summary

The moral theory of cultural relativism began with Xenophanes, who held that our common notions of god are culturally shaped. Philosophers of the skeptical tradition, beginning with Pyrrho, refined the notion of cultural relativism and drew attention to the broad diversity of cultural practices. Cultural relativists were typically moral skeptics insofar as they denied an objective foundation of morality. The principal argument for cultural relativism is based on social diversity. That is, cultural relativism is a better explanation of social diversity than is moral objectivism. Against this argument, Balfour maintained that moral objectivism is really a better explanation insofar as many accepted social practices are corrupt while true objective morality is intuitively clear. However, Balfour failed to provide an adequate test for distinguishing true morality from corrupt morality. The argument from social diversity has also been rightly criticized on the grounds that social practices are not as diverse as the relativist contends; in fact, some key moral values are cross-cultural.

There are two distinct approaches to cultural relativism: variable cultural relativism and nonvariable cultural relativism. Although the variable approach has problems, the nonvariable approach does not suffer from the same problems, and common arguments against it are not convincing. Indeed, nonvariable cultural relativism allows for the adoption of traditional moral values. It also does not lead to the establishment of horrible values any more than moral objectivism might. And, finally, it allows for the possibility of making universal moral judgments.

Study Questions

Introduction
1. Describe the practice of female genital mutilation.
2. Define "moral relativism," "cultural relativism," and "individual relativism."

Classic Cultural Relativism

Xenophanes and the Greek Skeptics
3. What is Xenophanes' view of cultural relativism regarding religion?
4. What was Pyrrho's view of morality?
5. What are some examples of culturally relative practices noted by Sextus Empiricus?
6. Describe the early Greek skeptics' view of tranquility.

Later Defenders of Cultural Relativism

7. What does Montaigne conclude about the power of social peer pressure in terms of moral practices?
8. For Sumner, what are the "folkways," and what is the connection between morality and a culture's folkways?
9. What does Mackie mean by "moral skepticism"?

The Argument from Social Diversity

10. Summarize the argument for cultural relativism from social diversity.

Balfour's Criticism: Many Customs Are Simply Depraved

11. According to Balfour, how do we determine whether a social practice reflects true morality or is simply depraved?
12. What is the problem with Balfour's argument?

Rachels's Criticism: Some Key Values Do Not Vary

13. Give some examples of rules of prudence.
14. According to Rachels, what are three values that are common to all societies?
15. What are some values that do in fact appear to vary from culture to culture?
16. What does Fieser conclude about the success of the argument from social diversity?

Common Arguments against Cultural Relativism

17. What is the difference between variable and nonvariable relativism?

Whether Cultural Relativists Deny All Moral Values

18. How does cultural relativism differ from moral nihilism?
19. What are the metaethical and normative ethical views of the cultural relativist?

Whether Cultural Relativism Leads to Horrible Values

20. What are Fieser's three responses to the criticism that cultural relativism leads to horrible values?

Whether Cultural Relativism Rules Out Universal Judgments

21. According to Fieser, how might the cultural relativist explain our tendency to make universal moral condemnations?

References

The quotations on female genital mutilation is from "Combatting Genital Mutilation in Sudan" by Sara Mansavage (UNICEF Feature No. 00109.SUD).

The quotations by Xenophanes are from Richard D. McKirahan, *Philosophy Before Socrates* (Indianapolis: Hackett, 1994), Chapter 7.

The quotation by Heroditus is from *The Histories,* translated by Aubery de Selincourt, (Harmondsworth, England: Penguin Books, 1972), p. 220.

The quotations by Sextus Empiricus are from *Outlines of Pyrrhonism,* 3.198–238, translated by R. G. Bury.

The quotations by Michel Eyquem de Montaigne are from "Of Custom, and That we should not Easily Change a Law Received" in his *Essays* (1580), adapted from the translation by Charles Cotton.

David Hume's "A Dialogue" is included at the end of his *Enquiry Concerning the Principles of Morals* (1751), which is available in several modern editions.

The quotations by William Graham Sumner are from *Folkways* (Boston: Guinn, 1906), Chapter 1.31; Sumner's discussion of incest is in Chapter 12.

The quotations by J. L. Mackie are from *Ethics: Inventing Right and Wrong* (New York: Penguin Books, 1977).

James Balfour's attack on cultural relativism is in his *A Delineation of the Nature and Obligation of Morality* (1753), Chapter 5. That specific chapter is reprinted in James Fieser's *Early Responses to Hume,* Vol. 1 (Bristol, England: Thoemmes Press, 1999).

James Rachels's critique of cultural relativism is in "The Challenge of Cultural Relativism," *Elements of Moral Philosophy* (New York: McGraw-Hill, 1993).

Suggestions for Further Reading

For discussions of the Pyrrhonian skeptical tradition, see J. Annas and J. Barnes, *The Modes of Scepticism* (Cambridge: Cambridge University Press, 1985); M. F. Burnyeat, ed., *The Skeptical Tradition* (Los Angeles: University of California Press, 1983); Diogenes Laertius, *Lives of the Philosophers,* trans. R. D. Hicks (Cambridge, MA: Harvard University Press, 1925), 9.69–116; R. J. Hankinson, *The Sceptics* (London: Routledge, 1995); C. L. Stough, *Greek Skepticism* (Los Angeles: University of California Press, 1969).

For discussions of cultural relativism and moral objectivism, see Ruth Benedict, *Patterns of Culture* (New York: Pelican, 1946); Gilbert Harman and Judith Jarvis Thomson, *Moral Objectivity* (Oxford: Blackwell, 1996); Michael Krausz, ed., *Relativism: Interpretation and Conflict* (Notre Dame, IN: University of Notre Dame Press, 1989); John Ladd, ed., *Ethical Relativism* (Belmont, CA: Wadsworth, 1973); Thomas Nagel, *The Last Word* (New York: Oxford University Press, 1997); Edward Westermarck, *Ethical Relativity* (Paterson, NJ: Littlefield, 1960).

2

Plato's Moral Objectivism

Introduction

Many people believe that reality is limited to the physical world that we see around us. In this view, rocks, rivers, plants, bugs, and all of the things that we experience throughout the day are physical in nature and can be fully explained through scientific investigation. Even human consciousness and social interaction are rooted in physical reality, and with enough investigation, science might fully unravel all of their mysteries, including the nature of morality. However, other people believe that the physical world is only the tip of the iceberg, that a grander reality exists beyond the immediate and superficial world of physical appearances. The New Age spiritualist movement today is a graphic example of this view, and New Age believers use a variety of paranormal techniques to help tap into that higher reality.

A vivid example is the recently conceived spiritualist technique of past-life therapy. A New Age version of psychoanalysis, past-life therapy involves uncovering traumas from one's previous lives. Past-life therapists argue that, by dredging up and resolving past-life traumas, we can heal ourselves of psychological discomforts and mental disorders in our current lives. Reported traumas from past-life experiences often involve moral components. For example, in one case study, a man with symptoms of schizophrenia revealed through hypnosis that in a past life during the Middle Ages he had been tortured by religious officials. After working through that lingering issue, the man allegedly became a normal functioning person. In a training manual on past life-therapy, William J. Baldwin explains the underlying psychology of the technique. He argues that our subconscious minds retain memories of everything that our spirit-being has ever experienced:

> This includes the present lifetime, prior lifetimes, potential future lifetimes, the nonphysical realms between incarnations, and the entire track of awareness back to and including the experience of separating or extending from Creator Source.

Many people in the United States would probably view past-life therapy with great skepticism. Part of the reason is that reincarnation is inconsistent with the notions of the afterlife expressed in traditional Judeo-Christian theology. Also, paranormal phenomena such as past-life experiences don't lend themselves to scientific scrutiny and so lack the kind of hard evidence that impels belief. Although we might doubt the validity of past-life therapy, we must recognize that it reflects a common conviction that truth resides in some higher realm. At one time in the history of Western philosophy, theories of higher reality were commonplace. The most influential of these was offered by the ancient Greek philosopher **Plato** (428–348 BCE).

By almost any standard, Plato ranks among the greatest philosophers of the world, and many scholars view him as the most important philosopher of Western civilization. We find in Plato a drive for absolute truth that goes beyond the merely popular opinions of the multitudes. We also find in Plato a conviction that the physical world around us is merely a pale copy of the true reality of things that exists on a higher objective plane. True knowledge—including true *moral* knowledge—involves an intimate encounter with this objective plane. Plato holds a position called **moral objectivism,** which is the view that morality has an objective foundation that is independent of human approval.

Over the centuries, philosophers have proposed a variety of theories of moral objectivism, arguing that morality is grounded in the creative will of God, or the laws of nature, or in eternal truths. Plato's theory, though, is the grandfather of all of these. Not only did Plato give the first detailed account of moral objectivism, but many moral objectivists after Plato incorporated his basic assumption into their own theories. That basic assumption is that moral standards are grounded in a higher and more perfect realm of moral truth. We will look at the central features of Plato's moral objectivism and assess some of the criticisms launched against his theory.

The Background of Plato's Moral Theory

Like most philosophers, Plato devised his theory in reaction to other views that he wasn't happy with. Plato was especially bothered by philosophers of his day who held that moral values are simply human inventions. A brief look at the intellectual climate of Plato's day will help illuminate the motivation behind his theory.

The Sophists and Socrates   Plato lived at a time when there was a special need for education in the Greek city-states. Governments required more administrators, so aristocratic parents hired freelance philosophers to educate their sons for this vocation. Although not members of any particular philosophical school of thought, these teachers were collectively known as **Sophists,** a term which means "one who makes people wise." They traveled widely throughout the ancient Greek world, contracting out their services in one city-state after another. Many Sophists claimed the ability to teach any subject, but they specialized in rhetorical skills, particularly the kind of arguing and persuasive speaking techniques needed in public debates. The Sophists had a skeptical attitude toward the pursuit of truth and, by and large, maintained that in many areas of inquiry truth is only a matter of persuasive argumentation. The *true* position in a debate is the *winning* position. To this end, they offered an argument strategy called "antilogic," which involved learning to argue both sides of a case as strongly as possible. Using this technique, students could turn the weaker argument into the stronger one. Not only did the Sophists have flexible attitudes toward truth, but many also had flexible attitudes about morality, holding that people create their own values to serve their particular needs. Civic leaders didn't always admire the Sophists' contributions to Greek society and often questioned their moral and religious integrity.

Plato's teacher was **Socrates** (469–399 BCE) who, like the Sophists, spent much of his life teaching aristocratic children in Athens. Unlike many of the Sophists, though, Socrates had a more optimistic view of morality, and Plato was directly influenced by this. Socrates left no writings, and the most reliable information we have about him comes from Plato. Plato's surviving writings consist mostly of dialogs, which, in modern editions, total around 1500 pages. In honor of his teacher, Plato introduces a character named "Socrates," who is the main speaker and hero of many of the dialogs. In the dialogs, Socrates moves among a strange cast of politicians, aristocrats, and Sophists—most also modeled after historical figures. Socrates typically tries to point out conceptual flaws in the views held by the other characters, although rarely do these rivals concede Socrates' position.

Scholars commonly divide Plato's writings into chronological groups of composition. The consensus for the past century has been that Plato's earliest dialogs present the views of the historical Socrates while the later dialogs use the Socrates character as more of a dramatic mouthpiece for Plato's own views. And, at times, Socrates is no longer a central character at all. Although it is nearly impossible to distinguish Socrates' actual views from those of Plato's even in the earlier dialogs, we may make a few generalizations about the historical Socrates' views on morality.

Historians of philosophy often credit Socrates with shifting the focus of philosophy from issues of cosmology to moral issues. Philosophers prior to Socrates were more like scientists, discussing the primary elements of the physical world and the way natural forces balance between perpetual change and regularity. Socrates, though, was principally concerned with moral choice—that is, with choosing to follow a lifelong path of courageous philosophical inquiry and a search for justice, rather than a path of conventional expectations. For Socrates, "The unexamined life is not worth living" and "Know yourself" are mottoes that encapsulate this quest. By continually picking away at the moral and religious views commonly held by Athenian society, Socrates alienated himself from Athenian leaders. In their eyes, Socrates was just another troublesome Sophist who threatened to undermine social order. For this reason, when Socrates was around 70 years old, he was put on trial for promoting atheism and corrupting the youth. He was found guilty and executed.

Protagoras's Individual Relativism   Socrates and Plato both strongly opposed the Sophists' moral relativism—that is, the view that moral values are simply human inventions. The undisputed champion of moral relativism in Socrates' day was the Sophist **Protagoras** (485–420 BCE). Protagoras expresses his moral relativism in his famous statement that "man is the measure of all things." Most simply, this means that people set their own standard of truth in all judgments. Only fragments of Protagoras's original writings survive, so we are left to speculate about the precise meaning of this statement. Plato gives his own interpretation about what Protagoras meant. First, when Protagoras states that "man is the measure of all things," "man" refers to individual humans, not to human society collectively. In this sense, then, *each person's* judgment, rather than *society's* judgment, constitutes the standard of truth. Therefore, in Plato's interpretation, Protagoras is a proponent of an **individual relativism,** which is the view that moral obligations are grounded in each person's own approval. This stands in contrast to a different form of moral relativism called **cultural relativism,** which holds that moral obligations are grounded in the approval of social cultures. A second point that surfaces in Plato's discussion concerns two possible interpretations of Protagoras's statement:

- Each person's private judgment constitutes the standard of truth *for everyone.*
- Each person's private judgment constitutes the standard of truth for *whoever makes that judgment.*

Plato inclines towards the second interpretation, which is less radical. A third point about Protagoras's statement concerns its longer and less familiar form, as we find it in Plato's discussion:

Man is the measure of all things—of things that are, that they are, and of things that are not that they are not.

Literally, Protagoras holds that individual people create their own truth, even to the extent that something exists or doesn't exist. In many ways, Protagoras's individual relativism presents no serious problems. For example, if I taste some honey and find it sweet, then my judgment that it is sweet *makes* it true for me. If you, by contrast, don't find honey sweet when you taste it, then it is true for you that honey is not sweet. In this situation, individual relativism makes sense, since I am describing how something tastes to me based on the physiology of my taste buds, and you are describing how it tastes to you based on your own physiology. But Protagoras pushes this individual relativism to an extreme, holding that the truth of *everything* is relative to the person. This is where many of us have problems with his individual relativism, since some truths don't seem to be relative. For example, suppose I believe it is true that "2 plus 3 equals 7" or "Tokyo is in France." According to Protagoras, these statements are true *for me,* even though our normal reaction is that these statements are just plain false. For Protagoras, the same individual relativism that applies to judgments about honey or addition or Tokyo also applies to judgments about morality. We all have our own perceptions about what things are good and evil, just and unjust. We can also defend our respective moral views with arguments. In this sense, each of our moral views is true for us respectively.

In short, according to Plato's interpretation of Protagoras, my personal beliefs constitute the standard of truth for me in all matters. We don't know precisely why Protagoras adopted individual relativism, but we can speculate based on a skeptical statement that he made about religion:

> Concerning the gods, I am unable to know either that they exist or that they do not exist, or what their appearance is like. For, there are many things that hinder knowledge, such as the obscurity of the matter and the shortness of human life.

Protagoras is arguing here that, given our human limitations, we are unable to penetrate religious reality. Because of this, he pleads ignorance on the subject of religion. Using parallel reasoning, he might also hold that we are unable to penetrate any ultimate *moral* reality and thus must plead ignorance on this matter as well. In the absence of any knowledge of a moral reality, we might emphasize the authority of our personal moral preferences.

Plato's Moral Theory

Although Plato presents Protagoras's individual relativism very meticulously, he nevertheless harshly rejected it. One problem that Plato had with this view is that he believed that it was self-defeating. In other words, said Plato, if I am the judge of what's true and false for me, then I can simply judge that Protagoras's theory of individual relativism is itself false, and it thereby becomes false. More precisely, Plato's criticism goes like this:

1. According to Protagoras, if I judge something to be false, then it is false for me.
2. Suppose that I judge it false that individual people are the measure of all truth.
3. Therefore, it is false for me that individual people are the measure of all truth.

Indeed, Plato hit the nail on the head with regard to Protagoras's theory of individual relativism. The central problem is with the sweeping claim that the truth of *all* things, which includes the theory of individual relativism itself, is relative to me. Although the truth of many things certainly is relative to me, such as how something tastes, it is simply false that the truth of *all* things is relative to me. The most that Protagoras can justifiably say, then, is that "man is the measure of *some* things."

Even though we must reject Protagoras's sweeping view of individual relativism, the question still remains about the status of moral truths. Is morality relative to individual people just as tastes are relative to individual people? In reaction to Protagoras, Plato maintains that moral truths aren't relative, but instead are grounded in a higher objective reality.

The Theory of the Moral Forms Plato develops his account of moral objectivism in what scholars call the *theory of the forms*. Plato's theory of the forms is complex, and different features of the theory emerge in various writings. It will help to begin with a simplified view of his theory and then to focus on some details.

According to Plato, the universe consists of two distinct realms. First, there is a visible world of appearances, which contains physical objects such as rocks, chairs, cars, and people. Second, there is an intelligible world of the **forms**, which contains universal abstracions, such as principles of mathematics and justice. Plato uses the Greek term *eidos* to refer to these abstract entities, a word that is often translated as "idea" or "form." "Idea," though, isn't the best translation since ideas exist only in the minds of people, whereas *eidos*, for Plato, exist independently of anyone's mind. The English word "form" avoids this pitfall and better captures Plato's view of abstract entities that are eternal and unchanging.

Imagine that we can take a tour of the realm of the forms—assuming that such a place exists. We first see that the form realm contains no physical things and, perhaps, not even any three-dimensional things. It is tempting to see it as a realm of spirit-beings, although we must avoid thinking of it as some heavenly domain containing the spirits of the dead. It is more like the unconscious furniture of the spirit realm. On our tour, we encounter mathematical relations such as 2 plus 3 equals 5. Although these aren't conscious spirits, they are nevertheless spiritual substances. We might think of these as eternal mathematical laws—and, for Plato, these are mathematical forms. Plato's notion of the forms was likely sparked by the universal and unchanging nature of such mathematical principles. People often refer to mathematics as the universal language since, regardless of where we are from, we rely on and understand the same basic mathematical notions. Not only do mathematical concepts cut across human cultures, but fans of science fiction believe that mathematics is the universal language of intelligent life elsewhere in the universe. In fact, a research organization called the SETI Institute (Search for Extraterrestrial Intelligence) attempts to eavesdrop on mathematically-based messages broadcast from outer space.

Moving beyond mathematical forms on our tour, we come across the essence of moral concepts such as justice, charity, honesty, and beauty. For Plato, these are the pure forms of moral traits that people have. For example, every person who exhibits the moral attribute of justice must possess a specific feature; according to Plato, that feature is "doing one's own business." Like mathematical and physical forms, moral forms function as ideal models for how we identify and categorize things. Specifically, we rely on moral forms to identify and categorize proper actions.

Finally, on our tour, we encounter the grandest form of all—namely, the form of **the Good**. Higher than justice and the other moral forms, the Good is the source of ultimate moral perfection in the other moral forms, and perhaps is even ultimate perfection in general. Plato himself struggles to explain the nature of the Good. He argues that we can't simply reduce the Good to qualities we commonly value, such as pleasure or wisdom. However, he argues, we all seek the Good and, like the sun, the Good illuminates everything that we know:

> In like manner [to the sun] the good may be said to be not only the author of knowledge to all things known, but of their being and essence, and yet the good is not essence, but far exceeds essence in dignity and power. (*Republic*, 509b)

The latter part of this passage is especially puzzling. Plato states here that the Good "far exceeds essence"; that is, the Good does not exist in the way that the other forms exist. One interpretation of this is that the regular forms have one kind of spiritual existence while the Good has an even more pure kind of spiritual existence.

Returning to the physical world, we see particular things, such as a bridge spanning a river or a man donating to charity. For Plato, these physical things are imperfectly molded from various mathematical and moral forms. For example, when building a bridge across a river, we rely on calculations about stress points and other mathematical components. In Plato's terminology, the particular physical things that we see *participate* (*methexis*) in different abstract forms. Thus, the structure of the bridge *participates* in abstract mathematical forms. The bridge, though, will never be perfect given the faulty material from which it is made. Similarly, when a person donates to charity, he *participates* in the moral form of charity; the morally good person participates in the form of the Good.

Recollection and Knowledge of the Forms

Perhaps the strangest part of Plato's theory is his explanation of how we obtain knowledge of the forms. Plato describes this as a recollecting process (*anamnesis*): In a previous existence, we were directly acquainted with all of the forms; but over the years, we've suppressed our knowledge of them. To know the forms, then, we must try to recollect them.

This component of Plato's theory places him in a spiritualist tradition that extends to the present New Age movement. Plato does not discuss the theory of past-life recollection in the *Republic* specifically. However, the theory of recollection appears so prominently in several of his other dialogs that we can't dismiss it as a fluke. His most graphic description of it is this:

> Thus the soul, since it is immortal and has been born many times, and has seen all things both here and in the other world, has the knowledge of virtue or anything else which, as we see, it once possessed. All nature is akin, and the soul has learned everything, so that when a man has recalled a single piece of knowledge—*learned* it, in ordinary language—there is no reason why he should not find out all the rest, if he keeps a stout heart and does not grow weary of the search, for seeking and learning are in fact nothing but recollection. (*Meno*, 81d)

The interesting thing about this passage is the statement that the soul "has seen all things both here *and in the other world*." For Plato, it is in the *other world* that we encountered the forms. Suppose that I had been born again and again in the physical world. If I couldn't gain knowledge of the forms through normal sense perception, then, even over a thousand lives, I would not be any closer to knowledge of the forms. By describing the procedure as *recollection* rather than *reacquaintance,* Plato implies that it is impossible for us to directly encounter the forms in our present worldly situation; all that we can do is recollect them. Our previous acquaintance with the forms, then, was in some other world.

Plato states that this other world is one in which we did not have a "human shape." More to the point, it is a world in which our souls were not restrained either by our bodies or by physical things. Plato has a low regard for both the physical human body and the visible world, and he blames them for our misfortunes. He writes that the body flusters, maddens, and imprisons the soul. It is diseased, it destroys the value of life, and the true philosopher despises it. By contrast, the other world in which we encountered the forms is spiritlike, which is better suited to the spiritual makeup of our souls.

To summarize, these are the key points of Plato's moral theory:

- Moral values are eternal, unchanging, and nonphysical forms.
- The highest moral value is the form of the Good, which is ultimate moral perfection.
- People become moral by participating in the moral forms.
- We gain moral knowledge by recollecting the moral forms from a past-life encounter.

Criticisms of Plato's Theory

From Plato's own day to the present, critics have exposed problems with various aspects of his moral theory. Shortly after his death, Plato's pupil **Aristotle** (384–322 BCE) took issue with the Platonic theory of the forms. Aristotle's main dispute with Plato is vividly represented in a famous painting by High Renaissance artist Raphael (1483–1520) entitled *The School of Athens.* In this painting, an elderly Plato and a young Aristotle are walking side by side down a staircase. Plato is pointing up at the sky to express his view that ultimate reality exists above and beyond the physical world. Aristotle, though, is pointing down at the ground to express his view that ultimate reality is embedded right here in the physical and tangible world. For Aristotle, there simply is no higher objective realm of the forms. In his book *Metaphysics,* Aristotle launches a stream of attacks on Plato's theory, two of which we will look at here.

Aristotle's First Criticism: The Forms Do Not Add to Our Knowledge
Plato is convinced that true knowledge about anything consists of knowledge of the relevant forms. For example, to truly understand the nature of charity, I must understand the form of charity. According to Aristotle, however, introducing the idea of the forms neither explains the nature of nor helps us better understand particular things:

> Above all one might discuss the question what on earth the Forms contribute to sensible things, either to those that are eternal or to those that come into being and cease to be. For they cause neither movement nor any change in them. But again they help in no wise either towards the knowledge of other things . . . or towards their being . . . (*Metaphysics,* 1.9)

Aristotle suggests that the theory of the forms simply confuses things by introducing unneeded concepts. Suppose that I want to better understand the notion of charity, and I read in Plato that the true nature of charity rests in the *form* of charity. Not only does this fail to advance my understanding of charity, but it also clutters my head with unneeded metaphysical entities. Insofar as we understand a "form" of charity, we do so by studying specific instances of it. The medieval philosopher **William of Ockham** (c. 1285–1349) recommended that we avoid multiplying entities beyond what we actually need. According to this principle, known more popularly as "Ockham's Razor," we should stick with our most metaphysically simple explanation. Aristotle anticipates Ockham's recommendation by pointing out that Plato's account of the forms merely adds useless metaphysical baggage.

Aristotle and Ockham are correct that, as a rule, our theories should contribute to our knowledge and that we should rid our theories of pointless complications. However, this criticism loses sight of an important motivation behind Plato's theory. The physical world around us is highly imperfect. If we try to understand the concept of charity by surveying this world, we will arrive at an inadequate concept. Most people are not as charitable as they should be. And even when we are charitable, we often act from ulterior motives, such as to enhance our reputation. There may be very few truly representative examples of charity upon which we can draw. Nevertheless, in spite of the inadequacy of our real-life experiences of charity, we have in fact formed a more perfect conception of charity. For Plato, we need *standards* before we can evaluate specific instances. We need to know what charity ideally is before we can evaluate alleged instances of it. This requires more reflection than observation, and perhaps even requires that we cast our vision away from this imperfect world toward a more perfect one. By proposing the theory of the forms, Plato offers us a perfect world upon which we can contemplate. So, Plato's hypothesis of the realm of the forms isn't as pointless as Aristotle charges.

Aristotle's Second Criticism: Participation Is Not Explained   We've seen that the notion of participation is a key element of Plato's theory. For example, I am a charitable person to the degree that I *participate* in the form of charity. In our discussion of participation, the concept was explained in terms of "molding"; that is, I am charitable to the extent that I *mold* myself after the moral form of charity. However, Aristotle objects that no such descriptions adequately explain how physical things get their attributes from the realm of the forms:

> All other things cannot come *from* the Forms in any of the usual senses of "from." And to say that they are patterns and the other things participate in them is to use empty words and poetical metaphors. (*Metaphysics,* 1.9)

Here, Aristotle argues that Plato's reliance on the notion of participation does not help explain the connection between forms and physical things. He argues that Plato uses the notion of participation metaphorically and that Plato never moves beyond the metaphor to give a more rigorous explanation.

Taken literally, the term *participation* means that one thing shares in or takes part in another thing, such as when I participate in a game of checkers. This implies an activity of giving or receiving. In this sense, clearly, particular sets of charity, for example, do not literally give or receive anything with respect to the forms. Aristotle is correct, then, that Plato uses the term participation metaphorically, which only hints at the point he wants to make. We might try to help Plato out by using other notions instead of participation, such as molding, mimicking, copying, or instantiating. But these, too, are only metaphors. We still lack a descriptive procedure that explains how the forms impact the physical world. What is worse, though, is that the nature of the issue itself will never allow for a literal and direct description. Plato is offering a theory concerning the interaction between two levels of reality—the physical and the nonphysical. Our words and experiences are firmly grounded in how things interact within the physical realm, and we lack the conceptual framework to literally denote features of a nonphysical realm.

Plato's theory of the forms isn't necessarily refuted by the fact that his notion of participation is unavoidably metaphorical. We are locked into metaphors in much of our daily conversation, as when we talk about mental events such as a "splitting headache" or a "painful thought." Religious believers are similarly locked into metaphors when saying anything about God or the spirit realm. In these arenas, we accept metaphors without demanding a more precise account. However, we also recognize that there is great margin for error in what we say on these subjects when using metaphors. The metaphorical nature of Plato's description places his theory in the same camp as talk about mental events or religion: Although we may allow his metaphors, we must also recognize the high margin of error.

Mackie's First Criticism: The Concept of the Forms Is Queer   In recent decades, Plato's moral theory has come under sharp attack by Australian philosopher J. L. Mackie (1917–1981). For Mackie, there is something "queer," or counterintuitive, about any description that we might give of Plato's realm of the moral forms:

> This [argument from queerness] has two parts, one metaphysical, the other epistemological. If there were objective values, then they would be entities or qualities or relations of a very strange sort, utterly different from anything else in the universe. Correspondingly, if we were aware of them, it would have to be by some special faculty of moral perception or intuition, utterly different from our ordinary ways of knowing everything else.

For Mackie, the *metaphysical* problem with Plato's theory of the forms concerns its strange, spiritlike realm. Where is this realm? How many dimensions does it have? Mackie argues that the strangeness of this realm alone is a compelling argument against its existence. The *epistemological* problem with Plato's theory concerns how we gain knowledge of these spiritlike things. We gain knowledge of the physical world through our five senses. But by what faculty do we gain knowledge of this spiritlike realm? Plato says that it involves a faculty of recollection—similar to our memory faculty—that dredges up knowledge from past-life experiences. However, few of us would claim to have this type of recollective faculty. Even if we say that it is a type of rational faculty, this presumes that it is like a mental eyeball that peers into another realm. But we don't seem to have this kind of mental faculty either. The crux of the problem, for Mackie, is that it isn't clear how the peculiar, non-natural realm of the forms has any connection with natural objects and human actions; the two realms are too distinct.

How might Plato respond to this charge? Here's one possible response: A classic issue in philosophy is the **mind-body problem**, which wrestles with how mental events—which are nonphysical in nature—connect with bodily acts—which are physical in nature. Suppose, for example, that I pull my hand away from a flame because of the pain that I experience. For this to occur, the signal of pain must first travel through my nerves from my hand to my brain. At some point, then, this physical signal mysteriously jumps into my mental awareness. I then mentally decide to remove my hand, and this decision mysteriously translates into another physical act as my hand moves. The point is that mental experiences seem to be different from merely physical events, and the connecting links between the two are a mystery. Thus, Plato might argue that, since we accept the mystery of the mind-body connection, then we can also accept the mystery concerning the connection between the natural realm and the realm of the forms.

The problem with this response, though, is that the two situations are not truly parallel. With the mind-body connection, I have clear experience of both my mind and my body, and I can't reasonably question the existence of either. However, as Plato himself acknowledges, I don't have direct experience of the realm of the forms; at best, I recollect the forms. This means that I can reasonably doubt the existence of that realm. It also means that anything I say about that realm will sound strange and far-fetched. So, the objection that Mackie raises seems valid, and it is here that we find the biggest problem with Plato's moral theory. The questions that Mackie asks are, in fact, pertinent to *any* theory of moral objectivism, and not simply Plato's theory of the forms. A variety of moral theories, just like Plato's, maintain that moral values are grounded in an objective reality that is independent of human approval. With any of these, we may rightly inquire about the metaphysical nature of that reality and how we gain access to it. Whatever answer the moral objectivist gives to our inquiry, the odds are good that it will be as counterintuitive as Plato's theory of the forms.

Mackie's Second Criticism: Tendencies to Objectify Can Be Psychologically Explained   In a second criticism of Plato, Mackie offers a psychological explanation for why people erroneously believe that there are objective

values of any kind. According to Mackie, people naturally tend to objectify values that are actually subjective in origin. For example, if I smell a rotten orange and it disgusts me, then I automatically think that the rotten orange *itself* is disgusting in nature. Clearly, though, the element of disgust is a subjective quality pertaining to my reaction; it isn't really a feature of the orange itself. I erroneously project the quality of disgust *onto* the orange. One reason that we make this mistake is because *something* is, in fact, external—namely, the orange itself. We then mistakenly think that *everything* pertaining to the orange is also external.

Mackie suggests that the same psychological projection takes place with moral values. Society places external constraints on me to behave morally, such as society's demand that I not run around naked. This societal demand itself is external to me; that is, I didn't invent it myself. Since this societal demand is external, I then erroneously think that everything about the demand is external, including the moral value in question, such as that it is wrong to run around naked in public. Mackie concludes that it is more reasonable to adopt this psychological projection theory than to accept the alternative view that moral values have a genuine external existence in a spiritlike realm of the forms.

Mackie's argument strategy here is appropriate. That is, it is relevant to consider a psychological explanation for why we might hold to an erroneous view. To illustrate, suppose that my neighbor wrongly believes that a hideous monster is stalking him. One way of exposing his error is to hire a surveillance team to continually watch him; presumably, they wouldn't detect a monster. However, another way to expose his error is to offer a cogent explanation of why he is having these delusions. I might, for example, show that there is a history of schizophrenia in his family and that he is another unlucky victim. My neighbor himself may not be convinced by this; instead, he may think that I'm plotting with the monster against him. However, to an impartial observer, this would be decisive evidence that my neighbor was in error about the monster. Similarly, a follower of Plato might not be persuaded by Mackie's theory of psychological projection. However, to the extent that we can consider the issue impartially, Mackie's theory of psychological projection is reasonable enough to make us think long and hard about why we might hold to a conception of objective moral forms.

The Legacy of Plato's Moral Theory

In spite of criticisms such as Aristotle's, Plato's theory of the forms had a strong impact on philosophers for more than 2000 years. His theory of moral objectivism in particular was kept alive by one generation of philosophers after another.

Plato's Influence   The fate of Plato's theory in the years immediately following his death is one of the great ironies in the history of philosophy. Plato was very optimistic about our ability to know truth, and he was very bold in his assertion about the existence of an ideal world beyond our immediate perceptions. He opened a school called the **Academy** to perpetuate his views, and when he died leadership of the Academy was passed on to his nephew. However, Plato's nephew quickly rejected the doctrine of the forms and transformed the Academy into a mathematical school. A few generations later, the new leaders of the Academy completely abandoned Plato's optimistic philosophy, replacing it with a radical skepticism that emphasized suspending judgment. The tradition of skepticism started by the new Academy reaches down to our present day, and Mackie among others is part of that tradition. Although the Academy in later years set skepticism aside, it never returned to a pure Platonic tradition, but instead adopted an eclectic approach to philosophy that blended the views of many philosophers. The Academy was eventually shut down in 529 CE by the Roman emperor Justinian.

The demise of Plato's theory in the Academy by no means put an end to the influence of Plato's philosophy in ancient times. Religious philosophers especially were attracted to Plato's theory. The realm of the forms coincided with religious conceptions of the spirit realm, and the notion of the Good coincided with the role that God plays as the most perfect being that permeates all things. The best examples of this are Plotinus (205–270), an Egyptian-born mystical philosopher, and Augustine (354–430), a bishop and theologian of the early Christian Church. Both of these philosophers offered moral theories that paralleled Plato's, and their respective moral views inspired religious philosophers throughout the Middle Ages. During much of this time, only one of Plato's writings—the *Timaeus*—was accessible to scholars. More of Plato's writings surfaced in the late Middle Ages and Renaissance, and with them came a revived appreciation of Plato's moral theory.

In seventeenth-century England, a group of philosophers educated at Emmanuel College in Cambridge championed a movement called **Cambridge Platonism**. These philosophers were especially turned off by Puritan and Calvinist Christian theologians who held that God somewhat arbitrarily ruled the universe according to divine whims. Instead, the Cambridge Platonists argued that there was a rational order to the universe and that God, as a rational being, followed that rational order.

The most influential of the Cambridge Platonists was **Ralph Cudworth** (1617–1688). Cudworth argued that moral principles are eternal truths that depend on no one's will—not even God's. Following Plato, Cudworth insists that moral truths have a reality in a spiritual realm, which is greater than the reality that physical things have in the "stupid and senseless" material realm:

> Those things which belong to Mind and Intellect, such as Morality, Ethicks, Politicks and Laws are, which Plato calls, The Offspring and Productions of Mind, are no less to be accounted natural Things, or real and substantial, than those things which belong to stupid and senseless Matter. (*Treatise concerning Eternal and Immutable Morality,* 4.6.8)

Cudworth departs from Plato somewhat in explaining how we gain knowledge of eternal moral truths. Plato believed that the moral forms exist outside of anyone's mind and that, in a previous existence, we encountered them directly.

Cudworth, though, believes that we gain knowledge of eternal moral truths by tapping into God's understanding of those truths. Even though God didn't invent these eternal moral truths, God nevertheless thinks about them, and this knowledge is then passed on to us.

Cudworth's view of eternal moral truths was widely adopted during the eighteenth century, and advocates clearly attributed the origins of this theory to Plato. We see this in the following passage by 18th-century moral philosopher Catherine Macaulay (1731–1791):

> [Morality involves] a necessary and essential difference of things, a fitness and unfitness, a proportion and disproportion, a moral beauty and a moral deformity, an immutable right and wrong, necessarily independent of the will of every being created and uncreated, explained by the philosopher Plato under the form of everlasting, intelligent ideas [i.e., forms], or moral entities, coeval with eternity. . . .

Macaulay continues by describing this Platonism as the "Catholic opinion in the creed of the moralist." That is, from Macaulay's perspective, the Platonist account of morality was *the* accepted view of the time. Macaulay's observation is important in two ways. First, she indicates that moral objectivism was the standard philosophical view of morality in her time. Second, she indicates that—in spite of different terminology—the moral objectivism of her day was essentially Plato's.

Skepticism about Plato's Moral Objectivism

The theory of morality that we find in Plato—and those he inspired—requires a unique belief in higher objective levels of reality. Traditional Christian believers distinguish between an earthly realm and a higher heavenly realm. Nontraditional religious believers, such as advocates of New Age religion, also think that reality has higher levels than what we see around us. These religious believers may very likely feel that Plato and his successors have accurately captured the higher and objective nature of morality. Others of us, however, may feel that the physical world around us is all that we can be sure of, and notions of the forms or eternal truths don't resonate with our earth-grounded view. This seems to be the conviction underlying the criticisms of Plato by Aristotle and Mackie. Aside from these earth-grounded criticisms, a skeptically-minded person might see an even greater problem with Plato's assertions about objective moral reality. For the skeptic, the true nature of morality is completely inaccessible to us. We strive to be moral, but we will never know *exactly* what morality is or why we approve of some actions and not others.

To illustrate, imagine that someone gives you a box that you can't open but that has something inside. If you shake the box in one direction, you can feel its weight shift and hear a rattling noise. If you shake it in other directions, its weight shifts differently and it makes thumps, crackles, or squeaks. You and your friends come up with different theories about what exactly is inside the box, but none of you knows for sure. When philosophers investigate the nature of reality, they frequently find themselves in a similar situation, lacking direct access to the thing that they want to explain. Philosophers have recognized this to be so with a variety of things. For example, I don't have direct access to the actual physical objects in front of me, such as rocks, trees, or houses. Instead, my knowledge of them is restricted to what appears to my five senses, and my senses are limited in what they can tell me about these objects. Similarly, when I'm speaking with other people, I don't have access to their thoughts; for all I know, they may not have any thoughts at all and may simply be unconscious biological robots. Even my own thinking process is to a large extent beyond my reach. When I go to the grocery store and buy vanilla ice cream rather than chocolate, I don't know exactly what is behind my decision to select one over the other. In all of these cases, we devise theories to help explain the nature of external objects, or other people's minds, or our own mental processes. Often, these theories are a bit too aggressive, making claims that go beyond the available facts.

According to the skeptic, to this list of inaccessible things we need to add the nature of morality. We struggle to uncover the true nature of morality, but all that we end up with is a wide range of theories. These theories sometimes locate the nature of morality in our individual preferences, such as Protagoras suggested, or in higher objective levels of reality, such as Plato suggested. These explanations are not only diverse but can't easily be reconciled with each other. There's a point at which we can reasonably abandon the quest for the true nature of morality and simply accept that the nature of morality is inaccessible to us. Theories such as Protagoras's and Plato's are interesting speculations about the hidden nature of morality. But, like other philosophical theories, these theories frequently venture too far from the available facts. The skeptic's approach to philosophy introduces its own set of problems, which we'd have to sort out before completely agreeing with the skeptic about the inaccessible nature of morality. Nevertheless, most philosophers agree that a dose of skepticism is a good thing insofar as it helps restrain us from becoming too aggressive with our theories.

The upshot of the situation for Aristotle, Mackie, and the skeptic is that, although we regularly read and admire Plato, it is difficult for us to actually believe in his theory of objective moral forms. When we can't accept a *literal* interpretation of a theory, a common tactic is to salvage something of the theory through a *metaphorical* interpretation. With past-life therapy, for example, William J. Baldwin suggests that for it to work, the therapist does not have to literally believe in reincarnation:

> Whether these [past-life] are memories of actual events or metaphoric, symbolic, even archetypal images, the therapist must work with the imagery and narrative and emotions as if they were real. They are real for the client, and the emotional impact of these memories can seriously disrupt a person's life.

We may adopt a similar strategy in handling Plato's theory. Rather than seeing the forms as objectively existing spiritual things, we might simply see them as expressing a *demand* for unchanging standards for moral judgment. Protagoras's "man is the measure" doctrine is simply inadequate; in its place, we require a more fixed criterion of morality.

We can also take Plato's theory metaphorically as a statement about our own moral state as we strive for perfection. Most of us try to be good people. We avoid stealing, we try to be polite, and we try to help others in need. Unfortunately, most of us fall short of moral perfection. We behave selfishly, disregard other people's feelings, speak unkind words about others, and perform a host of other negative acts. However, in spite of our failed efforts to be morally good, we always know that there is a more perfect version of each of us. If I am truly concerned about moral improvement, I will think about what that "more perfect me" is like. How might that more perfect me be more generous, courageous, or even-tempered than I am now? What are the key features of justice or charity that I lack and that the more perfect me should master? Plato and his successors all warn against limiting ourselves to what we see when looking in a mirror. They also warn that moving beyond the present physical world is a very difficult task. By reading objectivist accounts of morality such as Plato's, I may learn from philosophers who have struggled to look beyond the present world, and I may discover the features of that more perfect me.

Summary

Prior to Plato, Protagoras articulated the view that "man is the measure of all things." Plato interpreted this as a statement of individual relativism—namely, that whatever one may judge to be true is true for that person. Against Protagoras's individual relativism, Plato offered a theory of moral objectivism. According to Plato, moral truth is located in the spirit realm of the forms. We gain moral knowledge through past-life recollection of the moral forms, especially the form of the Good. Aristotle criticized Plato for offering a theory that was unnecessarily complex. However, given the state of moral imperfection around us, Plato was justified in offering his complex theory of the forms. Aristotle also objected that Plato does not adequately explain the key notion of participation but simply offers a metaphor. Plato's use of metaphors may be justified, although such metaphors have the disadvantage of being imprecise. Mackie criticized Plato's theory as "queer" with regard to the nature of the forms and how we gain knowledge of the forms. Indeed, this is a central problem for other theories of moral objectivism. Mackie also offered a psychological projection theory that explains why philosophers such as Plato wrongly believe that moral values are objective.

Influenced by Plato's moral theory, Cudworth claimed that we access eternal moral truths by seeing them in God's mind. Religious believers have an affinity with Plato's notion of a higher moral realm. However, more earth-bound people have difficulty accepting his theory literally and may wish to view it more metaphorically as a demand for unchanging moral standards or a vision of a more perfect self.

Study Questions

Introduction
1. What is past-life therapy?
2. What is the definition of "moral objectivism"?

Background of Plato's Moral Theory

The Sophists and Socrates
3. Who were the Sophists, and what was their function in Greek society?
4. Describe the Sophist's technique of "antilogic."
5. Why did many people of the time not like the Sophists?

Protagoras's Individual Relativism
6. What is Protagoras's famous saying?
7. What is "individual relativism"?
8. What was Plato's interpretation of Protagoras's individual relativism?
9. Why was Protagoras a religious skeptic?

Plato's Moral Theory

Theory of the Moral Forms
10. Briefly describe Plato's theory of the forms.
11. According to Plato, where do moral values exist?
12. What is "the form of the Good"?

Recollection and Knowledge of the Forms
13. How do we become acquainted with the various forms?

Criticisms of Plato's Theory

Aristotle's First Criticism: The Forms Do Not Add to Our Knowledge
14. What is "Ockham's Razor," and how does that notion constitute a criticism of Plato's theory?
15. How might you defend Plato against Aristotle's first criticism?

Aristotle's Second Criticism: Participation Is Not Explained
16. According to Fieser, what is the problem with the metaphorical nature of Plato's notion of participation?

Mackie's First Criticism: The Concept of the Forms Is Queer
17. According to Mackie, what are the "queer" aspects of Plato's theory of the forms?

Mackie's Second Criticism: Tendencies to Objectify Can Be Psychologically Explained
18. According to Mackie, why do people tend to objectify values?

The Legacy of Plato's Moral Theory

Plato's Influence
19. According to Cudworth, what are moral values?

Skepticism about Plato's Moral Objectivism
20. For the skeptically-minded person, what is the problem with Plato's theory?

21. What are two metaphorical ways of understanding Plato's theory of the moral forms?

References

William J. Baldwin, *Past Life Therapy: A Training Manual* (Elkhart, IN: Bethel Publishing Co., 1997).

The Sophists are discussed in Richard McKirahan's *Philosophy Before Socrates* (Indianapolis: Hackett, 1994).

Protagoras's views are described in Plato's *Theaetetus*, 152a, 161–173; his statement about the existence of the gods is from Diogenes Laertius, *Lives of the Philosophers*, ix.52.

Plato's distinction between the physical and intellectual realms is vividly illustrated in his analogy of the divided line in the *Republic*, 6.510–511; his theory of recollection is presented in *Phaedo*, 75; the analogy between sense perception and knowledge appears in the *Republic*, 6.507–509, and *Theaetetus*, 185–187. The quotations are from *The Dialogues of Plato*, translated by Benjamin Jowett (New York: Collier, 1901).

Aristotle's criticisms of Plato's theory of the forms are found in *Metaphysics*, 1.9, which is available in several recent translations.

J. L. Mackie's criticisms of Plato are in *Ethics: Inventing Right and Wrong* (New York: Penguin Books, 1977).

Plotinus's discussion of morality is from *Enneads*, 1.2.1, the best translation of which is by A. H. Armstrong, *Plotinus*, 7 vols. (Cambridge, MA: Heinemann, 1966–1988).

Augustine's discussion of virtue is from *City of God*, 19.25, which is available in several recent editions.

The quotation by Ralph Cudworth is from *Treatise concerning Eternal and Immutable Morality*, 4.6.8, which was recently edited by Sarah Hutton (Cambridge: Cambridge University Press, 1996).

The quotation by Catherine Macaulay is from *A Treatise on the Immutability of Moral Truth* (London: Dilly, 1783); there is no recent edition of this work.

Thomas Kuhn's discussion of paradigm shifts is in his *The Structure of Scientific Revolutions* (Chicago: University of Chicago Press, 1962).

Suggestions for Further Reading

For discussions of Plato's moral theory, see Terence Irwin, *Plato's Ethics* (New York: Oxford University Press, 1995); Terence Irwin, *Plato's Moral Theory* (Oxford: Clarendon Press, 1977); Richard Kraut, ed., *The Cambridge Companion to Plato* (Cambridge: Cambridge University Press, 1992).

For discussions of Plotinus, see Lloyd P. Gerson, ed., *The Cambridge Companion to Plotinus* (Cambridge: Cambridge University Press, 1996); Dominic J. O'Meara, *Plotinus: An Introduction to the Enneads* (Oxford: Clarendon Press, 1993).

For discussions of Augustine's theory of knowledge and ethics, see E. Portalie, *A Guide to the Thought of Saint Augustine* (Chicago: Regnery, 1960); C. Kirwan, *Augustine* (London: Routledge, 1989).

For a discussion of Cudworth, see J. A. Passmore, *Ralph Cudworth, an Interpretation* (Cambridge: Cambridge University Press, 1951).

3

Virtue Theory

Introduction

The media recently have focused on a phenomenon called "road rage" in which drivers become enraged at offending motorists and confront them. In Durham, North Carolina, a driver's education teacher became incensed when his car was cut off by another vehicle:

> [David] Cline was teaching two female students how to drive when the other car cut them off, according to police. Cline instructed the student driver to chase down the car, police said. They caught up to [Jon David] Macklin, and Cline got out and punched him, police said. Macklin then took off, and the instructor allegedly had the student chase him again.

The teacher was charged with simple assault and was suspended from his job; he later resigned from his middle school position. Although this particular situation has an element of irony, many other stories of road rage are nothing but tragic. On Virginia's George Washington Parkway, two motorists confronted each other when changing lanes, and the dispute erupted in a high-speed battle. Both drivers lost control of their vehicles, crossed the centerline, and killed two innocent motorists. Studies by the AAA suggest that about thirty deaths in a one-year period were *directly* attributable to road rage. However, the National Highway Traffic Safety Administration stated that, in a one-year period, two-thirds of 41,000 total highway deaths were at least *partly* attributable to road rage. In any case, most such deaths result from assailants using their vehicle as a weapon or using guns they have with them.

The circumstances that spark road rage are mostly trivial. A motorist might brake abruptly, swerve into another lane, or honk the horn. This prompts shouting, tailgating, obscene gestures, high-speed chases, and direct physical confrontations. There are several psychological explanations for the road rage phenomenon. Traffic is continually becoming heavier and thereby causing sensory overload. Many assailants are in large sports utility vehicles, which perhaps gives them a false sense of invulnerability. The root of the problem, however, is that the assailant experiences a strong emotion of anger and seemingly loses the ability to control it. Many relatively minor events in our daily lives have the potential to make us angry. The cat might knock over a plant, the new stereo might malfunction, a store clerk might be rude, or the neighbors might be too noisy. We learn to combat our angry urges, though, and react in a civilized manner.

Anger is just one strong feeling that we must keep in check. Others include lust, hunger, envy, malice, hatred, resentment, fear, pride, and desire. Imagine what life would be like if people never restrained *any* of these emotions. We would constantly clash with others, and society as we know it would collapse. Controlling strong emotions is a matter of training. Our parents and teachers begin training us when we are young. As we get older, we continue the training process on our own. Eventually, we develop habits that become fixed character traits of our personality. In short, we acquire what moral philosophers call virtues—positive character traits that regulate emotions and urges. Typical virtues include courage, temperance, justice, prudence, fortitude, liberality, and truthfulness. Vices, by contrast, are negative character traits that we develop in response to the same emotions and urges. Typical vices include cowardice, insensibility, injustice, and vanity. As a fully developed moral theory, **virtue theory** is the view that the foundation of morality is the development of good character traits, or virtues. A person is good if he or she has virtues and lacks vices.

Early Greek View of Virtues   Historically, virtue theory is one of the oldest moral theories in Western philosophy, having its roots in ancient Greek civilization. The Greek term for virtue is *arete,* which means "excellence." Greek epic poets and playwrights, such as Homer and Sophocles, described the morality of their heroes and antiheroes in terms of their respective virtues and vices. Their characters' successes and failures hinged on their virtuous or vicious character traits. For example, in Sophocles's tragedy *Oedipus Rex,* King Oedipus's life crumbles after he unknowingly kills his father and sleeps with his mother. These tragic acts themselves, though, are a consequence of his character flaws, particularly pride and overconfidence.

Discussions of the virtues become more formalized in the writings of Plato, who stressed four particular virtues: wisdom, courage, temperance, and justice. Early Christian theologians dubbed these the *cardinal virtues,* given their central role for Plato, especially regarding Plato's description of the human psyche. According to Plato, the human psyche has three distinct parts: one that reasons, one that wills, and one that has appetites. The job of our reason is to make sound judgments, and the job of the will is to ally itself with reason rather than appetite. We have *wisdom* when our reason is informed by general knowledge of how to live. We have *courage* when our will always obeys our reason, regardless of what our appetites say. We have *temperance* when our reason governs our appetites. We have *justice* when each of the three parts of our psyche performs its proper task with informed reason in control. Plato believed that these virtues are unified insofar as all four require a properly developed reason. So, for Plato, if I have one of these virtues, I will necessarily have them all. Although Plato's vision of reason's involvement in virtues influenced later theorists, the details of his four cardinal virtues had limited impact given their somewhat forced reliance on his specialized theory of the psyche. The more developed analysis of virtues was left to his student, Aristotle (384–322 BCE).

Aristotle's Theory

Aristotle's account of virtue is found in his work *The Nichomachean Ethics,* which he named in honor of his son Nichomachus. The work is long, at around 200 pages, and only the highlights of his theory can be presented here.

Appetite-Regulating Habits   There are three main components in Aristotle's discussion of virtues. The first involves establishing the fact that we all strive after an ultimate good that defines who we are. The subject of ethics is an attempt to discover this goal. For Aristotle, our ultimate good is an end that we seek in and of itself, and not merely for the sake of something else. In general, we call this ultimate end "happiness" (*eudamonea*), although this term is used in so many ways that we need to specify more precisely what it involves. Human happiness is different from the contentment that dogs experience, for example, and such happiness is unique to our human construction and purpose.

The second component in Aristotle's discussion involves discovering our uniquely human purpose by analyzing our uniquely human psyche. He offers this division of the human psyche:

		Calculative (logic, math, science)
	Rational <	
Psyche		Appetitive (emotions, desires)
	Irrational <	
		Vegetative (nutrition, growth)

According to Aristotle, the psyche has an irrational element that is similar to that found in animals and a rational element that is distinctly human. The highest aspect of the rational part is *calculative* in nature and is responsible for the uniquely human ability to contemplate, reason logically, and formulate scientific principles. At the other extreme is the *vegetative* faculty, the most primitive and irrational element of our psyche, which is responsible for our physical nutrition and growth. This element is present in all life forms, and not just in humans and other animals. Between the two extremes is an additional faculty that is by nature irrational but is guided by reason. This is the *appetitive* faculty, which is responsible for our emotions and desires. The appetitive faculty is irrational since even lower animals experience desires. However, this faculty is rationally guided in humans since we have the distinct ability to control these desires with the help of reason. The human ability to properly control these desires is called "moral virtue" and is the focus of ethics.

The third and final component in Aristotle's discussion involves describing the moral virtues themselves. Aristotle makes three general observations about the nature of moral virtues. First, he argues that the ability to regulate our desires isn't instinctive; rather, it is learned and is the outcome of both teaching and practice. Second, he suggests that desire-regulating virtues are character traits, or habitual dispositions, and shouldn't be seen as either emotions or mental faculties. Third, he notes that moral virtues are desire-regulating character traits that fall at some mean between more extreme character traits. If we regulate our desires either too much or too little, then we create problems. For example, in response to our natural emotion of fear when facing danger, we should develop the virtuous character trait of courage. If we develop an excessive character trait by curbing fear too much, then we are said to be rash, which is a vice. If, on the other extreme, we develop a deficient character trait by curbing fear too little, then we are said to be cowardly, which is also a vice. The virtue of courage, then, lies at the mean between the excessive extreme of rashness and the deficient extreme of cowardice. Aristotle notes that this is similar to how "excess or deficiency of gymnastic exercise is fatal to strength."

According to the doctrine of the mean, most moral virtues, and not just courage, fall at the mean between two accompanying vices. Aristotle describes eleven virtues in particular that follow this model. Each virtue and vice arises in reaction to some specific appetite or desire we have. His analysis is summarized in this table:

Appetite	*Vice of Deficiency*	*Virtuous Mean*	*Vice of Excess*
Fear danger	Cowardice	Courage	Rashness
Pleasure	Insensibility	Temperance	Intemperance
Give money	Stinginess	Generosity	Extravagance
Spend money	Pettiness	Magnificence	Vulgarity
Self-worth	Humility	Self-respect	Vanity
Honor	No ambition	Right ambition	Overambition
Anger	Spiritlessness	Good Temper	Ill temper
Social life	Unfriendliness	Friendly civility	Bootlickingness
Truth	False modesty	Sincerity	Boastfulness
Amusement	Humorlessness	Wittiness	Buffoonery
Fear dishonor	Immodesty	Modesty	Bashfulness

Of these eleven virtues, the pinnacle for Aristotle is self-respect, which is also translated as "pride" or "high-mindedness." It involves having a respectful attitude about our self-worth in everything that we do. For example, it is unbecoming for a self-respecting person to be cowardly when facing danger, or to be insensible with pleasure, or to be stingy about giving money.

Aristotle notes that there weren't enough terms in his language to adequately name all the virtues and corresponding vices. This is also the case with the English language, and it may be difficult at first to grasp the relation between the various virtues and vices on the preceding chart. Aristotle notes as well that not all virtues fall at a mean between two more extreme dispositions. One such virtue is that of justice, which simply has injustice as its contrary. The virtue of justice involves being lawful and fair; the unjust person, by contrast, is unlawful and unfair, and greedily grasps at things.

Practical Wisdom   Although Aristotle's analysis of the eleven virtues fits into a nicely organized scheme, in real-life situations it can be difficult to pinpoint the mean between two extreme dispositions. Suppose I am a soldier, and I know in theory that if my fear gets the best of me I will be a coward, and if I completely ignore my fear I will be rash. Somewhere in the middle lies courage. But how many bullets need to zip past my head before I can courageously crawl back into my foxhole for safety? Or suppose I am a college student, and I understand that temperance involves knowing how to regulate my desire for pleasure. Am I insensible if I completely avoid going to fraternity parties? And if I do go, how many beers can I have before I am intemperate? Or suppose that, in my drive to succeed at my job, I understand that lack of ambition will get me fired but that too much ambition will destroy my home life. How much devotion should I show at my job?

Aristotle confesses that it is indeed difficult to live the virtuous life primarily because of the challenges involved in finding the mean between the extremes. He notes that calculating the mean isn't simply a matter of taking an average. For example, if drinking twenty beers at a party is too much and drinking no beers is too little, this doesn't imply that I should drink ten beers, which is the mathematical mean. Fortunately, there is a solution to this problem. Aristotle explains that an aspect of our calculative reasoning called **practical wisdom** (*phronesis*) helps us find the virtuous mean. There are two components to practical wisdom. First, it involves an intuitive knowledge of our ultimate purpose in life. In a nutshell, our ultimate purpose is to be community-oriented, rational creatures, and each properly formed virtue contributes to fulfilling this ultimate purpose. Second, practical wisdom involves deliberating about and planning the best way of attaining this ultimate purpose. As a soldier, cowering in my foxhole won't help me attain my community-oriented purpose; being too rash won't help me either. Practical wisdom will help me to assess the risks in different combat situations and to see when it would be most prudent for me to charge or to flee the enemy. Similarly, practical wisdom will help me figure out how many beers I should drink at a party and how much ambition I should have at my job. With each dilemma we face, then, our practical wisdom will help us chisel out the appropriate conduct that will facilitate our ultimate purpose.

In spite of the assistance that we receive from practical wisdom, we shouldn't see it as an "inner voice" that tells us for each action whether that action hits the mean or one of the extremes. First, when we are in the process of developing virtuous habits, practical wisdom doesn't pronounce judgment on each of our actions. Instead, through our life experiences, we gradually develop a sense of our ultimate purpose, and just as gradually we cultivate virtuous hab-

its. Second, once our virtuous habits are developed, we act spontaneously without step-by-step rational prompting. For example, once I learn how to be a safe
driver, my roadway manners become second nature, and I slow down before
approaching a stop sign without consciously thinking about it.

If I successfully acquire virtues, then I attain the status of a good person. As
a good person, each of my actions will reflect the virtuous character traits that
I have developed. However, Aristotle argues, each action must be freely chosen.
That is, each action must have its causal origin within me; it can't be imposed
on me by other people. Further, for my choice to be truly free, I must know
all of the important details pertaining to the action in question. He argues
that freedom of the will is a factor with both virtuous choices and vicious
choices.

Good Temper   Given the problem of road rage, let's look at Aristotle's discussion of the virtue of good temper, the seventh virtue listed in our chart. Good
temper properly curbs one's appetite of anger. If I curb my anger too much, I
have the vice of spiritlessness; if I don't curb it enough, I have the vice of ill
temper. For Aristotle, there are five factors involved in our appropriate response
to anger. We should become angry only (1) at the appropriate person, (2) for an
appropriate offense, (3) to an appropriate degree, (4) with appropriate quick-
ness, and (5) for an appropriate length of time. He concedes that it is difficult to
define precisely what counts as "appropriate" in these five circumstances. But
he also maintains that good-tempered persons won't allow themselves to be
ruled by their passions; instead, they will be guided by practical wisdom. Aristotle believes that it is appropriate to get angry when someone callously insults
us. However, good-tempered individuals aren't vengeful, and to a degree they
accept their situation.

As for the vice of spiritlessness, there are several reasons it is bad for us to
completely lack expressions of anger. If we never react in anger even when there
is proper cause, then it will appear to others that we will tolerate injustice, that
we won't defend ourselves, and that we will put up with insult after insult
against our loved ones and ourselves. In a word, people will see us as fools. In
spite of how bad it is to be completely unaffected by anger, Aristotle believes
that it is better to err on the side of spiritlessness than on the side of ill temper
since spiritless people are easier to live with.

At the other extreme, ill-tempered people express anger inappropriately
with regard to at least one of the five factors given previously. In fact, Aristotle
notes, we have different names for ill-tempered people based on the combination of factors in which they fail. Hotheaded people get angry too quickly, with
the wrong people, for the wrong reason, and to the wrong degree (factors 1–4).
However, they get over their anger quickly (factor 5), which is the best thing
about them. Choleric people get angry quickly at everything on every occasion
(factors 1, 2, and 4). Brooding people fail mainly with the fifth factor, hanging
on to their anger far too long. Bad-tempered people get angry at the wrong
things for a long period of time (factors 2 and 5) and won't be satisfied until
they inflict punishment on the offender. How would Aristotle view the person

who exhibits road rage? The enraged driver has perhaps picked out the appropriate person for an appropriate offense, and perhaps he is angry for an appropriate length of time. But the *degree* of his reaction is far too extreme, and he becomes angry far too quickly. His principal failure, then, is with factors 3 and 4.

To recap, these are the main points of Aristotle's virtue theory:

- Moral virtues are habits that regulate the desires of our appetitive nature.
- Most virtues fall at a mean between two vicious habits.
- Our practical wisdom guides us in developing moral virtues by gradually informing us of our ultimate purpose and showing us the best means of attaining it.
- Our moral actions are freely chosen and are an extension of our virtuous habits.

Aristotle himself summarizes his notion of moral virtue in this way:

> Virtues are means between extremes; they are states of character; by their own nature they tend to the doing of acts by which they are produced; they are in our power and voluntary; they act as prescribed by right governance [i.e., practical wisdom]. (*Nicomachean Ethics*, 1114b, 25)

Virtue Theory after Aristotle   For almost 2000 years, Greek notions of virtue—and Aristotle's theory in particular—were central to Western conceptions of morality. The details were sometimes different, but moral philosophers consistently emphasized the need to acquire good character traits that guide our actions and thereby make us good people. Immediately after Aristotle, the rival philosophical schools of Epicureanism and Stoicism offered competing views of morality and the virtues. **Epicurus** (341–270 BCE) identified the virtuous life with the pursuit of pleasure and the avoidance of pain. By contrast, **Zeno of Citium** (334–262 BCE), the founder of Stoicism, emphasized the importance of resigning ourselves to fate and suppressing our desires for things beyond our control. For Zeno, virtue is intimately connected with our knowledge of the physical world, and to this end, the virtuous person develops four knowledge-oriented virtues. Through intelligence, she knows what is good and bad. Through bravery, she knows what to fear and what not to fear. Through justice, she knows how to give what is deserved. And through self-control, she knows what passions to ignore.

With the arrival of Christianity, the Apostle Paul endorsed the virtues of faith, hope, and charity, which were later dubbed the **theological virtues,** in contrast to Plato's four cardinal virtues. Medieval theologians sometimes referred to the "seven virtues," combining the three theological virtues with the four cardinal virtues. Medieval theologians such as Aquinas held Aristotle in especially high regard and wrote commentaries on the *Nichomachean Ethics,* which helped perpetuate Aristotle's analysis of the virtues. By the time of the Renaissance, philosophical discussions of virtue were mainly analyses of Aristotle's theory.

Traditional Criticisms of Virtue Theory

In the seventeenth century, interest in Aristotle's version of virtue ethics declined. His theory wasn't rejected outright; instead, leading moral philosophers argued that virtues were only of secondary importance in explaining moral obligation. Of primary importance was the need to follow rational moral rules and make sure that our actions abided by those rules.

Grotius's Criticism: Many Virtues Are Not at a Mean   In his work *The Law of War and Peace* (1625), Dutch philosopher **Hugo Grotius** (1583–1645) began the attack on Aristotle by arguing that his theory fails as a systematic account of morality. Grotius focuses specifically on Aristotle's doctrine of the mean. For Aristotle, virtues regulate our desires insofar as we form middle-ground habits between more extreme habits. According to Grotius, some virtues do indeed control our passions through a middle course, but not all virtues do this. In fact, some virtues are actually extreme dispositions. For example, Aristotle lists insensibility—or contempt for pleasure—as a vice, but Grotius sees this as a virtue. Aristotle lists ambitionlessness—or contempt for honor—as a vice, but Grotius sees this, too, as a virtue. In religious matters, Grotius believes that it is impossible to worship God too much, or to seek heaven too much, or to fear hell too much. The larger point, for Grotius, is that morality involves following the rational rules of natural law, and not scouting about for an elusive middle ground of behavior. Grotius believes that everyone has access to the rules of natural law, and our reason will quickly tell us when we should seek a middle ground and when we should do something in the extreme.

At face value, Grotius's criticism seems plausible: We can understand how Aristotle might have forced a number of virtues into a mold that they didn't quite fit. However, if we carefully examine the specific cases that Grotius cites, Aristotle's account of middle-ground virtues seems on target. Are contempt for pleasure and honor really virtues as Grotius claims? For average people in average social situations, these extreme behaviors don't seem appropriate. By having contempt for all pleasure, we cut ourselves off from many of life's best things, such as romance, good food, and entertainment. By having contempt for all honor, we feel incomplete in what we try to accomplish in life. Grotius also believes that it is virtuous to be extreme in our worship of God, fear of hell, or desire for heaven. Similarly, though, for average people in average social situations, if we focus too much on religious matters, then we may neglect our earthly responsibilities.

When praising these extreme character traits, perhaps Grotius has in mind religious believers, such as monks, who devote their lives to austerity. Monks deny all bodily pleasures and any emotional pleasure that comes from personal accomplishment. Scottish philosopher **David Hume** (1711–1776) discusses what he calls "monkish virtues," and unlike Grotius, he readily calls them vices:

> Celibacy, fasting, penance, mortification, self-denial, humility, silence, solitude, and the whole train of monkish virtues . . . server to no manner of

purpose. . . . We justly, therefore, transfer them to the opposite column, and place them in the catalogue of vices . . . (*Enquiry Concerning the Principles of Morals*, 9.1)

For Hume, these monkish qualities are actually vices since they don't make life more agreeable for ourselves or other people. Instead, they inhibit our happiness. Perhaps, like Grotius, Hume has also gone too far in assessing extreme monkish character traits. Although these may be vices for people in normal social situations, they are not vices for the monks themselves. The monks themselves believe that they are bettering themselves through their more extreme behavior. And—most significantly for Aristotle's theory—the monks will likely feel that they, too, are following a middle-ground lifestyle. Even a zealous monk could become too extreme and starve himself to death, or whip himself to death, or pray to the point of insanity.

So, contrary to Grotius, it seems appropriate to discover virtues through middle-ground dispositions—both for ordinary people and for monks. Many Eastern religions provide two separate lists of moral codes, one for monks and one for nonmonks, and each of these codes is reasonable in its own context. The key issue, then, is identifying one's social context and finding the appropriate mean in that context.

Kant's Criticism: Without Moral Principles, Misapplied Virtues Become Vices
German philosopher **Immanuel Kant** (1724–1804) recognized that virtues are important for developing our worth as people. However, he argues that virtues have no moral value unless they are directed by rational moral principles. In fact, for Kant, if our virtues are not guided by moral principles, then they actually become vices. For example, according to Kant, "The coolness of a villain makes him not only much more dangerous but also immediately more abominable in our eyes than he would have been regarded by us without it." That is, we typically think that it is a virtue to be cool-headed; but when a villain is cool-headed, this actually makes him seem more evil than he would have been otherwise. Although Kant does not reject virtues, he believes that they are secondary to our need to follow moral principles. Our primary moral task is to discover the rules of morality and then to shape our character based on these rules.

Philosophers before Kant also recognized that misapplied virtues become vices. One of the most dramatic illustrations of this is given by French statesman Maximilien de Béthune (1559–1641) in this description of a man he knew who had an extraordinary number of virtues:

His genius was so lively that nothing could escape his penetration, his apprehension was so quick, that he understood every thing in an instant, and his memory so prodigious, that he never forgot anything. He was master of all the branches of philosophy, the mathematics; particularly fortification and designing. Nay, he was so thoroughly acquainted with divinity, that he was an excellent preacher. . . . He applied this talent to imitate all sorts of persons, which he performed with wonderful dexterity; and was accordingly the best comedian in the world. He was a good poet, an excellent musician, and sung with equal art and sweetness. . . . His body was perfectly proportioned to his mind. He was well made, vigorous and agile, formed for all sorts of exercises. He rode a horse well, and was admired for dancing, leaping, and wrestling. He was acquainted with all kinds of sports and diversions, and could practice in most of the mechanical arts.

As de Béthune continues his description, he suggests that all of these virtues become tainted when we consider the horrible qualities of the same person:

Reverse the medal: He was a liar, false, treacherous, cruel, and cowardly, a sharper, drunkard and glutton. He was a gamester, an abandoned debauchee, a blasphemer and Atheist. In a word, he was possessed of every vice, contrary to nature, to honour, to religion, and society: he persisted in his vices to the last, and fell a sacrifice to his debaucheries, in the flower of his age; he died in a public stew, holding the glass in his hand, swearing, and denying God.

Both de Béthune and Kant expose a central problem for virtue theory: Virtuous character traits by themselves are not necessarily good. Indeed, Kant gives one successful solution to this problem—namely, that we should develop our virtues in response to general moral principles that we follow. Although a possible solution, this isn't the best solution.

Many moral philosophers—including Cicero, Hutcheson, Balfour, and Beattie—distinguish between two groups of character traits, the first being more important than the second:

Moral virtues: benevolence, fidelity, integrity, justice, humanity, generosity

Intellectual abilities: courage, coolness, industry, intelligence, wit, good manners, eloquence

According to these philosophers, it is ethically more important for me to develop moral virtues, such as benevolence, than intellectual abilities, such as courage. In fact, my overall moral goodness depends on my developing moral virtues rather than intellectual abilities. So, if I first develop moral virtues, such as benevolence, then I won't be able to misapply intellectual abilities, such as courage. We can see this by returning to Kant's example of the cool-headed villain. Kant's villain lacks moral virtues but has the intellectual ability of coolness, which he misapplies. But suppose that the villain has a moral conversion and acquires moral virtues such as justice. As a morally virtuous person, his coolness then becomes a moral asset rather than a moral liability; it is difficult to imagine how a just person could ever misapply the intellectual virtue of coolness. The distinction between moral virtues and intellectual abilities also solves the puzzle raised by de Béthune's example. The man's "virtues" are really only intellectual qualities, and his "vices" are mostly genuine moral vices.

In short, to solve the problem of misapplied virtues, we don't have to subordinate virtues to moral rules, as Kant argues. Instead, we can recognize and adopt a superior class of truly moral virtues, and this will prevent us from misapplying our intellectual abilities.

Mill's Criticism: Morality Involves Judging Actions and Not Character Traits   British philosopher John Stuart Mill (1806–1873) recognized the importance of virtues in forming our personal character and influencing our opinion of people. Good people, he says, are people who have virtues, such as charity. Mill also argues that virtues are important for inclining us to act properly. If I have the virtue of charity, for example, then I will be more inclined to help others in need. Nevertheless, Mill says, the job of morality is to assess people's *actions,* and not their *character:*

> No known ethical standard decides an action to be good or bad because it is done by a good or a bad man, still less because done by an amiable, a brave, or a benevolent man, or the contrary. These considerations are relevant, not to the estimation of actions, but of persons . . . (*Utilitarianism,* Ch. 2)

According to Mill, I am morally guilty only for what I *actually* do, and not for what I am *inclined* to do. Suppose, for example, that I dive into a river to rescue someone from drowning and that I'm motivated by the hope of getting a reward. Mill believes that I did the morally right thing. What matters is that I rescued that person; it doesn't matter what specifically inclined me to do it. So, since virtues are only inclinations, they are not relevant in our assessment of the actions themselves.

Although we should disregard virtuous inclinations when making moral judgments, Mill is quick to point out that we must recognize the immediate *intention* behind an action. The intention involves the action's specific purpose. For example, when I dive into the river, my intention is to rescue you, not to drag you out of the river and torture you to death. My intention to rescue you will be the same regardless of whether I am motivated by greed or benevolence. Mill recognizes that he might be going too far by devaluing the importance of virtues, but he believes that it is best to err on the side of caution and rigidly judge individuals for each of their intended actions.

Mill is correct in pointing out that we often judge people's intended actions, and not their predispositions. This is similar to how we legally judge criminals for the crimes that they actually commit, and not for their criminal predispositions. However, contrary to Mill, there are clear cases in which both moral and legal judgments go beyond the intended action and focus also on predispositions—for example, in the case of repeat offenders who show a predisposition toward immoral or illegal actions. Suppose that you are typically a mild-mannered person, but on one occasion you get into a bar fight and break a guy's nose. This is certainly bad, but not as bad as if you were predisposed to violence—and especially if you displayed this predisposition by routinely getting into bar fights. Sometimes, we carry our moral track record around with us, and we expect that people will judge our actions based on the kind of person we've become.

The upshot of the situation is that moral judgments are more multifaceted than Mill allows, and we often look beyond the intended action to the actual virtue or vice.

Contemporary Discussions of Virtues and Rules

Continuing the trend set by Grotius, Kant, and Mill, moral philosophers during the late nineteenth and early twentieth centuries typically assigned virtues a secondary place within their theories. In 1958, philosopher **Elizabeth Anscombe** published an influential article entitled "Modern Moral Philosophy" in which she harshly criticizes the direction of moral philosophy since the days of Grotius. According to Anscombe, modern moral theories inconsistently advance moral rules without any notion of a rule giver. She advises that we abandon the entire rule-based approach in favor of the virtue-based approach offered by Aristotle, which avoids this inconsistency.

Anscombe and other critics suggest that there are essentially two approaches to morality: virtue-based theories and action/rule-based theories. According to virtue-based theories, (1) greater importance is placed on developing good character traits than on acting in accordance with moral rules; (2) good actions are those that flow from our virtuous character traits; and (3) morality is a matter of being a *good person,* which involves having virtuous character traits. By contrast, according to action/rule-based theories, (1) emphasis is placed on proper actions, which conform to moral rules; (2) although good character traits might help us perform good actions, they don't define good actions; and (3) people are judged based on their actions, not on whether they are good people.

Feminine Ethics and Virtue Theory Virtue-based theories have received an extra boost recently from some feminist philosophers, who argue that action/rule-based morality is male-centered. Contemporary feminist writers express a wide range of ideas, and it is a mistake to associate any particular moral theory with the entire group. However, a theme popular with many feminist writers is that, historically, the creation of strict moral rules has been modeled after practices that were traditionally male-dominated, such as acquiring property, engaging in business contracts, and governing societies. The rigid systems of rules required for trade and government set a pattern for creating equally rigid systems of moral rules, such as lists of moral rights and duties. Some of this may have been the result of a male instinct to organize and pigeonhole things. It may also have been the result of self-serving male interests, which involved creating moral rules that subverted the interests of women, such as requiring women to be obedient, industrious, servile, and silent. Men not only created the rules of morality itself but also the rules that govern proper *discussion* of morality, so input from women became almost impossible.

Women, by contrast, traditionally had a nurturing role, raising children and overseeing domestic life. These tasks require less rule following and more spontaneous and creative interaction. Proponents of a view called **feminine ethics** argue that we should use women's experience as a model for moral theory, and the basis of morality should be caring for others as would be appropriate in each unique circumstance. According to this view, we should first listen to people's concerns and try to understand the total situation; we then can respond to the diversity of needs and perspectives reflected in the situation. This would involve acquiring nurturing character traits and allowing our actions to flow from these. This stands in sharp contrast to male-modeled morality, in which the agent mechanically performs his duty as moral laws require. Some feminist philosophers argue that a morality based on female virtues should *replace* male-modeled moral systems that emphasize rules. More moderate writers argue that it should only be a *supplement.*

Although many feminists endorse virtue-based approaches to ethics in general, contemporary philosopher Nel Noddings argues that Aristotle's specific account needs modification. Aristotle's list of specific virtues comes from an elite social class, as opposed to the social classes of slaves and women, who had more subservient roles in society. For Noddings, feminine ethics represents a quest for new virtues based on traditional women's practices that we see in everyday experiences. For example, accepted women's occupations today are cooking, cleaning, nursing, secretarial services, and childhood education. Although these are roles that women should rise above, they nevertheless reflect a caring mentality, which Noddings believes is inherent to women.

Virtues with or without Rules?   Anscombe and some feminine ethicists suggest that virtue theory should be completely independent of moral rules. Is this plausible? Proponents of one side of the dispute, which we will call *strong* virtue theory, maintain that rules must be eliminated from all notions of virtue. That is, morality is founded entirely on virtuous character traits such as courage, and these virtues are independent of ideal principles. Proponents of the other side of the dispute, which we will call *weak* virtue theory, maintain that there is either a single rule or a core set of rules that determine whether a character trait is good or bad. Some of the appeal of strong virtue theory undoubtedly stems from a frustration with the inadequacies of various action/rule-based approaches to morality, such as those proposed by Kant and Mill. As some feminists argue, rigid rules seem so contrary to the nurturing dispositions needed for genuine morality that we should simply reject them. However, in spite of the appeal of strong virtue theory, it isn't clear that classical virtue theorists held to this strong notion when devising their theories. Three aspects of Aristotle's theory in particular suggest that rules are at least part of virtue-based morality.

First, Aristotle's doctrine of the mean is itself a general principle, which some followers of Aristotle call the "principle of the golden mean." According to this principle, right or virtuous actions are those that fall between extreme responses. This rule is somewhat flexible and depends on our specific circumstances and the guidance of practical wisdom. Nevertheless, it is still the standard in determining virtuous conduct.

Second, each specific virtue is a standard by which we assess the correctness of our own actions, as well as those other people. This is clear in Aristotle's discussion of the virtue of good temper noted previously. We praise people who abide by the virtuous mean of good temper and condemn those who don't. He also advises us as individuals to "cling to the middle state" of good temper so that we become praiseworthy. Similarly, the virtues of courage, temperance, generosity, and self-respect all become standards by which we praise or condemn actions.

A final "rule" aspect of Aristotle's theory involves the intimate connection he establishes between ethics and politics. Ethics involves the discovery of our ultimate human purpose as developed in virtuous character traits. Politics extends directly from this and involves legislating "what we are to do and what we are to abstain from" (*Nichomachean Ethics,* 1.2). Part of this process involves establishing just actions and just punishments (*Politics,* 7.13). Virtues, then, are only the starting point; the next step is to create governing bodies, social classes, and the obligations of both rulers and citizens, all of which is rule-oriented. In view of these "rule" aspects of Aristotle's theory, he is best seen as a weak virtue theorist.

Contemporary Criticisms In spite of the recent strong support for virtue-based morality, defenders of action/rule-based approaches point out several limitations with virtue theory. However, most of these are attacks on strong virtue theory. Because of the popularity of such criticisms, it is important to see how defenders of weak virtue theory quickly respond to these charges. First, critics charge that there is a problem with determining precisely who is virtuous. It doesn't help to look for some external criterion, such as visible indications in the person's action, since outward actions are no guarantee that the person's inner self is virtuous. It also doesn't help to look for some internal criterion, such as the individual's self-respect or integrity, since we don't have the ability to read people's minds. In response, weak virtue theorists say that we look at people's actions as indicators of their character traits—for example, whether a given action appears ill-tempered. We then praise or blame the action based on whether it approaches the virtuous mean.

Second, critics argue that some acts, such as murder, are so intolerable that we must devise a special list of prohibited offenses. Strong virtue theory doesn't provide such a list, but it is easy for the weak virtue theorist to construct a list of prohibited actions. When we assess how well a person's actions conform to the virtuous mean, it becomes evident that some actions are more blameworthy than others are. We then make a list of these actions. Although Aristotle didn't provide a definitive list, he does note that certain vices are worse than others. For example, in his discussion of good temper, he argues that the vice of ill temper is worse than the vice of spiritlessness. Also, other virtue theorists do provide short lists of prohibited actions that stem from serious vices, the most famous of which is the medieval list of the seven deadly sins.

Finally, critics argue that virtue theory permits us to occasionally act badly, as long as the virtue in question remains intact. For example, virtue theory emphasizes long-term character traits, such as honesty or generosity. Because of this long-term emphasis, we might overlook specfic lies or acts of selfishness on the grounds that they are only temporary departures from our overall dispositions. The weak virtue theorist has two responses to this charge. First, once we set virtues up as standards of praise and blame, we are in a position to judge *every* action that departs from a given virtuous standard. The occasional lie, for example, will stand out and call for judgment. Second, it may be a mistake to think that occasional departures, such as white lies, don't compromise virtuous character traits. With many virtues, to be virtuous means to *always* display exemplary conduct. For example, even a single act of marital infidelity sufficiently signals a lack of virtue. A politician who publicly lies even once loses the trust of the people. It may sometimes seem as though we can still be virtuous while occasionally acting nonvirtuously, but this may only mean that we have compromised our standards of morality.

The Value of Virtue Theory

Virtues play a role in most traditional moral theories, and even Grotius, Kant, and Mill don't suggest that we should completely abandon interest in them. The issue becomes, first, how prominent a role virtues should play in a theory, and, second, what specific virtues we should adopt.

Incorporating Virtue Theory into Other Moral Theories   Regarding the first issue—how prominent a role virtues should play—our discussion so far suggests that they certainly deserve a central role, but not the only role. First, even the simple task of listing various virtues involves at least some rules. To determine whether a given character trait is virtuous as opposed to vicious, we will likely fall back on some rule, such as the principle of the golden mean. We are also likely to see each specific virtue itself as a standard and rule that indicates proper conduct. So, at a minimum, we should prefer weak virtue theory to strong virtue theory. Second, moral judgments are quite varied, and even weak virtue theory can't adequately explain this diversity without bringing in other theories. Suppose that, when driving down the highway, I accidentally cut off another driver, who then flies into a rage and runs me into a ditch. Aristotle would say that the other driver was immoral largely because he had the vice of intemperance. This, though, is only one kind of moral assessment, and it isn't even the most natural assessment that we might make. Instead, I might say that the driver was immoral because he caused me emotional pain for no justifiable reason. I might also say that the driver violated my rights—specifically, my right not to be physically attacked. If I am religious, I might say that the man sinned by going against God's will.

Contemporary virtue theorist **Alasdair MacIntyre** would say that I'm uttering nonsense with these other moral assessments—regardless of how commonly we speak about personal happiness, individual rights, or the will of God. MacIntyre believes that today we have only fragments of conflicting moral traditions:

> We continue to use many of the key expressions [of morality]. But we have—very largely, if not entirely—lost our comprehension, both theoretical and practical, of morality. (*After Virtue,* 1)

To make sense of morality, says MacIntyre, we need to adopt Aristotle's view of virtues. Contrary to MacIntyre, though, it isn't reasonable to simply dismiss most of our moral vocabulary simply because it doesn't draw on virtue theory. More importantly, it is not even possible for us today to abandon these other moral notions in exclusive favor of virtue theory. Notions of moral rights are firmly imbedded into American moral consciousness, particularly the natural rights to life, liberty, and the pursuit of happiness as endorsed by the Declaration of Independence. Religious believers who ground morality in God's will are not likely to shift to Aristotle's virtue theory anytime soon. To best understand and theorize about morality, we should begin by acknowledging the wide range of approaches that people actually do take to the subject. Virtue theory is only one of many approaches.

Regarding the second issue—what specific virtues we should focus on— clearly, Aristotle's short list of virtues is incomplete. Whereas Aristotle stopped at about a dozen virtues, seventeenth- and eighteenth-century virtue theorists expanded the list to include as many as 100 distinct virtues. Today, we should modify the list even more. Feminist critics such as Noddings correctly point out that Aristotle's list reflects an aristocratic bias that we should reject, and they rightly observe that we should include more feminine and nurturing qualities. As social trends shift and we become more receptive to racial, ethnic, and gender diversity, we should adopt virtues of social tolerance and acceptance. With growing interest in animal rights and environmental issues, we should cultivate virtues that display a sensitivity to these concerns. Part of the task of moral philosophers is to sift through social trends and update moral theories in this way.

The Best Teacher of Morality   Although we want to view virtue theory as only one of many approaches to morality, we should keep in mind virtue theory's unique asset. Imagine that, as a parent, you want to teach your child that it is wrong to become inappropriately enraged. When your child is older, you don't want him to give in to road rage, beat his wife, or perform any other action that is the consequence of inappropriate anger. Imagine further that you have two teaching methods available. The first method established meticulous rules for what counts as inappropriate anger in virtually every circumstance. It also included rules describing the kinds of punishments that are justified for each type of violation. According to this first teaching method, your child memorizes all these rules so that, for each situation that arises, your child immediately knows the right thing to do. The second method doesn't involve memorizing specific rules but instead focuses on instilling good habits. Using various techniques, such as behavior modification, you teach your child to avoid inappropriate action and become habituated toward appropriate action. You also give him techniques so he can properly modify his behavior on his own, without your constant monitoring. All other factors being equal, which of these two methods would work best in preventing inappropriate anger? The habit-instilling method appears to be the winner.

Virtue theorists capitalize on the benefits of teaching morality through creating virtuous habits. They argue that the most important thing about studying ethics is its impact on conduct. Aristotle himself said that he wrote the *Nichomachean Ethics* "not in order to know what virtue is, but in order to become good." Detailed lists of rules in and of themselves don't make us better people, but instilling good habits does. In 1993, attorney William J. Bennett edited an anthology entitled *The Book of Virtues,* which quickly became a best-seller. The work contains classic stories and folktales highlighting ten virtues, including self-discipline, compassion, responsibility, and friendship. Bennett says that the work is meant to assist in the "time-honored task of the moral education of the young." Among the essential elements of moral training, he notes that "moral education *must* provide training in good habits. Aristotle wrote that good habits formed at youth make all the difference."

In our actual lives as we raise our children, we will likely adopt a hybrid approach to teaching morality that involves both teaching rules and instilling good habits. The fact remains, though, that it is a mistake to completely ignore the benefits of virtue theory in moral instruction. Society needs all the help it can get in improving its moral climate. To that end, moral philosophers of all traditions should welcome the contributions of virtue theory.

Summary

Aristotle offered the view that morality consists of developing virtuous habits that are a mean between extreme vicious habits. Philosophers during the Middle Ages adopted Aristotle's view, although virtues were reduced to a secondary status by seventeenth- and eighteenth-century moral philosophers. Grotius argued that Aristotle's doctrine of the mean fails since some virtues, such as religious worship, actually require extreme behavior. But virtues do in fact occupy a middle ground, although the middle ground must be seen within particular social contexts. Kant argued that some virtues—such as cool-headedness—might become vices if they aren't guided by higher moral principles. We've seen, however, that we can avoid misapplying virtues by distinguishing between more important moral virtues, such as justice, and less important intellectual qualities, such as cool-headedness. By acquiring the more important moral virtues, we thereby avoid misapplying the less important intellectual qualities. Mill argued that morality involves judging a person's *actions* and not a person's *character.* Contrary to Mill, though, at least sometimes it is relevant to consider a person's character when judging actions, especially with repeat offenders.

Contemporary discussions of virtue assess the relative merits of virtue-based versus action/rule-based morality. Some feminist philosophers reject the action/rule-based approach for being too masculine in orientation and suggest instead that morality involves acquiring more feminine virtues such as nurturance. We can distinguish between strong virtue theory, which rejects all rules, and weak virtue theory, which involves some rules. Aristotle himself is a weak virtue theorist, and weak virtue theory sidesteps many common criticisms against virtue theory in general. In any case, virtue theory is only one of many approaches to moral philosophy, although virtue theory is uniquely suited for teaching morality.

Study Questions

Introduction

1. What are some of the reasons for road rage?
2. Define "virtue," "vice," and "virtue theory."

Early Greek View of Virtues

3. List the four cardinal virtues in Plato's theory

Aristotle's Theory

Appetite-Regulating Habits

4. What are the three faculties of the psyche?
5. How is the appetitive faculty both rational and irrational?
6. What are "moral virtues," and what are Aristotle's three general observations about them?
7. What are the two vices associated with the virtue of courage?
8. List the eleven virtues that Aristotle covers.

Practical Wisdom

9. For Aristotle, what are the two contributions of practical wisdom in the development of virtues?

Good Temper

10. In Aristotle's discussion of good temper, what are the five factors involved in our appropriate response to anger?

Virtue Theory after Aristotle

11. What are the three theological virtues?

Traditional Criticisms of Virtue Theory

Grotius's Criticism: Many Virtues Are Not at a Mean

12. Give one of Grotius's examples of a virtue that is not a mean between extremes.
13. What is Hume's view of the "monkish virtues"?

Kant's Criticism: Without Moral Principles, Misapplied Virtues Become Vices

14. Give an example of a misapplied virtue that might become a vice.
15. How does Kant suggest that we resolve the problem of misapplied virtues?

Mill's Criticism: Morality Involves Judging Actions and Not Character Traits

16. Mill argued that virtues are irrelevant when we judge a person's actions. What is Fieser's response to Mill?

Contemporary Discussions of Virtues and Rules

17. What are the key differences between action/rule-based morality and virtue-based morality?
18. In defending virtue theory, what is Anscombe's criticism of action/rule-based morality?

Feminine Ethics and Virtue Theory

19. According to many feminists, what are some key features of male ways of thinking and female ways of thinking?
20. According to many feminist moral philosophers, what will morality involve when it is modeled after women's experiences?
21. What is Noddings's criticism of Aristotle's list of virtues?

Virtues with or without Rules?

22. What is the difference between strong and weak virtue theory?
23. What are the three "rule" aspects of Aristotle's theory?

Contemporary Criticisms

24. What are the three contemporary criticisms of virtue theory?

The Value of Virtue Theory

Incorporating Virtue Theory into Other Moral Theories

25. What does MacIntyre say about the moral vocabulary that we use today?

The Best Teacher of Morality

26. According to contemporary author William J. Bennett, what must moral education provide?

References

The quotation on road rage is from *The Washington Post,* October 16, 1997.

Plato's discussion of the divisions of the soul is in the *Republic* 4.435, and his account of the unity of the virtues is in the *Protagoras,* 349b.

The discussion of Aristotle's theory presented here is from *Nichomachean Ethics,* 1–5, which is available in several modern translations.

Grotius's discussion of Aristotle is from *On the Law of War and Peace* (1625), Prolegomena, 43–45. The best current translation of this work is that by Francis W. Kelsey (Oxford: Oxford University Press, 1925).

Hume's discussion of monkish virtues is from his *Enquiry Concerning the Principles of Morals,* 9.1. The best current edition of this work is edited by Tom Beauchamp (Oxford: Oxford University Press, 1999).

Kant's criticism of virtue theory is from his *Foundations of the Metaphysics of Morals* (1785), which is available in several modern translations.

The quotation from Maximilien de Béthune, duc de Sully (1559–1641), appeared in his *Mémoires des sages et royales oeconomies* (Amsterdam, 1652–62), translated into English in *Memoirs of Maximilian de Bethune, duke of Sully, prime minister to Henry the Great* (London, printed for A. Millar, 1756). The quotation is as appears in James Balfour's *A Delineation of the Nature and Obligation of Morality* (1753), Chapter 5, which is available in a recent facsimile reprint (Bristol, England: Thoemmes, 1989).

Mill's criticism of virtue theory is in Chapter 2 of *Utilitarianism* (1863), which is available in several modern editions.

Elizabeth Anscombe's contemporary defense of virtue theory is in "Modern Moral Philosophy," *Philosophy,* 1958, Vol. 33; this article is reprinted in her *Ethics, Religion and Politics* (Oxford: Blackwell, 1981).

Nel Noddings discussion of feminist ethics and virtue theory is in "Ethics from the Standpoint of Women" in *Woman and Values,* edited by Marilyn Pearsall (Belmont, CA: Wadsworth, 1986).

Some of the contemporary criticisms of virtue theory are taken from Robert Louden, "On Some Vices of Virtue Ethics," *American Philosophical Quarterly,* 1984, Vol. 21.

Alasdair MacIntyre's contemporary defense of virtue theory is in *After Virtue,* 2nd ed., (Notre Dame, IN: Notre Dame University Press, 1984).

Suggestions for Further Reading

Commentaries on Aristotle's ethical theory include John M. Cooper, *Reason and Human Good in Aristotle* (Cambridge, MA: Harvard University Press, 1975); W. Hardie, *Aristotle's Ethical Theory* (Oxford: Oxford University Press, 1980); H. H. Joachim, *Aristotle: The Nichomachean Ethics* (Oxford: Oxford University Press, 1954); Martha Nussbaum, *The Fragility of Goodness* (Cambridge: Cambridge University Press, 1986); Amelie Rorty, ed., *Essays on Aristotle's Ethics* (Berkeley: University of California Press, 1980).

John Duns Scotus discusses various medieval philosophers on the subject of the interconnectedness of virtues (*Ordinatio* III, suppl. dist. 36), in *Duns Scotus on the Will and Morality,* trans. Allan B. Wolter (Washington, DC: Catholic University of America Press, 1986). James Beattie discusses early virtue theorists who distinguished between moral virtues and intellectual abilities; see Beattie's *Essay on the Nature and Immutability of Truth* (1770), Part 3, Chapter 2, recently edited by James Fieser (Bristol, England: Thoemmes Press, 2000). For a discussion of 18th-century philosophers who also made this distinction, see James Fieser, "Hume's Wide View of the Virtues," *Hume Studies,* November 1998.

J. B. Schneewind describes the post-Renaissance decline of virtue theory as a matter of continual revision, rather than a matter of complete rejection; "The Misfortunes of Virtue," *Ethics,* 1990, Vol. 101.

For contemporary discussions of virtue theory, see Philippa Foot, *Virtues and Vices* (Berkeley: University of California Press, 1978); William Frankena, *Ethics* (Englewood Cliffs, NJ: Prentice-Hall, 1963), Chapter 4; R. Kruschwitz, ed., *The Virtues: Contemporary Essays on Moral Character* (Belmont, CA: Wadsworth, 1987); Greg Pence, "Recent Work on the Virtues," *American Philosophical Quarterly,* 1984, Vol. 21.

4

Natural Law Theory

Introduction

Richard Cooper, an artist from Pennsylvania, often put images of himself in his paintings. In one work, he painted a woman on the left side of the canvas, a man on the right side, and himself between the two. He depicted himself pivoting away from the woman and reaching toward the man. The painting represents a moment in Cooper's life when he resolved an ongoing struggle with his gender orientation. Although attracted to men even in his youth, he followed society's expectations and dated women. Eventually, the inner tension became too great, and he acknowledged his homosexual leanings.

Social attitudes about homosexuality have varied greatly throughout history. Some ancient Greek literature, such as Plato's *Symposium,* describes homosexual relations between a master and his apprentice as commonplace. In a recent controversial work, John Boswell argues that during the early Middle Ages the Catholic Church endorsed same-sex unions, which may have been a cover for homosexual activity. On the other hand, passages in the Jewish Old Testament take strong stands against homosexuality, stating, "Do not lie with a man as one lies with a woman; that is detestable" (Leviticus 18:22). A medieval Eastern religious text states in even stronger terms that it wouldn't be murder if someone saw two men having sex with each other and, in a fit of rage, smashed their skulls with a rock.

American society today is somewhere in between these two extremes. We appreciate the social contributions of our openly gay friends and acquaintances. Reflecting the value system of political correctness, several recent TV sitcoms teach gay toleration and gay rights as a running theme. Yet, at the same time, most Americans resist the idea of officially endorsing homosexual marriages, and some even publicly express revulsion at homosexual behavior. How we deal with homosexual family members is also revealing: One-third of American teenagers who inform their parents of their homosexuality are thrown out of their houses.

The most common criticism against homosexual behavior is that it is unnatural or abnormal for "properly functioning" people. But in what sense is homosexuality "unnatural" or "abnormal"? It can't merely mean that homosexual behavior falls outside the statistical mean of human behavior. Although it is true that we find regular homosexual activity in only a small percentage of the population, many practices that we find morally acceptable are also statistical aberrations. For example, stamp collecting, deep-sea fishing, hang gliding, and thousands of other pastimes are practiced by only a small segment of the population. Similarly, we often condemn many behavioral practices even when they are practiced by a statistical majority of the people, such as premarital sex. So, if homosexuality is wrong because it is "unnatural," it must be for reasons other than mere statistics. The **natural law theory** of morality offers a detailed account of what it means for an action to be natural or unnatural, and discussions of natural law often focus on homosexuality as an example of unnatural conduct.

It is difficult to succinctly define natural law theory. It isn't a single theory per se, but a system of several smaller theories. Further, over the years, natural law philosophers have proposed different systems, and it is hard to find features common to them all. However, common themes of natural law theory are these:

- God endorses specific moral values and pronounces them as "law" by fixing them in human nature.
- There is one highest principle of natural law, which we discover by looking at aspects of our human nature (such as "people ought to be sociable").
- We rationally deduce subsidiary moral rules from this highest principle (such as "we ought not murder").
- These subsidiary rules carry the force of natural law to the degree that they are necessary for fulfilling the highest principle of natural law.

The notion of moral deduction is central to natural law theory. For example, suppose that God plants within me the intuition that "people ought to be sociable." I recognize that there are many kinds of actions that run contrary to this, such as murder, stealing, and lying. I can then deduce that murder, stealing, and lying are wrong because they are contrary to the intuition that I ought to be sociable.

Origins of Natural Law Theory   Natural law theory has its roots in ancient Greek thought, particularly Stoicism, which maintained that we should live in agreement with nature. Stoic philosophers believed that God permeates the entire world and strictly regulates all events. Everything in life—including natural disasters, the rise and fall of governments, and human conflicts—happens according to a preordained rational plan. Our moral responsibility is to conform our expectations to this preordained plan, and, thus, to live in agreement with nature. Inspired by the Stoic view of nature, Roman philosopher **Cicero** (106–43 BCE) gives an early account of the key ingredients of natural law:

> True law is right reason in agreement with nature; it is of universal application, unchanging and everlasting; it summons to duty by its commands, and averts

from wrong doing by its prohibitions. . . . We cannot be freed from its obligations by senate or people, and we need not look outside ourselves for an ex-
pounder or interpreter of it. And there will not be different laws at Rome and
at Athens, or different laws now and in the future, but one eternal and unchanging law will be valid for all nations and all times and there will be one
master and ruler, that is, God, over us all, for he is the author of this law, its
promulgator, and its enforcing judge. (*The Republic,* 3:22)

According to Cicero, God establishes within nature one eternal and unchanging
moral law that applies to all countries. Whether we are from Rome or Athens,
we are under the command of the same natural law. We discover this natural
law by looking within ourselves, not by consulting any external political governing bodies, such as the Roman Senate. The commanding force of natural law
is so strong that we are compelled to obey it.

The natural law tradition also has its roots in Roman law, which developed
over a 1000-year period—from about 500 BCE to 500 CE. Emperors, statesmen,
and legal experts all contributed to evolving discussions about laws pertaining
to everything from marriage contracts to slave ownership. In the 6th century CE,
these discussions were gathered together into a multivolume collection called
The Body of the Civil Law (*Corpus iuris civilis*). Although this great work focused mainly on practical legal matters, it also had a philosophical side. Specifically, it makes the philosophical distinction between three realms of law: civil
law, law of nations, and natural law. Civil law (*ius civile*) concerns the laws
created by a particular society, such as the Roman Empire, that apply mainly to
its own citizens. For example, specific laws of the Roman Empire determined
who could buy or sell slaves. Law of nations (*ius gentium*) concerns international laws that apply to citizens and foreigners alike. For example, laws of
various nations establish the institution of slavery in general. Natural law (*ius
naturale*) concerns laws that apply to animals as well as humans. For example,
animals and humans alike are born free by natural law, although we may become enslaved according to the laws of nations.

With the collapse of the western Roman Empire in 476 CE, the Christian
Church stepped in as the dominant political and intellectual force in Western
Europe. As Christian philosophers and jurists turned to the issue of natural law,
they viewed it from a distinctly Christian perspective. According to Christian
doctrine, humans are inherently corrupt because of our sinful heritage, which
began with Adam and Eve's first sin. Virtually everything that we do carries
some sinful taint, so even the best human laws that we devise will be flawed.
Christian philosophers argued that, because of our sinful nature, we need to
distinguish between the perfect *divine* law as mandated by God and the more
imperfect *human* laws that we devise on our own. For these philosophers, natural law is part of the perfect divine law. Early medieval discussions of natural
law were often sketchy. That changed, though, with Italian Christian monk
Thomas Aquinas (1225–1274), who systematically explored the topic of natural law and offered what quickly became the definitive medieval account of the
subject.

Aquinas's Natural Law Theory

Aquinas's account of natural law appears in his "Treatise on Law," a section of his several-thousand-page *Summa Theologica* (1a2ae q. 90–144). Drawing on discussions by his predecessors, Aquinas begins his analysis by distinguishing between different kinds of law.

Four Types of Law: Eternal, Natural, Human, and Divine

Aquinas argues that there are four distinct kinds of law: eternal law, natural law, human law, and divine law. *Eternal* law is the most perfect and complete set of God's laws, which govern "the whole community of the universe." Similar to earlier Stoic notions of divine order, Aquinas also argues that God's rule permeates the universe. We might view eternal law as something like a master database of all of God's laws. From a moral standpoint, these laws include both general moral rules of conduct, such as "Murder is wrong," and more particular rules, such as "Angry employees shouldn't gun down their bosses." Only God has access to the complete list of rules, and we humans will at best have only partial knowledge of this list. *Natural* law, for Aquinas, is a subset of eternal law and includes only general rules of conduct, such as "Murder is wrong." In different ways, these rules are embedded in our human nature, and we access them through rational intuition.

Human law represents our attempt to deduce more specific rules from the general rules of natural law. For example, from the general rule that "murder is wrong," we might deduce the more specific rule that "angry employees shouldn't gun down their supervisors." According to Aquinas, it is all too easy to make mistakes when deducing specific rules, and for that reason, we commonly assign this task to legislators and other legal experts. As long as governing bodies carefully and rationally deduce specific laws from natural law, then these specific laws will conform to eternal law. However, even the slightest error of reasoning may result in improper human laws, and these would clearly not be contained in eternal law. Finally, *divine* law is a special subset of eternal law that God reveals to us in divinely inspired texts, such as the Ten Commandments in the Hebrew Bible. The purpose behind divine law is to help eliminate human error when searching for moral rules. For example, we might not correctly grasp the general principle of natural law that "murder is wrong"; similarly, we might incorrectly deduce particular rules of human law. Divine law is a safeguard that helps us confirm our results.

In short, for Aquinas, all moral laws are ultimately grounded in God's unchanging eternal law, and we discover general rules of natural law through intuition. Legal experts then deduce more specific rules of human law from these, and in scriptural divine laws, we find examples of both general and specific rules. Since we don't have access to the complete list of eternal laws, morality begins, from our limited human perspectives, with a search for the general rules of natural law. But where do we begin looking for the general rules of natural law? Aquinas says that we must look to human nature as a guide:

[Each human being] has a share of the Eternal Reason, whereby it has a natural inclination to its proper act and end: and this participation of the eternal law in the rational creature is called the natural law. (*Summa Theologica*, 1a2ae, 90.2)

According to Aquinas, when God created us, he gave us natural instincts that reflect the general moral principles of natural law. There are two distinct levels of morally relevant instincts. First, God implanted in us an instinctive intuition that we should pursue our proper human end. Second, God implanted in us a series of instincts that define our proper end as living, reproducing, and rational creatures.

The Synderesis *Principle*   Concerning the first level of morally relevant instincts—the intuition to do good and avoid evil—Aquinas says that we get this through an intuitive faculty called *synderesis*. The word *synderesis* is a Greek term that means "innate moral consciousness." Christian theologians described it as a "spark" that ignites our conscience or the "fuel" that feeds our conscience. But Aquinas has a more precise psychological analysis of the *synderesis* faculty. First, he describes it as an instinctive habit. According to Aquinas, some human habits are very strong, such as the ability to acquire language, and others are much weaker, such as our inclination to be religious. For Aquinas, *synderesis* is a weak habit.

Second, Aquinas describes it as a component of our reason. According to Aquinas, sometimes we reason about things simply as a matter of speculation, such as whether 2 plus 3 equals 5. Other times, though, we reason about things for the practical purpose of performing an action, such as whether to get a drink from the refrigerator. For Aquinas, *synderesis* is an aspect of practical reasoning, and it involves reasoning about performing moral actions.

Third, as a habit of practical reasoning, *synderesis* involves reasoning from principles. Aquinas argues that reasoning always begins with general principles, and from these we deduce more specific things. For example, I may begin with the general principle that "all men are mortal" and deduce from that the more particular statement that "Bob is mortal." Practical reasoning similarly involves starting with the general principles and moving to specific things.

The *synderesis* faculty feeds us a *single* general principle of natural law, which commentators conveniently call the *synderesis* principle. Aquinas explicitly states the *synderesis* principle here:

Every agent acts on account of an end, and to be an end carries the meaning of to be good. Consequently the first principle for the practical reason is based on the meaning of good, namely that it is what all things seek after. And so this is the first command of law, "that good is to be sought and done, evil to be avoided." All other commands of natural law are based on this. Accordingly, then, the commands of natural law extend to all doing or avoiding of things recognized by the practical reason of itself as being human goods. . . . As converging on one common primary precept these various precepts of natural law all take on the nature of one natural law. (*Summa Theologica*, 1a2ae, 94.2)

In this passage, Aquinas states that the highest principle of natural law is that "good is to be sought and done, and evil to be avoided." At first, we might think that the *synderesis* principle is so general that it is almost useless. In fact, some critics of Aquinas say that his *synderesis* principle is an empty concept since it is true by definition; they claim that "doing good and avoiding evil" is simply built into the definition of "what is to be done and avoided."

However, the *synderesis* principle isn't as meaningless as critics charge, particularly because Aquinas defines "good" and "evil" in a very specialized sense. Specifically, "good" is that which conforms to our proper human end, and "evil" is that which does not. Using somewhat technical jargon, Aquinas makes this point here:

> The good or evil of an action, as of other things, depends on its fullness of being or its lack of that fullness. Now the first thing that belongs to the fullness of being seems to be that which gives a thing its species. (*Summa Theologica,* 1a2ae, 18.2)

The *synderesis* principle tells us that we should do those things that are conducive to our proper end and avoid those things that are not conducive to our proper end. More precisely, the *synderesis* principle contains two distinct parts:

1. If X is for our proper human end, then X ought to be done.

2. If X is not for a proper human end, then X ought not to be done.

From these two parts of the *synderesis* principle, we can deduce two separate lists of actions: (1) those that we should perform and (2) those that we should avoid. For simplicity, let's refer to these two parts of the *synderesis* principle as the "pursue good" and "avoid evil" clauses respectively.

The upshot of Aquinas's account of the *synderesis* principle is that it is a divinely implanted habit of practical reason that tells us to act according to our proper end. This is the highest principle of natural law, and from this we are to deduce more specific moral principles. There is clearly a religious element to Aquinas's theory insofar as God creates in us the instinctive *synderesis* faculty. However, according to Aquinas, we don't actually need to believe in God for the *synderesis* faculty to give us knowledge of natural law. We are all created with this instinct in spite of our individual religious views, and we all have the ability to grasp its meaning, just as we have the ability to grasp any other general rational principle.

Primary, Secondary, and Super-Added Principles

We've seen that the first instinctive component of natural law is our innate knowledge of the *synderesis* principle—namely, that we should act according to our proper end. The second instinctive component of natural law involves a series of human instincts that define our proper end as living, reproducing, and rational creatures. Aquinas argues that we must discover our proper human end by considering our most basic human natural inclinations. Following Aristotle's theory of human nature, Aquinas lists our basic inclinations according to three distinct faculties of the human psyche: the vegetative, appetitive, and rational faculties.

First, our *vegetative* faculty is responsible for keeping us alive through nutrition and growth. Arising from this faculty, then, we have an inclination for self-preservation. Second, our *appetitive* faculty provides us with an array of emotions and desires that prompt us to act out in different ways. From our appetitive faculty, we have an inclination to reproduce through heterosexual activities and to educate our offspring. Third, our *rational* faculty sets us apart from other animals, and from this we have inclinations to be rational, know God, and live in society. In total, then, Aquinas lists six human inclinations: (1) self-preservation, (2) heterosexual reproduction, (3) education of offspring, (4) rational thought, (5) knowledge of God, and (6) participation in society. Just as God implanted the *synderesis* principle within us, God also implanted these six inclinations within us. At this point, God's task is done, and it is up to us to discover the moral implications of the *synderesis* principle combined with our natural inclinations.

Aquinas argues that, from these six natural inclinations, we will discover six primary principles of natural law: (1) preserve human life, (2) have heterosexual (as opposed to homosexual) intercourse, (3) educate children, (4) shun ignorance, (5) worship God, and, (6) avoid harming others. Aquinas notes specifically that divine law corroborates the last two of these: "You should love the Lord your God" and "You should love your neighbor." For Aquinas, we arrive at these six primary principles by logically deducing each of them from the *synderesis* principle. For example, with the sixth primary principle—avoid harming others—we can see the precise deduction process here:

1. All acts that are unsuitable for human ends are acts that we should not do.
2. All acts that harm others are acts that are unsuitable for human ends.
3. Therefore, all acts that harm others are acts that we should not do.

Premise 1 in this argument is the "avoid evil" clause of the *synderesis* principle; premise 2 is based on the observation that humans instinctively live in society. Following the rules of syllogistic logic, from these two premises we deduce the primary principle of natural law: that we should avoid harming others. We deduce all six of the primary principles of natural law in a similar way. Aquinas believes that these deductions are so intuitive that any reasonable person can arrive at these six primary principles.

Aquinas argues that the deduction process does not stop here with the six primary principles of natural law. Rather, we must continue to draw out more precise secondary moral principles. At this stage, we leave the domain of natural law and enter the domain of human law. For example, from the primary principle "avoid harming others," we can deduce a secondary principle that we should not unjustifiably kill others:

1. All acts that harm others are acts that we should not do.
2. All acts of unjustified killing are acts that harm others.
3. Therefore, all acts of unjustified killing are acts that we should not do.

Premise 1 in this argument is the primary principle that we should avoid harming others—which we previously deduced from the *synderesis* principle. Premise 2 is the observation that we harm others when we unjustifiably kill people. For Aquinas, this is a premise that is supplied through the "careful reflection of wise people." Following the rules of syllogistic logic once again, from these two premises we deduce the secondary principle of human law that we should not kill people unjustifiably. When deducing secondary principles of human law, any mistake of reasoning will pervert its connection with natural law. For this reason, unlike the primary principles that can be deduced by everyone, secondary principles of human law require "careful reflection of wise people." To guard against errors at this level, divine law has confirmed the most general precepts of human law in the Ten Commandments.

Aquinas argues that the deduction process continues further by drawing out even more specific principles, which he calls "super-added principles." We derive these directly from secondary moral principles. At this stage, we leave the domain of natural law and enter the domain of human law. For example, from the secondary principle "do not kill people unjustifiably," we can deduce a super-added principle that employees should not kill their bosses:

1. All acts of unjustified killing are acts that we should not do.
2. All acts of killing one's boss are acts of unjustified killing.
3. Therefore, all acts of killing one's boss are acts that we should not do.

Premise 1 in this argument is the secondary principle that we should not kill others unjustifiably. Premise 2 is an observation by legal experts that we are not justified in killing our bosses at work. From this we deduce the super-added principle that we should not kill our bosses. The force of natural law diminishes as we move to increasingly specific principles. The reason, according to Aquinas, is that specific cultures have their own views as to what counts as harm or unjustified murder. For example, if I am an indentured servant in a Third World country and my boss routinely tortures me, I may indeed be morally justified in killing that person. So, as we move further away from the self-evident primary principles of natural law, we must rely more and more on the judgments of wise people and legal experts.

To summarize, the key points of Aquinas's theory of natural law are these:

- Natural law consists of general principles of eternal law that God fixes in human nature.
- Our instinctive *synderesis* faculty informs us of the highest principle of natural law: We should act according to our proper end.
- Six specific natural inclinations define our proper end and give us six primary principles of natural law.
- From primary principles of natural law, we deduce secondary and super-added principles of human law.

Here is a final illustration that links together all the deductive stages, beginning with the "avoid evil" clause of the *synderesis* principle, on through primary, secondary, and super-added principles:

1. All acts that are unsuitable for human ends are acts that we should not do. ("avoid evil" clause of the *synderesis* principle)

2. All acts that harm others are acts that are unsuitable for human ends. (based on the inclination of humans to live in society)

3. Therefore, all acts that harm others are acts we should not do. (primary principle of natural law)

4. All acts of stealing are harmful acts. (observation by wise people)

5. Therefore, all acts of stealing are acts we should not do. (secondary principle of human law)

6. All acts of fraud are acts of stealing. (observation by legal experts)

7. Therefore, all acts of fraud are acts we should not do. (super-added principle)

Revisions and Criticisms of Natural Law Theory

Aquinas was canonized by the Catholic Church about fifty years after his death, and his writings became enormously influential. Aquinas's conception of natural law in particular became the dominant view of morality throughout Europe for the next 300 years. Medieval moral philosophers after Aquinas took issue with minor points of his theory, but the general scheme remained intact: By looking at human nature, we understand the primary moral principles of natural law, and we deduce more specific principles from these. During the seventeenth century, however, a new wave of natural law philosophers questioned more central features of Aquinas's theory, especially the role that Aquinas assigns to our six human inclinations.

Suarez's Revision: Knowledge of Natural Law Is Based on Conscience, Not Natural Inclinations   Spanish monastic philosopher **Francisco Suarez** (1548–1617) was one of the more devoted followers of Aquinas, and in his *On Law and God the Law Giver* (1612), Suarez discusses and expands on Aquinas's theory of natural law. On the issue of our natural human inclinations, though, Suarez parts company with Aquinas. Aquinas believed that we discover the primary principles of natural law by looking at our six natural inclinations, which define our purpose. For example, I first recognize my natural inclination to live in society, and only then do I discover the primary principle of natural law: that I must avoid harming others. However, according to Suarez, the connection between natural law and human inclination is actually reversed. I must *begin* with an independent knowledge of natural law, and this knowledge will then help me regulate my six natural inclinations:

> The natural law brings man to perfection, with regard to every one of his tendencies and, in this capacity, it contains various precepts. . . . all these pro-

pensities in man must be viewed as being in some way determined and elevated by a process of rational gradation. For, if these propensities are considered merely in their natural aspect, or as animal propensities, they must be bridled, [so] that virtue may be attained[.] [A]nd on the other hand, if the same propensities are considered with respect to their capacity for being regulated by right reason, then proper and suitable precepts apply to each of them. (*On Law and God the Law Giver*, 2.8.4)

Suarez argues here that, by themselves, natural inclinations are animalistic, and we must perfect them through natural law. And we perfect our inclinations by following moral precepts, which are supplied by "right reason," that is, conscience.

Although the difference between Aquinas and Suarez is subtle, it is important in two respects. First, Suarez is more pessimistic than Aquinas about the value of human nature. According to Aquinas, natural inclinations do a good job of reflecting our true human purpose. For Suarez, natural inclinations are little better than animalistic urges. Second, Aquinas and Suarez differ concerning how we learn about natural law. According to Aquinas, we discover natural law through observation and experience—specifically, by surveying the natural inclinations of our human nature. But Suarez argues that we discover natural law more intuitively: Our conscience rationally dictates primary moral principles to us.

We might commend Aquinas both for his optimistic view of human nature and for his attempt to bring the subject of morality into the arena of public observation. However, there are serious and perhaps irresolvable problems with Aquinas's emphasis on natural inclinations, and Suarez appears correct in his suspicions about them. The central problem is that Aquinas's list of natural inclinations is too contrived. To reiterate, Aquinas lists six specific inclinations: (1) self-preservation, (2) heterosexual reproduction, (3) education of offspring, (4) rational thought, (5) knowledge of God, and (6) participation in society. However, a true list of human inclinations would be much longer. For example, if our list includes the inclination to have sexual intercourse, then we should also include our inclinations to eat food, to excrete waste outside of our sleeping area, to get angry, to laugh, to cry, and to perform any other act that is linked with the natural release of hormones. By preselecting only these six, Aquinas reveals that he has a specific moral agenda, and if we adopt his restricted list, then we will have a subjective survey of human inclinations. Not only is Aquinas's list too short, but at least one of the six items isn't really a "natural" inclination—namely, knowledge of God. Rather than being a *natural* inclination, this seems more like a *culturally shaped* inclination, which not everyone has and which also differs dramatically depending on one's religious affiliation and conception of God. Again, by listing this as a natural inclination, Aquinas advances a special moral agenda, not present an objective list of human inclinations.

In short, it appears that a purely objective understanding of human inclinations won't give us the knowledge of natural law that Aquinas supposes. Suarez offers one possible solution to this problem: Abandon all natural instincts as a source of natural law, and look to conscience instead. This, though, is only one of many approaches taken by natural law philosophers.

Grotius's Revision: Natural Law Is Rooted Only in the Instinct of Sociability   Shortly after Suarez, Dutch philosopher **Hugo Grotius** (1583–1645) took natural law theory in a different direction. Suarez consciously endorsed Aquinas's basic theory and saw himself as part of Aquinas's philosophical tradition. This is not so for Grotius. In the opening of his landmark book *The Law of War and Peace* (1625), Grotius announces that he aims to systematize Roman law since "the welfare of mankind demands that this task be accomplished." By analyzing Roman law directly, Grotius was looking at a natural law tradition that predated Aquinas, and Grotius thereby avoided many of the assumptions that Aquinas made. Specifically, Grotius does not attempt to base natural law on a wide range of human inclinations, such as Aquinas's list of six. Taking his lead from Stoicism, Grotius considers only one human inclination—sociability:

> Among the traits characteristic of man is an impelling desire for society, that is, for the social life—not of any and every sort, but peaceful, and organized according to the measure of his intelligence, with those who are of his own kind; this social trend the Stoics called "sociableness." (*On the Law of War and Peace*, Prolegomena, 6)

According to Grotius, we are naturally inclined to live in peaceful societies with other intelligent and like-minded humans. This basic fact of human sociability is the foundation of natural law:

> This maintenance of the social order, which we have roughly sketched, and which is consonant with human intelligence, is the source of law properly so called. (*On the Law of War and Peace*, Prolegomena, 8)

For Grotius, then, the highest principle of natural law is simply to *be sociable*. Like previous natural law theorists, Grotius also believed that we can deduce more specific rules of natural law from this highest principle. He lists five particular rules: (1) Do not take things that belong to others, (2) restore to other people anything that you might have of theirs, (3) fulfill promises, (4) compensate for any loss that results through your own fault, and (5) punish people as deserved. These more specific rules focus largely on issues of personal property and punishment, and it seems clear that the list is not complete. For example, we don't see rules about sexual behavior, family responsibilities, religious obligations, and similar moral issues that philosophers of the time commonly addressed. However, Grotius is not interested in offering a handbook of morality for use in our ordinary lives. Instead, he wants to explain the foundation of international laws that apply to warring nations around the world. What are the causes of war? When are wars justified? How can we maintain peace? Grotius's five specific rules of natural law help answer these questions, and they set the standard of proper conduct for all countries around the world.

Although Grotius didn't draw out the implications of natural law for our day-to-day moral behavior, he set the agenda for natural law philosophers after him. In Grotius's view, as we search for the rules of natural law that govern our personal lives, we should look toward our instinct of sociability, and not the broader list of six instincts that Aquinas suggested.

Hobbes's and Pufendorf's Revision: Natural Law Is Rooted in the Instinct of Self-Preservation

Hobbes's and Pufendorf's Revision: Natural Law Is Rooted in the Instinct of Self-Preservation British philosopher **Thomas Hobbes** (1588–1679) was one of the many writers influenced by Grotius's account of natural law. Like Grotius, Hobbes sees laws of nature as the basis for establishing peaceful societies and ending armed conflicts. However, unlike Grotius, Hobbes explains in great detail how laws of nature impact our daily moral behavior. As Hobbes begins his account of natural law, he immediately parts company with Grotius concerning the instinct of sociability: For Hobbes, humans simply have no such natural inclination. Not only do we lack instinctive sociability, but our human nature continually hinders our ability to live sociably with one another. We have differing likes and dislikes in virtually everything—from our favorite foods to our political views. From these differences arise "disputes, controversies, and at last war." Hobbes also explains how we differ from other, more sociable animal species, such as ants, which naturally live peacefully in groups. Unlike ants, we humans continually compete with one another for honor, and we take great pleasure in acquiring more things than our neighbors. We also commonly think that we are smarter than our leaders, and we have rhetorical skills that enable us to make evil things appear to be good.

Having rejected the instinct of sociability, Hobbes finds another instinct upon which to base natural law: the instinct of self-preservation. Self-preservation is so central to Hobbes's account of natural law that he even defines "law of nature" as a rational principle that mandates self-preservation:

> A *Law of Nature* (*lex naturalis*) is a precept or general rule, found out by reason, by which a man is forbidden to do that which is destructive of his life or taketh away the means of preserving the same, and to omit that by which he thinketh it may be best preserved. (*Leviathan*, 1.14)

Hobbes lists twelve specific laws of nature, each of which is rooted in our inherent need to survive. His first and most important law of nature is "to seek peace, and follow it . . . [and] by all means we can, to defend ourselves." Hobbes believes that the best way to preserve ourselves is to live in peace with other people, but if we can't do this, then we should defend ourselves any way we can.

Hobbes's view of self-preservation had a direct impact on German philosopher **Samuel von Pufendorf** (1632–1694), the most widely published natural law theorist of the seventeenth century. Echoing Hobbes, Pufendorf argues that we are naturally unsociable and that self-preservation drives us more than all of our other natural inclinations. However, striking a compromise between Grotius and Hobbes, Pufendorf argues that our instinct of self-preservation ultimately forces us to be sociable:

> So, then, man is an animal which is very desirous of his own preservation. He is liable to many wants, unable to support himself without the help of others of his kind, and yet wonderfully fit in society to promote a common good. But then his is malicious, insolent, and easily provoked, and not less prone to do

harm to his fellow man than he is capable of executing it. From this it must be inferred that to attain our self-preservation, it is absolutely necessary that we be sociable. (*The Duty of Man and Citizen,* 1.3)

According to Pufendorf, we are too weak to survive on our own, and so we must rely on help from others. Pufendorf finds sociability so important to our survival that, following Grotius, he makes sociability the highest principle of natural law: "From what has been said, it appears that this is a fundamental law of nature: to the extent that we can, every person ought to preserve and promote society, that is, the welfare of mankind." In short, although Pufendorf denies instinctive sociability, he endorses the mandate to be sociable in our instinct to survive.

The trend in natural law theory from Suarez onward shows a growing discontentment with using natural inclinations as a source of moral guidance. Although they abandoned Aquinas's optimistic view about the wide range of human inclinations, these philosophers nevertheless used at least some of our natural inclinations as foundations of moral laws. Eventually, though, even this more cautious view of human inclinations came under fire.

Hume's and Bentham's Criticism: Natural Law Theories Erroneously Derive Ought from Is
Scottish philosopher **David Hume** (1771–1776) argued that there is a big difference between statements of fact, such as "Stealing is harmful to society," and statements of obligation, such as "You should not steal." We establish statements of fact through observation and scientific investigation. For example, a sociologist could confirm the claim that "stealing is harmful to society." By contrast, Hume believes that we cannot establish statements of obligation through observation or scientific investigation. For example, no sociological study can establish the moral mandate that "you should not steal." According to Hume, moral theories commonly err by beginning with statements of fact and concluding with statements of obligation.

Philosophers today sum up Hume's point with the motto "We cannot derive *ought* from *is.*" After reading Hume, British philosopher **Jeremy Bentham** (1748–1832) was convinced that natural law philosophers made the blunder that Hume describes:

> Some fourscore years ago, by *David Hume,* in his *Treatise on Human Nature,* the observation was, for the first time, (it is believed,) brought to light—how apt men have been, on questions belonging to any part of the field of *Ethics,* to shift backwards and forwards, and apparently without their perceiving it, from the question, what *has been done,* to the question, what *ought to be done,* and *vice versa*: more especially from the former of these points to the other. . . . Such it has been in general, for example to the writers on *International Law;* witness *Grotius* and *Puffendorf.* In their hands, and apparently without their perceiving it, the question is continually either floating between these two parts of the field of Ethics, or shifting from one to the other. (*Chrestomathia,* Appendix 4, Section 20, note)

Although Bentham mentions Grotius and Pufendorf by name, his criticism applies equally to most natural law philosophers from Aquinas onward. Aquinas begins with *facts* about our six human inclinations and concludes that we *ought* to follow the six primary principles of natural law. Grotius begins with the *fact* about our instinctive sociability and concludes that we *ought* to be sociable. Hobbes begins with the *fact* of self-preservation and concludes that we *ought* to seek peace to preserve ourselves. Finally, Pufendorf begins with the *fact* of self-preservation and concludes that we *ought* to be sociable to survive.

Bentham is certainly correct that natural law philosophers derive *ought* from *is,* and they do so more blatantly than most other moral philosophers. However, we need to ask, what is so bad about deriving *ought* from *is*? One key problem is that there is too much flexibility in how we deduce *ought* statements from *is* statements. For example, from the natural inclination toward self-preservation, Aquinas infers that we should *always* preserve our lives and *never* resort to suicide, even when terminally ill. However, there are more modest inferences that we could make. For instance, we might reasonably deduce that we should preserve our lives in cases of self-defense, but we are morally permitted to end our lives when terminally ill. For every instinct mentioned by natural law philosophers, there are both extreme and modest conclusions that we can draw, and the differences between the two can be dramatic. It seems, then, that something more than mere facts guides us in selecting the extreme versus the modest recommendation. We might be guided by our intuitions, our personal feelings, or our social customs, and, if so, the pure facts are far less important than natural law philosophers believe. So, although it may *appear* as if we are simply deducing obligations of moral law from facts about natural inclination, we are not really doing this. Rather, we are relying on some other means of moral assessment. We should then just drop the factual facade in our moral theories and instead highlight the true basis of moral assessment—whether that is intuition, personal feeling, social custom, or something else.

The Value of Natural Law Theory

It seems that nature does not magically hand us moral principles through our natural inclinations in the way that natural law theorists believe. Natural law theorists themselves disagree about which natural inclinations are relevant for morality, and this disagreement itself is an argument against distilling morality from natural inclinations. Hume and Bentham appear correct that we cannot simply deduce moral obligations from facts about natural inclinations. One of the attractive features of natural law theory is that it aims to provide a clear, universal standard of morality that any reasonable individual can grasp. Unfortunately, natural law theory does not fulfill this promise. The limitations of natural law theory become especially clear when we examine the standard argument from natural law against homosexuality.

Natural Law and Homosexuality   We noted early in the chapter that natural law philosophers often focus on homosexuality as an example of unnatural and immoral conduct. This is specifically so with Aquinas and his followers since they believe that heterosexual reproduction is one of the six natural inclinations that define our purpose. We can reconstruct Aquinas's argument against homosexuality here, beginning with the "avoid evil" clause of the *synderesis* principle:

1. All acts that are unsuitable for human ends are acts that we should not do.
2. All acts of homosexuality are acts that are unsuitable for human ends.
3. Therefore, all acts of homosexuality are acts that we should not do.

The success of this argument rests on the claim in premise 2 that all homosexual acts are unsuitable for human ends. Aquinas would defend premise 2 by noting that humans have a natural inclination toward sexual reproduction and that this partly defines our proper end as human beings. The continuation of our species depends on sexual reproduction, and our heterosexual inclinations are designed for this purpose. Homosexual activity clearly runs contrary to our natural inclination to reproduce through heterosexual activity, and so homosexuality is unsuitable for our proper human end. There are two distinct assumptions in this defense: (1) Humans have a natural inclination towards heterosexual activity, and (2) sexual activity is exclusively for the purpose of reproduction. There are problems with both of these assumptions.

Concerning Aquinas's first assumption—that humans have a natural inclination toward heterosexual activity—researchers today believe that sexual orientation is largely a matter of genetic predisposition. Although most humans are indeed genetically predisposed to a heterosexual orientation, around 1 percent of the human population is genetically predisposed to a homosexual orientation. For that 1 percent, the homosexual orientation is indeed their natural inclination, and heterosexual activity is as foreign to them as homosexuality is foreign to heterosexuals. Contrary to Aquinas, then, humans don't have a single natural predisposition regarding sexual activity, and it is a mistake to talk about "human ends" as though there is a single end that applies to everyone. Therefore, we must reject premise 2 since it is based on the false assumption that there exists a uniform sexual inclination that defines a single human end. At best, we are only justified in saying for premise 2 that "all acts of homosexuality for heterosexuals are acts that are unsuitable for heterosexual human ends." That is, for people naturally predisposed to heterosexual activity, it is unsuitable for them to engage in homosexual acts since it is contrary to their human end of heterosexual reproduction.

Concerning Aquinas's second assumption—that sexual activity is exclusively for the purpose of reproduction—this seems like an overstatement. Again, for Aquinas, the continuation of the human species depends on reproduction, and our sexual inclinations are there for that purpose. Aquinas is correct that a large amount of sexual activity must be devoted to the continuation of the human species. On average, a man and a woman who want children must repeatedly engage in intercourse for almost an entire year before the woman successfully conceives. Although that certainly is a lot of sexual activity, it does not account for many sexual activities that aren't devoted to reproduction, such as oral sex, phone sex, cybersex, sex with contraception, and sex after menopause. A defender of Aquinas might see some of these as mating rituals that, in the long run, serve the purposes of reproduction, such as phone sex for couples who temporarily live far away from each other. However, even for married couples, this still leaves a large amount of sexual activity that is unrelated to reproduction. Should we see all of these sexual acts as distortions or violations of the reproductive purpose of sexual activity? Few of us would probably go that far. Although our sexual nature serves a fundamental task in propagating the species, it also serves nonreproductive tasks by shaping our identities, our intimate relationships, and our conceptions of happiness. These other tasks may certainly overlap with the reproductive tasks, but they don't *need* to for most people. We must then reject Aquinas's assumption that sexual activity is exclusively for the purpose of reproduction. And once we reject that assumption, we can't single out homosexuality for violating the reproductive purpose of sexual activity.

The upshot of Aquinas's argument against homosexuality is that it fails because it makes unwarranted assumptions about the existence of a universal natural inclination and the purpose of such an inclination. If we closely examined the other natural inclinations listed by Aquinas, we'd likely find similar problems with these.

The Legacy of Natural Law Theory   During the 17th and 18th centuries, there were essentially two distinct traditions of natural law theory: one started by Aquinas and another started by Grotius. Aquinas's specific theory was perpetuated by philosophers in the Roman Catholic tradition who held that we discover our proper human end by considering a wide range of natural inclinations. To this day, Aquinas's theory plays a vital role in Roman Catholic moral philosophy. However, non-Catholic philosophers perpetuated the theory that was first forged by Grotius and later developed by Pufendorf. This approach draws more selectively from our human nature and bases natural law only on a specific human inclination, such as sociability. By the nineteenth century, though, moral philosophers lost interest in Grotius's tradition of natural law. In spite of this decline in interest, the impact of natural law theory on moral philosophy was so strong that it left a legacy that is still with us today. We find this continuing legacy principally in minor themes of the natural law theory, which have since become major themes in moral philosophy.

One of these themes involves natural rights and duties. Grotius and Pufendorf argued that natural law dictates both a list of natural rights that protect me from the hostility of other people and a list of specific moral duties that obligate me toward other people. The U.S. Declaration of Independence, for example, draws on this notion of natural rights in its claim that God endows us with unalienable rights to "life, liberty, and the pursuit of happiness." Another theme of natural law theory is that of the **social contract**. Hobbes argued that the principles of natural law compel us to create peaceful societies through social contracts. That is, we mutually agree to set aside our hostilities and live in peace since this is the best way for each of us to preserve our own lives. Again, the

Declaration of Independence rests on social contract theory, particularly in its view that "governments are instituted among men" to bring about our "safety and happiness."

Another child of natural law theory is the notion of a supreme moral principle. Aquinas believed that the highest principle of natural law is to "do good and avoid evil." Grotius and Pufendorf believed it is to "be sociable." Natural law philosophers during the 18th century offered similar supreme principles, and, influenced by this tradition, later moral philosophers such as Immanuel Kant and John Stuart Mill offered their own highest principles of morality. A related notion in natural law theory is the idea that we deduce specific moral rules from more general ones. Many moral philosophers today believe that this kind of deduction is a normal part of moral reasoning.

Although moral theories today regularly incorporate these secondary features of natural law theory, we should not simply assume the validity of these features. Just as we scrutinized the natural law conception of human inclinations, so, too, should we scrutinize the notions of rights, duties, social contracts, and supreme moral principles.

Summary

We find the first hints of natural law theory in the Stoic notion that we should live in agreement with nature as mandated by God. Roman law introduced the term *natural law* in contrast to more narrow notions of civil law and law of nations. The first systematic account of natural law, though, was offered by Thomas Aquinas. Aquinas argued that natural law is a subset of God's eternal law that rules the universe. Specifically, natural law consists of general principles of morality that God embeds in our human nature. Through the faculty of *synderesis,* we receive knowledge of the highest principle of natural law: Do good and avoid evil, as defined by our proper human end. By reflecting on this principle and our six main human inclinations, we deduce six primary principles of natural law, such as "avoid harming others." And from these six principles, we deduce more specific principles of human law. As natural law theory developed in the sixteenth and seventeenth centuries, philosophers abandoned Aquinas's view that we gain knowledge of natural law by inspecting our six natural inclinations. Francisco Suarez believed that our conscience gives us knowledge of the principles of natural law, and this helps us regulate our six natural inclinations.

Returning to earlier Stoic and Roman notions of natural law, Hugo Grotius argued that we gain knowledge of natural law through our inclination toward sociability, and the highest principle of natural law is simply to be sociable. Thomas Hobbes believed that natural law is based on our instinct to survive, and the highest principle of natural law is to preserve our lives by seeking peace and defending ourselves. Influenced by both Hobbes and Grotius, Samuel Pufendorf argued that natural law is based on our survival instincts, and the best way to survive is to be sociable. Following Hume, Bentham criticized the natural law tradition for deriving *ought* from *is*—that is, for beginning with facts about human nature and concluding with statements of moral obligation.

Using the example of homosexuality, we see how natural law theories can make unwarranted assumptions about the existence and purpose of some human inclinations. Although interest in natural law theory declined during the nineteenth century, its influence lives on in moral theories involving rights, duties, social contracts, and supreme moral principles.

Study Questions

Introduction

1. What are some contemporary attitudes about homosexuality?
2. What is wrong with morally condemning homosexuality as "unnatural" simply because homosexual behavior is statistically limited?

Origins of Natural Law Theory

3. In Roman law—particularly in *The Body of the Civil Law*—what does "natural law" refer to?

Aquinas's Natural Law Theory

Four Types of Law: Eternal, Natural, Human, and Divine

4. Describe Aquinas's distinctions between eternal law, natural law, human law, and divine law.

The Synderesis Principle

5. What are the two parts of Aquinas's *synderesis* principle?
6. List the six human inclinations and their corresponding six primary precepts of morality.

Primary, Secondary, and Super-Added Principles

7. Give an example of how we deduce secondary moral principles from primary principles.
8. What is a "super-added principle" of morality?

Revisions and Criticisms of Natural Law Theory

Suarez's Revision: Knowledge of Natural Law Is Based on Conscience, Not Natural Inclinations

9. According to Suarez, how should we view natural inclinations by themselves?
10. According to Fieser, what is the central problem with Aquinas's list of natural inclinations?

Grotius's Revision: Natural Law Is Rooted Only in the Instinct of Sociability

11. According to Grotius, what is the highest principle of natural law?
12. What are the five specific rules that Grotius deduces from his highest principle of natural law?

Hobbes's and Pufendorf's Revision: Natural Law Is Rooted in the Instinct of Self-Preservation

13. According to Hobbes, what is a law of nature?
14. For Hobbes, what is the first law of nature?

15. What was Pufendorf's compromise position between Grotius's and Hobbes's view?

Hume's and Bentham's Criticism: Natural Law Theories Erroneously Derive Ought from Is

16. Explain Hume's view that we cannot derive *ought* from *is*.
17. How do natural law philosophers derive *ought* from *is*?

The Value of Natural Law Theory

Natural Law and Homosexuality

18. According to Fieser, what is wrong with Aquinas's first assumption that humans have a natural inclination toward heterosexual activity?
19. According to Fieser, what is wrong with Aquinas's second assumption that sexual activity is exclusively for the purpose of reproduction?

The Legacy of Natural Law Theory

20. What are the three themes of natural law theory that are still with us today?

References

John Boswell's account of medieval church attitudes toward homosexuality is in *Same-Sex Unions in Pre-Modern Europe* (New York: Villard, 1994).

The quotation by Cicero is from *The Republic (De Re Publica)*, 3.22, translated by Clinton Walker Keyes (Cambridge, MA: Harvard University Press, 1928).

The quotations by Aquinas are from "The Treatise on Law" (1a2ae, q. 90–144) and other portions of *Summa Theologica,* translated by Laurence Shapcote, Fathers of the English Dominican Province (London, 1911–36).

For a more detailed account of the deductive process in Aquinas's theory, see James Fieser's "The Logic of Natural Law in Aquinas' 'Treatise on Law,'" *Journal of Philosophical Research,* 1992, Vol. 17, pp. 147–164.

The quotation by Suarez is from *On Law and God the Lawgiver (De Legibus ac Deo Legislatoro,* 1612), 2.8.4, translated by Gladys Williams et al., in *Selections from Three Works of Francisco Suarez* (Oxford: Clarendon Press, 1944).

The quotation by Grotius is from *On the Law of War and Peace (De jure belli ac pacis,* 1625), Prolegomena, translated by Francis W. Kelsey (Oxford: Oxford University Press, 1925).

The quotation by Hobbes is from *Leviathan* (1651), 1.14, which is available in several modern editions, the best of which is edited by Edwin Curley (Indianapolis: Hackett, 1994).

The quotations by Pufendorf are adapted from *The Whole Duty of Man according to the Law of Nature* (London, 1691), a seventeenth-century English translation of his book *De officio hominis et civis juxta legem naturalem* (1673). Pufendorf also presents his theory in a longer and more detailed work, *Of the Law of Nature and Nations (De Jure Naturae et Gentium,* 1762).

Hume's view about not deriving *ought* from *is* can be found in his *Treatise of Human Nature* (1739–40), 3.1.1, which is available in several recent editions.

The quotation from Bentham is from *Chrestomathia: being a collection of papers* (1816), Appendix 4, Section 20, note, from *The Works of Jeremy Bentham,* edited by John Bowring (London, 1838–43).

Suggestions for Further Reading

For discussions of Aquinas's theory of morality and natural law, see R. A. Armstrong, *Primary and Secondary Precepts in Thomistic Natural Law Teaching* (The Hague: Martinus Nijhoff, 1966); Alan Donagan, *Human Ends and Human Action* (Milwaukee: Marquette University Press, 1985). D. J. O'Connor, *Aquinas and Natural Law* (London: Macmillan, 1968); Ralph McInerny, *Aquinas on Human Action* (Washington, DC: Catholic University of America Press, 1992).

For discussions of the history of natural law theory, see Lloyd L. Weinreb, *Natural Law and Justice* (Cambridge, MA: Harvard University Press, 1987); J. B. Schneewind, *The Invention of Autonomy* (Cambridge: Cambridge University Press, 1998).

5

Morality and the Will of God

Introduction

On April 19, 1993, around eighty members of a religious sect called the Branch Davidians burned to death in their communal home in Waco, Texas, at the close of a siege initiated by the FBI and other government organizations. The siege was prompted by the FBI's concern about weapons that the group had stockpiled. The FBI was also concerned that the Davidians' 34-year-old leader, David Koresh, was sexually and physically mistreating children in the group. During the siege, Koresh admitted to fathering more than twelve children by different wives, who were around 12 or 13 years old when they became pregnant. At earlier Bible study sessions, Koresh had taught that the younger girls in the compound would have the privilege of having sex with him once they reached puberty. Koresh also had harshly disciplined the children by beating them and withholding food from them. The FBI became increasingly frustrated by the Davidians' failure to surrender and, on day 51 of the siege, the FBI launched an assault against their communal home. Rather than comply, the Davidians set themselves on fire and died.

The theology of the Branch Davidian group is complex, but many of their views hinge on their belief in divinely inspired prophecies. According to their view, we find some divine prophecies in the Bible, which foretell of events leading to the end of the world. Other divine messages, though, come from recent prophets—including David Koresh himself. Koresh believed that as a prophet he was in a unique position to know God's plan for the world. In a taped message during the siege, he explains that God's saints know how to slowly uncover God's truth, one precept at a time:

> If she [i.e., God's bride] has the righteousness of saints, we as saints, should we not know rightly how to divide the Word of God (line upon line, precept on precept; to see here, there; and a little here, and there a little) the Truth of God? (Taped message of March 2, 1993)

More specifically, Koresh believed that God's plan involved a bloody confrontation between the church and the U.S. government—which was his reason for stockpiling weapons. He also believed that God directed him to father children with his various young brides.

An underlying component of Koresh's prophecies is that God is a law unto himself and can order things as he sees fit. This appears to include God's ability to create moral standards. Although at one time God might tell us to cooperate with our government, at another time he might tell us to resist our government with military force. Although at one time God might give us specific rules regarding marriage and children, at another time he might instruct a special person—such as David Koresh—to defy these rules in a manner that we would ordinarily find morally repugnant. Theological positions such as Koresh's prompt us to think more closely about the relation between morality and the will of God. Does God simply invent moral rules as he sees fit, or does God himself answer to a higher standard? A long-standing tradition in Christian philosophy holds that God does indeed create moral rules purely as a function of his free will. We will look at the central arguments for and against this position.

Plato and the Euthyphro Puzzle The philosophical issue surrounding morality and the will of God first came to light in the writings of the Greek philosopher Plato (428–348 BCE) in his dialog *Euthyphro*. In this dialog, a character named Euthyphro is prepared to turn his father over to the authorities for mistreating and causing the death of a slave. In ancient Greece, children were expected to show unconditional loyalty to their parents, and so, by turning in his father, Euthyphro would be violating the standard code of morality. Nevertheless, Euthyprho believes that he is following the will of the gods and therefore doing the right thing. On his way to the courthouse, Euthyphro bumps into Socrates, and the two start debating on the connection between morality and religious obedience. Socrates then poses this question to Euthyphro: "Are good things good because the gods approve of them, or do the gods approve of them because they are good?"

In this **Euthyphro puzzle**, Socrates presents two options regarding the relation between the gods and morality. The first option is that something becomes good when the gods *will* that it is good. For example, the gods might will that children should show unconditional loyalty to their parents, and, by so willing, it is thereby morally good and obligatory that children should show unconditional loyalty to their parents. In this view, the gods invent morality and, in a sense, create morality completely from scratch without any source of guidance. If the gods will that something should be morally good, then it simply becomes morally good.

The second option Socrates presents is that good things are objectively good, and the gods merely *recognize* them as such. For example, it may be objectively good and obligatory for children to show unconditional loyalty to their parents, and the gods simply endorse this moral standard. In this view, morality is grounded in a preexisting standard of moral goodness, which the gods themselves have no control over and must adopt. The genius of Plato's puzzle is that—assuming that God has an interest in morality—these are the only two choices available for explaining the connection between God and morality: God either invents it from scratch or abides by a preexisting standard. Further, since we can't endorse both of these options at the same time, we are locked into choosing one over the other. Plato himself believed that morality is grounded in external and preexisting standards, and so he went with the second option. Many philosophers after Plato followed his lead and held that there exists an external and independent standard of morality.

Traditional Voluntarism

During the Middle Ages, Christian philosophers thought about the connection between God and morality and considered more seriously whether God might be the author of moral standards. The philosophers who debated this issue were all part of the natural law tradition of moral philosophy. That is, they all roughly held that God endorses specific moral standards and fixes them in human nature. We then discover these natural laws of morality through our conscience or through reflection on our natural human inclinations. Although natural law philosophers agreed on these basic points, they disagreed about where God got moral standards to begin with. Aquinas, for example, believed that, although God endorses the moral principles of natural law, God doesn't literally *author* these principles. Instead, moral principles are rational laws that exist independently of God. God simply *adopts* moral principles because, as a rational being, God has a kinship with rational notions such as moral principles. Since God created humans as rational creatures, we, too, have the capacity to rationally grasp these moral principles. This position is commonly called **intellectualism**, insofar as it emphasizes the view that moral principles issue from God's intellect. Other medieval philosophers took the opposing view, called **voluntarism**. According to this view, moral principles of natural law are not independent rational principles, but instead are creations of God's will (in Latin, *voluntas*). In recent years, the voluntarist position also has gone by the name of **divine command theory**.

Scotus's Voluntarism   One of the great defenders of voluntarism in the Middle Ages was Scottish-born philosopher **John Duns Scotus** (c. 1266–1308). There are two components to Scotus's view. First, Scotus believed that God has a genuinely free will in the sense that God could have willed things differently than he actually did. Suppose, for example, that God willed to create the planet Mars at a specific point in time. At the precise moment that he willed to create Mars, God could have willed instead to *not* create it. Scotus's notion of God's will is substantially stronger than the views of God's will held by intellectualist philosophers before him. Aquinas, for example, believed that God's will is intimately bound up with God's rational abilities, so that God wills things that are rational. For Aquinas, when God willed to create the laws of morality, he did so because such laws involve a rational and orderly way for moral beings to conduct their lives. But Scotus believed that Aquinas's notion of God's will is inadequate since it constrains God's will with prior reasons or causes. A genuinely free will, for Scotus, is unconstrained.

The second component of Scotus's view is that God has **absolute power** in the sense that God can bring about anything that he wants, so long as it doesn't involve a logical contradiction. Scotus makes this point here:

> God, therefore, insofar as he is able to act in accord with those right laws he set up previously, is said to act according to his ordained power; but insofar as he is able to do many things that are not in accord with, but go beyond, these [divinely] preestablished laws, God is said to act according to his absolute power. For God can do anything that is not self-contradictory or act in any way that does not include a contradiction (and there are many such ways he could act); and then he is said to be acting according to his absolute power. (*Oxford Commentary*, 1.44)

In this passage, Scotus explains that God has two kinds of powers: ordained and absolute. God's *ordained* power involves a basic ability for God to act in accord with laws that he previously sets up, such as laws of salvation or laws of physics. By contrast, God's *absolute* power involves a stronger ability to act contrary to his previously established laws, and God can do this in any way that he wants, so long as there is no logical contradiction. A statement is logically contradictory when it both asserts and denies the same thing. Take, for example, the statement that "Bob is a married bachelor." Since the definition of "bachelor" includes being unmarried, this statement is contradictory insofar as it implies that Bob is both married and unmarried. Similarly, the statement "Bob has a tattoo of a round square" is contradictory since it implies that a specific shape simultaneously contains and lacks 90-degree angles.

When we combine God's free will with his absolute power, we see that God is *free* to do what he wants and that he has the *power* to do what he wants—so long as there are no logical contradictions. We can better understand the scope of God's free will and absolute power by considering three kinds of laws:

- Physical laws, such as the law of gravity
- Mathematical laws, such as "$2 + 2 = 4$"
- Logical laws, such as the law of identity (the Empire State Building is the Empire State Building)

According to Scotus, God's absolute power gives him control over some of these laws, but not others. Concerning physical laws, Scotus and most theologians quickly grant that God has creative control over the structure of the physical world and the rules that govern it. For any physical law that we pick, such as gravity, God could change it without logical contradiction. However, mathematical and logical laws can't be changed without logical contradiction. If we say that God has the power to make 2 plus 2 equal 4, then God would also have the power to make 2 plus 2 equal 5. And this seems absurd. Similarly, if we say that God has the power to create logical laws such as the law of identity, then he also has the power to institute the opposite law. So, for example,

God could make the Empire State Building not identical to itself, or, for that matter, God could make *himself* not identical to himself. Since Scotus holds that God can't perform logically contradictory tasks, he would reject the view that God has power over mathematics and logic. Most medieval philosophers also held this view. However, medieval philosophers didn't see this as a restriction on God's absolute power, since *no* possible being can perform logically contradictory tasks.

When we turn to the issue of moral laws, we must determine whether moral laws are more like physical laws, which God has control over, or mathematical and logical laws, which God doesn't have control over. For Aquinas, moral laws, such as "Murder is wrong," are more like mathematics and logic, which God has no control over. Scotus, though, sees moral laws as more like physical laws, which God does have control over. For Scotus, God first freely wills a specific conception of morality and then institutes these values through his absolute power. He creates these without reliance on any preexisting external standards, and he implants knowledge of them in our human nature.

Scotus's voluntarism creates a paradox: If morality is a creation of God's will, then God could will whatever moral values he wants, even the exact opposite of present moral values. For example, although God in fact mandates that stealing is wrong, God could have made stealing morally permissible—and so, too, for killing, lying, and marital infidelity. Therefore, God's moral commands seem arbitrary. Scotus is willing to accept this paradox and all of its strange implications. In fact, he believes that at specific points in history God actually did reverse the rules of morality to suit his own special purposes. Scotus draws attention to three particular stories from the Hebrew Bible in which several of the Hebrew patriarchs commit seemingly immoral acts at God's command:

> To kill, to steal, to commit adultery, are against the precepts of the decalogue, as is clear from Exodus [20:13]: "You shall not kill" [etc.]. Yet God seems to have dispensed from these. This is clear in regard to homicide from Genesis 22, regarding Abraham and the son he was about to sacrifice; or for theft from Exodus 11[:2] and [12:35] where he ordered the sons of Israel to despoil the Egyptians, which despoilment is taking what belongs to another without the owner's consent, which is the definition of theft. As for the third, there is Hosea 1: "Make children of fornications." (*Oxford Commentary*, 3.37)

The first story depicts how God commands Abraham to offer his son as a human sacrifice. At the last minute, as Abraham raises his knife, God provides an animal as a substitute. Nevertheless, Abraham's intent is already fixed, and he attempts to carry out the act in accord with God's will. The second story relates how, just before the Israelites leave Egypt, God commands them to steal vessels from their Egyptian neighbors. In the third story, God commands Hosea to have sex with an adulteress.

Scotus believes that these are genuine examples of God granting a special dispensation or privilege for these people. By granting such dispensations, God is temporarily revoking a specific moral law and setting up a new and possibly opposite standard in its place:

> Any legislator dispenses unconditionally when he revokes a precept of positive law made by himself. He does not allow the prohibited act or precept to remain as before, but removes the prohibition or makes what was formerly illicit now licit. (*Oxford Commentary*, 3.37)

Scotus concludes that God could alter virtually all of the moral laws if he wanted. The only exceptions are moral laws involving our subservience to God, such as the commands to worship and obey God. To alter these, God would need to stop being the infinitely great God that he is, and because doing so would be in contradiction to God's nature, God cannot do this.

To recap, these are the main points of Scotus's view of voluntarism:

- God has a genuinely free will, which is unconstrained by prior reasons or causes.
- God has absolute power insofar as he can do anything that is logically possible.
- Moral standards are creations of God's will, and God can alter them without logical contradiction.
- Some biblical stories depict God revoking previously established moral standards.

Voluntarism after Scotus   In the centuries after Scotus, advocates continued to line up on both sides of the intellectualism/voluntarism debate. The dispute became so central to moral theory that virtually every moral philosopher felt compelled to weigh in on whether morality is a creation of God's will. One of the more dramatic defenders of voluntarism after Scotus was English-born philosopher **William of Ockham** (1285–1349). Like Scotus, Ockham believed that God could revoke any moral law he wanted. For example, Ockham argued that, although God will in fact punish us for being immoral, nothing requires him to do so. And, supposing that we didn't repent, God could still grant us forgiveness and not punish us, if that's what God wanted to do. Ockham pushes this line of reasoning further and argued that, although God commands us to *love* him, God could command us to *hate* him instead:

> Every will can conform to the commands of God. God can, however, command a created will to hate Him. Therefore, the created will can do this. Moreover, any act that can be just on earth could also be just in heaven. On earth the hatred of God can be just, if it is commanded by God Himself. Therefore, the hatred of God could also be just in heaven. (*Fourth Book of the Sentences*, 13)

Ockham argues here that, if God did command us to hate him, then this would in fact be the morally right thing to do. Ockham's statement was so controversial that it contributed to his excommunication from the Catholic Church in 1328.

During the Protestant Reformation of the sixteenth century, German reformer **Martin Luther** (1483–1546) came down strongly on the side of voluntarism. In a statement that sounds like a direct answer to Plato's Euthyphro
puzzle, Luther writes, "What God wills is not right because he ought or was
bound so to will; on the contrary, what takes place must be right, because he
wills." Following Luther's lead, French Protestant reformer **John Calvin** (1509–
1564) argued that God's will is the highest authority for morality:

> God's will is so much the highest rule of righteousness that whatever he wills,
> by the very fact that he wills it, must be considered righteous. When, therefore,
> one asks why God has so done, we must reply: because he has willed it. But if
> you proceed further to ask why he has so willed, you are seeking something
> greater and higher than God's will, which cannot be found. (*Institutes of the
> Christian Religion,* 3.23.2)

Calvin argues here that God's will is the final authority behind everything that
God does, including God's pronouncements about morality. If we attempt to
explain why God chose this or that moral standard, our only answer is that God
simply willed it that way. Luther's and Calvin's statements were important for
moving the voluntarist position beyond its Catholic origins and establishing it
within the Protestant philosophical tradition.

Within a century after the Reformation, though, several Protestant moral
philosophers resisted the idea that God creates moral standards. The trend
started with Dutch philosopher **Hugo Grotius** (1583–1645), who stated directly that God cannot change moral standards:

> The law of nature, again, is unchangeable—even in the sense that it cannot be
> changed by God. Measureless as is the power of God, nevertheless it can be
> said that there are certain things over which that power does not extend; for
> things of which this is said are spoken only, having no sense corresponding
> with reality and being mutually contradictory. Just as even God, then, cannot
> cause that two times two should not make four, so he cannot cause that that
> which is intrinsically evil be not evil. (*Law of War and Peace,* 1.10.5)

In this passage, Grotius appears to accept the notion of God's absolute power
as Scotus defined it—namely, the ability to do anything that is not logically
contradictory. However, Grotius rejects voluntarism by suggesting that moral
laws are similar to mathematical laws, which can't be altered without logical
contradiction. As we've seen, voluntarists such as Scotus believe that moral laws
are more like physical laws, which can be changed without contradiction. Grotius, then, does not technically ascribe less power to God's abilities, but instead
elevates the status of moral standards, placing them beyond God's reach.

We don't know why Grotius was motivated to elevate moral standards to
the level of mathematical laws. However, shortly after Grotius, a group of philosophers known as the **Cambridge Platonists** gave very clear reasons for their
rejection of voluntarism. Cambridge Platonists like **Ralph Cudworth** (1617–
1688) were bothered by followers of Calvin who made God's will the final authority in all moral matters. According to Calvinists, God somewhat arbitrarily
chooses some people for salvation and other people for damnation, and nothing

that we do on our own can change God's choices. Like Plato, Cudworth believed that there exists an objective standard of moral goodness that humans must submit to. This moral standard is independent of God's will, and everyone can grasp it through the use of reason. Thus, for example, I don't have to worry about whether God arbitrarily chose me for salvation. Instead, as long as I follow this objective standard of morality, then I will be in God's favor.

Over the next 150 years, dozens of critics of voluntarism similarly claimed that moral standards are eternal and immutable, and even God can't change them. Although rejecting voluntarism per se, many of these philosophers believed that God's will still plays at least some role in morality. Suppose, for example, that by using my reason I learn the eternal moral truth that I should not steal from other people. Although I now *know* that I should not steal, I nevertheless may not be *motivated* to actually follow this moral rule. And that's where God's will enters the picture. If God wills that we should all follow these eternal moral truths—and we don't want to disappoint God—then we'll all be motivated to follow those moral truths. So, even though God does not willfully *create* moral truths, he willfully *mandates* them on humans, and this motivates us to be moral.

Voluntarists and intellectualists differed about whether God creates moral standards, but both held equally that God is an important component in morality. Virtually no one publicly questioned the existence of God until the eighteenth century, and philosophers commonly held that no true atheists either did exist or could exist. So, the climate was well suited for mixing morality and religious belief. Since the eighteenth century, however, the tables have turned regarding the connection between religion and morality. Scientifically-minded moral philosophers of the eighteenth century attempted to create a science of ethics, which, like the physical sciences, stands independently of religious doctrines. During the nineteenth century, several philosophers and scientists publicly affirmed atheism or agnosticism, and this further established a secular agenda for moral philosophy. We've inherited this agenda, and an academic book on ethics published today might not mention "God" even once.

Arguments for and against Voluntarism

Traditional voluntarists offer two central arguments for the position that God freely creates moral standards: an argument from revoking established moral standards and an argument from absolute power. We will examine each of these in turn.

Defense: The Argument from Revoking Established Moral Standards

Scotus and like-minded voluntarists often argue that the Bible and other sacred texts give us examples of how God temporarily revokes previously established moral standards for special purposes. Since God has the ability to revoke previously established moral standards, this implies that these standards must be creations of God. Put more precisely, the argument is this:

1. If God has the ability to temporarily revoke a moral standard, then he has the power to freely create moral standards.
2. Some divinely inspired texts depict God as temporarily revoking a previously established moral standard.
3. Therefore, God has the power to freely create moral standards.

The success of this argument depends on the truth of premises 1 and 2. However, both of these premises have problems.

Premise 1 makes the basic claim that, if someone has the power to revoke a standard, then that person had the initial power to create that standard. Suppose, for example, that the state of Tennessee decided to raise the speed limit on its highways from 70 miles per hour to 80 miles per hour. If state government officials have the authority to revoke the 70-mile-per-hour limit, then it is reasonable to assume they are the ones who created that speed limit to begin with. However, although this is a reasonable inference, it isn't absolute. It is possible that some other governing body, such as the federal government, established the original 70-mile-per-hour limit and simply assigned power to the state of Tennessee to revoke that standard if it saw fit. Similarly, it is possible that something other than God set in place our basic moral values, and God simply has the power to revoke those standards. For example, perhaps the fabric of the cosmos itself created our basic moral values, and God uses his power to override them on occasion. Alternatively, perhaps human societies invented our basic moral values, and sometimes God enters into the moral decision-making process and uses his power to override the values that we invented. So, just because someone has the power to *revoke* moral standards, this does not necessarily mean that he or she had the power to *create* those standards.

Premise 2 states that some divinely inspired texts depict God as temporarily revoking a previously established moral standard. The stories of Abraham sacrificing his son, the Israelites fleeing Egypt, and Hosea having sex with an adulteress seem to be examples of this. The most obvious problem with these examples is that they carry weight only for believers within religious traditions that recognize the authority of specific scriptures. In the case of stories from the Hebrew Bible, these principally carry weight for Jews and Christians, who constitute only a minority of the world's population. Hindus, Buddhists, Muslims, and members of other religions might find these stories interesting but not authoritative.

For the sake of argument, let's confine our discussion to the stories from the Hebrew Bible and to the Jews and Christians who see these stories as authoritative. Even so, there is still a major problem with premise 2: These stories don't conclusively illustrate God revoking moral standards. Take, for example, the story of Abraham preparing to kill his son. Although murder is certainly wrong, it is often difficult to determine whether an act of killing is unjustified to the point that it constitutes murder. If an intruder breaks into my house and threatens my family, I may be justified in killing him and, so, it may not count as murder per se. To determine if an act of killing rises to the level of murder, we must examine the context of a person's act and consider his or her motivations.

If Abraham slaughtered his son for no good reason, then that would certainly appear to be murder. However, Abraham does have a reason for preparing to kill his son, and this reason involves a complex relationship with God. In addressing the story of Abraham, Aquinas argues that Abraham's act was justified in view of God's ultimate role in the life-and-death process:

> All men alike, both guilty and innocent, die the death of nature: which death of nature is inflicted by the power of God on account of original sin, according to 1 Kings 2:6: "The Lord killeth and maketh alive." Consequently, by the command of God, death can be inflicted on any man, guilty or innocent, without any injustice whatever. (*Summa Theologica*, 1a-2ae, q. 94.5)

According to Aquinas, God has ultimate authority over when and how anyone dies. Therefore, although it might be wrong for Abraham to kill his son on his own, it would not be wrong for Abraham to carry out God's orders since God is and always was the final authority over human life.

Aquinas similarly rationalizes the situations of the Israelites' leaving town with the property of their Egyptian neighbors and Hosea sleeping with an adulteress. Once again, although stealing and adultery are immoral, Aquinas argues that God ultimately owns all property and spouses, and he can assign them to whomever he wants. Even if we don't agree with Aquinas's precise explanations, his larger point is still valid: The biblical stories don't conclusively depict God revoking previously established moral standards. So, there are serious problems with premise 2—problems that, like those with premise 1, force us to reject the argument from revoking established moral standards.

Defense: The Argument from Absolute Power   Scotus and other voluntarists offer a second argument for the position that God freely creates moral standards, an argument that is grounded in the notion of God's absolute power. If God has absolute power, then he can do basically anything, including create moral principles in any way that he sees fit. The more precise argument is this:

1. If a being is absolutely powerful, then that being can freely create moral standards without contradiction.
2. God is absolutely powerful.
3. Therefore, God can freely create moral standards without contradiction.

Again, the success of this argument rests on the truth of premises 1 and 2. Premise 1 draws on Scotus's notion of absolute power—namely the ability to do anything that doesn't involve a contradiction. Premise 1 also claims that, in principle, moral standards can be created and altered in various ways without logical contradiction. For example, according to Scotus, it is not logically contradictory to state that "we are morally obligated to murder, steal, or commit adultery." This statement may be false, and it certainly sounds strange when we say it out loud, but it contains no logical contradiction, such as we find in the statement "Bob is a married bachelor."

A critic of Scotus might argue that prohibitions against murder, theft, and adultery are actually *built into* our notion of moral obligation. That is, when we speak about our moral obligations, we actually refer to a specific collection of moral obligations, which include our obligations not to commit murder, theft, and adultery. So, according to the critic, a contradiction is lurking beneath the surface in the statement that "we are morally obligated to murder, steal, or commit adultery." In response, Scotus would deny that we define the notion of "moral obligation" in terms of a specific collection of moral obligations. Instead, "moral obligation" has a much more general meaning and is linked to what God freely wills. It is too soon in the argument to grant Scotus's point that God himself defines the nature of moral obligation. Nevertheless, Scotus's view is at least logically possible, and this by itself shows that prohibitions against murder, theft, and adultery are not logically part of the definition. Although we've gotten used to linking "moral obligation" with prohibitions against murder, theft, and adultery, these prohibitions are not *logically* included in the notion of moral obligation.

Premise 1, then, seems acceptable. That is, moral standards seemingly might be created and altered in various ways without logical contradiction. The success of the argument, then, rests on premise 2: God is absolutely powerful. According to this premise, there exists a God who has the power to do anything that doesn't involve a logical contradiction. Should we accept this premise? Medieval philosophers devised proofs to demonstrate that God exists and that God has infinitely great qualities—including the power to do all logically possible things. Scotus himself formulated one of the most elaborate proofs ever for God's existence. Suppose, though, that we are not convinced by such proofs or that we aren't even interested in wading through the details of these proofs to see if they work. We might instead wish simply to grant that God exists and then consider as a matter of personal faith whether God has absolute power. For traditional believers, the idea of a God with limited power doesn't make much sense. Who would want to believe in a puny God with restricted abilities? Instead, a dedicated believer motivated by a sense of devotion should *want* to attribute as much power to God as possible, including creative power over moral principles. So, a strong sense of religious devotion should incline the believer to accept premise 2.

There are two problems with this devotion-based endorsement of premise 2. First, just because we *want* to attribute absolute power to God, that doesn't mean that an absolutely powerful God actually exists. Our devotion may be misdirected, and we may be only thinking wishfully—just as we might hope to hit the big lottery jackpot. Wishful thinking isn't a strong enough basis for concluding that God freely creates morality. Second, it is not clear that, as a matter of devotion, we should *want* to attribute absolute power to God. How much power must we ascribe to God before we are psychologically content in our devotion toward him? A believer may certainly be psychologically compelled to believe in a God who is very powerful. But as the believer heaps more and more powerful abilities on God, there is a point at which ascribing that extra power is unnecessary for spiritual contentment and even collapses into self-indulgence.

Suppose, for example, that I love to eat apples, and for the next month I vow to eat nothing but apples. During this one-month period, there would be physical limits to the number of apples I could eat—say, about 1000 apples. Suppose, too, that a local apple grower decides to support my efforts during that one-month period and drops off a truckload of 1000 apples. Ungraciously, I protest, "That's not good enough, and I demand 2000 apples even though I won't be able to eat them all!" Like my desire for more apples than I can eat, a believer can stipulate more divine power than the believer actually needs to be spiritually satisfied, and anything beyond that is something like spiritual gluttony.

The least admirable form of religious faith is that which is directed by the believer's personal cravings, such as the desire for heavenly rewards. The Hindu *Bhagavad Gita* makes this point here:

> The foolish utter flowery speech, and rejoice in the letter of the Vedas [i.e., Hindu scriptures]. For them there is nothing but a desire for the self with only the intent on reaching heaven. (*Bhagavad Gita,* 2)

This passage condemns established religious practices that are rooted in the believer's selfish desires. The *Bhagavad Gita* recommends instead that we distance ourselves from any personal benefit that our faith might give us. Although traditional Christians may resist taking spiritual advice from Hindu texts, this particular point in the *Bhagavad Gita* is universal: Selfish interests shouldn't guide faith. Accordingly, it isn't appropriate for us to grant God creative power over moral principles when we are motivated by spiritual gluttony.

In the absence of a convincing proof for the existence of an all-powerful God, we should be suspicious of premise 2 and thereby reject the argument from absolute power. So, we've rejected both the argument from revoking established moral standards and the argument from absolute power. Although both of these arguments fail, it is important to note that this does not necessarily mean that voluntarism is false; it only means that these *specific* arguments fail as proofs for the view that morality is a creation of God's will. The voluntarist may offer other, more successful proofs or simply hold to voluntarism as a matter of faith in spite of the criticisms.

Criticism: Voluntarism Implies That Divine Goodness Is Meaningless

Although voluntarism is no longer part of mainstream moral philosophy, some Christian philosophers today continue to argue that God creates morality. Like their medieval predecessors, contemporary voluntarists often rely on both the argument from revoking established moral standards and the argument from absolute power. This continued interest in voluntarism has sparked a number of critical reactions. The most commonly discussed contemporary criticism is that, if God does create moral goodness, then we can't meaningfully say about God himself that "God is morally good." According to voluntarism, "moral goodness" simply means "that which God ordains." This definition by itself does not present problems when we make moral statements about humans.

Suppose, for example, that I say, "Bob is morally good." Based on the voluntarist's definition of moral goodness, this statement translates as "Bob does that which God ordains," and this is a perfectly meaningful statement. However, suppose that I next say, "God is morally good." Based on the voluntarist's definition of moral goodness, this statement translates as "God ordains that which he ordains," and here the notion of divine moral goodness is lost. The critic's general point appears correct: If voluntarism is true, then moral statements about God aren't as meaningful as moral statements about humans. It also seems clear that the voluntarist's notion of divine moral goodness isn't as meaningful as the intellectualist's. According to intellectualism, "moral goodness" means "that which conforms to an independent moral standard." If I then say that "God is morally good," for the intellectualist this translates "God conforms to an independent moral standard"—and this is perfectly meaningful.

For the critic, then, the voluntarist implicitly abandons any meaningful notion of divine moral goodness. This is a problem since, without moral goodness, God wouldn't be much more than an all-powerful bully. The heart of this issue involves a tension between the notions of divine power and divine goodness. On the one hand, if God has absolute power over moral principles, then the notion of divine moral goodness is not meaningful. On the other hand, if we wish to preserve the notion of divine moral goodness, then we must deny God's absolute power over moral principles. The intellectualist critic advises that we should take this second option and preserve God's goodness at the expense of God's power. Should the believer follow the critic's intellectualist advice? The question appears to hinge on the believer's differing levels of psychological comfort. Presumably, according to the critic, it is more comforting to retain a meaningful notion of divine goodness than it is to retain the notion of God's absolute power over morality.

However, we run into problems when basing arguments on issues of comfort. We've already seen that endorsing the notion of absolute power may simply be motivated by spiritual gluttony, which isn't very admirable. Similarly, if we examine the intellectualist's psychological motivation for retaining a meaningful notion of divine goodness, we may find something equally unadmirable. Intellectualism retains a meaningful notion of divine goodness because it sets up a standard of morality that is external to God. Perhaps this is motivated by a sense of distrust in God. If God creates moral standards on his own, then who knows what whimsical commands he might come up with? And if we instead view morality as grounded in an independent standard from God, then we are free from God's moral authority. To a degree, this was the motivation behind the endorsement of intellectualism by the Cambridge Platonists.

In short, the worst-case motivation for voluntarism is spiritual gluttony and the desire to heap more power on God than is necessary. The worst-case motivation for intellectualism is a distrust of God and the desire to have a more reliable standard of morality. Neither of these are particularly good motives for a believer to have. If believers hope to resolve the dispute between intellectualism and voluntarism, they will need to find more pure motives for adopting one of these options over the other. Without a more pure motive, the dispute collapses into self-indulgent assertions. The safest route for the believer, though, is to set the whole issue aside and concede the inability to mark off the boundaries between God's absolute power and God's moral goodness. Whether God creates moral principles or not, it should be sufficient for the believer to see that God *endorses* these principles.

God and Morality

In recent years, the tables have turned against religious morality so much that contemporary moral philosophers view with suspicion, simply dismiss, or even ridicule those who vocalize any religious ethics. What, though, is so bad about linking morality with God? On one level, the religious ethics of Aquinas and Scotus is a purely academic issue with little immediate practical implication. For Aquinas, God simply endorses the same rational moral standard that any other rational being, including humans, would endorse. Aquinas contends that we don't even need to believe in God to rationally uncover moral standards. To a degree, this is also the case for Scotus. Even though God freely creates moral standards as he pleases, Scotus argues, we gain knowledge of these divinely created moral standards through our conscience, which is a natural faculty that we all possess. Since I have this faculty regardless of whether I personally believe in God, then, just like the believer, I will intuit these proper moral standards. Aquinas and Scotus both believe that God *encourages* us to be moral and will punish us for immoral conduct, which has an impact on our motivation to be moral. However, as long as our moral views are firmly grounded in our conscience, then the component of divine punishment simply adds an exclamation point to their views of morality. It is like saying, "Stealing is wrong and, by the way, God will punish you if you steal." This, though, isn't much different from saying, "Stealing is wrong and, by the way, the cops will get you if you steal."

Lingering Problems with Religious Ethics   Critics don't seem upset with those aspects of religious ethics that are found in Aquinas's and Scotus's theories. The big problem for critics, though, is when believers merely stipulate that God morally endorses a particular type of conduct. For example, David Koresh claimed that God morally endorsed him to have sex with 12-year-old girls for the purpose of siring children. The mere mention of this is likely to make anyone cringe—believer and nonbeliever alike. Critics, though, have the same negative response when believers appeal to God's authority concerning a wide range of moral issues, such as abortion, homosexuality, interracial marriages, and handgun ownership. When pressed, the believer might justify his views by appealing to the Bible, to religious tradition, or to his religious conscience. Again, though, we must ask, what is so bad about this? There are three problems that the critic of religious ethics might point out.

First, according to the critic, appealing to religious intuitions on moral issues is a conversation stopper. We would like to at least open a dialog on an issue, but we can't since the believer quickly appeals to his foundational and non-negotiable religious assumption. In response, the believer maintains that there *is* room for dialog within his religious tradition but that the *critic* stops the conversation with her secular viewpoint. In one fell swoop, the critic shuts off an entire range of religious-based discourse because of her own foundational and non-negotiable secular assumptions. If there is a stoppage of conversation, much of the fault rests with the critic.

Second, the critic might argue that the believer's chain of reasoning isn't long enough and rests too quickly on his foundational religious assumption. Proper ethical decisions involve detailed reasoning, but the typical believer has a one-step reasoning process. Abortion, for example, is wrong because the believer's religious intuitions tell him so. However, other nonreligious moral theories also have a one-step reasoning process. A utilitarian, for example, might argue that it is wrong to torture animals since this increases the quantity of pain in the world. A rights theorist might argue that stealing a car is wrong since it violates individuals' property rights. What is relevant in these cases is (1) the strength of the initial moral standard, such as the importance of reducing pain, and (2) the applicability of the moral standard to a given issue, such as torturing animals. So, if we dismiss religious ethics because it involves a one-step reasoning process, then we must also dismiss many secular theories.

Finally, the critic might argue that the believer blindly perpetuates bigotry when pronouncing, for example, that God commands men to be in charge of women. Bigotry is certainly bad, but if there is a link between bigotry and religious ethics, it is at most a sociological connection, and not a logical one. Religious intuitions don't logically entail that one single out and unjustly condemn specific groups of people. And even from a sociological perspective, it isn't immediately clear that believers in religious ethics tend more toward bigotry than does the population as a whole. Unless such a connection can be established through responsible sociological studies, then it is bigotry itself to dismiss proponents of religious ethics as bigots simply on the basis of a hunch.

Critics of religious ethics may be bothered by appeals to religious intuitions for additional reasons. However, critics aren't justified in declaring a monopoly on the field of ethics by restricting it to only nonreligious approaches, which historically are relatively recent and geographically are confined mostly to Western culture. In today's secular environment, the religious believer undoubtedly limits his audience by appealing to religious intuitions in moral matters. For example, if I debate the issue of women's rights with a Muslim and he appeals to the Koran to support his perspective, his appeal will carry little weight for me. However, we must distinguish between arguing to win a debate and arguing to justify a moral view. We can expect only the latter from anyone making ethical choices, and in their own contexts, at least some religious appeals are legitimate justifications.

There are, however, limits to religious appeals. First, religious appeals won't be morally binding for nonbelievers who question fundamental points about religion, such as the existence of God. Second, believers should consider that there are limits to the authority of religious appeals even for *themselves*.

Interpretations of scripture change, religious organizations redefine their doctrines, and individuals' religious consciences often shift over the years. For example, throughout much of its long history, the Roman Catholic Church held that slavery was morally permissible since it reflected a natural hierarchy in social groups. In more recent times, though, the Catholic Church has harshly condemned slavery. Several centuries ago, the Catholic Church and many early Protestant denominations believed that they were morally justified in torturing and killing vocal members of rival Christian denominations. Today this idea is appalling to all Christian groups. And when contraceptive devices became widely available in the early twentieth century, most Protestant denominations harshly condemned their use since that would thwart God's plan for human reproduction. Within fifty years, though, virtually all Protestant denominations reversed their views. So, even for the believer, religious assessments of moral matters should be viewed in light of this changing backdrop.

Summary

Medieval Christian philosophers hotly debated the relation between morality and God's will. Intellectualist moral philosophers such as Aquinas believed that moral standards are independent of God and that God endorses them because of his rational nature. By contrast, voluntarist moral philosophers such as Scotus argued that moral standards are created by God and don't exist independently of God. Scotus believed that God has a genuinely free will and absolute power to create anything that does not involve a logical contradiction. For Scotus, moral principles fall under the domain of God's absolute power. Scotus and other voluntarists offered two arguments for this position. First, voluntarists argue that, insofar as religious texts depict God as revoking previously established moral laws, God has creative power over these moral laws. But we've seen that the power to revoke moral laws does not necessarily imply the power to create moral laws. We've also seen that the specific biblical stories discussed by voluntarists are not clear illustrations of God revoking moral standards. Second, voluntarists argue that, insofar as God has absolute power, God has the ability to create moral standards. In theory, moral standards might be created and altered in various ways without logical contradiction. However, there are problems with granting that God is absolutely powerful. In the absence of a proof, belief in God's absolute power may be driven by either wishful thinking or spiritual gluttony.

A common contemporary argument against voluntarism is that, if God creates moral standards, then the notion of divine moral goodness becomes meaningless. That is, the statement "God is morally good" simply means "God ordains that which he ordains." The issue involves a tension between God's goodness and God's absolute power. According to the intellectualist, it is best for us to preserve God's moral goodness even though this means reducing God's range of power. However, both sides of the dispute may have questionable motives: the voluntarist by spiritual gluttony and the intellectualist by distrust of

God. The safest way to address the dispute is simply to concede ignorance about the nature of God's goodness and power and to contend only that God endorses moral principles. Although religious-based ethics is currently unpopular in secular discussions of morality, there is nothing wrong with religious morality as long as believers recognize that there are limits to this approach.

 ## Study Questions

Introduction
Plato and the Euthyphro Puzzle
1. What is the puzzle regarding the relation between God and morality that Plato presents in the *Euthyphro*?

Traditional Voluntarism
2. What are the definitions of "intellectualism" and "voluntarism"?

Scotus's Voluntarism
3. What does Scotus mean by the view that God has a genuinely free will?
4. What does Scotus mean by "absolute power"?
5. For Scotus, what kinds of laws are moral laws most similar to?
6. Scotus maintained that God temporarily revoked established moral standards. What are some examples of this?
7. According to Scotus, what are the only kinds of moral laws that God cannot alter?

Voluntarism after Scotus
8. What controversial claim did Ockham make about God's ability to change moral laws?
9. According to Calvin, what is the highest authority behind everything that God does?
10. According to Grotius, what kinds of laws are moral laws most similar to?
11. Why did Cambridge Platonists side with intellectualism?

Arguments for and against Voluntarism
Defense: The Argument from Revoking Established Moral Standards
12. Premise 1 of the argument from revoking established moral standards is this: "If God has the ability to temporarily revoke a moral standard, then he has the power to freely create moral standards." What is the problem with this premise?
13. How does Aquinas interpret the story of God commanding Abraham to kill his son?

Defense: The Argument from Absolute Power
14. Premise 1 of the argument from absolute power is this: "If a being is absolutely powerful, then that being can freely create moral stan-

dards without contradiction." Why does Fieser accept the truth of this premise?

15. What is Fieser's view about absolute divine power and spiritual gluttony?
16. What point does the *Bhagavad Gita* make about selfish desires?

Criticism: Voluntarism Implies That Divine Goodness Is Meaningless

17. Explain the critic's view that voluntarism implies that divine goodness is meaningless.
18. By enhancing the notion of divine power, what does the voluntarist sacrifice?
19. According to Fieser, what are the worst-case motivations for voluntarism and intellectualism, respectively?

God and Morality

Lingering Problems with Religious Ethics

20. In what respect are Aquinas's and Scotus's views on religious ethics purely an academic question with little immediate practical implication?
21. What are the three main criticisms that the opponent of religious ethics might give?
22. In matters of morality, what are some limitations on the authority of religious appeals as pertains to religious believers themselves?

References

Plato's statement of the Euthyphro puzzle is in the dialog *Euthyphro,* 10a–11b, translated by Benjamin Jowett in *The Dialogues of Plato* (New York: Collier, 1901).

The quotations by Scotus are from *The Oxford Commentary on the Four Books of the Sentences,* translated by Allan B. Wolter in *Duns Scotus on the Will and Morality* (Washington, DC: Catholic University of America Press, 1986).

The quotation by Ockham is from *Fourth Book of the Sentences,* Question 14, as translated by Lucan Freppert in *The Basis of Morality According to William Ockham* (Chicago: Franciscan Herald Press, 1988).

The quotation by Luther is from *Martin Luther: Selections from his Writings,* edited by John Dillenberger (Garden City, NY: Anchor Books Doubleday, 1961), p. 196.

The quotation by Calvin is from *Institutes of the Christian Religion,* translated by Ford Lewis Battles (London: SCM Press, 1961).

The quotations by Aquinas are from "The Treatise on Law" (1a2ae, q. 90–144) in *Summa Theologica,* translataed by Laurence Shapcote, Fathers of the English Dominican Province (London, 1911–36).

The *Bhagavad Gita* is available in several modern translations; the quotation here from Chapter 2 is rendered from the translation by Annie Wood Besant (London: Theosophical Publishing Society, 1895).

Suggestions for Further Reading

For a discussion of Scotus's moral theory, see Allan B. Wolter, *Duns Scotus on the Will and Morality* (Washington, DC: Catholic University of America Press, 1986); B. M.

Bonansea, *Man and His Approaches to God in John Duns Scotus* (Lanham, MD: University Press of America, 1983).

For a discussion of Ockham's moral theory, see Lucan Freppert, *The Basis of Morality According to William Ockham* (Chicago: Franciscan Herald Press, 1988).

For contemporary defenses of divine command theory, see Robert M. Adams, "A Modified Divine Command Theory of Ethical Wrongness," in *The Virtue of Faith* (Oxford: Oxford University Press, 1987); Richard J. Mouw, *The God Who Commands* (Notre Dame, IN: University of Notre Dame Press, 1990); Philip L. Quinn, *Divine Commands and Moral Requirements* (Oxford: Clarendon Press, 1978).

For a contemporary criticism of divine command theory, see Kai Nielsen, *Ethics Without God* (London: Pemberton, 1973).

6

Social Contract Theory

Introduction

On April 19, 1995, a terrorist car bomb exploded outside of a nine-story federal office building in Oklahoma City. The explosion was so powerful that people in buildings several blocks away were thrown from their chairs, and people 30 miles away could feel the blast's vibration. About 550 people were inside the federal building at the time, and 168 of those people were crushed to death by the collapsed structure, making the explosion the worst terrorist act ever on U.S. soil. The FBI immediately distributed composite drawings of two bombing suspects, and within days the bombers were identified as 27-year-old Timothy McVeigh, a former Army mechanic, and 39-year-old Terry Nichols. Both McVeigh and Nichols had ties with antigovernment paramilitary organizations. These organizations opposed government gun control efforts and were hostile to any freedom-restricting activities of the federal government. For McVeigh and Nichols, the message behind the bombing was that the federal government should not take away our freedoms.

The Oklahoma City bombing is among the most tragic events in recent U.S. history, and the bombers' callous disregard for human life violates everything we know about morality. One troubling aspect of this tragedy is its underlying ideological message, part of which we accept as freedom lovers, and part of which we reject for its extremism. According to many antigovernment groups, we establish governments to perform only a narrow range of tasks, principally protection from foreign invasion. However, the U.S. government pushes its authority beyond its established purpose by unjustly restricting people's freedoms. This justifies resistance, which even the U.S. Declaration of Independence endorses: "Whenever any form of government becomes destructive to these ends [i.e., rights to life, liberty and happiness], it is the right of the people to alter or to abolish it, and to institute new government. . . ."

The underlying philosophy of such antigovernment groups is that of **social contract theory**. In its less extreme form, social contract theory is both a legitimate and a historically important account of political and moral obligation. Briefly, social contract theory describes a disease and then proposes a cure. The disease is that humans have unsociable tendencies and are unable to construct and live in cooperative societies. The cure is that we contractually agree to be civil to one another under threat of punishment from a governing body that we establish for this purpose. This mutual contract then becomes the backbone for our moral obligations to each other.

Social contract theory has a long but spotty history. Plato hints at a social contract theory in his great dialog the *Republic*. A skeptical character in that dialog named Glaucon argues that people are naturally inclined to exploit one another. Since people also don't like being exploited, they agree not to exploit others on the condition that others don't exploit them:

> When men have both done and suffered injustice and have had experience
> of both, not being able to avoid the one and obtain the other, they think that
> they had better agree among themselves to have neither; hence there arise laws
> and mutual covenants; and that which is ordained by law is termed by them
> lawful and just. (*Republic*, 2.358e)

For Glaucon, the mutual contracts that we create are the basis of the rules of justice. Plato himself didn't accept this skeptical view of the origins of morality; instead, he argued that moral truths are fixed in a higher and more eternal realm of the universe. For almost 2000 years, most moral philosophers largely agreed with Plato's view. In particular, they believed that both morality and governmental authority are grounded in objective natural laws that God himself endorses. During the seventeenth century, a few skeptically-minded philosophers offered alternative explanations of morality that were grounded more in the human than the heavenly realm. One of these was British philosopher **Thomas Hobbes** (1588–1679), who offers the first detailed account of social contract theory.

Hobbes's Theory

Hobbes presents his social contract theory in a series of works, the most famous of which is *The Leviathan* (1651). For Hobbes, the powerful governing body that we establish for protection is like the "Leviathan," a large mythological sea creature as depicted in the Hebrew Bible and earlier Canaanite mythology. The Hebrew Bible describes the great sea creature as the "king over all the children of pride." Similarly, Hobbes saw that the government as the king over prideful people, insofar as our human pride forces us to create a government for our own protection.

The State of Nature   A common story line in science fiction sagas is that modern society crumbles because of a nuclear world war or a colossal ecological disaster. A few isolated surviving humans forage through the ruins of destroyed cities, hoping to find a stray can of food, a container of gasoline, or a box of bullets. Every contact with another human is a life-or-death struggle to acquire the other person's goods. Rather than looking into the future to describe a post-apocalyptic world, Hobbes looks to the distant past and asks us to imagine what life might have been like before there were any governing bodies. The condition that Hobbes describes is as selfish and brutal as any science fiction story. Hobbes calls this primitive condition the **state of nature**. Hobbes isn't describing an actual time in human history; he offers this thought experiment only to highlight the limits of our human nature and the effects of our unsocial inclinations on our interactions with others.

Hobbes argues that, in this state of nature, we are roughly equal to one another in both intellectual cunning and physical strength. Intellectually, we all gain knowledge through experience, and given enough time and effort, we can all rise to a comparable intellectual level. Physically, although a bigger person might be able to beat me in an arm wrestling contest, with a little cunning I can overpower him. Hobbes writes that "as to the strength of body, the weakest has strength enough to kill the strongest, either by secret mechination, or by confederacy with others that are in the same danger with himself." Although intellectual and physical equality might seem like good things, in the state of nature they only perpetuate struggle. If someone stood out with superhuman physical abilities, such as Superman, then he could simply take control and force people to cooperate. Perhaps the same thing could happen if someone stood out with superhuman intellectual abilities. But since we're all more or less equal in the state of nature, no one will naturally emerge to take charge.

In view of our equality, Hobbes notes three factors that immediately cause us to quarrel. First, we equally desire things that are in limited supply. All of us seek after basic necessities such as food, clothing, and shelter. If all of our physical needs in life could be met simply by reaching up and picking things off a tree, then there would be no need to engage in conflict with anyone. The reality of the situation, though, is otherwise. Necessities are in limited supply, and as we compete for the same things, we quickly come to view one another as enemies. Through violence, then, we seek to subdue "men's persons, wives, children, and cattle."

The second cause of quarrels is that, once we acquire some goods, we immediately become distrustful of people who approach us, and so we attack them. This isn't merely paranoia, but a necessary means of protecting things that we've acquired. For example, when people win large amounts of money in a lottery, they are often targeted by scam artists who try to defraud them of their winnings with shady investment opportunities. The more distrustful we are of outsiders, the better we'll be able to retain what we've acquired. In the state of nature, this distrust translates into violence.

The third cause of quarrels is that we will attack others simply to preserve our reputations as tough guys that people shouldn't mess around with. If our reputations diminish, then others will see us as easy prey.

The consequence of all this is a state of war pitting all against all. It includes actual as well as anticipated wars that, similar to the cold war between the United States and the former Soviet Union, involve constant military posturing. Hobbes's description of this state of war is one of the most famous passages in philosophy:

> In such condition there is no place for industry, because the fruit thereof is uncertain, and consequently, no culture of the earth, no navigation, nor use of the commodities that may be imported by sea, no commodious building, no instruments of moving and removing such things as require much force, no knowledge of the face of the earth, no account of time, no arts, no letters, no society, and which is worst of all, continual fear and danger of violent death, and the life of man, solitary, poor, nasty, brutish, and short. (*Leviathan*, 13)

For Hobbes, in the state of nature, we would lack all social comforts that come about through mutual cooperation. We wouldn't even attempt to grow food, import goods, or build dwellings on our own since we would thereby make ourselves targets of attack by other people. Our rivals would see what we have, desire it, and kill us to acquire it. We would have no "knowledge of the face of the earth" since the only geographical area that counts is the one immediately around us as we seek to survive attacks by others. We would have "no account of time" since the only time that matters is the present moment in which we struggle to survive. We would have no arts and no literary compositions since these are luxury items that humans create only after we secure our survival. We would have no society since social interaction requires trust and cooperation, which we wouldn't be capable of. In essence, our human lives would be "solitary, poor, nasty, brutish, and short."

What kind of morality is there in this state of nature? In a word, none! Hobbes argues that in this condition the "notions of right and wrong, justice and injustice have there no place." It is a moral free-for-all in which we can do whatever we want, in which "every person has a right to everything, even to one another's body." Hobbes offers several examples from ordinary-life situations to support his gloomy description of human nature. When we go on trips, we take guns with us for protection against robbers. When we go to bed at night, we lock our cabinets to prevent our housekeepers and even our own children from stealing from us. We take these extra steps to protect ourselves in addition to the protection we get from the police and court systems. And individual countries, like individual people, are always poised to defend themselves against invaders who want to plunder their resources.

The Laws of Nature   The state of nature that Hobbes describes is so disturbing that it gives us strong motivation to want to rise above that condition if possible. None of us wants to die violently; we all want decent living conditions; we also carry hopes that we can improve our living conditions through work. But we can't fulfill any of these desires until we achieve peace, and Hobbes next describes what we need to do to secure such peace. This part of his discussion is influenced by natural law theory, particularly the version developed by Dutch philosopher **Hugo Grotius** (1583–1645). In his work *The Law of War and Peace* (1625), Grotius explains that there are fixed moral laws of nature that are binding on everyone worldwide. Further, according to Grotius, we set up governing bodies to ensure that we follow these moral mandates of natural law and thus live peacefully. Hobbes not only follows Grotius's basic solution to securing peace but also adopts the language of natural law theory. For Hobbes, then, we get out of the state of nature by following the laws of nature.

Hobbes lists fifteen distinct laws of nature that facilitate ending conflict and securing peace, the first three of which are the most important. Hobbes describes the first law of nature as this:

> Every man ought to endeavour peace, as far as he has hope of obtaining it, and when he cannot obtain it, that he may seek and use all helps and advantages of war. (*Leviathan*, 14)

This first law of nature tells us that we should seek peace but that we should defend ourselves if we can't achieve peace. The binding nature of this law is clear: We all wish to survive, and peace is the best way to survive. When peace fails, however, we need to defend ourselves.

The second law of nature describes more precisely how we achieve peace with one another. We saw that in the state of nature "Every person has a right to everything, even to one another's body." Imagine that each of us carried around a bag with slips of paper that listed all of our respective rights in the state of nature. The rights that I would have in the state of nature are almost infinite in number and allow me complete liberty. For example, I might pull one slip out of my bag that says I have a right to hop around on one foot. I might pull another slip out that says I have the right to kill you—which surely would worry you. However, in your rights bag, you would have a similar slip of paper that says you have the right to kill me, and that certainly would worry me. And as long as we both hold onto our rights to kill each other, we can never achieve peace.

The second law of nature, then, says that you and I should agree to give up those specific rights that threaten each of us respectively:

> A man [should] be willing, when others are so too, as far-forth as for peace and defence of himself he shall think it necessary, to lay down this right to all things, and be contented with so much liberty against other men, as he would allow other men against himself. (*Leviathan*, 14)

According to this law of nature, if you're willing to remove from your bag the slip of paper that grants you the right to kill me, then I should be willing to remove from my bag the slip of paper that grants me the right to kill you. We should do this with all rights that breed hostility—such as the right to kill, steal from, lie to, or assault others—and enlist any person who is willing to cooperate with us. In short, the second law of nature tells us, "Do not do to others what you would not want done to yourself." Why should I be willing to give up any of my personal rights? Because my survival depends on it. However, Hobbes implies that we should only mutually give up those rights that are *necessary* for securing peace. For example, my right to hop around on one foot has no bearing on the peace process, so I shouldn't give up that right.

The third law of nature is simply that "people perform their covenants made," since our agreements are empty words if we don't keep them. For

Hobbes, even if you and I have the best of intentions and plan on giving up our hostile rights forever, we must actually abstain from those hostilities; otherwise, we will remain in the state of nature. Assuring that we abide by our agreements is tricky. I will always be looking for ways to cheat the system, and I can only assume that you will, too. Our verbal agreement alone isn't enough, and we both need some extra motivation to follow through on our agreements. The solution is that we both agree to give unlimited power to a political authority that will punish us if we break our agreements. This means that you and I must give up a few more of our rights, handing them over to this political authority. But it is worth it if this is the only way to guarantee our contractual arrangement, which in turn ends the state of nature.

Hobbes's remaining twelve laws of nature are principally rules of diplomacy that preserve peaceful coexistence once it is established. For example, the fourth law tells us that we should show gratitude toward others who comply with contracts. If we don't, then others might regret participating in the contract. The fifth law says that we should compromise on minor issues that serve the larger interests of society. If we have to debate every little issue, then the peace process will grind to a halt.

Political Theory and Moral Theory   Hobbes's social contract theory serves double duty: as (1) a political theory that justifies the existence of a government and (2) a moral theory that specifies our moral obligations. As a political theory, Hobbes's social contract theory maintains that governments are the creations of people, and not the creations of God. The complete justification for a government's existence is its role as preserver of the peace. However, even though we are the ones who create governments, we are never allowed to overthrow them once they are established, even if we're not happy with the job that they're doing. The reason for this is that, to guarantee that governments will be effective in their peacekeeping mission, we must give them absolute and irrevocable authority over us. For Hobbes, if governments have anything less than this, then they will be unable to enforce the laws.

The governments that we establish can be monarchies, aristocracies, or democracies. However, Hobbes believed that monarchies are the most effective in preserving the peace, for several reasons. Monarchs will receive better counsel since they can select experts and get advice in private. Monarchs' policies will also be more consistent since they are operating as individuals, unlike other forms of government that have many leaders. Similarly, there is less chance of a civil war with a monarchy since monarchs will not disagree with themselves.

Although scholars debate the precise details of Hobbes's view as a moral theory, two features seem prominent. First, morality isn't a permanent feature of the nature of things but is only a creation of the social contract. We saw that, in the state of nature, "Notions of right and wrong, justice and injustice have there no place." The notions of morality that emerge through the laws of nature are contractual agreements. In this regard, Hobbes is a moral skeptic insofar as he holds that moral principles have no objective foundation independent of human society.

The second feature of Hobbes's moral theory is that our specific moral obligations are intimately linked with the fifteen laws of nature. For example, the third law of nature states that we should keep our contracts. When we do this, we have the moral virtue of justice; when we fail to do this, we have the moral vice of injustice. Similarly, the fourth law of nature states that we should show gratitude toward those who keep their contracts. When we follow this fourth law, we have the virtue of gratitude; when we fail to do so, we have the vice of ingratitude. Other virtues that Hobbes lists include sociability, modesty, equity, and mercy, with each linked directly to one of the fifteen laws of nature. Hobbes also notes that his theory recognizes the same virtues as traditional virtue theories, such as Aristotle's, which includes courage and fortitude. So, Hobbes writes that "the science of virtue and vice is moral philosophy, and therefore the true doctrine of the Laws of Nature is the true moral philosophy." There are two specific implications to Hobbes's virtue account of morality. First, the job of moral philosophy is to find out specifically which virtuous character traits facilitate adherence to the various laws of nature. Second, our job as morally responsible people is to cultivate virtuous character traits since, if we don't, we place the peace of society at risk.

To summarize, here are the main points of Hobbes's theory:

- The prepolitical state of nature for humans is a condition of mutual conflict that contains no objective moral values.
- We achieve peace by mutually agreeing to give up our rights to harm one another.
- To ensure compliance, we create governments that punish those who break the agreements.
- To further secure compliance we recognize various laws of nature and acquire moral virtues.

Social Contract Theory in the Seventeenth and Eighteenth Centuries

Shortly after Hobbes's writings appeared, theologically-minded critics attacked Hobbes for eliminating God's role in mandating morality and establishing political authority. Accusations of atheism and irreligion were common, and several bishops reportedly even discussed burning Hobbes to death. Fortunately for Hobbes, threats like this never materialized. In spite of these harsh reactions, Hobbes's general notion of the social contract captured the imagination of philosophers after him, and for 150 years, social contract theory was a dominant theme among political philosophers. These social contract theorists modified features of Hobbes's theory to make it less skeptical, but they all accepted the basic concept of an original state of nature, and a social contract that addresses limitations of our natural state. For example, German philosopher **Samuel von Pufendorf** (1632–1694) agreed with Hobbes that the state of nature is fairly miserable and that, to survive, we enter into a social contract and establish political authorities to punish contract violators. However, Pufendorf argued that God sets the basic terms of the social contract by mandating that we should be sociable. For Pufendorf, then, the social contract is grounded in God's author-ity, and not simply in the authority of people.

British philosopher **John Locke** (1632–1704) also put a more positive spin on social contract theory. According to Locke, the state of nature isn't a condi-tion of moral anarchy as Hobbes supposed; instead, it is an environment in which we have God-given natural rights to life, health, liberty, and possessions. Locke agreed that we need to contractually form governments to punish rights violators. However, whereas Hobbes believed that governments should have absolute authority once we put them in place, Locke argued that citizens may overthrow their government if it fails at its peacekeeping role. So, in Locke's version of social contract theory, political revolutions are sometimes justifiable. The British Whig party quickly adopted Locke's version of social contract theory and its justification for revolution. This, in turn, provided the intellectual climate to justify the American Revolution and the rights expressed in the Dec-laration of Independence.

As in Great Britain, social contract theory played a vital role in 18th-century French political thought, especially in the writings of French philoso-pher **Jean-Jacques Rousseau** (1712–1778). Contrary to Hobbes, who described the state of nature as a condition of mutual conflict, Rousseau argued that it is a condition of individual freedom in which creativity flourishes. According to Rousseau, in this state of nature people can't avoid interacting with one an-other, and so citizens set up a social contract to regulate this interaction. The contract specifically establishes an absolute democracy that is ruled by the gen-eral will of the people, which, for Rousseau, involves what is best for all people. Just as social contract theory offered a philosophical justification for revolution-ary activity in Great Britain, it similarly offered justification for the French Revolution of 1789.

Criticisms of Hobbes

For decades after his death, Hobbes was the principal target of criticism among moral and political philosophers, and dozens of negative reactions were pub-lished that criticized almost every part of his theory. We will look at three criti-cisms that are directed at central features of Hobbes's account of morality.

Hyde's Criticism: Hobbes Denies That Morality Is Immutable and Eternal   We saw that, for Hobbes, traditional moral values are nonexistent in the state of nature and morality is a creation of the social contract. Although Hobbes boldly denies morality in the state of nature, he fudges the issue a little when describing the invented status of morality within the social contract. In fact, he goes so far as to say that "the Laws of Nature are immutable and eter-nal." Traditionally, when philosophers such as Grotius claimed that morality is "eternal" and "immutable," they meant that moral values are universal and unchanging, and are not creations of human convention. Hobbes's choice of the words "immutable" and "eternal" was probably politically motivated, repre-senting an attempt to avoid condemnation by conservative critics. If so, his ruse wasn't successful. **Edward Hyde** (1609–1674), a British politician and acquaintance of Hobbes, charged that Hobbes's laws of nature are not at all "immutable" and "eternal" in the usual philosophical sense:

> If nature has thus providently provided for the peace and tranquillity of her children, by laws immutable and eternal that are written in their hearts, how come they to fall into that condition of war, as to be every one against every one, and to be without any other cardinal virtues, but of force and fraud? (*A Survey of Mr. Hobbes*)

According to Hyde, even the content of Hobbes's laws of nature reveal that they are not immutable and eternal in the traditional sense:

> But where are those maxims to be found—which Mr. Hobbes declares and publishes to be the laws of nature—in any other author before him? That is only properly called "the law of nature" [when] that is dictated to the whole species. . . . (*A Survey of Mr. Hobbes*)

Hyde has two complaints against Hobbes. First, he accuses Hobbes of actually denying the immutable and eternal nature of morality, as seen in Hobbes's depiction of the state of nature. Second, he claims that Hobbes tries to flimflam us by describing the laws of nature as immutable and eternal when Hobbes clearly doesn't mean it. Hobbes must plead guilty to both of these charges. However, from today's perspective, neither of these "crimes" are as bad as Hyde makes them out to be. As to Hyde's first charge, philosophers today typically don't describe moral principles as "immutable" and "eternal." To do so requires that we postulate some eternal realm in which moral principles permanently exist—a realm completely outside of human society. This calls for more metaphysical speculation than philosophers today are comfortable with.

As to Hyde's second complaint, even flimflamming on key terminology is defensible. Between the sixteenth and eighteenth centuries, philosophers, theologians, and scientists could be imprisoned, tortured, and even executed for publishing controversial ideas. The most famous example of this is the case of Italian astronomer Galileo (1564–1642), who, under threat of torture, retracted his claim about a sun-centered solar system. Sometimes, controversial authors could appease religious and political authorities simply by being diplomatic in their choice of words. Hobbes was concerned about negative reactions from the authorities, and it is reasonable to interpret his choice of the terms "immutable" and "eternal" as an act of diplomacy.

We can also see Hobbes's choice of these words as an attempt to reformulate the traditional moral vocabulary. Like astronomers and other scientists of his time, Hobbes hoped to break from medieval traditions and set his area of inquiry on a new and more scientifically rigorous course. The context of Hobbes's comments about the immutable and eternal nature of morality shows how he tried to redirect discussions on the nature of morality:

> The Laws of Nature are immutable and eternal. For injustice, ingratitude, arrogance, pride, iniquity, acception of persons, and the rest, can never be made lawful. For it can never be that war shall preserve life, and peace destroy it. (*Leviathan,* 15)

Hobbes argues here that the laws of nature are "immutable and eternal" to the extent that they are required for preserving life through making peace. Hobbes, then, shifts the discussion of moral truths from a mysterious eternal realm to the observable realm of human nature and our desire for survival. In the end, the history of philosophy shows that the terms "immutable" and "eternal" didn't take to being redefined and simply were dropped.

Clarke's Criticism: Punishment Alone Won't Motivate Us to Always Keep Contracts   Suppose that I agree to participate in the social contract. Although I understand that I'm supposed to keep the agreements that I've made, I occasionally see potential opportunities to violate these agreements when it might benefit me. For example, while my neighbor isn't looking, I could sneak next door, steal his lawnmower, and sell it to a pawnshop. If I'm careful, I won't get caught. So what should stop me from violating the social contract if I can get away with it?

British philosopher **Samuel Clarke** (1675–1729) draws attention to this problem and contends that ultimately Hobbes's theory offers no safeguard to ensure that we will keep our agreements in such situations:

> If the Rules of Right and Wrong, Just and Unjust, have none of them any obligatory force in the State of Nature, antecedent to positive Compact, then, for the same Reason, neither will they be of any force after the Compact, so as to afford men any certain and real security; (Excepting only what may arise from the Compulsion of Laws, and Fear of Punishment, which therefore, it may well be supposed, is all that Mr. Hobbes really means at the bottom.) (*Discourse*, 1)

Clarke argues here that, if we aren't motivated to follow moral rules in the state of nature, then we won't be any more motivated to follow moral rules once we enter into the social contract. Clarke recognizes that fear of punishment may provide some motivation to follow the rules, but he claims that this isn't enough. For Clarke, our main motivation to follow moral rules comes directly from an awareness of eternal and immutable moral truths themselves—and Hobbes denies this as a source of moral obligation. In short, according to Clarke, fear of punishment is the only source of motivation that Hobbes provides, and that is not sufficient to motivate us to always keep our agreements.

Hobbes addresses this issue himself, agreeing that someone might reason as follows: "There is no such thing as justice . . . [and that for someone] to make or not make, keep or not keep, covenants was not against reason, when it conduced to one's benefit." However, Hobbes suggests that this line of reasoning is flawed:

> He, therefore, that breaketh his covenant, and consequently declareth that he thinks he may with reason do so, cannot be received into any society that unite themselves for peace and defense but by the error of them that receive him; nor when he is received, be retained in it without seeing the danger of their error; which errors a man cannot reasonably reckon upon as the means of his security . . . (*Leviathan*, 15)

In other words, it isn't reasonable for the sneaky contract breaker to base his own security entirely on his ability to go undetected. If he is caught, then he will be expelled from society, and, it is just not reasonable for him to take this risk. So, for Hobbes, fear of punishment is sufficient to restrain the sneaky contract breaker.

Hobbes is probably right that we won't take the risk if there is a good chance that we'd be detected. But what if we plan the perfect crime, with no reasonable chance of getting caught? In this case, Hobbes needs another source of moral obligation that goes beyond an immediate fear of punishment. Perhaps we can rescue Hobbes from this dilemma by drawing on the virtue component of his theory. Suppose that I carefully scheme to steal my neighbor's lawnmower, and I succeed without getting caught. As a creature of habit, I am likely to plan similar crimes against other neighbors, and each time I do I increase the risk of being detected. By starting down the initial path of theft, then, I am taking an unreasonable risk since the odds of my getting caught are increased. To eliminate this risk, the reasonable thing for me to do is develop the virtue of justice so that I will habitually avoid stealing and never even start down that risky path. So, when I recognize my tendency to fall into dangerous habits, my fear of punishment should motivate me to develop consistent virtues, which in turn will keep me from breaking the rules. Hobbes's actual comments on the role of virtues are brief, and he doesn't offer this specific solution there. However, given Hobbes's view that "the science of virtue and vice is moral philosophy," this virtue-based solution fits neatly into his overall theory.

Hume's Criticism: We Don't Even Tacitly Agree to a Social Contract

Hobbes didn't believe that there was an actual point in history when people got together and signed a social contract. However, if the social contract isn't a specific historical agreement, then serious questions are raised about what kind of agreement it actually is and how it forms the basis of morality and governance. Hobbes himself tries to address this problem, noting that we can agree to contracts in either of two ways. First, we may agree through a concrete verbal expression, such as "I hereby agree to abide by the terms of the contract." Second, we may indicate agreement by inference, whereby, through either our silence or actions, others will understand that we've agreed to something. Social contract theorists after Hobbes emphasized this second method, which they dubbed **tacit consent**. Locke provided the definitive description of what counts as tacit consent:

> Every Man, that hath any Possession, or Enjoyment, of any part of the Dominions of any Government, doth thereby give his *tacit Consent,* and is as far forth obliged to Obedience to the Laws of that Government, during such Enjoyment, as any one under it . . . (*Two Treatises of Government*, 2.119)

Thus, according to Locke, if I obtain any possession or benefit from a government, then I've tacitly agreed to abide by the rules of that government. For example, if I rely on protection from the local police or the U.S. military, then I'm receiving a benefit from these government agencies and thereby tacitly agree to their rules.

Scottish philosopher **David Hume** (1711–1776) wasn't satisfied with this notion of tacit agreement. According to Hume, willful consent is the key element in *any* agreement—including tacit agreements—and virtually no one has willfully consented to the authority of their governments:

> A tacit promise is, where the will is signified by other more diffuse signs than those of speech; but a will there must certainly be in the case, and that can never escape the person's notice who exerted it, however silent or tacit. But were you to ask the far greatest part of the nation, whether they had ever consented to the authority of their rulers, or promised to obey them, they would be inclined to think very strangely of you: and would certainly reply, that the affair depended not on their consent, but that they were born to such an obedience. (*Treatise of Human Nature*, 3.2.8)

Hume argues that most people believe they were simply born into a condition of obedience. In fact, according to Hume, based on the idea of a line of succession, politicians try hard to trick people into believing that governments have natural authority over their citizens. Our current rulers claim that many years ago an earlier generation of citizens tacitly consented to a specific government, and governments today inherit that authority over us. Since we can't go back in time and interview that first generation of citizens, we accept the politicians' story and see ourselves as born into a condition of obedience. In short, we are tricked into accepting governmental authority, and neither we nor earlier generations of citizens ever tacitly agreed to a social contract. Ironically, Hume feels that this deception is actually a good thing. We need governments for our own protection, and if governments are forced into tricking us into accepting their authority, then so be it. The fact remains, though, that there neither is nor ever was a valid social contract that people tacitly consented to.

Hume is correct that people don't willfully consent to the terms of a social contract—either explicitly or tacitly. Critics after Hume recognized this problem, and British political philosopher William Godwin (1736–1836) highlights a range of related conceptual problems:

> Upon the first statement of the system of a social contract various difficulties present themselves. Who are the parties to this contract? For whom did they consent, for themselves only, or for others? For how long a time is this contract to be considered as binding? If the consent of every individual be necessary, in what manner is that consent to be given? Is it to be tacit, or declared in express terms? (*Enquiry Concerning Political Justice*, 3.2)

According to Godwin, not only is there a problem with whether the contract is tacit or explicit, but there are also questions about who is involved in the contract, how long the contract is binding, and what the precise terms of the contract are. Suppose that a defender of Hobbes concedes all of these problems and grants that there is no *actual* contract in place. Instead, according to the defender, the contract is only *hypothetical*. That is, we are only considering how a rational person would respond *if* that person were placed in the state of nature and presented with a social contract agreement.

However, appealing to hypothetical contracts leads to yet another problem. It doesn't make sense to say that *I* specifically am obligated to the terms of a source contract simply because some imaginary rational person would agree to those terms. We don't convict real people for crimes that imaginary people commit. We don't reward real people for heroic deeds that imaginary people perform. Why, then, should real people be contractually bound by an agreement made by an imaginary person? We simply aren't. In short, we must reject the idea of an actual social contract that we supposedly agree to tacitly. We must also reject the idea of an hypothetical social contract that an imaginary person agrees to.

Recent Social Contract Theory

Serious interest in social contract theory declined during the nineteenth and early twentieth centuries. In recent years, though, scholars have turned again to this theory, particularly Hobbes's version. Contemporary discussions usually expand on three central aspects of the social contract. First, there is a description of a hypothetical environment in which we interact. This involves an account of the limits of our human rationality, the levels of risk that we take in making decisions, the way we balance our short-term versus long-term interests, the extent to which we are self-regarding versus other regarding, and the degree to which we are physically and mentally equal. Second, in view of this hypothetical environment, there is a description of conflicts that inevitably arise. According to one explanation, our emotions drive us to act selfishly, in ways that conflict with other people's interests. According to another explanation, conflicts arise based on how we rationally calculate what is in our respective best interests. Third, in view of the inevitable conflicts, there is a description of the type of political authority that is reasonable for us to create.

The Prisoner's Dilemma   One of the best-known contemporary discussions of social contract theory is the **prisoner's dilemma,** which describes how conflicts inevitably arise in a hypothetical state of nature. Specifically, the prisoner's dilemma clarifies how our rational calculations lead to conflict. Imagine that you and I are caught robbing a bank, but the district attorney doesn't have quite enough evidence to guarantee a conviction. He needs us to confess to our crime, so, using a common interrogation tactic, he puts us in separate rooms and tries to get each of us to turn on the other. In this case, he offers a plea bargain based on various confessions that we might make:

- If I confess and you do not, then I will get only a 3-month sentence, but you will get a 10-year sentence.
- If you confess and I do not, then you will only get a 3-month sentence, but I will get a 10-year sentence.
- If neither of us confesses, then we will both get a 1-year sentence.
- If both of us confess, then we will both get an 8-year sentence.

If you and I could communicate, then the best arrangement would be for both of us to not confess, since then we'd each get only a 1-year sentence. Since we can't communicate, though, I can't trust that you'll keep your mouth shut. Even if you and I are friends, I need to calculate what the best deal is for me, regardless of how you respond to the district attorney's offer. So, in spite of what you decide to do, I'll clearly be better off by confessing, since it is better to serve 3 months or even 8 years than it is to serve 10 years.

The point of this illustration is that, although mutual cooperation is the best *mutual* deal, I will still be rationally motivated to pursue the best deal for me *individually*. That is, since I can't trust your decision, I have to look out for my own interests and do what's best for me. In Hobbes's terminology, since I can't trust you in the state of nature, then I'll have to look out for my own interests and attack you before you attack me. If I eliminate you first, then I serve my interests better than if I sat around passively. Ultimately, cooperation in the state of nature isn't reasonable for any of us individually, and we will always be poised for war.

The original prisoner's dilemma scenario rests on the assumption that I can't communicate with you about devising the best mutual strategy to shorten our stays in jail. The parallel in Hobbes's state of nature is the assumption that I can't trust you even if you say that you won't attack me. Is this distrust justified? My reasons for distrust in the state of nature rest on a variety of intricate questions about human nature—specifically, whether we can be naturally kind to strangers. Hobbes believed that we just aren't psychologically designed to be naturally kind to people whom we don't know. If we agree with Hobbes's pessimistic view about human kindness, then we are justified in distrusting all strangers in the state of nature in spite of the good intentions that they express. However, this pessimistic view is a matter of debate; in fact, this is among the more hotly debated issues in ethics. The best we can say is that, if the pessimists are correct, then—as the prisoner's dilemma suggests—the state of nature will be a perpetual state of conflict.

Rawls and Social Contract Theory   The most influential contemporary proponent of social contract theory is **John Rawls,** as he develops it in his book *A Theory of Justice* (1971). Paralleling Hobbes's state of nature, Rawls describes a hypothetical **original position.** In the original position, we are neither at war with one another nor trying to start a government. Instead, we are merely a group of rational, equal, and self-interested people who want to devise mutually beneficial moral guidelines for reforming our social system. To help us arrive at the most impartial moral guideline, we temporarily ignore our actual status in society, such as the size of our bank accounts and the amount of property that we own. Metaphorically, it is as though we voluntarily stand behind a **veil of ignorance.** This assures that I won't try to rig the system and create moral guidelines that benefit me the most—whether I am rich or poor.

According to Rawls, after some back-and-forth discussion, we will eventually arrive at two rules of justice. We will then use these two rules to generate a longer and more specific list of obligations. The two rules of justice are these:

- Each person is to have an equal right to the most extensive basic liberty compatible with a similar liberty for others.
- Social and economic inequalities are to be arranged so that they are both (1) reasonably expected to be to everyone's advantage and (2) attached to positions and offices open to all.

The first rule tells us that we should give one another as much freedom as we can. This includes moral liberties such as free speech and free movement. It also includes economic liberties, such as acquiring property and making money. Finally, it includes political liberties, such as voting and holding public office.

So far, none of this is controversial from the standpoint of American society, which was founded on broad notions of liberty. However, we sometimes need to place limits on the wealth and power that we individually accumulate from our various liberties. Economic liberty is nice, but when we look at the vast fortunes accumulated by entrepeneurs like Bill Gates, we might feel that enough is enough.

The second rule is a guideline for regulating the accumulation of wealth and power. According to this rule, Bill Gates can have an unequal amount of money only if such a capitalist economic system is *to everyone's advantage*—including poor people. This aspect of Rawls's theory is controversial. The default economic arrangement is that Bill Gates should get only an *equal* share of wealth. The burden of proof, then, is on the capitalist businessperson to show that even poor people benefit when an entrepreneur can pursue his economic dreams unimpeded. This, though, is a tough case to support, which makes socialism the default economic policy. Rawls clearly thinks that this socialistic orientation is the most impartial way to distribute wealth. However, Bill Gates and other capitalist businesspeople would simply reject Rawls's second rule of justice as too biased toward socialism.

The Value of Social Contract Theory

Since the seventeenth century, social contract theory has been a useful tool for justifying political revolutions when governments fail to do their jobs. In the years ahead, political revolutionaries will likely continue to draw on social contract theory to justify overthrowing incompetent governments. Social contract theory also helps us understand why we allow our governments to have so much control over our lives. Take, for example, the power that we give our local police officers. We permit them to walk around with guns and even shoot us if necessary. We give them the authority to kick down our doors, storm through our homes, haul us to jail, and interrogate us for hours. Why would we want to give someone this kind of power over us? Social contract theory offers the best, and perhaps only reasonable, answer: We give the police this power in exchange for protection. In spite of social contract theory's strong points, there are two distinct limitations to the social contract tradition.

Social Contract versus Social Reciprocation

Social Contract versus Social Reciprocation   The first limitation of social contract theory is that it is naive to take the notion of a contract literally. We noted in our discussion of Hume's criticism that a literal social contract requires consciously willful consent, and in point of fact, no one really gives this kind of consent to social contracts. Even Rawls's theory suffers from this problem. When people negotiate the rules of justice, they willfully consent to step behind the veil of ignorance. In reality, though, neither we nor our legislators do this. We may not even be psychologically *capable* of doing this.

Although we may not be able to fully rescue social contract theory from this problem, we might recast the theory in a more modest form as a theory of social reciprocation. That is, instead of seeing our situation as involving a formal contract that we consciously consent to, it is more plausible to see it simply as a kind of social reciprocation that we are content with. We pay our taxes, follow the laws, and acknowledge the authority of our government; what do we get in return? We receive governmental protection and some governmental benefits, such as free education and the use of public highways. Most of us are content with this give-and-take relationship, and we may not really care about who established the relationship to begin with. We're happy to leave that issue to the historians. From our individual perspectives, we don't object to keeping the social relationship going, and many of us are even grateful for this relationship when we consider the horrible alternatives that we find in war-torn countries around the world. For example, without strong governmental protection, members of ethnic or religious factions might rise up and slaughter each other. To the extent that we are content with this reciprocal relationship, we will routinely follow the moral and legal rules of the relationship to keep the social machine working.

The key difference between a social contract and social reciprocation is that a contract involves a distinct mental act of consent that occurs at a distinct time. Philosophers today refer to this kind of psychological act as an *occurrent* mental state, which means that it principally occurs during a short and fixed period of time. By contrast, a merely reciprocal relationship requires only a long-term mental viewpoint of contentment. We might compare this mental viewpoint to the outlook of someone who is persistently happy. Suppose, for example, that you are a persistently happy person, and I ask you when you first became happy. You answer, "As far as I know I've *always* been happy, and I don't remember any distinct point in time when I wasn't." Philosophers today refer to this as a *dispositional* mental state insofar as it is long-term and persistent within a person's mind. Such is the case concerning our mental contentment with the give-and-take relationship between ourselves and society. Insofar as we've been consistently content with this reciprocal relationship, then we will follow the required rules.

Traditional social contract theorists might object that mere contentment isn't strong enough to assure that we consistently abide by society's rules. Even if I am content today, I may become discontent a week from now and then stop following the rules. Granted, the words "contract" and "consent" are much stronger than the words "reciprocation" and "contentment." However, peppering our moral vocabulary with these stronger words won't necessarily make us take our moral obligations more seriously. The Oklahoma City bombing is a good illustration of this. A traditional social contract theorist would say that earlier in their lives Timothy McVeigh and Terry Nichols tacitly consented to the terms of the contract, but later in life they both violated those terms. In spite of the weighty implications of the word "contract," McVeigh and Nichols nevertheless didn't take their moral obligation seriously. A less cumbersome explanation would be that, early in life, McVeigh and Nichols were dispositionally content with the give-and-take relationship between themselves and society. Later, though, they became dispositionally discontent and no longer felt compelled to continue the relationship or to abide by the rules.

Mixing Moral Theory and Political Theory A second limitation of social contract theory is that it does not adequately account for moral obligations that go beyond our political obligations. Social contract theories commonly weave together issues of political authority and moral obligation. Hobbes, for example, believed that we have no moral obligations outside of the social contract, and morality emerges as a tool for preserving a peaceful society under the absolute authority of a ruler. From one perspective, this is an advantage of social contract theory since it reduces the conceptual clutter of two separate theories explaining our distinct moral and political obligations. Moral theories and political theories both talk about the behavioral obligations that we have to our fellow humans, and it makes sense to connect these obligations. From another perspective, though, the close relationship between political theory and moral theory is a liability of social contract theory, particularly Hobbes's version. Issues of political authority and political obligation are important in all of our lives, and if we ignore these issues, then we create legal problems for ourselves. However, political issues are not the only important issues in our lives, and for many of us, they are not even among our most important issues. Moral issues permeate our lives, and every encounter we have with other people involves a proper and an improper way of behaving. Although some of these obligations have direct ties to political issues, many have only a very remote connection.

Suppose, for example, that you cheat on your spouse and continually lie to your family and friends concerning your secret life. Suppose also that you wipe out your family bank account on personal pleasures and that, when you're home, you are drunk most of the time. Although all of these actions are immoral, they don't violate any laws, and they pose no threat to political authorities and the continuation of a peaceful political society. So, issues of political obligation only go so far in defining the scope of our moral obligations. The Oklahoma City bombing illustrates this point, too. Most of us feel that McVeigh and Nichols were grossly misdirected in their belief that the U.S. government unjustly overstepped its authority. For the sake of argument, though, let's concede their bizarre political point and grant that the U.S. government forfeited its status as a legitimate authority. Does this make the bombing any less of an immoral deed? Certainly not. Completely apart from the political issue, there remains the moral issue concerning the value of the 168 victims' lives, which McVeigh and Nichols callously ignored.

Summary

Thomas Hobbes presented the first systematic account of social contract theory. According to Hobbes, our human nature prevents us from naturally living at peace with one another. Hobbes depicts this by describing a prepolitical state of nature in which people constantly war. To move beyond this state of nature, we recognize the need to seek peace, the need to give up our hostile rights, and the need to keep our agreements. Accordingly, we enter into a social contract with one another and establish a government with absolute authority over us to assure that we abide by our agreements. Morality, for Hobbes, involves acquiring virtues that habitually incline us to do what the terms of the social contract require of us. Edward Hyde criticized Hobbes for denying the immutable and eternal status of morality. But contemporary moral philosophers have abandoned the specific concepts of immutability and eternality because of the metaphysical difficulties that they create. Samuel Clarke criticized Hobbes for thinking that fear of punishment would sufficiently motivate people to follow the rules of the social contract. If we plan a perfect crime and face no risk of getting caught, then fear of punishment alone will fail as a motivation. As creatures of habit, we are inclined to repeat crimes, and this continually increases our chances of getting caught and punished. To eliminate all risk, we should develop virtues that habitually incline us to follow the rules in all situations.

Hume criticized social contract theory on the grounds that people don't willfully consent to the terms of the contract; and, without willful consent, there is no contract. Social contract theorists can't rescue themselves by claiming that the contract is only hypothetical. Many recent discussions of social contract theory draw on the scenario of the prisoner's dilemma, which helps explain why people are so uncooperative in the state of nature. But the prisoner's dilemma works as an explanation only if we grant that people are not naturally kind to strangers. Rawls offers a contemporary version of social contract theory, which involves a group of rational people devising rules of justice in an original position. Rawls's theory is controversial since it leans towards socialism.

There are two limitations of social contract theory. First, we must abandon the idea of a contract involving an occurrent mental state of willful consent. Instead, we should see the relationship as involving a dispositional mental state of contentment. More precisely, we are simply content to have a reciprocal relationship with governing bodies whereby we follow rules in exchange for protection and benefits. Second, we should recognize that social contract theory does not adequately account for moral obligations that rise above our politically-based obligations.

Study Questions

Introduction

1. According to some antigovernment groups, what is the principle reason that we establish governments?
2. What is the "disease" and what is the "cure" as described by social contract theory?
3. According to Glaucon in Plato's dialog, under what conditions do I agree not to exploit you?

Hobbes's Theory

4. Why does Hobbes refer to the government as a "leviathan"?

The State of Nature

5. Why does Hobbes think that we are equal both physically and intellectually in the state of nature?
6. What are the three causes of quarrel in the state of nature?
7. What examples does Hobbes give to prove his gloomy description of human nature?

The Laws of Nature

8. What are the first three laws of nature?

Political Theory and Moral Theory

9. According to Hobbes, why can't we overthrow governments?
10. What are the two features of Hobbes's account of morality?

Social Contract Theory in the Seventeenth and Eighteenth Centuries

11. What is the state of nature like according to Pufendorf, Locke, and Rousseau, respectively?

Criticisms of Hobbes

Hyde's Criticism: Hobbes Denies That Morality Is Immutable and Eternal

12. What are Hyde's two main complaints about Hobbes?
13. In Hobbes's attempt to scientifically redefine traditional moral vocabulary, what does he mean when he says that the laws of nature are "immutable and eternal"?

Clarke's Criticism: Punishment Alone Won't Motivate Us to Always Keep Contracts

14. According to Fieser, what is the virtue theory solution to the problem that Clarke points out?

Hume's Criticism: We Don't Even Tacitly Agree to a Social Contract

15. According to Locke, when do we tacitly agree to a social contract?
16. According to Hume, how do governments trick us into accepting authority?

Recent Social Contract Theory

The Prisoner's Dilemma

17. What is the point of the prisoner's dilemma?

Rawls and Social Contract Theory

18. What is the "original position" for Rawls?
19. What does Rawls's first rule of justice tell us?
20. According to Rawls's second rule of justice, what is the main rule by which we regulate the unequal accumulation of wealth and power?

The Value of Social Contract Theory

Social Contract versus Social Reciprocation

21. Explain the difference between occurrent and dispositional mental states.
22. What is the difference between consenting to a social contract and being content with social reciprocity?

Mixing Moral Theory and Political Theory

23. Give an example of a moral obligation that is not typically linked with a political obligation.

References

Plato hints at social contract theory in both the *Republic,* Book 2, and in *Crito.* Both dialogs are available in several modern editions.

The quotation by Hobbes is from *Leviathan* (1651), 1.14, which is available in several modern editions, the best of which is edited by Edwin Curley (Indianapolis: Hackett, 1994). Hobbes also wrote a trilogy of works covering similar issues: *On the Citizen* (1642), *On the Body* (1655), and *On Man* (1658). Early drafts of Hobbes's thoughts were published without his permission in *On Human Nature* and *On the Political Body* (1650). Spelling and punctuation in the quotations have been modernized for clarity.

The quotations by Edward Hyde's criticism of Hobbes is in *A Survey of Mr. Hobbes* (1676), in *Leviathan: Contemporary Responses,* edited by G. A. J. Rogers (Bristol, England: Thoemmes Press, 1994), pp. 201–202. Spelling and punctuation in the quotations have been modernized for clarity.

The quotations by Samuel Clarke are from *A Discourse Concerning the Unchangeable Obligations of Natural Religion* (1706). This text is available in reprints of Clarke's collected *Works* (1738) and in *British Moralists,* edited by D. D. Raphael (Indianapolis: Hackett, 1991).

The quotation by Locke is from *Two Treatises of Government* (1690), 2.119, which is available in several modern editions. The best current edition is the critical edition by Peter Laslett (Cambridge: Cambridge University Press, 1963).

The quotation by Hume is from *Treatise of Human Nature* (1739–40), 3.2.8, which is available in several modern editions.

The quotation from William Godwin is from *An Enquiry Concerning Political Justice* (1793), 3.2, the most recent edition of which is edited by Mark Philip (London: William Pickering, 1993).

Suggestions for Further Reading

For discussions of Hobbes's moral theory, see David Boonin-Vail, *Thomas Hobbes and the Science of Moral Virtue* (Cambridge: Cambridge University Press, 1994); Arnold W. Green, *Hobbes and Human Nature* (New Brunswick, NJ: Transaction, 1993); Samuel I. Mintz, *The Hunting of Leviathan* (Bristol, England: Thoemmes Press, 1996); George Shelton, *Morality and Sovereignty in the Philosophy of Hobbes* (New York: St. Martin's Press, 1992).

For social contract theories after Hobbes, see Samuel von Pufendorf, *Of the Law of Nature and Nations* (*De Jure Naturae et Gentium*, 1762), and *The Duty of Man and Citizen according to Natural Law* (*De officio hominis et civis juxta legem naturalem*, 1673); John Locke, *Second Treatise of Government* (1690), ed. Peter Laslett (Cambridge: Cambridge University Press, 1960); Jean-Jacques Rousseau, *The Social Contract* (1762), trans. Maurice Cranston (Harmondworth, England: Penguin Books, 1968).

For a discussion of the prisoner's dilemma and other contemporary contractarian issues, see Jody S. Kraus, *The Limits of Hobbesian Contractarianism* (Cambridge: Cambridge University Press, 1993).

For discussions of Rawls, see Chandran Kukathas, *Rawls: A Theory of Justice and Its Critics* (Stanford, CA: Stanford University Press, 1990); Thomas W. Pogge, *Realizing Rawls* (Ithaca, NY: Cornell University Press, 1989).

7

Duty Theory

Introduction

Some years ago, a popular philosophy professor at Florida State University named Michael Bayles killed himself. Having put the final touches on a book manuscript a few days before, Bayles went to a nearby national forest and shot himself with a handgun. The area was one where he and his wife had gone walking in the past. The event was a great shock to his family, friends, colleagues, and students. Bayles was having some personal problems, but he refused therapy since he feared that it would undermine his freedom. In a letter to a philosophy publication, a former student of Bayles's commented on the suicide. According to the former student, preserving one's freedom—even in the face of suicide—shows an integrity of choice:

> I believe that for oneself it's better to be—whatever, than to survive as a treated half-person. Once therapeutized, the self of moral action is lost. The life that asserts the meaningfulness of moral reflection, the life that animates moral choice, is itself no longer there by reason of choice. In the worst case one is maintained as the effect of a drug—and then what can anything one does mean?

In this view, it is better to be internally tormented and retain one's ability for moral choice than it is to therapeutically relieve this torment—presumably through antidepressant or antipsychotic drugs—yet live like a zombie with lost freedom.

In response to the former student's depiction, a jointly written letter appeared in the same publication, which harshly criticized the former student for portraying Bayles's suicide as an act of moral heroism. The authors argued that suicide "is typically an act that is the product of mental illness and which usually originates from a chemical imbalance." The patient is not reduced to a "half-person" by treating chemical imbalances with drug therapy; instead, the patient has his or her autonomy and moral agency restored. The former student's view of mental illness and psychiatry, they conclude, is tragic since it might prompt some to heroically embrace suicide rather than seek treatment.

The position on drug therapy taken by the authors of this joint letter is more responsible than the view advocated by the former student. The number of suicides that occur each year is staggering. A recent study by the Centers for Disease Control reports that, in one recent year, 31,284 Americans died of suicide, which surpasses the 22,552 homicides for that same year. This makes suicide the ninth-leading cause of death in the United States. Even if we could find a few examples of a genuinely heroic suicide, the vast numbers are nothing but tragic.

Although we might reject the view that suicide is an act of moral heroism, we can still ask whether it is *morally permissible* to kill oneself, or whether acts of suicide are essentially wrong. Philosophers from the earliest days have taken different stands on this issue. Plato, for example, believed that suicide is wrong since it "frustrates the decree of destiny." By contrast, Roman philosopher Seneca argued that suicide is permissible when age destroys our faculties one by one. During the seventeenth and eighteenth centuries, a common argument against suicide was that it violates a duty we have to ourselves—specifically, a duty to survive. Proponents of this view believed that all of our moral obligations fall into one of three groups: duties to God, duties to oneself, and duties to others. Although suicide might violate some duties to God and others, duty theorists argued that it is wrong principally because it violates a duty to oneself. According to **duty theory,** we all know that we have this duty, and we know this *intuitively,* without deriving it from any more basic moral principles. Duty theorists listed as many as 100 moral duties that we have to God, oneself, and others. For these philosophers, to be moral *means* to understand and act according to our long list of duties. We will look at the key elements of traditional duty theory and consider problems that it encountered.

The Development and Popularity of Traditional Duty Theory   Moral philosophers from ancient Greek and Roman times offered lengthy lists of moral duties. The best surviving example of this is a work entitled *The Offices* by Roman philosopher **Cicero** (106–43 BCE), in which he discusses hundreds of duties in every capacity of our private and social lives. Medieval philosophers continued this tradition and sometimes emphasized distinct duties to God, self, and neighbors. However, an explicit three-part list of duties to God, oneself, and others emerged in the seventeenth century. By the mid-eighteenth century, this approach had become so popular that it would have been difficult to pick up an ethics book that didn't discuss that three-part scheme. In fact, many ethics texts were structured *entirely* according to that scheme. We also find this scheme in reference works of the time, such as the 1773 *Encyclopedia Britannica* article on "Moral Philosophy." One reason for the popularity of this approach is that it provides a convenient way of classifying an otherwise cumbersome list of moral obligations. Another reason, though, is that duty theorists believed that the three-part list of duties serves as a checklist by which a person could determine whether a given action is right or wrong. In that way, the list of duties to God, oneself, and others perform much the same function as the Ten Commandments or the Golden Rule.

An example may help illustrate the popularity and function of the three-part division of duties. Scottish philosopher **David Hume** (1711–1776) wrote a short defense of suicide that rests squarely on this concept of duties. Hume opens his defense by stating that "if Suicide be criminal, it must be a transgression of our duty either to God, our neighbour, or ourselves." Going against the trend of his time, Hume continues by arguing that suicide does *not* violate duties in any of these three groups. What is most interesting about Hume's discussion is that, in another book, he formulates an entirely different checklist of moral conduct that doesn't rest on the traditional division of duties. However, rather than using his newly devised litmus test, Hume felt that, if he wanted to make his case in defense of suicide, he had to proceed from what at the time was the accepted criterion of moral permissibility—namely, duties to God, oneself, and others.

Pufendorf's Theory of Duties

The first fully developed account of traditional duty theory was given by German philosopher **Samuel von Pufendorf** (1632–1694). Pufendorf was directly influenced by two great moral philosophers of his time. From Thomas Hobbes (1588–1679), Pufendorf adopted the notion of an original condition of humans and the need for us to bond together through contracts. From Dutch philosopher Hugo Grotius (1585–1645), Pufendorf adopted the notion of laws of nature from which we derive our moral obligations.

Survival and Mutual Cooperation   In his book *The Duty of Man and Citizen according to the Law of Nature* (1673), Pufendorf argues that all of our moral duties spring from our instinctive drive for survival. Like other animals, we humans have a sense of our own existence and we value our individual selves more than anything else. We learn every manner of self-preservation that we can, and we will set aside all other human inclinations when our survival is at stake. When anyone makes an attempt on our lives, we develop a deep hatred toward them and seek revenge. Although survival is the first order of business for us, we must rely on the cooperation of other people to survive. Pufendorf paints a gloomy picture of the isolated man who tries to survive on his own:

> He has nothing left but herbs and roots to pluck and the wild fruits to gather; to quench his thirst at the next spring, river or ditch; to shelter himself from the injuries of weather by creeping into some cave or covering himself with any sort of moss or grass; to pass away his tedious life in idleness; to jump at every noise, and be afraid at the sight of any other animal. In a word, he will ultimately perish either by hunger or cold or some wild beast. (*The Duty of Man and Citizen,* 1.3)

To keep from starving to death or being eaten by wild animals, we must band together with other people, spend years of our lives learning time-honored survival skills, and rely on others for protection from dangers that even the best of us can't handle alone.

In spite of this obvious need to cooperate with others, we have other natural instincts that block the path to mutual cooperation. We are very cruel, and we exhibit a stronger tendency to harm each other than does any "wild" animal. We are also very picky. When satisfying our need for food, it isn't enough to simply eat—we must *enjoy* what we eat. When obtaining clothing for protection, our sense of vanity inclines us to acquire ornamental or stylish clothes. We are driven to possess much more than we ever need, as we see from the history of invasions and wars that have plagued human society. We are predisposed to insult other people, which only antagonizes them. Because of our higher intelligence, we are also capable of doing more harm than other animals. Each human is also motivated by a different set of desires: "There are as many minds as there are heads, and everyone has his unique opinion." This makes us unpredictable.

These unsociable inclinations make it all the more important for us to cooperate with others. In view of the importance of mutual cooperation, Pufendorf proposes this as the fundamental law of nature: "To the extent that we can, every person ought to preserve and promote society, that is, the welfare of mankind." For Pufendorf, it is one thing simply to recommend mutual cooperation, and quite another to command mutual cooperation as a law. A mere recommendation won't do the trick since we could adopt or abandon the recommendation as it suits our needs. To attain the status of law, according to Pufendorf, this law must be authored and commanded by God. God also instills in us a natural knowledge of this law, which we progressively acquire in the same manner that we progressively acquire language.

Duties to God, Oneself, and Others   Pufendorf argues that our knowledge of the law of mutual cooperation involves duties to God, oneself, and others. We don't have a master list of all of these duties stamped into our minds, but we deduce them through a natural reasoning process.

Duties to God, for Pufendorf, are of two basic kinds: (1) the duty to know God and (2) the duty to obey God. Our duty to know God first means that we should know that he exists. During the Middle Ages, theologians offered a variety of proofs for God's existence, some based on the idea that God is the first cause of everything and others on the idea that God is the master designer of all the order that we see in the universe. Philosophers and theologians in Pufendorf's day refined these arguments, and Pufendorf himself offers five distinct proofs for God's existence. As for our duty to obey God, Pufendorf argues that this involves first honoring God with our internal thoughts and then expressing God's will in our external actions.

Pufendorf, like most traditional philosophers, holds that we have both a soul and a body; so, duties to oneself are directed at one or the other of these. As far as our souls are concerned, we have a duty to develop our talents and learn a trade that will make us useful to human society. If we don't, then "we will become a useless burden to the earth, cumbersome to ourselves, and troublesome to others." As far as our bodies are concerned, we should first keep ourselves healthy through proper nourishment and exercise, and avoid "gluttony, drunkenness, [and] the immoderate use of women." Not only do these excesses harm ourselves, but they frequently disturb society as well. More important than staying *healthy*, though, is staying *alive*; that is, we should not kill ourselves. In some special situations—if it benefits society—we may engage in a demanding occupation that potentially will shorten our lives, such as hard labor or military service. However, as a rule, suicide is not permissible for reasons of infirmity, indignity, fear of pain, or bravery:

> Some voluntarily put an end to their own lives, either for being tired with the many troubles which usually accompany this mortal state; or from an abhorrence of indignities and evils which yet would not make them scandalous to human society; or through fear of pains or torments (although by enduring them with fortitude they might become useful examples to others); or out of a vain ostentation of their fidelity and bravery. All these are to be certainly reputed as sinners against the law of nature.... (*The Duty of Man and Citizen*, 1.4)

The final category of obligations is that of duties to others, and Pufendorf's discussion of these is longer and more detailed than the previous two categories. Pufendorf first distinguishes between *absolute* and *conditional* duties to others. The absolute duties are common obligations that every person has, regardless of his or her situation. Our first absolute duty is that "one do no wrong to another" through physical harm or the destruction of another's property. Our second absolute duty is that "every man respect and treat another as naturally equal to himself." In practical terms, this means that we treat people justly, such as fairly compensating those we hire for their labor, and that we treat people equally when distributing wealth. The third and final absolute duty is that "every man ought to promote the good of another as far as conveniently he may." That is, we should actively try to benefit others, such as through acts of charity.

Our conditional duties to others arise from contracts that we make with others. Some of us are not inclined to perform good deeds simply from the goodness of our hearts. Instead, we will do good deeds only if we know exactly what we will receive in return. For this reason, we devise contracts with other people. The principle duty surrounding contracts is that "every man keep his word, or fulfill his promises and make good his contracts." If we don't, then contracts are useless, and we lose out on the social benefits that we might otherwise obtain.

To summarize, these are the main points of Pufendorf's theory:

- The principal law of nature mandates that we should be sociable in order to survive, which we fulfill through duties to God, self, and others.
- Duties to God include the duty to know that God exists and the duty to conform our actions to his will.
- Duties to oneself include duties of the soul (develop one's talents) and duties of the body (stay healthy, don't kill oneself).
- Duties to others include absolute duties (don't harm, acknowledge equality, promote the good of others) and conditional duties (keep one's contracts).

Intuitionism and Other Features of Duty Theory Pufendorf discusses additional issues about duties, which were adopted and refined by moral philosophers after him. One issue is the *intuitive* nature of duties. If I asked you, "Why should we be kind to other people?" you might answer, "We simply *should* be kind to others, and there is no 'why' about it." Duty theorists give the same answer, and this has become the most distinctive feature of duty theory. According to duty theorists, our core notions of duty are *foundational* in the sense that they are not derived from any more basic notions. It is much the way that we instinctively recognize the color blue, and it makes no sense for us to trace our notion of "blue" back to any more basic concept. Pufendorf, for example, believed that knowledge of all of our duties originates from an instinctive mandate to be sociable, which God implants in us all.

Duty theorists after Pufendorf were even more explicit about the intuitive nature of duties, and they often described these as *commonsense intuitions.* Scottish philosopher James Beattie (1735–1803) defines this notion of common sense here:

> The term *Common Sense* . . . [is a] power of the mind which perceives truth, or commands belief, not by progressive argumentation, but by an instantaneous, instinctive, and irresistible impulse; derived neither from education nor from habit, but from nature; acting independently on our will . . . (*An Essay on the Nature and Immutability of Truth,* 1.1)

According to Beattie and many other duty theorists, God implants commonsense moral instincts in us, and we cannot search for a justification of morality beyond these instincts. We don't logically deduce moral duties from rational principles or infer them from any human experience. We simply *know* them as they are, with absolute certainty, and we can trust that they are true since we have complete confidence in God, who implanted these intuitions in us. The intuitive component of duty theory became so prominent that during the 19th century duty theory was often simply called **intuitionism.**

A second issue in duty theory concerns its connection with other traditional notions of morality—specifically, moral virtues and moral rights. Virtues are good habits that we develop, that incline us toward the morally right thing. Philosophers beginning with Plato and Aristotle placed the notion of virtue at the center of their moral theories. Pufendorf and other duty theorists also emphasized the importance of virtues and argued that for each duty there is a corresponding virtue. In this view, virtues are simply the good habits that we develop to assure that we comply with our various duties. For example, if we have a duty to worship God, then we should develop the virtue of piety. If we have a duty to keep our promises, then we should develop the virtue of fidelity. This connection between duty and virtue was so fixed that many duty theorists used the terms "duty" and "virtue" interchangeably.

Duty theorists also held that there is an intimate relationship between moral duties and **moral rights.** The basic notion of a right is that it is a justified constraint that we have on another person's actions. For example, if I have a right to life, then other people are morally constrained from killing me. Pufendorf and other duty theorists held that, for every right I have, someone else has a corresponding duty. My right to life implies that others have a duty not to kill me. My property right to my car implies that others have a duty not to steal my car. The distinction between rights and duties is largely one of perspective. When I talk about my rights, I refer to what other people owe me; when I talk about my duties, I refer to what I owe other people. By linking moral duties with both virtues and rights, traditional duty theory became especially versatile, which contributed to its popularity.

A third issue of duty theory involves some technical distinctions between various duties—specifically, distinctions between perfect and imperfect duties and between direct and indirect duties. The distinction between perfect and imperfect duties traces back to ancient Greek and Roman philosophy. Cicero describes perfect duties as obligations that are complete and beyond dispute, whereas imperfect duties are those that require special justification or argument. Cicero's distinction is a little obscure, and he doesn't give examples, but Pufendorf gives us a much clearer account. **Perfect duties** for Pufendorf are those requiring or prohibiting precise behavior, such as our duty not to kill others and to keep our contracts. If we violate these duties, we may be punished. **Imperfect duties,** by contrast, involve less precisely defined behavior, such as helping others through good advice or generosity. Even if we violate these, we would not ordinarily be punished.

Concerning the distinction between direct and indirect duties, we may illustrate this by considering the care that we take in laying to rest the bodies of our dead relatives. In theory, if your uncle died, you could throw his body out with the trash. You wouldn't do that, though, because you have a clear duty to treat his body respectfully. But this duty isn't directly owed to your uncle, since your uncle no longer exists, and nonexisting things can't make moral demands on us. Instead, your direct duty in this case is to avoid insulting your uncle's living relatives; your duty to properly bury your uncle, then, is indirect. So, a **direct duty** is a moral obligation toward someone who has his or her own claim against us, and an **indirect duty** is a moral obligation toward someone because of a claim that a third person has against us.

Revisions and Criticisms of Duty Theory

For over 100 years, Pufendorf's basic arrangement of intuitive moral duties was the accepted view of the subject. No one offered a serious objection to the scheme, and even the most original moral philosophers of the time incorporated that division into their systems. Eventually, though, critics—both within and outside of the duty theory tradition—chiseled away at its central components.

Kant's Revision: We Have No Duties to God Because We Cannot Know God   Pufendorf clumps duties to God together with the moral duties that we have to humans. But this seems strange since—assuming that God exists—God is an entirely different kind of being from you and me. German philosopher

Immanuel Kant (1724–1804) drew attention to this problem. Kant himself falls squarely within the intuitionist tradition of duty theory. From his earliest to his most mature writings on ethics, Kant argued that moral duties are divided between those to oneself and those to others. However, Kant was more suspicious about whether we have moral duties to God. He believed that we have any number of *religious* duties to God, but none that are genuinely *moral.*

Kant's specific views on the subject evolved over the years. In an early set of lectures on ethics, he attacks the view that we have duties to higher spiritual beings—such as angels or demons—on the grounds that we have no real knowledge of them:

> Spirits may exist or they may not; all that is said of them may be true; but we know them not and can have no intercourse with them. This applies to good and to evil spirits alike. (*Lectures on Ethics*)

In these early lectures, Kant does not use this reasoning to argue directly against our having any duties to God. However, in a later work he does:

> As far as reason alone can judge, a human being has duties only to human beings (himself and others), since his duty to any subject is moral constraint by that subject's will. Hence the constraining (binding) subject must, *first,* be a person; and this person must, *secondly,* be given as an object of experience, since the human being is to strive for the end of this person's will and this can happen only in a relation to each other of two beings that exist (for a mere thought-entity [i.e., God] cannot be the cause of any result in terms of ends). (*The Metaphysics of Morals,* 442)

Kant himself believed in God, and he argues that we need to act as though there is a God. His point here, though, is that God exists in a world that transcends the world of experience around us, and we can't acquire knowledge of God in that transcendent realm. In fact, Kant says, it is nonsensical to even talk about knowledge of God. Since we have no experiential knowledge of God, we don't know if we have duties to him, let alone what they might be.

A century before Kant, **Thomas Hobbes** (1588–1679) made a similar point about God's inaccessibility, and by looking at Hobbes's statement, we may better understand Kant's criticism. Hobbes considers the kinds of beings with which humans can make agreements or contracts. He writes that we can't make agreements with God because we don't know whether God accepts the agreements that we devise:

> To make covenant with God is impossible, but by mediation of such as God speaketh to (either by revelation supernatural or by his lieutenants that govern under him and in his name); for otherwise we know not whether our covenants be accepted or not. (*Leviathan,* 14.23)

According to Hobbes, communication with humans is two-way: I can speak directly to you, and you can speak directly back to me. However, except in rare cases when God communicates through revelation, communication with God is one-way: I can speak to God, but God doesn't directly speak back to me. Agreements require two-way communication, such as when I offer to sell you my car and you agree to purchase it. I may try to make an agreement with God, such as "If God cures my cancer, then I promise to be a better person." But if I don't know whether God accepts my proposal, then no genuine agreement has been reached. Kant similarly feels that we must have some access to God in order to determine whether we have duties toward him. For Kant, philosophy can't give us such knowledge of God.

Religious mystics disagree with Kant and Hobbes about our ability to directly access God. For mystics, our life's goal should be to encounter God, realize our inherent connection with God, and thereby acquire immediate knowledge of God's nature. Similarly, rationalist theologians believe that we can rationally deduce knowledge of God's nature and thereby gain access to God. Hobbes holds open the possibility of accessing God through supernatural revelation, but this concession isn't a real option for either Hobbes or Kant. So, whose intuition should we follow on this issue: Kant's or the religious mystic's?

The heart of the issue concerns the extent to which we may dispute the existence and nature of the person to whom we might owe a moral duty. We can't dispute the existence of other humans and the moral demands they place on us. Clearly, then, we all have duties toward other humans. However, many people do dispute God's existence and nature. It is not clear, then, that we have duties to God. To resolve the issue of duties to God, we need to strike a compromise. People who doubt knowledge of God should follow Kant, and people who assert knowledge of God should follow the mystic and allow for duties to God to the degree that their knowledge of God requires. In formulating this compromise, we are not so much granting permission to the religious believer as simply acknowledging what many believers are already doing. That is, many believers feel duty-bound to God's expectations and will follow those moral duties, regardless of Kant's objection. Unless we are prepared to challenge the believer's claim to know God, we must recognize that the believer may accept special moral duties that stem from this knowledge.

Mill's Criticism: Duties to Oneself Reduce to Only Self-Respect and Self-Development

A 21-year-old man recently died in a dirt bike accident. Riding in a wooded area, he launched his bike off an embankment and collided in midair with another biker. A friend of the deceased biker commented that "he died exactly the way he wanted, doing what he loved." The friend's statement reflects a common attitude that society shouldn't interfere in our private leisure activities, even if they put our lives at risk. Nineteenth-century British philosopher John Stuart Mill (1806–1873) defended this view of personal freedom in his book *On Liberty* (1859). In a famous passage, Mill argues that society may rightfully constrain us only when our actions harm others, but not when they only harm ourselves:

> That the only purpose for which power can be rightfully exercised over any member of a civilized community, against his will, is to prevent harm to others. His own good, either physical or moral, is not a sufficient warrant. . . .
> The only part of the conduct of any one, for which he is amenable to society, is that which merely concerns others. In the part which merely concerns himself, his

independence is, of right, absolute. Over himself, over his own body and mind, the individual is sovereign. (*On Liberty,* 1)

According to Mill, when our actions don't affect others, we have absolute independence over what we do to both our bodies and minds.

Mill's principle of liberty—as we now call it—has implications for the traditional view of duties to oneself—namely, that duties to oneself are not socially obligatory:

> What are called duties to ourselves are not socially obligatory, unless circumstances render them at the same time duties to others. The term duty to oneself, when it means anything more than prudence, means self-respect or self-development; and for none of these is any one accountable to his fellow-creatures, because for none of them is it for the good of mankind that he be held accountable to them. (*On Liberty,* 4)

Mill argues here that duties to ourselves are not socially binding on us unless they spill over into the arena of duties to others. Technically, Mill doesn't deny that we have duties purely to ourselves; he only argues that society can't force us to abide by these duties. For example, Mill would have argued that the dirt biker did nothing socially wrong by harming himself, although he did do something socially wrong to the degree that he harmed the other biker in the collision. The person who disregards duties to him- or herself may displease or disgust us, and even cause us to pity him or her. Think of a town drunk who wallows in his own filth but is harmless to other people. In spite of our negative reaction to people like this, Mill believed that we would not be justified in punishing them.

For the sake of argument, let's grant Mill's political point that we don't want society to interfere in this arena of our personal lives and enforce duties to oneself. Lurking beneath the surface of Mill's political point, though, is an interesting ethical point—namely, that duties to oneself are relatively insignificant. Traditional duty theorists believed that duties to oneself were as urgent and inflexible as duties to others. Pufendorf, in particular, believed that duties to oneself rest on both religion and societal necessity and that we cannot willfully dispense with duties to ourselves:

> The duties a person owes to himself arise jointly from religion and from the necessity of society. Thus, no person is completely lord of himself, but, instead, there are many things relating to himself which are not to be disposed altogether according to his will. This is partly because of the obligation he lies under for being a religious worshiper of the Deity, and partly so that he may keep himself a useful and beneficial member of society. (*The Duty of Man and Citizen,* 1.3)

Mill agrees that duties to others are indeed significant and relatively inflexible, insofar as they are firmly grounded in the greater good of humankind. The case is different, though, with duties to oneself. Why, asks Mill, aren't duties to oneself socially obligatory? The answer he gives is that they are simply matters of "self-respect or self-development." And, for Mill, we define our personal notions of self-respect and self-development based on our *individual* conceptions of what is good—conceptions that are flexible. For example, the dirt biker may have been morally justified in his death-defying behavior if, based on his personal conception of goodness, he believed that his behavior was an expression of self-respect and self-development. Heroic suicides, such as we described early in the chapter, might also be morally permissible in view of that person's concept of self-respect. In short, insofar as duties to oneself hinge on self-respect, self-development, and individual good, they rest on matters of personal preference, and this is more flexible and less urgent than duties to others.

In his other writings, Mill may not have consistently held to this reduced status of duties to oneself, but the implications in his discussion here are clear. Mill is probably right that moral duties to oneself have a less urgent and more flexible foundation than duties to others. However, we still might find a common theme that underlies our duties to ourselves and to others—and also any possible duties to God. Our duties to others are informed by our knowledge of what other people demand of us. Our duties to God—if there are any—are informed by the extent to which we know what God demands of us. Using parallel reasoning, our duties to ourselves should be informed by what demands we make on ourselves. Those who choose to make special demands on themselves, then, have special duties to themselves. Those who choose not to make demands don't have those duties. If the harmless town drunk claims that he has no duties to himself, then I must accept him at his word unless I am prepared to show that he in fact makes special demands on himself. However, this would be difficult for me to show since the information that I need exists mainly in the mind of the town drunk, which I don't have direct access to.

Sidgwick's Criticism: Commonsense Moral Intuitions Are Imprecise

We noted that perhaps the most distinctive feature of duty theory is its view that we have intuitive knowledge of our duties. In *Methods of Ethics* (1874), British philosopher **Henry Sidgwick** (1838–1900) criticizes this aspect of duty theory, contending that we cannot base our moral obligations on commonsense intuitions. Specifically, Sidgwick explains that there are two possible ways to discover our moral intuitions, and both of these have serious problems. According to the first way, simply survey the specific moral beliefs of ordinary people, which will supposedly reflect the underlying moral instincts within us. However, Sidgwick objects that the moral opinions of the ordinary person are "loose, shifting, and mutually contradictory." For example, the average person would think it wrong to take items from a grocery store without paying. But that same person might have no problem with taking home pencils that are the property of her employer or failing to report miscellaneous income on her income tax return. Sidgwick is probably right in his negative assessment about the ordinary person's moral views. However, no duty theorist would recommend that we discover our moral intuitions in such a crass manner. Rather than asking an average *real* person "How do you feel about stealing?" duty theorists suggest that we should instead consider how a hypothetical *reasonable* or *impartial* human would answer this question. This leads us to the second way of discovering our commonsense moral intuitions as noted by Sidgwick.

According to the second way, we should look beyond the specific attitudes of the ordinary person to find "clear and precise principles commanding universal acceptance." That is, we should search for universal moral principles that underlie common moral beliefs. But Sidgwick argues that, when we attempt to precisely define these principles, several problems emerge. Some principles that we arrive at may not be universally accepted. In other cases, "moral notions seem to resist all efforts to obtain from it a definite rule." In still other cases, the duty becomes so complicated that it is no longer self-evident. A rule against suicide would be a good example. Once we say that it is wrong to kill oneself, we then need to consider cases in which a person is dying of a painful disease, or creates a life-threatening situation through reckless behavior, or is about to be captured and tortured by an enemy, or goes on a suicide mission in military combat. The moral rules on suicide become so complex that they are no longer intuitively obvious. Sidgwick concludes with a fairly pessimistic statement of commonsense moral intuitions:

> In each case what at first seemed like an intuition turns out to be either the mere expression of a vague impulse, needing regulation and limitation which it cannot itself supply . . . or a current opinion, the reasonableness of which has still to be shown by a reference to some other principle. (*Methods of Ethics,* 3.11)

Most traditional duty theorists such as Pufendorf and Beattie believed that our moral intuitions are fixed and universal since God implants them in us that way. However, Sidgwick's judgment about the looseness and inconsistency of moral intuitions seems more realistic, and most moral philosophers today agree with Sidgwick's assessment. For the sake of argument, let's accept Sidgwick's dismal portrayal of moral intuitions, and let's assume further that we cannot systematically make them any more fixed and universal. As inconsistent as they may be, it may still be premature to reject outright our commonsense intuitions as a guide for moral conduct. Philosophers such as Sidgwick are convinced that true morality requires consistency and universality. In fact, the usual way of attacking any proposed moral theory is to expose inconsistencies or to show that the theory cannot be universally applied. Perhaps there is a moral theory out there that can live up to this standard. Or perhaps not. In either case, we can't put our actions on hold while we search for that perfect theory. In the meantime, we know for a fact that we have commonsense moral intuitions, despite their looseness and flexibility. It seems reasonable—and inevitable—to use these intuitions as the default guide for moral conduct until something better comes along. We might merely rely on commonsense intuitions as our guide but avoid generalizing our duties beyond our current circumstances.

Duty Theory Today

Since the late 19th century, few moral philosophers have defended lists of intuitive duties to God, oneself, and others. The criticisms by Kant, Mill, and Sidgwick are partly responsible for the decline in interest. Another reason is the advent of newer moral theories that encapsulate moral obligation in single principles rather than lists of duties.

Ross's Theory of Prima Facie Duties   Perhaps the last major proponent of traditional duty theory was British philosopher **W. D. Ross** (1877–1971) in his book *The Right and the Good* (1930). Dissatisfied with the newer moral theories of his time, Ross proposed a list of intuitive duties that form the basis of our moral judgments. There are two key features of Ross's theory, the first of which is the list of duties itself. Unlike traditional duty theorists who offer dozens of duties to God, oneself, and others, Ross pares the list down to seven types of duty:

- Duties of fidelity: Keep promises, tell the truth.
- Duties of reparation: Make good on previous harm done.
- Duties of gratitude: Show thanks for services done to us by others.
- Duties of justice: Distribute happiness in accord with a person's merit.
- Duties of beneficence: Help improve the lives of others.
- Duties of self-improvement: Develop virtue or intelligence.
- Duties of noninjury: Avoid actively harming others.

Ross's list of duties differs from earlier lists in several important respects. First, duties to God don't appear on the list; in fact, Ross does not discuss religious issues at all in his book. Second, although Ross includes a duty to oneself—self-improvement—he does not list the survival duty to not kill oneself. It seems, for Ross, that we can kill ourselves if we so choose, but if we don't kill ourselves, then we need to improve our lives. The remaining duties on Ross's list are standard duties similar to others that we find on earlier lists. Like earlier duty theorists, Ross, too, believes that these duties are self-evident intuitions, which we naturally develop as we mature. And, like his predecessors, Ross suggests that we discover these duties by looking at "the moral convictions of thoughtful and well-educated people," and not by surveying the attitudes of ordinary people.

The second key feature of Ross's theory is his distinction between one's *prima facie* duty and one's *actual* duty. This distinction arises from the occurrence of moral dilemmas—that is, situations in which, if we follow one moral duty, then we necessarily violate a different moral duty. Suppose, for example, that I borrow your gun and promise to return it when you ask for it. The next day you have a fight with your boss and ask me to return your gun. Should I give you back your gun? I am clearly torn between two duties: (1) the duty of fidelity, which requires me to keep my promise and return it to you, and (2) my duty of noninjury, which requires that I not participate in harming your boss. Cicero believed that conflicts such as this weaken both duties and make them less "perfect" than they would otherwise be. Ross, too, feels that all moral duties are somewhat diminished by possible conflicts with competing duties. For Ross, all duties are tentatively binding on us; that is, they are **prima facie duties**. The Latin term *prima facie* literally means "at first appearance" and implies that this is how something appears immediately. Even though these duties are immediately clear, they are still open for consideration in the face of moral dilemmas. If there is no moral dilemma, then the duty becomes my actual duty. However, if there is a moral dilemma, then only the stronger of the competing duties emerges as my actual duty.

According to Ross, there is no clear formula for determining which duty in a moral dilemma emerges as my actual duty. He suggests that we are guided once again by our intuitions. In the case of the borrowed gun, it seems intuitively obvious that my actual duty is to prevent injury to my neighbor's boss and my duty to keep promises essentially disappears. However, Ross argues that intuitions about our actual duties are not self-evident and are subject to error. For Ross, then, there are two distinct intuitive components to his theory: (1) a self-evident intuition that we tentatively have the seven prima facie duties listed above, and (2) an error-prone intuition about our actual duty in moral dilemmas.

The Value of Duty Theory   Since Ross, philosophical discussions of moral duties have been few and far between. Technically, contemporary moral philosophers haven't *rejected* the theory of moral duties. Given the intimate connection between moral duties and moral rights, as long as we believe in moral rights, then we implicitly hold to moral duties. However, discussions of duties have taken such a remote back seat to discussions of rights that they are almost invisible. The key difference between moral duties and moral rights is that duties involve what *I owe others* and rights involve what *others owe me*. Although it is risky to speculate about shifts in social trends, we appear to be more self-oriented today than in past centuries; to that extent, I may be more inclined to think about what others owe me than what I owe others. That is, asserting my moral rights will come easy to me, and I may not even think about the moral duties that I owe others.

Although the difference between moral rights and moral duties is only a matter of perspective, it is an important psychological difference, and the decreased emphasis on duties is a great loss. If I focus on my moral rights, then I will principally think about what other people owe me. But this won't necessarily make me a better person—even criminals assert their moral rights. By contrast, if I focus on my moral duties, then I will be forced to think about what I owe other people, and this will make me a better person. This is probably why Pufendorf and other early theorists emphasized the *duty* component of morality more than the *rights* component. By focusing on moral duties, we not only awaken within us a sense of what we owe others but also may awaken within us a sense of what we owe ourselves. With the issue of suicide, for example, rather than focusing on my moral right to die, I may instead think about my duty to live.

Duties and Suicide   We opened the chapter with the issue of suicide, and we may now close by considering whether suicide is wrong for violating any possible duty to God, oneself, or others. Two notions in our earlier discussion are central to answering this question. First, we noted that our duties arise in recognition of reasonable demands that someone places on us—demands by either God, ourselves, or others. To see if we have a duty to avoid ending our lives, then, we must see if there is a reasonable demand on us to stay alive. Second, following Ross, we should recognize that each of our duties is only tentative in view of competing duties that arise in moral dilemmas. So, even if we do have a duty to stay alive, this may be overridden by a competing duty.

Concerning duties to others, we recognize a variety of demands to stay alive, some of which are weak and others of which are strong. Insofar as suicide is illegal, the government demands that we stay alive. But given the impersonal and often artificial nature of governing bodies, this is among the weakest demands, and the corresponding moral duty may be negligible. We have a stronger demand to stay alive from our friends, but even this demand is limited. In crisis situations, friends often distance themselves from us, and when they are available, it is typically for only limited amounts of time. If my friend says, "You mustn't kill yourself," but then doesn't contact me for a few weeks, then the force of my friend's demand won't be very strong. Clearly, the strongest demand that we have to stay alive comes from our family, especially family members who depend on us emotionally or financially. In this case, the resulting duty to stay alive is so strong that it overrides most conceivable considerations to the contrary.

Concerning duties to God, these are restricted to people who claim to know some demand that God makes of them. Many believers look to organized religion as a way to discover God's demands. Since virtually all organized religions around the world condemn suicide, followers of these religions may claim to have a duty to God to stay alive. More mystically-inclined believers may claim to access God's demands more directly. In either case, the strength of one's religious belief will determine the comparative strength of a divinely-mandated duty to stay alive. For devout believers, this duty may be very strong.

Finally, concerning duties to oneself, these are restricted to people who make special demands on themselves to stay alive. Interestingly, this may be one of our stronger duties to not commit suicide. The strength of this duty rests in the fact that one's private demand to stay alive is by its very nature irrevocable. Suppose that when I was 20 years old I vowed to never commit suicide. Implicit in this vow is a demand on myself to never commit suicide *at any future stage* of my life, regardless of how I feel later on. Suppose that, at age 50, a series of misfortunes pushes me to consider suicide. If I did kill myself, I would be violating the duty that I placed on myself thirty years earlier. It is true that I may be an entirely different person at age 50, but that makes my earlier vow no less binding on me. In matters of morality, we assume a continuity of personal identity over a person's entire life. One example of this is long-term punishment of criminals. We are comfortable in handing out prison sentences that last a person's entire life, regardless of how many changes the prisoner goes through. Marriage is another example of a long-term duty that may continue throughout one's life. Although parole hearings and divorce courts allow us to undo the long-term nature of punishment and marriage, we purposefully make these procedures exceedingly difficult.

In many ways, then, the important moral events that occur early in life stay with us over the long haul. Not many of us literally vow to stay alive by uttering the words "I hereby place a demand on myself to never commit suicide." However, we may come very close to this. We denounce suicide as an option for other people, which implies that we denounce it for ourselves. When having a conversation about suicide with someone, we may say, point blank, "I would never kill myself." These are implicit demands and vows. They are also very *strong* implicit demands and vows, and so our corresponding duty to stay alive would be equally strong.

Although there are plenty of opportunities to reject suicide from our duties to God, ourselves, and others, we must again reiterate the limitations of this theory. A person who doesn't believe in God will have no duty to God to stay alive. A person without friends, relatives, or social connection will have no duty to others to stay alive. And a person who never vows against suicide will have no duty to him- or herself to stay alive. Further, even if a person has duties to God, self, and others to stay alive, these will only be *tentative* duties that might be overridden by stronger duties to God, self, or others.

Summary

During the seventeenth and eighteenth centuries, the most consistently adopted notion of moral responsibility consisted of a list of self-evident and intuitively known duties to God, oneself, and others. Pufendorf argued that these duties stemmed from a divine mandate to be sociable in view of our dependence on others for survival. Kant revised traditional duty theory by arguing that we have no duties to God since we lack knowledge of God. However, believers who claim to have knowledge of God may have special duties to God that spring from such knowledge. Mill objected that duties to oneself reduce to self-respect and self-development; this makes duties to oneself largely a matter of personal preference. Duties to oneself are indeed more flexible and less urgent than duties to others, but individuals who make special demands on themselves may have special duties to themselves. Sidgwick criticized duty theory for its reliance on shifting and inconsistent commonsense intuitions. However, it is reasonable to rely on such unstable commonsense moral intuitions in the absence of a moral standard that is more consistent and universally applied. In the early twentieth century, Ross offered a shorter list of intuitively known duties. These *prima facie* duties are all tentatively binding on us, but when two duties compete in moral dilemmas, we intuitively recognize the strongest duty as our actual duty. The key value of duty theory is its emphasis on what we owe others, rather than what others owe us. There is also the possibility of deriving a tentative obligation against suicide from our duties to God, ourselves, and others.

Study Questions

Introduction

1. Why, according to Bayles's former student, was Bayles's suicide heroic?

The Development and Popularity of Traditional Duty Theory

2. According to Fieser, what is a reason for the popularity of the three-part scheme of duties to God, oneself, and others?

Pufendorf's Theory of Duties

Survival and Mutual Cooperation

3. According to Pufendorf, what happens when we try to survive on our own?

Duties to God, Oneself, and Others

4. What are our duties to God?
5. Give an example of a special situation in which we may engage in a demanding occupation that potentially shortens our lives.
6. What are our absolute duties to others?

Intuitionism and Other Features of Duty Theory

7. Explain Beattie's notion of common sense.
8. Explain the intuitionist aspect of moral duties.
9. What is the connection between duties and virtue?
10. What is the connection between duties and rights?
11. Explain the difference between perfect and imperfect duties.
12. Explain the difference between direct and indirect duties.

Revisions and Criticisms of Duty Theory

Kant's Revision: We Have No Duties to God Because We Cannot Know God

13. Why did Kant believe we cannot know God?
14. Why did Hobbes believe that contracts with God are not valid?
15. What is Fieser's compromise view regarding duties to God?

Mill's Criticism: Duties to Oneself Reduce to Only Self-Respect and Self-Development

16. According to Mill, what is the only condition in which society may rightfully constrain us?
17. According to Fieser, what is the result of basing duties to others on self-respect and self-development?

Sidgwick's Criticism: Commonsense Moral Intuitions Are Imprecise

18. According to Sidgwick, what are the two possible ways of discovering our moral duties?
19. What is Fieser's response to Sidgwick's criticism?

Duty Theory Today

Ross's Theory of Prima Facie Duties

20. What are Ross's seven prima facie duties?

21. According to Ross, what is the difference between a prima facie duty and an actual duty?

The Value of Duty Theory

22. What is the key difference between moral duties and moral rights?

Duties and Suicide

23. According to Fieser, what might be the basis of a duty to oneself against suicide?

References

An initial memorial announcement of Bayles's death by Alan K. Mabe appeared in the *Proceedings and Addresses of the American Philosophical Association,* "Michael D. Bayles: 1941–1990," June 1991, Vol. 64, No. 7, pp. 30–31. The sympathetic response from a former student was by Thomas Steinbuck, Letter to the Editor, *Proceedings and Addresses of the American Philosophical Association,* September 1991, Vol. 65, No. 1, p. 33. The joint critical attack on Steinbuck's response was by Joram Graf Haber, Lina Levit Haber, Jack Nass, and Bernard H. Baumrin, Letter to the Editor, *Proceedings and Addresses of the American Philosophical Association,* January 1992, Vol. 65, No. 5, p. 90.

Plato's views on suicide are in *Laws,* Book 8, 873c; Seneca's views on suicide are in *De Ira,* 1.15; Hume's view of suicide is in "Of Suicide," included in recent editions of *Essays, Moral, Political, and Literary.*

Cicero's discussion of perfect and imperfect duties is in *The Offices,* 1.3.

The quotations from Pufendorf are adapted from *The Whole Duty of Man according to the Law of Nature* (London: Charles Harper, 1691), a seventeenth-century English translation of his book *De officio hominis et civis juxta legem naturalem* (1673). Pufendorf also presents his theory in a longer and more detailed work entitled *Of the Law of Nature and Nations* (*De Jure Naturae et Gentium,* 1762).

Kant's early discussion of duties is in his *Lectures on Ethics,* given around 1780, translated by Louis Infield (London: Methuen, 1930), "Duties towards Inanimate Objects." Kant's later statement is from his *Metaphysics of Morals* (1785), translated by Mary Gregor (Cambridge: Cambridge University Press). In an even later statement on the issue in the *Critique of Practical Reason* (1788), Kant associates duties to God with a duty to the holiness of the moral law itself (Part 2, "Methodology").

The story of the young man on the dirt bike is from the *Tribune Democrat* (Johnstown, Pennsylvania), July 1999.

Beattie's discussion of commonsense is from *An Essay on the Nature and Immutability of Truth* (1770), the most recent edition of which is edited by James Fieser, in *Scottish Common Sense Philosophy* (Bristol, England: Thoemmes Press, 2000), Vol. 2.

Henry Sidgwick's critique of commonsense moral intuitions is from *The Methods of Ethics* (1874); the quotation is from the seventh edition of 1904, recently reprinted (Indianapolis: Hackett, 1981), Book 3, Chapter 11.

Ross's account of *prima facie* duties is from Chapter 2, "What Makes Right Acts Right," in *The Right and the Good* (Oxford: Oxford University Press, 1930).

Suggestions for Further Reading

For a discussion of Pufendorf's philosophy see J. B. Schneewind, *The Invention of Autonomy* (Cambridge: Cambridge University Press, 1998), Chapter 7.

Many ethics books from the eighteenth and nineteenth centuries discuss duties to God, oneself, and others. All of the following by British authors are available in recent editions or facsimile reprints: David Fordyce, *The Elements of Moral Philosophy* (London: 1754), Book 2; William Paley, *The Principles of Moral and Political Philosophy* (London, 1785), Books 3–5; James Beattie, *Elements of Moral Science* (London, 1790–93); Dugald Stewart, *The Philosophy of the Active and Moral Powers of Man* (Edinburgh, 1828), Books 3–4.

For a recent discussion of duties to ourselves, see Kurt Baier, *The Moral Point of View* (Ithaca, NY: Cornell University Press, 1958), Chapter 9.

For a recent discussion of W. D. Ross, see Martin Curd, "Ross's Intuitionist Theory of Prima Facie Duties," James Fieser, ed., in *Metaethics, Normative Ethics, and Applied Ethics* (Belmont, CA: Wadsworth, 2000).

8

Natural and Human Rights

Introduction

One of the worst things that we can say about a country today is that it violates the human rights of its citizens. We find reports of a broad range of human rights abuses in scores of countries around the world. Certain governments routinely torture and execute political dissenters. In other countries, women are little more than the property of their husbands and have only a fraction of the rights that men do. In some places, members of ethnic and religious minorities are rounded up, exiled, and often murdered.

Surprisingly, the practice of slavery—one of the grossest violations of human rights ever—continues today in some countries. A major offender is the West African country of Mauritania, which has a several-hundred-year slavery tradition. In Mauritania, wealthier, light-skinned Arab people historically have enslaved poorer black people and used them for labor; as with any other property, the slaves are bought and sold, given as gifts, traded for other items, and passed on through inheritance. Journalist Samuel Cotton describes the kinds of tortures to which the Mauritanian slaves are subjected:

> These black African slaves in Mauritania are subjected to mental and emotional torments that have always been concomitant with slavery. "Routine" punishments for the slightest fault include beatings, denial of food and prolonged exposure to the sun, with hands and feet tied together. "Serious" infringement of the master's rule can mean prolonged tortures, documented in a report by Africa Watch. These include 1. The "camel treatment," where a human being is wrapped around the belly of a dehydrated camel and tied there. The camel is then given water and drinks until its belly expands enough to tear apart the slave. 2. The "insect treatment," where insects are put in his ears. The ears are waxed shut. The arms and legs are bound. The person goes insane from the bugs running around in his head. 3. The "burning coals," where the victim is seated flat, with his legs spread out. He is then buried in sand up to his waist, until he cannot move. Coals are placed between his legs and are burnt slowly. After a while, the legs, thighs and sex organ of the victim are burnt. There are other gruesome tortures—none of which is fit to describe in a

family newspaper, states Africa Watch. Another report states that some slaves caught fleeing are often castrated or branded like cattle.

Slavery has been outlawed several times in Mauritania's recent history. However, there are no meaningful criminal penalties for owning slaves, and slave owners insist on retaining possession of the slaves until the owners can be financially compensated. Recent reports place the number of Mauritanian slaves at around 90,000, with perhaps another 300,000 living in near slavelike conditions.

Organizations such as Amnesty International and Human Rights Watch try to reduce the number of human rights abuses by publishing reports of atrocities. These reports not only expose and embarrass the perpetrators but also give ammunition to agencies such as the United Nations, which are in a position to help the human rights victims and punish the offenders.

The notion of "rights" is complex, and in addition to "human rights" we find discussions of "natural rights," "moral rights," "positive rights," "legal rights," and "civil rights." Implicit in all of these notions is that some rights are not invented by governments and that we all have certain rights regardless of which country we live in. The notions of *human* rights, *natural* rights, and *moral* rights all emphasize this universal feature. The universal right to be free from slavery is a concrete example of this kind of right. By contrast, other rights are grounded in the legislative decisions of specific governments and are more limited in whom they apply to. For example, my right to vote in a U.S. presidential election is established by U.S. law and wouldn't apply to elections in China. The notions of *positive* rights, *legal* rights, and *civil* rights emphasize this more limited feature. Often, these two groups of rights overlap, as with the right to be free from slavery, which is both a universal right and a more limited right that we find in the U.S. Constitution. Legal scholars and moral philosophers try to make sense of the different domains of rights. We will focus on the more universal concept of rights that we find in discussions of human rights.

Natural Rights and Natural Law   The term **human rights** was coined in the twentieth century to designate a group of rights that all humans around the world supposedly possess. Historically, the forerunner to the notion of human rights is the notion of **natural rights,** which emphasizes that some rights are grounded in nature rather than in governments. Influenced by the natural law tradition, proponents of natural rights believed that all rights—whether natural or legal—rest on laws. Suppose, for example, that a group of political radicals prevents me from voting in a U.S. presidential election by physically blocking an election booth. When I protest that my rights have been violated, my protest is based on U.S. laws that allow me safe passage to election booths. This is an example of how a **legal right** is grounded in a law created by a governing body. Natural law theorists believed that natural rights also emerge from a higher kind of law. Roman and medieval theorists drew a distinction between law of nature (*lex naturalis*) and right of nature (*ius naturale*). Thomas Aquinas (1225–1274) suggested that the laws of nature are the formulated *expressions* of natural rights.

The link between rights and laws remained important to natural law philosophers of later centuries and reached its peak in seventeenth- and eighteenth-century discussions. But the concept of natural rights went through an important change from medieval to more modern discussions; specifically, later theorists saw rights as permanent features of who we are. For Aquinas, my rights merely emerge in the face of some relation that I have with another person. For example, if you owe me money, then I have a right to be paid. However, if I were stranded alone on an island, then technically I wouldn't have any rights since no one would be there to have some relation with me. Dutch philosopher Hugo Grotius (1583–1645) first articulated the more modern notion of rights, describing them as moral qualities that attach to a person:

> There is another meaning of law viewed as a body of rights . . . which has reference to the person. In this sense a right becomes a moral quality of a person, making it possible to have or to do something lawfully. Such a right attaches to a person. . . . (*On the Law of War and Peace,* 1.1.4)

For Grotius, my rights are similar to an item of property that I carry around with me—like my shirt or shoes. In Grotius's view, then, even the lone island dweller retains his or her rights, although this isolation limits his or her opportunities to act on them.

Influenced by Grotius and the natural law tradition, British philosopher Thomas Hobbes (1588–1679) took the notion of natural rights further by viewing it principally as a liberty:

> The *right of nature,* which writers commonly call *ius naturale,* is the liberty each man has to use his own power as he will himself, for the preservation of his own nature, that is to say, of his own life, and consequently of doing anything which, in his own judgment and reason, he shall conceive to be the aptest means thereunto. (*Leviathan,* 14)

According to Hobbes, this right of nature implies a liberty to protect myself from attack in any way that I can. The next giant step in the development of natural rights theory was made by British philosopher **John Locke** (1632–1704). Like Grotius, Locke thought that rights were permanent features of who we are. Like Hobbes, Locke saw liberty as a key component of rights. However, for Locke, natural law dictates four principal natural rights: life, health, liberty, and possessions.

Locke's Theory

Locke was a physician by training and profession. In the later years of his life, though, he focused on philosophy and produced several works that made him among the most influential writers of the late seventeenth and early eighteenth centuries. One of these works is *Two Treatises on Civil Government* (1690), in which he presents his most mature view of natural rights.

Natural Rights within the State of Nature   Thomas Hobbes began his discussion of natural laws and rights by considering what humans would be like in a state of nature, prior to any form of government. For Hobbes, the state of nature is a horrible environment, with nothing to guide us but the desire to survive and the impulse to satisfy our various desires. Because we are equally powerful and resources are limited, we are in constant conflict with others as we pursue our desires. In this condition, "Every man has a right to everything, even to one another's body."

Locke, too, begins his account of natural rights by speculating about the state of nature before the establishment of governments. Like Hobbes, Locke sees it as a "state of perfect freedom" and a "state of equality." But, unlike Hobbes, Locke does not view it as a moral free-for-all. Instead, within this condition, we are guided by a law of nature to avoid harming others regarding their life, health, liberty, and possessions:

> The state of nature has a law of nature to govern it, which obliges every one: and reason, which is that law, teaches all mankind, who will but consult it, that being all equal and independent, no one ought to harm another in his life, health, liberty, or possessions . . . (*Two Treatises,* 2.2.6)

This law of nature, then, grants each of us the fundamental rights to life, health, liberty, and possessions. Locke believes that we get this law from God, and in one of his writings, he states that nobody would be so "brutish" as to deny that "God has given a rule whereby men should govern themselves." In *Two Treatises,* he argues further that the law of nature is grounded in our roles as God's servants and creations. Given that God made us all equal, we are not justified in bringing others under our power—and that is precisely what happens when we harm others regarding their life, health, liberty, or possessions.

Not only do we have natural rights to life, health, liberty, and possessions, Locke continues, we also have the right to punish those who violate our rights to these. Without the right to punish offenders, our other rights would be useless. This right to punish is very sweeping and entitles us to kill offenders. By violating my rights, the offender declares war on me, and at that point I can't reason with him any more than I can reason with a wild animal that attacks me. Just as I am entitled to kill an attacking animal, I can also kill the human offender who threatens my right to life. I can even kill a thief, whether or not the thief shows an immediate intention of killing me.

Locke's reasoning on this point is especially interesting. A thief who steals from me, such as the mugger who pulls a knife on me, is using force to get me into his or her power. Locke states, "I have no reason to suppose, that he, who would take away my liberty, would not, when he had me in his power, take away every thing else." That is, if the aggressor forcefully subordinates me to steal my money, I can only assume that he will also kill me. Not only can I kill the thief on the spot, but, because I am now in a state of war with the thief, I can hunt him down and kill him later. However, Locke notes that if there is a functioning government in place, then the state of war between the thief and me ends once the thief runs away. At that point, it is up to the laws to address the wrong. For this reason, Locke believed that the best way of minimizing "wars" with others is to form societies in which authorities take over the task of punishment.

Slavery and the Right to Life   Earlier natural law philosophers believed that slavery was justified. Aquinas argued that slavery is natural because society benefits from enslaving some people. Appealing to Hebrew and Roman law, Grotius argued that "to every man it is permitted to enslave himself to any one he pleases for private ownership." That is, I can voluntarily become a slave if it suits my purposes. Today, the notion of voluntary enslavement advanced by Grotius makes no sense, and it is difficult even to envision a scenario in which voluntary enslavement would be a real option. Hobbes, though, gives us one scenario. Suppose that our country is overrun by a despot who wants to control everything and who promises simply to kill those who don't comply. To save our lives, we agree to become his slaves for some period of time. While enslaved, we must obey the despot, and if we don't, then he can kill us for breaking the agreement. Hobbes believed that this kind of voluntary slavery is contractually binding.

Locke takes a middle ground on the subject, based on a specific definition of "slavery." Strictly speaking, if I am your "slave," then my entire existence is in your hands, and you can kill me as you see fit. This notion of slavery, for Locke, isn't morally acceptable: I cannot voluntarily *give* you the right to kill me since I myself don't have the right to dispense with my own life. Locke believes that the right to life is *inalienable* in the sense that we cannot simply cast it aside or give it to someone else. It is as though our right to life is on loan to us from God, and we don't have the authority to rid ourselves of it. For this reason, I cannot kill myself, since in doing so I wrongly assume that I have the authority to dispense with my right to life. Similarly, I cannot transfer my right to life to someone else in a voluntary slave contract.

However, even though I can't *transfer* my right to life to someone else, according to Locke, I can *forfeit* that right by harming someone. It is as though God loans me my right to life on the condition that I abide by the law of nature; if I violate that law by harming someone, then God revokes my right to life and gives it to my victim. In this case, I am not so much a slave as I am a justly condemned prisoner. My victim can then either kill me on the spot or delay killing me and force me to labor for him or her. Suppose that my victim delays killing me but makes my life so miserable through hard labor that I wish I were dead. Even at this point, I don't have the right to end my misery and kill myself since my victim still holds my right to life. The best that I can do is disobey my victim's orders and prompt him or her to kill me.

So, for Locke, although I can't voluntarily enslave myself, I can essentially make myself a prisoner on death row by harming someone and thereby forfeiting my right to life. There is yet another twist to Locke's view on slavery. Locke describes a more moderate form of servitude called "drudgery" that does not give the master control over the servant's right to life. The servant in drudgery loses his or her liberties and possessions—and his or her condition may be dreadful—but the servant still retains the right to life. Locke believed that we can voluntarily submit ourselves to drudgery.

Although there is certainly an important technical distinction between slavery and drudgery, most of us would still identify such drudgery as slavery in the broader sense of the term. It is disappointing that an original philosopher like Locke didn't condemn drudgery as he did the more severe form of slavery. But, with some modifications to Locke's theory, we can go that extra mile. Locke rejects the severe form of slavery because it violates our inalienable right to *life.* We might similarly reject drudgery on the grounds that it violates our inalienable right to *liberty.* That is, through drudgery, I lose my liberty to select my own occupation and to come and go as I please. But it would be hard to argue that *all* components of my right to liberty are inalienable. For example, when I sign an employment contract, I transfer over to my employer a large part of my liberties during my working hours. However, there is always a core set of liberties that I retain. For example, my employer can't chain me to an office computer and force me to balance the books under penalty of torture. The problem with drudgery, then, is that it violates this core set of liberties.

Locke didn't take this route to argue against drudgery because he had a different conception of liberty, confined mainly to issues of governmental authority. For Locke, the right to liberty involves the freedom from absolute and arbitrary power, and the freedom to act within the rules established by a consensually created government:

> Freedom of men under government is, to have a standing rule to live by, common to every one of that society, and made by the legislative power erected in it; a liberty to follow my own will in all things, where the rule prescribes not; and not to be subject to the inconstant, uncertain, unknown, arbitrary will of another man: as freedom of nature is, to be under no other restraint but the law of nature. (*Two Treatises,* 2.4.22)

The problem with Locke's account of liberty is that a consensually created government might agree to permit drudgery, in which case drudgery would not violate our liberty rights. To reject drudgery, then, we need to expand Locke's notion of liberty beyond the rules of a consensually created government. That is, we need a notion of liberty that meaningfully retains our ability to come and go, in spite of what a government decides. Rights theorists in more recent years have viewed the right to liberty in this expanded sense.

The Right to Property   Locke discusses the right to property in more detail than any of our other principal rights. Although this may seem unusual at first, it makes sense when we consider the impact that property ownership has on us all. We labor much of our lives to acquire possessions, most of which we could survive without. More wars break out over land disputes than for any other reason. In giving advice to political rulers, Italian political philosopher Nicolo Machiavelli (1469–1527) emphasized the importance of respecting an individual's property. Machiavelli dramatically states that "above all he [i.e., the ruler] must keep his hands off the property of others, because people more quickly forget the death of their father than the loss of their inheritance." Locke similarly believed that property is of the greatest importance to us.

Locke begins his discussion of the right to property by explaining how we first obtain property. In the original state of nature, everything in the world belonged in common to all humans. People then took some item from the common storehouse, altered and improved it through their labor, and thereby created something that was uniquely their own. For example, someone may have cut down a tree and carved it into a boat, which he then called his own. We first acquire property, then, by applying our labor to a commonly held object. In Locke's words, "Whatsoever then he removes out of the state that nature has provided, and left it in, he has mixed his labor with, and joined to it something that is his own, and thereby makes it his property." According to Locke, this is an activity that people could freely engage in on a first-come-first-served basis, without needing to get prior consent from others. If prior mutual consent were required, people would have starved to death while waiting for permission from everyone. Locke considers the objection that this formula for acquiring property will incite people to be greedy and apply their labor to as much as they can so as to acquire as many things as they can. The common storehouse of goods would then run out, and people would begin to fight over possessions. Locke counters that this worst-case scenario could never happen because God has provided such a bounty that the common storehouse of goods will never run out, regardless of our greed.

Locke's formula for acquiring property applies to land as well as to things like wooden boats. Locke writes that "as much land as a man tills, plants, improves, cultivates, and can use the product of, so much is his property. He by his labour does, as it were, enclose it from the common." Again, Locke argued that God has provided such an abundance of land that we all can take what we can use and there will always be more. It is as if each of us is drinking from an ever-flowing river that will never run dry. Today—with a world population ten times that of Locke's day—Locke's view seems naive. All the land on the earth is spoken for, and the best that we can hope for is to buy or inherit a tiny piece of land from someone else. Locke recognized that most of the land in modern European communities was already claimed and cultivated. However, he argued that in other parts of the world "there are still great tracts of ground to be found" that the local inhabitants don't make use of.

It is easy to see how Locke's view of property rights could justify the conquering of foreign lands by early explorers. In Locke's day, an explorer who landed on American shores would have found none of the signs of land cultivation that were common in Europe. The local inhabitants lived off the land and used primitive agricultural techniques, but none claimed "ownership" of the vast woodlands. So, to the explorer, the land was still part of the common storehouse, ready to be claimed and cultivated. Locke argues further that society actually benefits by claiming land and maximizing its use:

I ask, whether in the wild woods and uncultivated waste of America, left to nature, without any improvement, tillage or husbandry, a thousand acres [would] yield the needy and wretched inhabitants as many conveniencies of life, as ten acres of equally fertile land do in Devonshire, where they are well cultivated? (*Two Treatises*, 2.5.37)

So, not only were they *justified* in claiming the "uncultivated waste of America," but it was actually *good* for them to do this. Again, from a contemporary ecological perspective, Locke's view seems naive. We now know that the survival of life on earth depends on *not* cultivating large tracts of land. Also, we cringe at Locke's disrespect for indigenous cultural traditions that don't match European standards, particularly in areas of economics and property ownership.

Although there are serious problems with Locke's specific notion of land acquisition, his more general intuition about property acquisition rings true for other kinds of property. When we invest our time and labor into some project, we typically feel that we "own" the project. This sense of ownership is superbly reflected in U.S. copyright law, which states that we immediately own a literary or artistic work once we create it:

Copyright protection subsists from the time the work is created in fixed form. The copyright in the work of authorship immediately becomes the property of the author who created the work. Only the author or those deriving their rights through the author can rightfully claim copyright.

It is the job of governing bodies to work out the details of acquiring and transferring property. However, we find in Locke a convincing explanation of where I first get the right to call something *mine*.

Political Authorities and the Right to Liberty

We noted previously that the right to liberty, for Locke, is a freedom from the arbitrary rule of some political authority. For Locke, the reason we submit ourselves to any political authority is for protection. When we are off by ourselves or even with family clans, we can't completely protect ourselves from attack. The solution is to band together in larger communities by forming a compact, which requires that we give up some of our liberties. As we try to make political decisions within these communities, we cannot reasonably expect everyone to agree on every point, such as who should serve in the military or whether there should be rules against public drunkenness. We must, then, follow the will of the majority; otherwise, our compact will be meaningless. The will of the majority is the only legitimate political authority, and we usually determine the will of the majority by empowering representative assemblies to make decisions for us all.

Locke explains that the government that we form can fall apart in a number of ways. First, it may be squashed by an invading foreign power. Second, we may voluntarily disband it with the aim of replacing it with something better. Third, we may revolt. Locke believed that political revolutions are fully justified when a government acts contrary to its appointed purpose—namely, to protect our lives and our property. Here, the government forfeits its power, and the people essentially return to the state of nature in which they can form a new government:

> By this breach of trust they forfeit the power the people had put into their hands for quite contrary ends, and it devolves to the people, who have a right to resume their original liberty, and, by the establishment of a new legislative, (such as they shall think fit) provide for their own safety and security, which is the end for which they are in society. (*Two Treatises,* 2.19.222)

For Locke, this "breach of trust" justifies intense civil wars, as well as more minor insurrections.

Locke's position on the overthrowing of governments was very radical for its time. Although Hobbes similarly believed that governments are created by people in a social contract, Hobbes argued that we can't overthrow governments—even bad ones—since, to effectively keep the peace, governments must exercise absolute authority. In an early essay on the subject of natural law, written about thirty years before his *Two Treatises,* Locke also argued that we must show absolute obedience to political authorities. Locke states in this early work that "the law of nature decrees that princes and a law-maker . . . should be obeyed." However, Locke's view on the subject of absolute obedience changed during the English revolution of 1688, which was a revolution that Locke supported. Locke wrote his *Two Treatises* at this time, and as we saw, he valued the preservation of our natural rights more than obedience to political authorities.

To recap, here are the central points of Locke's theory:

- In the state of nature, we have the rights to life, health, liberty, and possessions, and we may rightfully punish people who violate these rights.
- We cannot voluntarily transfer our right to life to someone else, although we can forfeit this right by violating the rights of others.
- Our right to acquire property—including land—arises when we apply our labor with something that is held in common.
- Our right to liberty is a freedom from absolute and arbitrary power, and we may rightfully overthrow governments that violate our natural rights or fail to protect them.

Criticisms of Natural Rights Theory

Occasionally, a great philosopher will write a book that has an impact beyond the world of philosophers and also influences lives and events in the larger world. Locke is a case in point. Aside from influencing other moral and political philosophers of his time, Locke's view of natural rights directly impacted the views of political reformers and revolutionaries. The Virginia Declaration of Rights from June 12, 1776, is one example. Echoing Locke, the declaration opens by recognizing the natural rights of life, liberty, property, happiness, and safety:

> That all men are by nature equally free and independent, and have certain inherent rights, of which, when they enter into a state of society, they cannot by

any compact deprive or divest their posterity; namely, the enjoyment of life and liberty, with the means of acquiring and possessing property, and pursuing and obtaining happiness and safety.

The declaration continues in Lockean fashion, noting that governments are "instituted for the common benefit, protection, and security of the people" and that we may "reform, alter or abolish" a government when it fails in its purpose. We find these same points in the more famous U.S. Declaration of Independence from July 4, 1776:

We hold these Truths to be self-evident, that all Men are created equal, that they are endowed by their Creator with certain unalienable Rights, that among these are Life, Liberty, and the Pursuit of Happiness—That to secure these Rights, Governments are instituted among Men, deriving their just Powers from the Consent of the Governed, that whenever any Form of Government becomes destructive of these Ends, it is the Right of the People to alter or to abolish it, and to institute new Government, laying its Foundation on such Principles, and organizing its Powers in such Form, as to them shall seem most likely to effect their Safety and Happiness.

The Lockean notion of natural rights appears yet again in the Declaration of the Rights of Man and of Citizens, adopted by the French assembly in 1789 at the outset of the French Revolution:

Men are born and remain free and equal in rights . . . [and the] aim of all political association is the conservation of the natural and imperscriptable rights of man . . . [including] liberty, property, security, and resistance to oppression.

With real-world events tied to the notion of natural rights, early critics of natural rights theories focused less on Locke's actual words and more on the documents and manifestos of political movements that supported natural rights.

Burke's Criticism: Abstract Notions of Natural Rights Are Too Simplistic   Shortly after the French Revolution, Irish philosopher and politician **Edmund Burke** (1729–1797) harshly denounced the French uprising in his *Reflections on the Revolution in France* (1790). Although Burke supported the more moderate American Revolution, he believed that the French Revolution uprooted important social values involving religion, property, and the nobility. Part of Burke's attack focused on the revolutionaries' notions of natural rights. For Burke, their conception of natural rights was simply metaphysical speculation with no consideration of the complex manner in which societies actually operate. Although bold statements about our natural rights stir our emotions, the assertion of an abstract right to food, for example, is useless in resolving the practical issue of feeding people. In this case, Burke says, we are better advised to listen to a farmer or a physician:

What is the use of discussing a man's abstract right to food or medicine? The question is upon the method of procuring and administering them. In that deliberation I shall always advise to call in the aid of the farmer and the physician rather than the professor of metaphysics.

The underlying problem, according to Burke, is that notions of natural rights are simple, neat, and tidy, whereas "the nature of man is intricate; the objects of society are of the greatest possible complexity." Once we latch onto such simplistic concepts of natural rights, our "complicated mass of human passions" pulls those notions in any number of directions, and the original simplicity is entirely lost. So, in proportion as these notions of natural rights are "metaphysically true" because of their simplicity, "they are morally and politically false" for failing to apply to the real world. Burke didn't completely reject the notion of rights, but he believed that rights occupy a middle ground between purely abstract speculation and purely practical issues, such as starving people. Because rights are in a place of limbo, they are impossible to define. However, we can still recognize them when we properly apply them to real-world issues. For Burke, our true understanding of rights is shaped through the art of compromise as we balance different social interests through a kind of rational "computing principle."

In short, Burke has two observations about rights theory: (1) Discussions of natural rights in the 18th century were very abstract, with little real-world application; and (2) we gain a true understanding of rights by balancing different social interests. Burke is correct in both of these observations. In the years since Burke, though, rights theory has developed to the point that it now adequately addresses Burke's two points. As to Burke's first point—the overly abstract nature of rights—there is a reason early rights theorists such as Locke listed only a few general rights. Most proponents of natural law argued that nature mandates only one very general law, such as "Do that which is suitable for human ends" or "Be sociable" or "Don't harm others." It is then the job of politicians and legal experts to continue the deduction process until they arrive at very specific rules. Theorists such as Locke and documents such as the Declaration of Independence stopped with a short and general list of rights. However, since then, the legal machinery in the United States has carried out the deduction process and given us precise guidelines for applying rights in very precise situations. For example, I have the right to stand in front of a courthouse and protest against a corrupt judge. Discussions of human rights today typically draw on the subtle distinctions made in such discussions of legal rights.

As to Burke's second point—the issue of balancing different social interests—rights theory today does this exceptionally well. When you assert any right, such as your right to smoke, that right is only one claim that must be weighed against competing claims, such as my right to be free from secondhand smoke. Although the smoker's and the nonsmoker's rights may be equally legitimate, it takes a lot of compromise and real-world application to determine when one right overrides the other. The smoker/nonsmoker case is a good illustration of how many conflicts between rights emerge.

Rights theorists distinguish between two classes of rights that inevitably come into conflict. The first class involves a *freedom to* various liberties, such as the freedom to smoke, to speak publicly, to print and circulate information, to engage in religious worship, or to travel around. The second class involves a *freedom from* various harms, such as the freedom from being exposed to secondhand smoke, from being physically attacked, from being publicly insulted, or from having property stolen. If I exercise my *freedom to* speak out against a corrupt judge, this might conflict with the judge's *freedom from* public insult. Again, the legal process in the United States continually works out compromises between conflicting legal rights. In this case, my right to speak out against a public official has priority over that official's right to protect his or her reputation. In the case of smoker's versus nonsmoker's rights, our freedom from being harmed has priority over someone else's freedom to smoke. As these issues play out in the theater of legal rights, we have more concrete ideas for how to resolve moral conflicts between human rights.

Bentham's Criticism: Legal Rights Are Grounded in Fact, but Natural Rights Are Not

Burke held open the possibility that there are some sort of natural rights, although we cannot define them. British political philosopher Jeremy Bentham (1748–1832) rejected the notion of natural rights completely, calling it "nonsense on stilts." The heart of Bentham's critique is his view that real laws will give us real legal rights, but imaginary natural laws will give us only imaginary natural rights. He picturesquely makes this point here:

> Right . . . is the child of law; from *real* laws come *real* rights; but from *imaginary* laws, from laws of nature, fancied and invented by poets, rhetoricians, and dealers in moral and intellectual poisons, come *imaginary* rights, a bastard brood of monsters "gorgons and chimaeras dire." (*Anarchical Fallacies,* Conclusion)

Bentham believed that all rights—legal and natural—are fictions that we create for the convenience of discussion. We talk about rights as though they are personal possessions, but this is only symbolic language since we clearly don't possess rights as we possess other things, such as cars or houses.

Although all rights are fictions, Bentham concedes that *legal* rights are at least grounded in some kind of fact. People in power—presidents, lawmakers, and judges—all seek to uphold the laws upon which our legal rights are based. The "tangible facts" involved here are the psychological dispositions of these government officials concerning their interest in upholding the laws. However, Bentham argues, there is no tangible reality to natural laws that might form a factual basis for *natural* rights. Defenders of natural rights say that these rights are of divine origin and are factual in that sense. In the words of the Declaration of Independence, humans are "endowed by their Creator with certain unalienable Rights." But, Bentham argues, this explanation places the issue beyond the realm of fact, and we are simply left with the defender's private conviction. For Bentham, without a concrete factual foundation, the notion of natural rights is completely empty of meaning. Even if we grant in theory that a person has a natural right to something, "his condition is not in any respect different from what it would be if he had it not."

Bentham believes that we can help rid ourselves of natural rights language if we see exactly how politicians and philosophers first blundered into assertions about natural rights. He blames English-speaking people specifically for not being careful in how they used the term "right." Suppose that your own a coat; I then recognize that the coat is your property, and I say this:

1. You *ought* to possess your coat.

Here I am expressing my satisfaction at the idea of your owning the coat, and I also imply that you should have legal protection to your property. Suppose that I then say this:

2. It *is right* for you to possess your coat.

Here I am saying exactly the same thing as in (1): I am pleased with your owning the coat, and your property should be legally protected. Suppose that I next say this:

3. You *have a right* to your coat.

The words here are very similar to those in statement 2, but there is a big difference. In statement 3, I am implying that you can knock someone down who tries to take your coat, but I don't imply this in statement 2. For Bentham, statement 2 is the language of peace, and statement 3 is the language of mischief. Once I've asserted that you have a right to your coat, it is easy for me to start calling it a *natural* right if I think that you are naturally entitled to knock someone down who tries to take your coat. Given how close the wording is between statements 2 and 3, we quickly slide from one to the other and then add the word "natural." Again, Bentham recognizes that, for the purpose of some discussions, we need to use the word "right" in the sense of statement 3. However, we need to see it only as a *legal* right, and not a *natural* right.

Even if we don't find Bentham's linguistic explanation convincing, his larger point remains: Natural rights are not grounded in the kind of hard facts that legal rights are. How might we respond to Bentham? On the one hand, in the face of tragedies today like slavery in Mauritania, we want to assert a universal right not to be enslaved beyond what governments say. On the other hand, Bentham raises serious questions about the factual foundation of these alleged natural rights. It is unlikely that the dispute will be resolved anytime soon. In fact, scholars today still debate about whether there are any natural rights beyond the legal rights established by governments. However, we can offer one solution here that tries to preserve the meaningfulness of natural rights while at the same time acknowledging Bentham's skepticism about them.

Let's grant Bentham's point that natural rights aren't factually grounded in the authority of God or some other intangible realm as natural law theorists maintained. Nevertheless, we might be able to find a factual basis for natural rights that parallels legal rights—namely, a factual basis in some feature of human thinking. Perhaps this feature of human thinking is a culturally shaped intuition that is shared by everyone who lives in and appreciates humane societies. Or perhaps it is only an attitude shared by a smaller group of impartial and socially sensitive people. In either case, it is rooted in some fact of human psychology. And this is in the same ballpark as the psychological facts surrounding government officials who desire to uphold the laws upon which legal rights are based. We are, then, *inventing* natural rights just as we do legal rights. Locke would be horrified at the thought that he—or the spirit of his times—"invented" natural rights. Today, though, this idea isn't nearly so horrifying. A recent book on human rights opens by stating that "undoubtedly human rights are among the greatest inventions of our civilization." According to that author, the importance of natural rights is in no way diminished by the fact that they are invented.

Marx's Criticism: Natural Rights Emphasize Selfishness and Ignore Community

German political philosopher **Karl Marx** (1818–1883) had a long-standing dislike for social structures that allowed a ruling class of people to exploit an underclass. He spent his entire adult life in revolutionary politics, urging a revolution of the working class. In view of this, we might think that Marx would appreciate the theory of natural rights and its emphasis on equality. On the contrary, Marx believed that natural rights theory is seriously flawed, particularly as expressed in American and French political documents. For Marx, natural rights theories reinforce the selfish side of human nature and suppress our community-oriented side, which is our true identity. Marx makes this point by drawing a contrast between the egoistic man and the species-being. The egoistic man is what we are when we act in isolation of one another within the neutral territory of civil society, not knowing or caring who our neighbors are as long as they leave us alone. The species-being is what we are when we see ourselves connected with other members of our species in a kind of extended family.

Marx looks at each of the key natural rights as expressed in political documents and exposes their selfish orientation. For example, the right to liberty allows me to do what I want so long as I don't harm others. However, this separates me from other people rather than unites me with them. The right to property allows me to enjoy my own possessions and arbitrarily dispose of them without regard for other people. The right to equality allows me to be treated as a self-sufficient single person. The right to security simply preserves the status quo and guarantees that I will remain selfish. Marx concludes that "none of the so-called rights of man goes beyond egoistic man, man as he is in civil society, namely an individual withdrawn behind his private interests and whims and separated from the community." By following natural rights theory, we won't see ourselves as community-oriented species-beings, and the only bond that will hold us together is our selfish need for protection, especially the protection of our private property.

Marx is correct that 18th-century discussions of rights were exceptionally self-oriented, and it is no secret why this was so. Writers on natural rights were launching revolutions against oppressive rulers and social classes. By revolting against their oppressors, they were essentially saying, "Leave me alone!" The problem with Marx's critique, though, is that he wrongly assumes that we are *either* self-oriented *or* community-oriented, that we can't be both at the same time. Most of us have a mixture of selfish interests and community interests, and when oppressed by others, even the best of us occasionally shouts, "Leave me alone!" Eighteenth-century natural rights theorists successfully tapped into our self-oriented side while neglecting our community-oriented side. However, later rights theorists addressed that deficiency and in fact put forward a more community-oriented set of rights, which requires that we help others in need.

We can best understand this community-oriented set of rights by distinguishing between negative rights to be let alone and positive rights to our welfare. **Negative rights** are our rights to not be mistreated, as brilliantly expressed by 18th-century rights theorists. By contrast, **positive rights,** also called welfare rights, are our rights to be helped by others. If I am injured, I can rightfully demand medical help. If I am starving, I can rightfully demand food. In these cases, I don't want people to leave me alone; instead, I want them to *do* something for me. To the extent that I demand welfare rights for myself, I am duty-bound to assist others when they demand welfare rights for themselves. So, with one eye we look toward ourselves to protect our negative rights to be let alone, and with the other eye we look toward others to help secure our welfare rights. Some conservative rights theorists today question the legitimacy of welfare rights and argue instead that our true rights are limited to negative rights to be let alone. But to the extent that we agree with Marx that traditional natural rights are too selfish, we will want to endorse the more community-oriented set of welfare rights.

Human Rights Theory Today

Since the time of Burke, Bentham, and Marx, rights theory has only grown more influential, and we can't conceive of dismissing the theory as these early critics suggest. We noted that more recent rights theorists introduced distinctions between types of rights that help address some of the problems pointed out by early critics. These are the particular distinctions that we noted:

1. Negative rights: rights to be left alone
   a. Freedom to various liberties (such as smoker's rights)
   b. Freedom from various harms (such as nonsmoker's rights)
2. Positive (or welfare) rights: rights to other people's help

In the 20th century, rights theorists dropped the term "natural" with its somewhat dated reliance on natural law theory, and adopted the term "human rights," which simply designates that every person alive has a specific set of rights.

The Universal Declaration of Human Rights   The greatest single contribution to human rights theory in recent decades is the **Universal Declaration of Human Rights,** which the General Assembly of the United Nations adopted on December 10, 1948. The Universal Declaration is a short document that lists several dozen human rights that apply to all humans worldwide. Eighteenth-century political documents grounded natural rights in God's authority and natural law. By contrast, the Universal Declaration completely avoids these appeals and takes a more practical approach by founding human rights on our shared desire for peace. According to the Universal Declaration, by recognizing human rights, we bring about "freedom, justice and peace in the world." By disregarding human rights, we bring about "barbarous acts which have outraged the conscience of mankind" and oppressed citizens are compelled to rebel against tyranny.

The central theme of the Universal Declaration is that human rights are universal in the sense that everyone has the same rights, regardless of nationality or ethnicity:

> Article 1. All human beings are born free and equal in dignity and rights. They are endowed with reason and conscience and should act towards one another in a spirit of brotherhood.
>
> Article 2. Everyone is entitled to all the rights and freedoms set forth in this Declaration, without distinction of any kind, such as race, colour, sex, language, religion, political or other opinion, national or social origin, property, birth or other status.
>
> Furthermore, no distinction shall be made on the basis of the political, jurisdictional or international status of the country or territory to which a person belongs, whether it be independent, trust, non-self-governing or under any other limitation of sovereignty.

After establishing the universal nature of human rights, the Universal Declaration makes a statement similar to eighteenth-century declarations: "Everyone has the right to life, liberty and the security of person."

Unlike eighteenth-century political documents that stop with a short general list of rights, however, the Universal Declaration spells out very particular rights. At the top of the list is a prohibition against slavery and servitude: "slavery and the slave trade shall be prohibited in all their forms." Next is a prohibition against torture and "cruel, inhuman or degrading treatment or punishment." Targeting tyrannical governments, the Universal Declaration lists various rights to fair criminal trials, political asylum, and tribunals concerning human rights violations. Moving to more domestic issues, we have rights "to marry and to found a family" and to own property. We also have liberty rights to "freedom of thought, conscience and religion" and the right to "peaceful assembly and association." One of the boldest components of the Universal Declaration is its list of economic rights. These include the "free choice of employment," "equal pay for equal work," the right to "periodic holidays with pay," and various forms of social welfare including special assistance for childcare.

A common criticism of the Universal Declaration is that the standard of rights is set so high that few countries in the world can actually meet them. In fact, some of the economic rights are not realities here in the United States. However, this argument is akin to saying that all standards of morality are invalid since few people have perfect moral conduct. The important question is whether the human rights listed are (in the words of the Universal Declaration itself) "a common standard of achievement for all peoples and all nations." It is not clear what kind of person would answer no to this question.

The Interrelation between Human Rights and Legal Rights   The notion of rights is so firmly embedded into our thinking today that it is difficult for us to discuss moral issues without quickly citing various rights. If someone vandalizes your car, you may say that your property rights have been violated. If the police make you remove some old refrigerators from your backyard, you may say that your liberty rights have been violated. When asserting our rights, at various times we may be referring to our basic human rights or to our basic legal rights. However, many times we may not really know whether we're referring to our human rights *or* our legal rights. In our common thinking, the lines between the two have become blurred.

One of the reasons for this is that there is a unique interrelation between human rights and legal rights. On the one hand, discussions of legal rights draw from our more basic intuitions about human rights. Suppose, for example, that as a legislator I am trying to write something about the legal right to free speech. I will very likely draw from my intuitions about our *human* right to free speech and related liberties. On the other hand, our intuitions about human rights draw from the refined discussions of legal rights. Suppose, for example, that as a moral philosopher I want to say something about my human right to criticize government officials. I will be less abstract if I look at how this issue is addressed in the law and in court cases. Even if I don't fully agree with the laws and court decisions, my thoughts on this issue will be more appropriate to real-world situations than they would be otherwise.

So, the lines of distinction between human rights and legal rights seem to be blurred, and it seems that we need to accept them both as a package. The Universal Declaration of Human Rights blurs the distinction between human rights and legal rights even more. On the one hand, the Universal Declaration is an expression of our moral intuitions about human rights, and on the other, it is a legal document of a governing body with some power of enforcement. This extra blurring between human rights and legal rights has particular advantages when addressing major human rights violations today, such as the lingering practice of slavery in Mauritania. A simple moral condemnation may not be enough to end that abuse. But a condemnation by the United Nations, backed with sanctions, is more likely to have an impact.

Although the marriage between human rights and legal rights may be a good thing for society at large, it is a loss for moral philosophers. If we want to speak intelligently on a specific issue of human rights today, we may need an intimate knowledge of U.S. case law and perhaps even knowledge of international law. Without this knowledge, our abstract philosophical discussions risk being "morally and politically false" in Burke's terms or, even worse, "nonsense on stilts" in Bentham's terms. So, much of the discussion of specific human rights today is taken on by legal scholars and political scientists. The task that remains for moral philosophers is to show what is uniquely moral about our human rights intuitions.

Summary

Influenced by natural law theory, the theory of natural rights took its first distinctive form in Locke's *Two Treatises of Government.* Locke argued that we have basic natural rights to life, health, liberty, and possessions, and that we form governments to help protect our rights. According to Locke, slavery isn't justified since it violates our right to life insofar as our owners supposedly can kill us as they see fit. However, Locke held that drudgery is justified to the extent that our owners can't kill us. By expanding Locke's notion of the right to liberty, we can also make drudgery unjustified. Locke held that the right to property rests on mixing our individual labor with something that is held in common. There are problems in applying this principle to land acquisition, but it is a reasonable explanation for how we might acquire other kinds of property— such as intellectual property. For Locke, the right to liberty principally means the freedom from absolute and arbitrary power, and this forms the basis for justifying revolutions. Natural rights theories were adopted by 18th-century political revolutionaries, and critics of natural rights theory often focused on these statements.

Burke criticized natural rights theory for being too abstract and failing to see the importance of compromise in working out social problems in real-life situations. Burke rightly noted that the early advocates of natural rights were too abstract and stopped at short lists of rights; however, later rights theorists have indeed deduced more specific rights. Burke also correctly noted that we need to balance competing social interests; however, later rights theorists acknowledged this insofar as we need to balance "freedom from" rights against "freedom to" rights. Bentham criticized natural rights theory for failing to be grounded in fact and, in essence, for being a purely imaginative construct. Indeed, it is best to abandon the traditional idea of rights founded in natural law; however, it is nevertheless reasonable to base natural rights on psychological facts involving culturally-shaped intuitions. Marx criticized natural rights theory for being too egoistic and failing to be community-oriented. Early advocates of natural rights were principally interested in securing personal freedom; however, recent rights theory allows for the possibility of welfare rights, which involves a community-oriented duty to help other people. Finally, legal rights and human rights are interdependent: our intuitions about human rights prompt us to systematize and enforce them in the form of legal rights; the details of legal rights, then, help us refine our concepts of human rights.

Study Questions

Introduction

  1. Which notions of rights are associated with the view that some rights are *not* invented by governments?

Natural Rights and Natural Law

2. What is the relation between natural law and natural rights?
3. What is the uniquely modern notion of rights that was articulated by Grotius?
4. For Hobbes, what does a "right of nature" involve?

Locke's Theory

Natural Rights within the State of Nature

5. For Locke, what are the four principal rights that we have in the state of nature?
6. In the state of nature, why can I kill a thief even if he doesn't show any intention to kill me?

Slavery and the Right to Life

7. What is Locke's strict notion of slavery, and why does Locke oppose that form of slavery?
8. What is Locke's notion of drudgery?
9. According to Fieser, how might we alter Locke's theory to condemn drudgery?

The Right to Property

10. How do we acquire property?
11. Why does Locke believe that his formula for acquiring property also applies to acquiring land?

Political Authorities and the Right to Liberty

12. What does the notion of liberty involve?
13. How can governments fall apart?
14. Under what conditions can we overthrow a government?

Criticisms of Natural Rights Theory

15. What rights are listed in the Virginia Declaration of Rights?

Burke's Criticism: Abstract Notions of Natural Rights Are Too Simplistic

16. Burke states that in proportion as notions of natural rights are "metaphysically true," "they are morally and politically false." What does he mean by this?
17. Explain the distinction between freedom *from* and freedom *to*.

Bentham's Criticism: Legal Rights Are Grounded in Fact but Natural Rights Are Not

18. For Bentham, what are the "facts" in which legal rights are grounded?
19. According to Fieser, in what facts might we also ground natural rights?

Marx's Criticism: Natural Rights Emphasize Selfishness and Ignore Community

20. What does Marx mean by "egoistic man" and "species-being"?
21. Explain the distinction between negative rights and positive rights.

Human Rights Theory Today

The Universal Declaration of Human Rights

22. What is Fieser's response to those who maintain that the Universal Declaration of Human Rights sets too high a standard?

The Interrelation Between Human Rights and Legal Rights

23. What is the interrelation between human rights and legal rights?

References

Samuel Cotton, "The African Slave Trade," *The City Sun*, February 1–February 7, 1995.

Thomas Aquinas's views on natural rights and slavery are in *Summa Theologica*, 2a2ae, q. 57.

Hugo Grotius's views on natural rights and slavery are in *On the Law of War and Peace* (1625), 1.1.3–4. The best current translation of this work is that by Francis W. Kelsey (Oxford: Oxford University Press, 1925).

The best current edition of Locke's *Two Treatises* is the critical edition by Peter Laslett (Cambridge: Cambridge University Press, 1963). Locke's statement about God giving us a moral rule is from *An Essay Concerning Human Understanding*, 2.28.8. Locke's early views of natural law are from *Essays on the Law of Nature*, edited by W. von Leyden (Oxford: Clarendon Press, 1954).

Thomas Hobbes's views on slavery are discussed in *Leviathan*, Chapter 20 (paragraphs 10–13 in Curley's edition).

Nicolo Machiavelli's statement about property is in *The Prince*, Chapter 17, which is available in several recent editions.

The quotation on U.S. copyright law is from *Circular 1: Copyright Basics*, U.S. Copyright Office.

Bentham's critique of natural rights is in his *Anarchical Fallacies*, Conclusion (in *Works*, edited by John Bowring, Vol. 2, p. 522 ff.), and *Pannomial Fragments*, Chapter 3 (in *Works*, Vol. 3, p. 217 ff.). Both of these titles remained unpublished during Bentham's life.

The quotation that "human rights are among the greatest inventions of our civilization" is from Carlos Santiago Nino, *The Ethics of Human Rights* (Oxford: Clarendon Press, 1991).

Marx's critique of natural rights is found in his review article "On the Jewish Question," originally published in 1843 and is available in *Karl Marx: Selected Writings*, edited by David McLellan (Oxford: Oxford University Press, 1977).

Wesley Newcomb Hohfeld's articles on rights were collected in *Fundamental Legal Conceptions as Applied in Judicial Reasoning* (1919), more recently edited by W. W. Cook (New Haven, CT: Yale University Press, 1966).

The quotation from the Universal Declaration of Human Rights is taken from *Metaethics, Normative Ethics, and Applied Ethics*, edited by James Fieser (Belmont, CA: Wadsworth, 2000).

Suggestions for Further Reading

For a discussion of natural rights theories before Locke, see Richard Tuck, *Natural Rights Theories: Their Origin and Development* (Cambridge: Cambridge University Press, 1979).

For discussions on Locke's moral theory and the *Two Treatises,* see R. Ashcraft, *Locke's Two Treatises of Government* (London: Unwin and Hyman, 1987); J. Colman, *John Locke's Moral Philosophy* (Edinburgh: Edinburgh University Press, 1983); J. Dunn, *The Political Thought of John Locke* (Cambridge: Cambridge University Press, 1969).

An influential analysis of rights is given by Wesley Newcomb Hohfeld; his articles on rights were collected in *Fundamental Legal Conceptions as Applied in Judicial Reasoning* (1919), more recently edited by W. W. Cook (New Haven, CT: Yale University Press, 1966).

For recent discussions of rights theory, see Joel Feinberg, *Social Philosophy* (Englewood Cliffs, NJ: Prentice-Hall, 1973); Joel Feinberg, *Rights, Justice, and the Bounds of Liberty* (Princeton, NJ: Princeton University Press, 1980); R. Martin, *A System of Rights* (Oxford: Clarendon Press, 1993); Carlos Santiago Nino, *The Ethics of Human Rights* (Oxford: Clarendon Press, 1991).

9

Moral Reason versus Moral Feeling

Introduction

Approximately 12 million children die each year from diseases and hunger-related illnesses. Most of these children are from developing countries that lack adequate social and economic structures and that tend to be overpopulated. In those countries, farmers grow barely enough food to meet normal food demands, but during times of drought, food production drops sharply, and there's simply not enough to go around. Children are hit harder than adults in times of famine, mainly because adults can go longer without food than children. Charitable organizations in the United States and other industrial countries try to reduce the number of casualties by providing food and health supplies to needy families. The Save the Children organization is recognized as one of the most effective charities of this kind in America. Part of its success owes to the heart-wrenching descriptions it provides of needy and abused children around the world, such as this:

> Daniel was born in a small village in Mozambique and spent his first ten years there. . . . One summer night seven years ago, a band of armed rebels burst into their family compound, then kidnapped Daniel . . . at gunpoint. All night long he marched. He arrived at the rebel camp the next morning . . . his bare feet badly cut and swollen . . . his body shaking with fear. . . . Daniel was held captive for five years. He didn't see his parents or anyone he knew. Beatings were common. At first he took care of the cattle and served the soldiers. Later, he was given a gun, taught to use it and forced to kill.

The story continues that, after a peace treaty, Save the Children helped reunite Daniel with his family. Celebrity spokespeople for this organization—such as Sally Struthers, Brooke Shields, and David Bowie—make public appeals and tell us that for only a few dollars a month we can help these children. The appeals are convincing, and our hearts go out to the young victims. If we feel enough compassion for them, we might even donate money to the organization to support its efforts.

The appeals made by such charitable organizations are blatantly emotional. They tug on our heartstrings to prompt us to action—specifically, to get us to make a financial commitment. They imply that there is an intimate connection between our sympathetic feelings and our sense of moral obligation. We can *feel* that it is our duty to assist these needy children. However, some philosophers believe that such emotional appeals are manipulative and have nothing to do with morality. True morality, they argue, is purely rational and must be free from all emotional considerations. Although we naturally feel pangs of sympathy for people in need, true morality requires that we set these feelings aside and base our judgments on the cool and impartial dictates of reason. Other philosophers, though, disagree, arguing that moral judgments have little to do with human reason. We are morally motivated by emotions, and our moral assessments of other people are basically emotional reactions.

During the eighteenth century, British moral philosophers hotly debated the role of reason versus that of emotions in moral matters. Several philosophers of the early eighteenth century took the hard-line position that morality is strictly a matter of rational judgment. Perhaps the most famous advocate of this view is **Samuel Clarke (1675–1729)**. Clarke's chief opponent was **David Hume (1711–1776)**, who argued that moral approval is not a rational judgment, but a pleasing emotion that we experience when we observe someone's conduct. We will look at this eighteenth-century dispute between reason and emotion and consider the impact of this discussion on later moral philosophy.

Clarke's Rationalist Theory

Since the time of the Greek philosopher Plato, philosophers frequently have argued that moral truths exist in a spiritual realm and that we access these moral truths through a special rational faculty. The theory of natural law forged in the Middle Ages perpetuated this view, holding that moral truths are embedded in nature. Clarke lived during the tail end of this tradition. Many of the great figures in natural law theory, such as Hugo Grotius (1583–1645), emphasized the *political* implications of natural law—specifically, how we form governments and international laws. Clarke, though, focused mainly on the *moral* implications of natural law and on how we, as ordinary people, discover moral truths through the use of our reason.

Eternal Moral Relations   Clarke's central message is simple: Moral truths, like mathematical truths, are eternal. And just as we access mathematical truths through reason alone, we also access moral truths through reason alone. According to Clarke, mathematical truths rest on *relations* between numbers—in particular, the relations of "greater than," "less than," and "equal to":

> That there are differences of things; and different relations, respects or proportions, of some things towards others; is as evident and undeniable, as that

one magnitude or number, is greater, equal to, or smaller than another. (*Discourse*, 1)

Moreover, Clarke says, these mathematical relations have fixed and eternal meanings, which even God can't change. We rationally grasp these mathematical notions and use them in our ordinary lives. For example, I might state that "the money in my bank account is *less than* the money in my attorney's bank account." This statement is true if it lives up to the ideal mathematical meaning of "less than." In Clarke's words, my statement will be *fit* or *proportioned* with respect to the mathematical relation of "less than."

Clarke continues that there are also nonmathematical eternal laws, which he calls "laws of righteousness." Just as mathematical laws are grounded in eternal mathematical relations, moral laws are grounded in **moral relations.** Clarke lists three specific laws of righteousness, each of which involves a distinct moral relation. First, there is the law of righteousness toward God, which hinges on the relation of "infinite greatness." Since God is infinitely great in comparison to us, then it is fit or proportioned for us to worship and adore God. The second law of righteousness is the "law of equity," which involves dealing with others in ways that are right and just. For Clarke, the law of equity hinges on a relation of equity that exists between people, and this relation is simply the **Golden Rule:** "Whatever I judge reasonable or unreasonable for another to do for me; that, by the same judgment, I declare reasonable or unreasonable, and I in the like case should do for him." For example, it would be unreasonable for me to steal my neighbor's lawnmower, since I would find it unreasonable for him to steal my lawnmower. When I follow the Golden Rule, my actions are fit and proportioned to this relation of equity. By and large, the law of equity demands only that we avoid *harming* others in ways that we ourselves would not want to be harmed. However, Clarke argues that the third law of righteousness moves beyond the issue of harm and instead mandates us to more actively promote the well-being of others. This third law is the "law of benevolence," which hinges on a relation of doing the greatest good. This law requires us to help others in need and, more generally, to strive to make the world a better place.

Just as even God can't alter mathematical laws and their relations, Clarke argues, God can't alter the three laws of righteousness and their relations. Further, just as our knowledge of mathematical relations is self-evident and purely rational, so, too, is our knowledge of moral relations. In fact, Clarke says, these moral relations are so self-evident that it would be ridiculous to deny them:

> These things are so notoriously plain and self-evident, that nothing but the extremest stupidity of Mind, corruption of Manners, or perverseness of Spirit can possibly make any Man entertain the least doubt concerning them. For a Man endued with Reason, to deny the Truth of these Things, is the very same thing, as if a Man that has the use of his Sight, should at the same time that he beholds the Sun, deny that there is any such thing as Light in the World; or as if a Man that understands Geometry or Arithmetic, should deny the most obvious and known Proportions of Lines or Numbers, and perversely contend

that the whole is not equal to all its parts, or that a Square is not double to a triangle of equal base and height. (*Discourse*, 1)

In other words, it is as stupid for a rational person to deny the existence of moral relations as it is for a person with eyes to deny that the sun shines. Clarke goes on to note that these moral relations are binding on all beings who can rationally intuit them. And as a supremely rational being, God can flawlessly intuit these moral relations and will carry them out in practice. Humans are rational as well, and so can perceive moral relations and are bound by them. However, our reason is limited, and we are distracted by our human emotions. Also, through improper upbringing, our rational abilities might become corrupted. So, unlike God, we are morally fallible.

To summarize, here are the main points of Clarke's theory:

- There are three eternal laws of righteousness—namely, worship of God, equity, and benevolence, which rest on three related moral relations.
- Our knowledge of moral relations is purely rational and self-evident to all humans, just as is our knowledge of mathematical relations.
- We judge the fitness or unfitness of our actions in reference to these eternal moral relations.
- Although we are morally bound by these eternal moral relations, our finite reason and human emotions sometimes prevent us from realizing proper moral motivation.

Clarke didn't think that his list of the laws of righteousness was particularly original, and he states that a more detailed list of our various duties "may easily be supplied abundantly out of several late excellent writers." What is unique to Clarke, though, is his notion of moral relations and the way these parallel mathematical relations.

Hume's Criticisms of Clarke   Hume thought that natural law philosophers were wrong about the eternal status of moral truths and also about the role of reason in making moral judgments. In attacking this tradition, Hume focuses specifically on Clarke's theory of moral relations. According to Hume, moral assessments can't be judgments about relations since we find exactly the same relations in both moral and nonmoral situations. To make this point, Hume compares the case of a young tree killing its parent tree to that of a man killing one of his parents:

Let us chuse any inanimate object, such as an oak or elm; and let us suppose, that by the dropping of its seed, it produces a sapling below it, which springing up by degrees, at last overtops and destroys the parent tree: I ask, if in this instance there be wanting any relation, which is discoverable in parricide or ingratitude? (*A Treatise of Human Nature*, 3.1.1)

Hume suggests here that it is no moral crime when a young tree overgrows and kills its parent tree, but it *is* a moral crime when someone like the Roman emperor Nero kills his mother. Since both of these situations exhibit the same relation, then moral assessments must be different from rational judgments about relations. Stated more precisely, Hume's argument is this:

1. Anything that exhibits a given moral relation should be judged good or bad accordingly. (Clarke's target supposition)
2. A young tree overgrowing and killing its parent exhibits the same relation as Nero killing his mother.
3. Since Nero's act is morally bad, then so, too, is that of the young tree.
4. Clearly, this is absurd; hence, it is false that anything that exhibits a given moral relation should be judged good or bad accordingly.

On the face of it, Hume's argument appears weak, particularly regarding premise 2. There is a big difference between Nero killing his mother and a young tree overgrowing and causing the death of its parent. Nero acted with a *motive,* but young trees are not the kind of things that can have motives. In response to Hume's attack, then, Clarke would simply reject premise 2. But Hume anticipates this problem and challenges us to specify *exactly* the kind of relation exhibited between Nero and his mother. Suppose that Clarke says that the relation involves ill will in Nero's motive regarding his mother; young trees clearly don't have motives of ill will. According to Hume, that particular relation won't work since we would all be guilty of a moral crime any time we felt ill will toward another person, even when we never actually acted on that feeling. To avoid this conclusion, suppose, instead, that Clarke locates the relation in Nero's *action* toward his mother rather than his motive. For Hume, that relation won't work either since it would apply to nonhuman things that don't have motives, such as trees, and we are back where we started. So, premise 2 in Hume's argument is stronger than we might initially think.

However, there is a third option that Hume doesn't consider. Instead of looking at *either* motives *or* actions, suppose that we look at what philosophers call "intentional actions." Some of our actions are nonintentional, such as seizures, sneezes, and coughs; they just happen without any planning or purpose on our part. Other actions, though, are intimately connected with some intended goal, such as when I brush my teeth or when Nero kills his mother. Although trees might exhibit nonintentional movements, such as swaying in the wind or growing toward the sun, they certainly don't exhibit intentional action. Based on this understanding, Clarke could say that Nero's act is wrong since it displays the relation of an intentional act of killing an innocent person. This relation won't apply to people who simply have bad thoughts, nor will it apply to young trees. So, Hume's argument against Clarke fails.

Although Hume's young-tree argument doesn't successfully refute Clarke, Hume offers two additional arguments that are more compelling. First, Hume argues that, when we closely examine the contents of any morally significant action, such as a murder, we will never locate a special moral fact or moral relation about which we can make a rational judgment. All that we will find is our own feelings. Second, Hume asks us to consider whether moral assessments are more like rational judgments, such as "4 is greater than 3," or more like aesthetic pronouncements, such as "This painting is beautiful." Hume believes that moral assessments are clearly more like aesthetic pronouncements—and thus are feelings, and not rational judgments. Hume's point in both of these arguments is that we can easily see the emotional component of moral assessments, but we can't so easily articulate the rational component. Although a diehard rationalist like Clarke might still insist that the rational component is obvious, most of us will probably agree that the emotional component is more obvious.

Hume summarizes his attack on moral rationalism in what has become one of the most famous passages in Western moral philosophy, in which he lays out the *is/ought* problem:

> In every system of morality which I have hitherto met with, I have always remarked that the author proceeds for some time in the ordinary way of reasoning, and establishes the being of a God, or makes observations concerning human affairs. When [all] of a sudden I am surprised to find that, instead of the usual copulations of propositions, *is* and *isn't,* I meet with no proposition that isn't connected with an *ought* or an *ought not.* The change is imperceptible, but is, however, of the last [and greatest] consequence. For as this *ought* or *ought not* expresses some new relation or affirmation, it is necessary that it should be observed and explained. And at the same time, [it is necessary] that a reason should be given for (what seems altogether inconceivable) how this new relation can be a deduction from others, which are entirely different from it. (*A Treatise of Human Nature,* 3.1.1)

Hume's point is that rationalistic discussions of morality all begin with statements of fact, such as "Daniel is starving," and then conclude with statements of obligation, such as "We should help feed Daniel." According to Hume, we can't simply rationally deduce statements of obligation from statements of fact. Even if it is a fact that Daniel is starving, we need our emotions to make the assessment that we should help feed Daniel. Clarke's blunder is that he claims as a point of fact that there are eternal relations and then concludes that we ought to follow these relations as laws of righteousness. Contemporary moral philosophers encapsulate Hume's point with the slogan that, "We cannot derive *ought* from *is.*" That is, we can't rationally deduce statements of obligation from statements of fact. No collection of facts will ever entail a judgment of value, so values must come from another source.

Hume's Moral Theory

Once Hume dispenses with Clarke's notion of moral rationalism, he then explains in more detail how emotion is involved in moral assessments. Hume was inspired by several earlier British moral philosophers who proposed that we have a **moral sense** that enables us to perceive and assess right and wrong conduct.

Early Moral Sense Theories   The first British writer to use the term "moral sense" was **Anthony Ashley Cooper** (1671–1713), better known as the Earl of Shaftesbury. In his *Inquiry Concerning Virtue or Merit* (1699), Shaftesbury maintains that our moral sense perceives moral qualities in much the same way that our eyes perceive colors:

> The case is the same in mental or moral subjects, as in [our sense perceptions of] ordinary bodies, or the common subjects of sense. The shapes, motions, colors, and proportions of these latter being presented to our eye, there necessarily results a beauty or deformity, according to the different measure, arrangement and disposition of their several parts. So in behavior and actions, when presented to our understanding, there must be found, of necessity, an apparent difference, according to the regularity or irregularity of the subjects.

Although Shaftesbury doesn't give a detailed description of our moral sense, he apparently takes the notion of "sense" literally and is willing to classify it as a sixth sense. This literal understanding of the moral sense is in part based on a broad definition of "sense perception." For example, British philosopher John Locke (1632–1704) broadly defines the notion of sense perception here:

> When I say the senses convey into the mind, I mean, they from external Objects convey into the mind what produces there those *Perceptions*. (*Essay Concerning Human Understanding*, 2.1.3)

Based on Locke's definition, any mental faculty that can convey external qualities may be called a "sense."

Shaftesbury's suggestion took hold, and other moral philosophers developed the notion of the moral sixth sense in greater detail. The most influential of these was Irish philosopher **Francis Hutcheson** (1694–1747), who interpreted the notion of moral sense literally:

> [The] power of receiving these [moral] perceptions may be called a moral sense, since the definition [of "sense"] agrees to it, viz. a determination of the mind, to receive any idea from the presence of an object which occurs to us, independent on our will. (*Inquiry Concerning Moral Good and Evil*, 1.1)

According to Hutcheson, all of our senses involve two things: (1) an *object* that we perceive and (2) a mental *perception* that we form in response. For example, with my sense of sight, I am presented with a physical object, such as a chair, and I form a visual perception of that object in my mind. Similarly, the objects of my moral sense are benevolent actions that people perform, such as donating to charity; the mental perception that I form is a feeling of pleasure. For Hutcheson, then, my moral sense enables me to detect benevolence in an action, and my subsequent feeling of pleasure constitutes my approval of that benevolent action.

Hume not only read Hutcheson's description of the moral sense but knew Hutcheson personally and corresponded with him. In his own moral theory, Hume downplays the literal notion of "moral sense" proposed by Hutcheson, but he nevertheless agrees with Hutcheson's main point: Moral approval is a pleasing feeling, and not a rational judgment.

The Moral Spectator's Sympathetic Feelings Most simply, Hume's theory is that moral approval is only a pleasing feeling that we experience when we observe good conduct. When I see someone donate to charity, I sympathetically feel pleasure for the receiver of that donation. And if I see someone steal a car, I sympathetically feel pain for the car owner. The experience of pleasure *is* my moral approval, and the experience of pain *is* my moral disapproval. Hume states his basic view here:

> Moral distinctions depend entirely on certain peculiar sentiments of pain and pleasure, and that whatever mental quality in ourselves or others gives us a satisfaction, by the survey or reflexion, is of course virtuous; as every thing of this nature, that gives uneasiness, is vicious. (*A Treatise of Human Nature*, 3.3.1)

Hume's account of morality involves a complex chain of events featuring three players: a moral agent, a receiver, and a moral spectator. The **moral agent** is the person who performs an action, such as donating to charity or stealing a car. The **receiver** is the person directly affected by the agent's action, such as the person who receives charity or the victim who gets his or her car stolen. The **moral spectator** is the person who observes or imagines the receiver and makes a moral assessment about the agent. All moral assessments start with an agent's motivated action, extend through the consequences to a receiver, and end with sympathetic feelings of pleasure or pain in the mind of a spectator.

When moral spectators pass judgment on the actions of moral agents, there are distinct psychological events going on in the minds of all parties involved, which we can chart in this way:

Agent	*Receiver*	*Spectator*
Character trait leading to an action	Useful or agreeable consequences	Sympathetic pleasure/pain

To illustrate these various psychological components, suppose that you (the agent) donate to Save the Children specifically to help improve the life of Daniel (the receiver). I (the spectator) judge your act of charity to be morally good. According to Hume, my feelings of moral approval are in response to your character trait as reflected in your action. Hume also argues that your character trait is the motive behind your action, and your trait either will be instinctive or will have been acquired through social conditioning. In this case, your act of charity is motivated by benevolence, which, according to Hume, is largely an instinctive character trait.

If we suppose that Save the Children does its job properly, then your act of charity will have a direct impact on Daniel's life. Specifically, you will make him happier than he would otherwise be. According to Hume, there are two types of effects stemming from morally approvable actions: (1) The action will be *immediately agreeable* to the receiver and thereby directly give him or her pleasure, and (2) the action will be *useful* to the receiver and indirectly give him or her pleasure. In Daniel's case, he will be immediately pleased by your simple act of charity *in and of itself*, and he will also be pleased by the *use* that his family can make of the donated money, such as providing him with more food. In both cases, Daniel experiences pleasure from your charitable act.

As a spectator, I can personally witness or at least imagine the pleasure that Daniel experiences through your act of charity. Once I observe Daniel's pleasure, I, too, will experience pleasure for him vicariously or, in Hume's words, "sympathetically." Hume uses the term "sympathy" in a literal sense, as a human instinct by which a receiver's emotions are *transferred* to a spectator. An illustration from physics will help explain this literal notion of sympathy. Imagine that I have two acoustic guitars side by side. If I pluck the low E string on one guitar, then the low E string on the second guitar will automatically vibrate, without my even touching the second guitar. Physicists refer to this phenomenon as the "sympathetic vibration of strings." Analogously, Hume describes what we may call a "sympathetic transference of emotion." If Daniel experiences pleasure because of your donation, then that pleasure will be transferred to me, and I will be pleased as well. My sense of pleasure, then, constitutes my moral approval of your benevolent motive. That is, my feeling of pleasure *is* my moral approval of you. I then deem that your initial character trait is a virtue as opposed to a vice.

According to Hume, all moral assessments follow the preceding formula, even when we decide that a person is morally bad. Suppose you steal your neighbor's car. Again, you are the agent, but this time you are motivated to steal because you have an unjust character trait concerning property rights. Your unjust act of stealing has negative consequences for your neighbor's life. First, your neighbor will be immediately outraged simply because you took something of hers; second, she will be inconvenienced. For both of these reasons, she will experience emotional pain. And when I, as the spectator, see your neighbor's pain, I will experience her pain sympathetically. My pain, then, constitutes my moral condemnation of your unjust character trait, which I thereby deem to be a vice.

The radical part of Hume's theory is that moral assessments aren't rational judgments, as Clarke and other moral rationalists believed, but only feelings in the mind of the moral spectator. Hume boldly makes this point here:

> To have the sense of virtue, is nothing but to *feel* a satisfaction of a particular kind from the contemplation of a character. The very *feeling* constitutes our praise or admiration. We go no farther; nor do we enquire into the cause of the satisfaction. (*A Treatise of Human Nature,* 3.1.2)

For Hume, the spectator's feelings are the final authority in moral assessments, and we can't seek for a further explanation of moral assessment beyond these. In addition to his radical claims about the spectator's moral approval, Hume made equally daring claims about the nature of moral motivation and God's role in morality.

Moral Motivation and Morality without God   For the sake of argument, let's grant Hume's point that the spectator's moral approval is an emotion, and

not a rational judgment. There is still the question of what motivates the agent to perform a given action to begin with. For example, what specifically provokes you as an agent to donate to Save the Children or to perform any other moral action? According to Clarke, your *reason* tells you that it is the right thing to do, and so your *reason* motivates you to act. According to Hume, though, for any action that you perform as an agent, you are only motivated to act from *emotion,* and never from reason. Reason is inert and won't by itself incline us to do anything even if our lives depend on it. Hume illustrates his view here:

> It is not contrary to reason to prefer the destruction of the whole world to the scratching of my finger. It is not contrary to reason for me to chuse my total ruin, to prevent the least uneasiness of an *Indian* or person wholly unknown to me. It is as little contrary to reason to prefer even my own acknowledged lesser good to my greater, and have a more ardent affection for the former than the latter. (*A Treatise of Human Nature,* 2.3.3)

Although a little extreme, Hume's basic observation is correct: *Something* must motivate us to prefer one thing over another, but even a truckload of reasons won't motivate us. According to Hume, human reason addresses only issues of truth and falsehood, such as whether it is true or false that children are starving in Third World countries. However, reason is completely indifferent to what it determines, and reason won't get us to act in one way or another. So, without emotion, there is nothing to keep me from preferring the destruction of the whole world to the scratching of my finger.

Even though reason won't motivate us to act in any way whatsoever, Hume concedes that reason plays a minor role as an information gatherer. Specifically, reason helps us discover facts that we might emotionally respond to—such as facts about the specific countries in which people are starving. But I still need emotions to make me prefer to do something about it. In Hume's words, "Reason is, and ought only to be, the slave of the passions, and can never pretend to any other office than to serve and obey them."

In short, Hume believes that moral rationalists are misguided about both the spectator's evaluation of moral conduct and the agent's motivation for acting. Hume pushes this a step further and concludes that morality is a purely human phenomenon—involving only human emotion—and has no relation to God. Hume makes his case most clearly in one of his letters to Hutcheson:

> If morality were determined by reason, that [determination] is the same to all rational beings. But nothing but experience can assure us that the sentiments are the same. What experience have we with regard to superior beings? How can we ascribe to them any sentiments at all? They have implanted those sentiments in us for the conduct of life like our bodily sensations, which they possess not themselves. (March 16, 1740)

In this passage, Hume gives two reasons for denying that morality applies to superior rational beings, such as God or angels. First, moral feelings depend on a physical body, which God and angels lack. This means that spiritual beings cannot be emotionally motivated to act in the way that human moral agents are motivated. This also means that spiritual beings won't have sympathetic feelings of moral approval in the way that human spectators have such feelings. Second, it is only through experience that we can conclude that all *human* beings have similar moral feelings. Since we have no experience of *superior* beings, we cannot draw similar conclusions about their moral nature.

Hume's moral theory seems to be the first account of ethics since ancient Greece and Rome that doesn't involve the existence of God. Some philosophers during the modern period, such as Grotius and Hobbes, tried to minimize God's involvement in moral matters. However, these philosophers still maintained that God endorses the same moral values that we do and that God also urges us to be moral. According to Hume, though, even if God exists, morality doesn't appear to have anything to do with God.

To recap, here are the main points of Hume's theory:

- Moral agents perform actions that are motivated by either instinctive or acquired character traits and, in either case, are sparked by emotions, not reason.
- Receivers experience pleasure (pain) either immediately from the agent's action or from the usefulness (inconvenience) of that action.
- Moral spectators sympathetically experience pleasure (pain) when observing the receiver's pleasure (pain).
- The moral spectator's pleasure (pain) constitutes his or her moral assessment of the agent's character trait, thereby deeming the trait to be a virtue (vice).

Criticisms of Hume

When Hume's moral theory first appeared, reactions were almost unanimously critical. One opponent accused Hume of "sapping the foundations of morality" insofar as Hume links morality exclusively with human psychological makeup. Most moral philosophers agreed with Hume that feelings play *some* role in moral assessment, but they attacked him for making moral assessment *exclusively* a matter of emotion. The most articulate critic to make this point was Scottish philosopher **Thomas Reid** (1710–1796).

Reid's First Criticism: Hume Abuses Common Moral Language   Shortly after Hume's death, Reid published a detailed critique of Hume's moral theory, which, even today, remains one of the most insightful discussions of Hume. Reid agreed with Hume that the moral spectator in fact does have an emotional response to the agent's action. However, for Reid, the emotional reaction is only of secondary importance. Like Clarke, Reid held that true moral assessment is a rational judgment, and our emotional reaction is almost like an afterthought. According to Reid, Hume's theory fails because it blurs the distinction between the spectator's rational assessment and emotional response.

Reid makes his point with two distinct arguments. Reid's first argument is straightforward: Our common use of moral language shows that moral assessments are really *rational* judgments, and Hume abuses the language by linking moral terms with the spectator's feelings:

> When Mr Hume derives moral distinctions from a moral sense, I agree with him in words, but we differ about the meaning of the word *sense*. Every power to which the name of a sense has been given, is a power of judging of the objects of that sense, and has been accounted such in all ages; the moral sense therefore is the power of judging in morals. But Mr Hume will have the moral sense to be only a power of feeling, without judging: This I take to be an abuse of a word. (*Essays on the Active Powers of Man*, 5.7)

Reid argues that we all can clearly distinguish between a spectator's report about feelings and his or her rational judgment about an agent's action. And, based on how we in fact use common moral terms, we all clearly understand that moral assessment is a rational judgment, and not a report of feelings. Hume, though, abuses the moral language by giving key moral terms an unconventional meaning; specifically, he implicitly defines "moral sense" to mean only a power of feeling, without any rational judgment. Not only does Hume do this with moral sense but, Reid argues, he also does this with the terms "decision," "determination," "approbation," "praise," and several others. So, according to Reid, if Hume had paid attention to how we commonly use moral terms, then he would have seen that moral assessment is a rational judgment, and not a report about feelings.

But if Reid is correct that common language is so clear about moral assessment, then how did Hume manage to even get his theory published? According to Reid, Hume plays a trick with language by carefully selecting specific terms, such as "approval," that in English commonly involve both a rational judgment *and* an emotional reaction. So, if Hume says, "Moral assessment only involves a spectator's approval," we initially agree, since our common notion of approval has a rational component. However, Hume then pulls the wool over our eyes by explaining that "approval" means only that a spectator feels pleasure. We agree with this, too, since our common notion of "approval" also has an emotional component. As logicians say, Hume equivocates on the term "approval" by secretly playing off of two meanings of a single word.

For the sake of argument, let's grant Reid's point that Hume equivocates on key moral terms such as "approval" when Hume claims that moral assessments are *only* reports of feelings. However, we can accuse Reid and other moral rationalists of doing the same thing. As Reid himself notes, the common meaning of the word "approval" includes both a rational *and* an emotional component. When Reid and others emphasize the rational component of moral approval, they then ignore the built-in emotional component of this term. Even the term "judgment" has an emotional component in common language. For example, when I "judge" that a hamburger doesn't taste as good as a cheeseburger or that the blue curtains don't look as nice as the green curtains, these clearly involve emotional reactions. Almost any similar term that we use for moral assessment will include an emotional component. In our common moral discourse, we rarely use purely rational terms such as "deduce"—as in, for example, "I deduce that it is wrong for Smith to kill Jones." Instead, we select terms that have both an emotional and a rational component. So, our common moral language in fact indicates that moral assessment is not purely a matter of rational judgment but also involves an emotional response.

In short, although Reid attacks Hume for restricting moral approval to a spectator's emotions, at best Reid shows only that there is *some* rational component to morality along with an emotional component. And it isn't clear from Reid's observations whether reason or emotion play the dominant role. Perhaps reason plays only a secondary role as a "slave of the passions" as Hume suggests. Common language alone won't settle this.

Reid's Second Criticism: Reporting Feelings Differs from Approving

Reid's second argument against Hume is that reporting my feelings about an agent's conduct isn't logically equivalent to my approving of an agent's conduct. To make his point, Reid asks us to compare two statements such as these:

1. I (the spectator) *approve* of an agent's conduct.
2. An agent's conduct gave me (the spectator) an *agreeable feeling.*

According to Hume's theory, the two statements are essentially the same since my approval of an agent's conduct is *identical* to a specific agreeable feeling that I experience. However, contrary to Hume, Reid argues that the two statements are not at all the same. The first expresses an assessment about the agent, whereas the second merely testifies that the spectator had a feeling. This difference becomes more apparent when we examine the logical relation between the two statements, as Reid describes here:

> The first [statement] may be contradicted without any ground of offence, such contradiction being only a difference of opinion, which, to a reasonable man, gives no offence. But the second speech cannot be contradicted without an affront; for, as every man must know his own feelings, to deny that a man had a feeling which he affirms he had, is to charge him with falsehood. (*Essays on the Active Powers of Man,* 5.7)

Suppose, Reid suggests, that we negate the first sentence and at the same time assert the second:

1. *It is not the case that* I approve of an agent's conduct.
2. An agent's conduct gave me an agreeable feeling.

If Hume's theory is correct, then we would contradict ourselves if we asserted these two statements at the same time. For Reid, however, it is totally plausible that I could disapprove of an agent's conduct yet at the same time have an agreeable feeling about that agent's conduct. Take Robin Hood, for example, who stole from the rich and gave to the poor. I may disapprove of the fact that he stole, but I may still feel good about Robin Hood's actions if I sympathize with the plight of the poor. So, although Hume believes that statements 1 and 2 are identical, according to Reid they really *aren't* identical since we can meaningfully deny statement 1 even while asserting statement 2.

How might Hume respond? Reid poses a genuine problem that pushes Hume's theory to its limits. If we analyze the Robin Hood case in more detail, we can see precisely how the problem arises. In this situation, Robin Hood is the agent who steals from the rich with the intention of giving to the poor. I am the spectator who feels either pleasure or pain in sympathy with the receivers. Who, though, are the receivers? In this case there are *two* groups of receivers: the rich and the poor. The rich are victims of Robin Hood's thievery, and the poor are beneficiaries of his benevolence. This explains why I can disapprove of Robin Hood's conduct (on behalf of the rich) yet also feel good about it (on behalf of the poor). To be more precise, then, we must reword the two apparently contradictory statements as follows:

1. I disapprove of (i.e., feel bad about) Robin Hood's conduct on behalf of the rich.
2. I approve of (i.e., feel good about) Robin Hood's conduct on behalf of the poor.

Strictly speaking, statements 1 and 2 aren't logically contradictory, since the laws of logic don't prevent me from having mixed and competing feelings about something. So, once we speak more precisely about the object of our disapproval and the object of our agreeable feelings, the contradiction disappears.

Although this solves the apparent logical problem that Reid points out, our solution creates a different problem for Hume. Specifically, we still need to make some definitive moral pronouncement about Robin Hood's conduct: Should we approve of it or disapprove of it? Four options suggest themselves in cases like Robin Hood's, in which a single action has good consequences for one receiver and bad consequences for another receiver:

1. We should side with our feeling of approval (on behalf of the poor).
2. We should side with the feeling of disapproval (on behalf of the rich).
3. We should compare the approval against the disapproval, and side with the strongest one.
4. We should both approve and disapprove of Robin Hood's conduct at the same time.

Hume simply didn't address this issue. If we speak on behalf of Hume, though, the best solution seems to be option 3. That is, we should consider all the positive and negative consequences of the agent's action for all receivers affected and then endorse the action if it produces a stronger feeling of approval than disapproval.

The Value of Hume's Theory

Hume's moral theory involves an interplay between (1) the agent's character trait, (2) the consequences of the agent's action on the receiver, and (3) the spectator's sympathetic feeling of approval or disapproval. Hume's immediate critics, such as Reid, focused mainly on this third component in the belief that

Hume's fundamental contribution to moral theory concerned the role of the moral spectator. However, in the years following Reid, moral philosophers became more intrigued by the second component—specifically, Hume's view that an agent's actions have useful and agreeable consequences for the receiver. When Hume spoke about an agent's "useful" consequences, he often used the word "utility" as a synonym. So, according to this next generation of moral philosophers, the heart of Hume's theory was his **theory of utility**—namely, that morality involves assessing the pleasing and painful consequences of actions on the receiver.

Utilitarianism and the Fate of the Agent and Spectator   By the late eighteenth century—about ten years after Hume's death—many moral philosophers latched onto Hume's "theory of utility," as it was then commonly called. One of these was **William Paley** (1743–1805), a religiously conservative philosopher who made a name for himself by writing books that defended God's existence and the Christian faith. In his first published book, *The Principles of Moral and Political Philosophy* (1785), Paley adopts Hume's theory of utility and argues that we should act in ways that bring about the most pleasure. However, Paley gives his theory a Christian spin by arguing that we should maximize utility since God wants us to be happy. Paley's book quickly became a standard ethics textbook in many British and American universities, and this greatly increased the popularity of the theory of utility. A second important philosopher who was influenced by Hume was **Jeremy Bentham** (1748–1832). Bentham endorsed social contract theory in his youth but writes that, after reading Hume's account of utility, "I felt as if scales had fallen from my eyes." In his *Introduction to the Principles of Morals and Legislation* (1789), Bentham greatly enlarges on Hume's theory of utility and provides the foundation for nineteenth-century discussions of utilitarianism.

Although Paley and Bentham were advocates of Hume's general view of utility, they both strongly rejected the role of the spectator in moral decision making that Hume believed was so important. Bentham argued specifically that if you—as a spectator—appeal to your feelings as a way of determining morality, then you make right and wrong "just what you please to make them." According to Bentham, your feelings are too whimsical, and relying on them would make you despotic or dictatorial. Just as Paley and Bentham rejected the role of the spectator's sympathetic feelings, later utilitarian philosophers rejected the role of the agent's character traits. British philosopher **John Stuart Mill** (1806–1873) makes a clear argument for rejecting considerations of the agent's mental dispositions:

> It is often affirmed that utilitarianism renders men cold and unsympathizing; that it chills their moral feelings toward individuals; that it makes them regard only the dry and hard considerations of the consequences of actions, not taking into their moral estimate the qualities from which those actions estimate.... [I answer that] These considerations are relevant, not to the estimation of actions, but of persons ... (*Utilitarianism,* 2)

According to Mill, an act isn't made right simply because it is performed by someone who has a noble character trait. Instead, it is only the *consequences* of an act that make it right or wrong.

The thrust of the utilitiarian approach after Hume was that the only things that matter in morality are the *consequences* of an agent's action on the receiver. The agent's character traits are not particularly relevant, and neither are the spectator's feelings. In essence, utilitarians snipped off both the agent and the spectator parts of Hume's system, leaving only the pleasing and painful consequences as they affect receivers. Utilitarians such as Bentham and Mill believed that it is important to make moral judgments as scientific and objective as possible. Emphasis on the mental states of agents and spectators muddles the process, and the most objective procedure is simply to inspect the balance of pleasure and pain as affects all receivers. The outcome of this inspection then will constitute our moral judgment. This involves only a little observation and a little calculation, which anyone can do objectively. It is roughly the same kind of empirical assessment that I make when I say, for example, that "Smith has more hair on his head than Jones has on his head."

Time, though, seems to have vindicated Hume in the face of utilitarian efforts to eliminate the roles of agent and spectator from moral theories. In recent years, many moral philosophers have come to the defense of **virtue theory**—a theory that stresses the importance of the agent's character traits in moral assessment. For virtue theorists, when we judge people's actions, we in fact make pronouncements against their habitual traits, along with all the social history that contributed in forming those traits. Similarly, contemporary philosophers of language maintain that the role of the spectator is central to understanding the meaning of moral assessments. Some philosophers go so far as to say that morality involves *only* a consideration of the spectator's emotional response to a given situation. The genius of Hume's theory is that it links together the views of the virtue theorist concerning the agent, the utilitarian concerning the receiver, and the language philosopher concerning the spectator.

Summary

We can summarize the various views presented here by returning to the issue of charity. All moral theorists believe that charity is one of our chief moral obligations. Clarke believed that we're obligated to be charitable since there exists an eternal moral relation of benevolence, which we immediately grasp through our reason. As a moral agent, my sheer awareness of this relation should motivate me to act charitably. As a spectator, you have a rational ability to judge eternal truths, including eternal truths about charity. Hume criticized Clarke for deriving *ought* from *is*—that is, for beginning with the factual claim about eternal relations and concluding that we ought to follow these relations as laws of righteousness. Hume argued that charity begins with an instinctive motive in the mind of the spectator, has useful and agreeable consequences for the receiver, and produces a feeling of moral pleasure in the mind of the spectator.

Hume also argued that when I, as an agent, donate to charity, I am motivated completely by emotion, and not by reason. Hume maintained that morality has nothing to do with God since morality is rooted in human physical makeup, whereas God is a spirit and does not have any physical emotional makeup.

Reid criticized Hume for abusing common moral language by downplaying the rational component of terms like "approval." In response, we saw that rationalists such as Reid also abuse the language by downplaying the emotional component of such terms as "approval" and "judgment." Reid also criticized Hume for failing to distinguish between the act of moral approval and a report of one's feelings, but Hume consistently identifies the two. A key benefit of Hume's theory is that it connects together the concerns of virtue theorists, utilitarians, and language philosophers.

Study Questions

Introduction
1. What do some critics say about emotional appeals in moral matters, such as those used by Save the Children?

Clarke's Rationalist Theory
Eternal Moral Relations
2. What is an example of a *mathematical* relation as Clarke understands the notion?
3. What is an example of a *moral* relation as Clarke understands the notion?
4. What are the four main points of Clarke's theory?

Hume's Criticisms of Clarke
5. Explain Hume's argument regarding Nero and the young tree.
6. How does the notion of an "intentional action" refute Hume's argument comparing Nero and the young tree?
7. What are Hume's two additional arguments against Clarke?
8. What is meant by the statement "We cannot derive *ought* from *is*"?

Hume's Moral Theory
Early Moral Sense Theories
9. What is Locke's definition of a sense perception?
10. According to Hutcheson, what are the objects and mental perceptions of the moral sense?

The Moral Spectator's Sympathetic Feelings
11. Briefly describe the roles of the agent, receiver, and spectator in Hume's moral theory.
12. Explain what happens when I (as the spectator) morally approve of your charitable action (as an agent).

Moral Motivation and Morality without God

13. What does Hume mean by the statement "It is not contrary to reason to prefer the destruction of the whole world to the scratching of my finger"?
14. According to Hume, why is morality a purely human phenomenon that has no relation to God?

Criticisms of Hume

Reid's First Criticism: Hume Abuses Common Moral Language

15. What is Reid's main criticism of Hume's account of moral assessments?
16. As to Reid's first criticism, how does Hume "abuse" common moral language?
17. According to Fieser, how does Reid himself equivocate on moral terms?

Reid's Second Criticism: Reporting Feelings Differs from Approving

18. As to Reid's second criticism, how does the Robin Hood story illustrate the difference between reporting one's feelings about an agent, and approving the agent's conduct?
19. Hume's theory raises the problem of how we pass moral judgment on a single action that has both good and bad consequences for different receivers. According to Fieser, how might we resolve this problem?

The Value of Hume's Theory

Utilitarianism and the Fate of the Agent and Spectator

20. What reason does Bentham give for rejecting the role of the spectator in moral assessments?
21. What reason does Mill give for rejecting the role of the agent's character traits in moral assessments?
22. What do the recent virtue theory and language philosophy movements say about the roles of agent and spectator, respectively?

References

The quotations by Samuel Clarke are from *A Discourse Concerning the Unchangeable Obligations of Natural Religion* (1706). This text is available in reprints of Clarke's collected *Works* (1738) and in *British Moralists,* edited by D. D. Raphael (Indianapolis: Hackett, 1969).

The quotations by Francis Hutcheson are from *Inquiry Concerning Moral Good and Evil* (1725), included in Raphael's *British Moralists.*

David Hume's moral theory is found in *A Treatise of Human Nature* (1740), Book 3, and *An Enquiry Concerning the Principles of Morals* (1751). Both of these texts are available in several modern editions.

Thomas Reid's critique of Hume is found in his *Essays on the Active Powers of Man* (1788), Essay 5. Reid's text is available in several modern editions. The quotations are from Essay 5, Chapter 7.

The quotation by Jeremy Bentham concerning Hume's influence on him is from *A Fragment on Government* (1776), 1.36, footnote. The quotation concerning the despotism of moral spectator theories is from *Introduction to the Principles of Morals and Legislation* (1789), 2.14, footnote. Both of these are taken from the *The Works of Jeremy Bentham*, edited by John Bowring (London, 1838–43).

The quotation by John Stuart Mill is from *Utilitarianism* (1863), 2, which is available in several modern editions.

Suggestions for Further Reading

For selections from the writings of seventeenth- and eighteenth-century British moral theorists, see L. A. Selby-Bigge, ed., *British Moralists* (Oxford: Clarendon Press, 1897); and D. D. Raphael, ed., *British Moralists: 1650–1800* (Indianapolis: Hackett, 1969).

For a discussion of British moral theories, see W. D. Hudson, *Ethical Intuitionism* (New York: St. Martin's Press, 1967).

For 18th- and 19th-century commentaries on Hume's moral theory, see James Fieser, ed., *Early Responses to Hume's Moral, Literary and Political Writings* (Bristol, England: Thoemmes Press, 1999), Vol. 1.

For commentaries on Hume's moral theory, see Pall S. Ardal, *Passion and Value in Hume's "Treatise"* (Edinburgh: University Press, 1966); J. L. Mackie, *Hume's Moral Theory* (London: Routledge and Kegan Paul, 1980).

10

Kant's Categorical Imperative

Introduction

For 150 years, a section of New York City called the Bowery had a notorious reputation for being home to countless bums and vagrants. Originally a high-profile business district, after the Civil War business shifted to more northern districts of the city, and social and economic activity in the Bowery was confined to seedy entertainment and flophouses. The Bowery became the most famous Skid Row in the country and, in spite of recent economic revitalization, its homeless problems continue today. Here is a sketch of a modern-day Bowery vagrant:

> David was homeless for eight years. He slept in cardboard boxes in the dead of winter. He descended deep into dangerous subway tunnels where the screech of trains shook him from his sleep and where he competed with rats for food. Sometimes the police would chase him out of the subways—even on the coldest of winter nights.

What was typical of the Bowery for over a century is now typical of many parts of large U.S. cities such as Los Angeles, Chicago, Atlanta, and Washington, DC. If you live in or visit these cities, you can't help but notice homeless people camping on sidewalks, wandering the streets, and panhandling from pedestrians. On any given day, there are about 3 million homeless people in the United States, most of whom are male. In addition, there are a growing number of homeless families, which typically consist of a young mother with two children under the age of 6, usually fathered by different men. Because of the increase in such homeless families, about one in four homeless people today are children.

Most of the homeless are victims of circumstances beyond their control, such as domestic violence, poor education, and economic disadvantage. Contrary to stereotypes, only small numbers are mentally ill or drug users. Many have full-time jobs, but earning only the minimum wage, they cannot afford housing, and they may not have families to fall back on for assistance. The presence of this large group of homeless people, a product of irresponsible economic and social policies, should embarrass us all.

Aside from the vast majority of the homeless who clearly deserve our help, there remain about 6 percent of the homeless people who live that way by choice. That in itself is a very large number, totaling about 200,000 people. It is difficult to understand why someone would voluntarily become homeless since this mode of life is far from easy and the hardships probably outweigh any benefits. Perhaps these people simply hate to go to work, or they want the freedom to do nothing, or they don't want to commit themselves to anything stable. They then accept their homelessness as their default condition rather than their preferred way of life. We may not easily sympathize with this group of people and may feel that it is pointless to offer them any meaningful help. We may also feel that—in spite of their problems with organized social life—they have responsibilities to themselves and to society to develop their talents, better their lives, and become productive citizens.

German philosopher **Immanuel Kant** (1724–1804) believed that we have a clear moral responsibility to develop our talents. For Kant, our human reason makes moral demands on our lives. If we think rationally about how we should behave, then we will immediately see that some kinds of actions are unreasonable. Voluntarily living on the street, for Kant, is an unreasonable decision. Many philosophers before Kant also said that morality is linked with the rational part of human nature. Kant goes a step further, though, and formulates a supreme rational principle that tells us precisely whether a specific action is right or wrong. Kant calls this principle the **categorical imperative:** Act only on that maxim by which you can at the same time will that it should become a universal law. According to the categorical imperative, it is wrong for me to voluntarily live on the street since I couldn't reasonably want everyone to live on the street. Kant explains that "activity is part of life's sustenance" and "if a man has no occupation whatever, he loses some of his life-force, and by degrees grows indolent." So, it is unreasonable for me to wish this fate on humanity. If the categorical imperative succeeds as a true test of moral conduct, then it is the most important contribution to moral philosophy ever. All moral controversies would be quickly resolved, and no one could claim ignorance about their moral obligations. But does it succeed? We will look at Kant's account of the categorical imperative and discuss some of its limitations.

Kant's Moral Theory

Kant presents his moral theory in three principal books, published in the final two decades of his life: *Foundations of the Metaphysics of Morals* (1785), *Critique of Practical Reason* (1788), and *Metaphysics of Morals* (1797). The first of these, the *Foundations,* is the most influential, and our discussion of Kant's categorical imperative will come mainly from this.

Influences on Kant's Theory   To understand why Kant devised the categorical imperative as he did, it will help to look at his influences. It often takes detective work to discover the principal influences on major philosophers. Scholars might investigate where a great philosopher was educated and what texts were used in that school. They might comb through the philosopher's personal correspondences to find references to books that he read. They might also discover the contents of a philosopher's personal library by locating records of estate sales after his death. In Kant's case, the task of discovering his influences is easy. Kant was born in Königsberg, a Prussian city of about 70,000 people. He attended the University of Königsberg and later held teaching posts there for forty years. In his writings as both a teacher and scholar, Kant left a clear paper trail indicating various influences on his philosophy.

From the beginning of his university teaching career, Kant offered a course in ethics, and the contents of his lectures were eventually transcribed by some of his students. From these lectures, we know that Kant assigned two standard ethics textbooks written by German philosopher Alexander Baumgarten (1715–1762). Baumgarten's texts discuss in detail the various moral duties that we have to God, ourselves, and others. For example, we have duties to believe in and pray to God, to develop our own intellectual abilities, to be benevolent to others. Eighteenth-century moral philosophers commonly offered similar lists of duties to God, oneself, and others—an approach that was formalized a century earlier by Samuel von Pufendorf (1632–1694). Influenced by Baumgarten and this tradition, Kant also believed that the task of morality is to inform us of our various duties—specifically, duties to ourselves and others.

We also see in his lectures that Kant was influenced by the ethical writings of German philosopher Christian Wolff (1679–1754). Wolff believed that morality involves a quest to make ourselves and others more perfect. According to Wolff, I make myself more perfect by improving my body and mind, and I make others more perfect by helping and not harming them. For Wolff, all of my actions should be directed by this rule: "Do what makes you and your condition, or that of others, more perfect; omit what makes it less perfect." Following the natural law tradition of moral philosophy, Wolff sees this rule as the fundamental law of nature. He also argues that human reason informs us of this rule and guides us in applying it. In contrast to some earlier philosophers, such as Pufendorf, who believed that God invents morality, Wolff argues that this fundamental rule of morality would be obligatory even if God did not exist:

> Because this rule is a law because it obligates, and the obligation comes from nature, the law of nature is validated by nature itself and would hold even if man had no superior who could obligate him to it. In fact it would hold even if there were no God. (*Reasonable Thoughts on Human Action*, 1.1.23)

Kant adopted different components of Wolff's view of morality. First, like Wolff, Kant believes that we can express our moral obligation in a single principle. But Kant rejects Wolff's specific moral principle and instead proposes the categorical imperative, which Kant believes better captures our duty dictated by reason. Second, like Wolff, Kant wholeheartedly believes that morality comes from the authority of human reason and isn't simply invented by God. Kant states that "no one, not even God, can be the author of the laws of morality, since they have no origin in will, but instead a practical necessity." Both Wolff and Kant believe that morality cannot arise from authoritarian mandates. This is not surprising given that in the eighteenth century many writers rejected traditional authorities in a variety of areas including religion, politics, and academics. The only true guideline is human reason, and an enlightened person will follow his or her reason rather than the arbitrary edicts of self-proclaimed authorities. Kant clearly expresses this attitude in a brief essay on the subject of enlightenment:

> Nothing is required for this enlightenment, however, except *freedom;* and the freedom in question is the least harmful of all, namely, the freedom to use reason *publicly* in all matters. ("An Answer to the Question: What Is Enlightenment?")

Kant continues by noting that we hear authoritarian commands all the time: "The taxman says 'do not argue, pay!' The pastor says 'do not argue, believe!'" But Kant counters that we *should* argue and follow our reason.

Kant may have followed Baumgarten and Wolff, to some extent, but there were others whom he completely rejected. In his ethics lectures, he lists several philosophers who ground morality on emotions or feelings. For example, ancient Greek philosopher Epicurus (341–270 BCE) stressed that morality involves satisfying our senses and gaining selfish fulfillment. British philosopher Francis Hutcheson (1694–1747) believed that an internal moral feeling distinguishes between right and wrong conduct. Kant rejects these theories because they depend too much on the accidental physical makeup of humans and on the particular circumstances in which we find ourselves. Instead, Kant argues that morality is grounded in our reason, which is stable and universal.

Motives That Influence Our Human Will   The aim of Kant's book *Foundations of the Metaphysics of Morals* is, in his words, "to seek out and establish this supreme principle of morality"—that is, to explain the origin and function of the categorical imperative. Before presenting the categorical imperative, though, Kant says some things about human psychology and explains how the categorical imperative fits into the moral decision-making process.

We all recognize that morality involves choices between different courses of action. If I see an accident victim alongside the road, I can choose to either help that person or not. To understand morality, then, I need to understand the factors that influence my will when making decisions. Philosophers of the 18th century commonly viewed the human will as something like a switch that turned on and off specific actions. We have countless motives that incline us toward various actions. For example, my motive of thirst inclines me to act out by getting a drink. My motive of greed inclines me to act out by accumulating money and possessions. My motive of sympathy inclines me to act out by helping people. The function of the will is to select a specific motive and thereby switch on a specific action.

Kant similarly believes that various motives tug at our human will, prompting us to act in different ways. For Kant, motives fall into one of two classes: (1) selfish inclinations and (2) rational obligations. Unfortunately, most of our motives are of the selfish variety, and as long as we willfully select these motives, then our actions will never be truly moral. This is so even if I perform an action that appears to be morally proper. Suppose, for example, that I help an accident victim because I hope to get a reward. My motive in this case is selfish, so my act isn't truly moral. Kant believes that morally pure motives must be rational considerations, which are universal and not personal or selfish. Specifically, the motive must be a rationally informed duty toward the categorical imperative. Let's look more closely at Kant's reasoning here.

First, Kant believes that a moral choice must be a *rational* decision since morality involves what is *necessary* for us to do, and only rational considerations are necessary. For example, there is nothing necessary about my selfish inclination to obtain material wealth. At the same time, when we hear the moral command "Don't steal!" we recognize an element of necessity insofar as this command applies to everyone. Further, when we assess that anything in life is "necessary," such as the truth of mathematical formulas, we are making a rational assessment, and this applies to morality as well. Second, Kant believes that in moral choice our rational motive must be in the form of a *principle* since human reason operates by issuing principles. Our reason gives us universal and necessary principles of mathematics, principles of logic, and, in this case, a principle of morality. Third, the principle must be in the form of a *command* or *imperative* since morality involves commands, such as "Don't steal!"

To better clarify how the categorical imperative differs from selfish inclinations, Kant distinguishes the categorical imperative from **hypothetical imperatives.** Compare these two imperatives:

1. If you want to be a lawyer, then you must go to law school.

2. You must help others in need.

Although both of these statements are imperatives in the sense that they command us to perform some action, only the second is a *moral* imperative. The first is a *hypothetical* imperative in the sense that the commanded action (go to law school) applies to you only if you have a particular desire (to be a lawyer). Hypothetical imperatives will always be of the form "If you want *some thing*, then you must do *some act*." Since all people won't want the same things, hypothetical imperatives lack the element of necessity, and so are not truly moral commands. They are instead rules of personal preference. By contrast, the second imperative does not depend on whether you have some desire. Instead, it simply mandates, "You must do *some act*." This is the form that our moral obligations take when they arise from the categorical imperative.

The Formula of the Law of Nature

So much for the psychology behind the categorical imperative. The most important part of Kant's theory is the categorical imperative itself:

> Act only on that maxim by which you can at the same time will that it should become a universal law.

The categorical imperative offers us a step-by-step procedure for determining the moral status of particular actions. First, I take a specific action, such as stealing my neighbor's lawnmower. Second, I see what the guiding principle or "maxim" is behind the action, such as "I will steal my neighbor's lawnmower to gain material wealth." Third, I reflect on what that maxim would be like if it were a universal rule that everyone followed, such as "Everyone may steal his or her neighbor's lawnmower to gain material wealth." Fourth, if the universal rule is reasonable, then I accept the action as moral; if unreasonable, I reject the action as immoral. It is almost like asking "What would happen if everyone did this?" However, we don't want to consider what happens regarding our selfish inclinations, such as whether a universal rule would make me happy or not. Instead, we only want to look at what happens in our *reasoning process* as we think about a universal rule. Kant has a specific notion of reason in mind, with specific indicators about when a rule is rational or irrational. Kant gives four formulations of the categorical imperative that reflect different facets of human rationality.

The first and most famous formulation is sometimes called the **formula of the law of nature**: "Act as if the maxim of your action were to become through your will a universal law of nature." The wording of this is very close to that of the original statement of the categorical imperative. However, as Kant explains, the distinguishing feature here is that we consider whether our maxim could function as a law of nature—and specifically, whether it is free from contradiction. Suppose I tell you that gravity will make the rock in my right hand fall to the ground and will at the same time make the rock in my left hand hover in mid-air. You will think that this is impossible since laws of nature can't be inconsistent like this. Similarly, this formula of the categorical imperative instructs us to search for a contradiction within a universalized maxim.

To illustrate, Kant gives four examples that he thinks represent our main types of moral duties. The clearest of the four examples is this: Suppose I borrow money from you promising to return it later, but I know full well that I won't return it. The intended maxim or guiding principle behind my action is this: "Whenever I believe myself short of money, I will borrow money and promise to pay it back, though I know that this will never be done." Kant continues by noting that a contradiction arises once I view this maxim as a universal rule. Specifically, if such deceit were followed universally, then the whole institution of promising would be undermined and I couldn't make my promise to begin with. So, on the one hand, I state "I promise such and such" yet, on the other, once universalized the practice of promise keeping itself would be gone.

In another example, Kant explains why it is wrong for me to kill myself when misfortunes push me to the point of despair. The maxim of this action is "From self-love I make it my principle to shorten my life if its continuance threatens more evil than it promises pleasure." But a law of nature of this sort would be contradictory. The self-love principle inclines me to preserve my life, but according to this maxim, it also inclines me to end my life. In a third example, Kant explains why I must develop my talents rather than let them waste away. The maxim of the contrary action might be something like "I will let my talents decay and devote my life to idleness." Kant concedes that this maxim by itself isn't contradictory since in theory everyone could become an idle slug. However, the contradiction emerges when I willfully assert this maxim while at the same time acknowledging my inherent rational obligation to develop my talents. In a final example, Kant explains why it is wrong to be uncharitable. The maxim of this action might be "I will not help someone in need." Similar to the last example, a contradiction arises when I willfully assert this maxim while at the same time acknowledging my inherent rational obligation to receive charity when I am in need.

From these four examples, two different types of contradictions emerge. The first example in particular involves an internal contradiction *within* the proposed universal rule; the last two involve a contradiction *between* the proposed universal rule and another inherently rational obligation. The important point, though, is that a particular maxim fails as a universal law of nature if a contradiction arises at some point once a maxim is universalized.

The Formula of the End Itself   The second formulation of the categorical imperative is called the **formula of the end itself:** "Act in such a way that you always treat humanity, whether in your own person or in the person of any other, never simply as a means, but always at the same time as an end." In other words, we should not use people as objects, but instead recognize the dignity and value that we all have because of our freedom. It helps to understand Kant's point if we distinguish between things that have merely *instrumental* value and things that have *inherent* value. Some things in life are valuable only as instruments to obtain something else. My car keys, for example, are very valuable to me, and when I lose them, my life grinds to a halt. But my car keys are valuable only as tools that perform a task—namely, the task of starting my car. Even the value of my car itself is mainly instrumental insofar as it allows me to get from one place to another. By contrast, other things in life are inherently valuable, and we appreciate them for what they are, and not for what they enable us to do. Companionship and the enjoyment of music are good examples.

Kant believes that human beings have inherent value and should never be treated as instruments:

> In so [improperly] acting man reduces himself to a thing, to an instrument of animal amusement. We are, however, as human beings, not things but persons, and by turning ourselves into things we dishonor human nature in our own persons. (*Lectures,* "The Supreme Principle of Morality")

The reason we have inherent value, according to Kant, is because, unlike animals, we have the ability to rise above our brute instincts and to freely make crucial decisions in shaping our lives and the world around us. This ability to freely make such decisions is a feature of our human reason, and it confers on us an inherent dignity that is valuable in and of itself. We have a moral responsibility, then, to treat people in ways that reflect their inherent value, and not to reduce people to mere objects of instrumental value. So, when I treat someone as an *end,* I respect her inherent value; and when I treat someone as a *means,* I see him as having only instrumental value.

Kant explains that there is both a negative and positive component to this formula. The negative component is that we should *avoid* treating people as a mere means. But this tells us only to abstain from using people as instruments, which is a bare minimum obligation. The positive component is that we should *undertake* to treat people as an end in themselves. This tells us to actively assist or support others in retaining their dignity. It isn't enough simply to avoid abusing people; we must go a step further and help them, especially when misfortune strikes them.

Kant again illustrates this formula with the same four examples that we considered earlier. If I make a bad-faith promise to you with the intention of acquiring financial gain, then I'm treating you as a thing or instrument and not recognizing your inherent value. If I commit suicide, then I am using myself as a means to attain a tolerable state of affairs until the point that I'm actually dead. If I let my talents decline, then I am not acknowledging my inherent worth as a rational person who shapes the world through my decisions; I'm not treating myself as an end. And if I fail to help people in need, then I am not helping them maintain their dignity; I'm failing to treat them as an end. The first two examples illustrate the negative obligation to avoid treating people as a means, and the last two illustrate the positive obligation to undertake treating people as an end.

Kant's first two formulations of the categorical imperative are the most famous of the four and Kant devotes the most attention to these. The remaining two formulations draw from the central points of both the first and second formulations. The third is the formula of autonomy: "So act that your will can regard itself at the same time as making universal law through its maxims." The focus of this formula is the authority that rests within our human will to productively shape the world around us when following reason. As we act, we should consider whether our intended maxims are worthy of our status as shapers of the world.

The fourth formulation is the formula of the kingdom of ends: "So act as if you were through your maxims a law-making member of a kingdom of ends." The point here is that the moral fate of all people hangs together. We saw that Kant thinks of human beings as ends in themselves, and so, collectively, we are a "kingdom of ends" or, more simply, a moral community. As I act, I should consider whether my actions contribute to or detract from the moral community. Specifically, I should consider whether the intended maxim of my action could productively function as a universal rule in the moral community.

To summarize, here are the main points of Kant's theory:

- Motives behind true moral choices are not those of selfish inclination but instead those of a rational duty conforming to the categorical imperative.
- Hypothetical imperatives have the form "If you want *some thing,* then you must do *some act*"; the categorical imperative mandates, "You must do *some act.*"
- The general formula of the categorical imperative has us consider whether the intended maxim of our action would be reasonable as a universal law.

- Specific formulations of the categorical imperative focus on a particular feature of human rationality, such as the absence of contradiction, free choice, and inherent dignity.

Criticisms of Kant's Theory

Kant was an original thinker not only in the field of ethics but in virtually every area of philosophy. His reputation skyrocketed during the last two decades of his life, and during the nineteenth century his writings were more influential in Europe than those of any other philosopher. Many philosophers adopted his theories and perpetuated a specialized Kantian vocabulary. Others, however, were less happy with Kant's elaborate philosophical system and picked away at parts of it, including the categorical imperative.

Schopenhauer's Criticism: The Categorical Imperative Reduces to Egoism   Kant's writings were a source of inspiration for German philosopher Arthur Schopenhauer (1788–1860). Although Schopenhauer followed Kant in many particulars, in an appendix to his work *The World as Will and Representation* (1818), Schopenhauer politely critiques different aspects of Kant's philosophy that don't quite mesh with Schopenhauer's own. This includes Kant's categorical imperative. Schopenhauer believes that human conduct is guided sometimes by sympathy for other people and other times by selfish or *egoistic* concerns for oneself. Truly moral conduct, he argues, must be sympathetic, but Kant denied the role of sympathy as the motive behind truly moral action. Sympathy is a fellow feeling or sense of commiseration that we have with other people. Like other feelings—such as happiness and self-love—sympathy focuses on specific people and specific situations. All such feelings, Kant says, are too unstable and unreliable to be an effective foundation for morality.

According to Schopenhauer, if I shun my feelings of sympathy—as Kant recommends—then egoism will drive how I consider the universal implications of my actions in the categorical imperative. Without sympathy, the *real* step-by-step procedure of the categorical imperative is this: (1) I consider how willing I am to allow the egoism of others to encroach on my territory, and then (2) I recognize that this is as far as I can allow my own egoism to encroach on other people's territory. Schopenhauer makes this point here:

> This aim [concerning the well-being of all], however, still always remains [egoistic] well-being. I then find that all can be equally well off only if each makes the egoism of others the limit of his own. It naturally follows from this that I ought not to injure anyone, so that, since the principle is assumed to be universal, *I* also may not be injured. This, however, is the only ground on account of which I, not yet possessing a moral principle but only looking for one, can desire this to be a universal law. But obviously in this way the desire for well-being, in other words egoism, remains the source of this ethical principle. (*The World as Will and Representation*, Vol. 1, appendix)

For Schopenhauer, the categorical imperative simply reduces to the egoistic principle that "I shouldn't do to others what I don't want done to myself."

Schopenhauer believes that this is good enough for the purpose of establishing political laws that regulate how we behave as citizens, for political laws mainly limit how much we can encroach on other people's territory. However, Schopenhauer argues, this is not sufficient for establishing moral obligations that go beyond the bare minimum obligations that we find in legal codes. For example, morality may require that we more aggressively help others in need.

For the sake of argument, let's suppose that Schopenhauer is correct that either something like sympathy or something like egoism must be the driving force behind our consideration of the universal implications of our actions. How might we defend Kant from Schopenhauer's charge of egoism? Even though Kant rejects a specific notion of sympathy—that is, sympathy as a feeling toward particular people—he still believes that there is a humanitarian emphasis within human reason. Although reason cannot directly instruct me to sympathize with this or that person, it does instruct me to sympathize with the whole race of humans. This more generalized notion of sympathy emerges in the formula of the end in itself, which tells us to respect the inherent value of all people. We've seen that this formula includes the positive mandate to treat people as ends in themselves by helping them when in need. This goes beyond the purely negative mandate to avoid treating people as a means or using them as an instrument. This reflects Schopenhauer's precise point that there is more to morality than simply not encroaching on other people's territory. The solution, then, to Schopenhauer's egoistic spin on the categorical imperative is to accept a more generalized notion of sympathy toward humanity.

We must note, though, that there is a drawback to this solution. If sympathy is directed only toward humanity at large, then there will be a distinct lack of personal feelings toward individual people. For example, if I visit my friend in the hospital, then, in Kant's view, my action should be motivated by a concern for humanity at large, and not by a concern for my friend specifically. This, though, seems both cold and unrealistic.

Mill's Criticism: The Categorical Imperative Reduces to Utilitarianism

British philosopher **John Stuart Mill** (1806–1873) developed a theory of morality that was about as contrary to Kant's theory as one could imagine. Kant believed that our moral duties spring immediately from human reason, without any consideration of the actual effects of our actions on our personal happiness. For Kant, the categorical imperative is a method of directly accessing the commands of our reason, independent of other considerations. By contrast, Mill believes that our moral obligations spring only from considerations of how our actions affect human happiness. Mill proposes his own principle of morality, which he calls the "utilitarian principle": "Actions are right in proportion as they tend to promote happiness; wrong as they tend to produce the reverse of happiness." According to this principle, we look at the consequences of our actions and assess whether they bring about more happiness than unhappiness.

Mill was aware of Kant's categorical imperative and the enormous influence that Kant's theory had on philosophers of the time. In a brief passage, Mill argues that the categorical imperative does not succeed as a purely rational source of obligation. Instead, he says, it is actually a disguised version of the utilitarian principle—which is the very last thing that Kant thought his principle was:

> This remarkable man [i.e., Kant], whose system of thought will long remain one of the landmarks in the history of philosophical speculation, does, in the treatise in question, lay down a universal first principle as the origin and ground of moral obligation; it is this: "So act, that the rule on which thou actest would admit of being adopted as a law by all rational beings." But when he begins to deduce from this precept any of the actual duties of morality, he fails, almost grotesquely, to show that there would be any contradiction, any logical (not to say physical) impossibility, in the adoption by all rational beings of the most outrageously immoral rules of conduct. All he shows is that the consequences of their universal adoption would be such as no one would choose to incur. (*Utilitariansim*, 1)

Although Mill cites the general formula of the categorical imperative, he directs his attack against the formula of the law of nature, which tells us that an action is wrong if a contradiction arises when universalizing the intended maxim. To illustrate Mill's complaint, suppose I want to borrow money from you, never intending to pay you back. Kant believes that this is immoral since my intended maxim is contradictory; specifically, I'm promising to do one thing, but when universalized the practice of promise keeping itself is undermined. According to Mill, the categorical imperative fails to reveal any logical contradiction in my universalized maxim. The only thing it reveals is that the consequences of universalizing my maxim involve more unhappiness than happiness, so I must reject the maxim. In this case, deceitful promises as a rule make us distrust each other; and distrust, in turn, makes life unhappy. So, although Kant thinks that we merely look for the presence of a contradiction, we actually are looking at the unpleasant effects of a universalized rule.

Mill is correct in noting that it is easy for us to look at the unpleasant effects of a universalized rule. However, Kant does not do this, and the contradictions that he exposes are genuine. The example of deceitful promises is a perfect illustration of how an immoral maxim may produce an internal contradiction when universalized. If we universally allow deceitful promises, this means that we may (1) keep our word and (2) not keep our word at the same time. This is as explicit a contradiction as one can get. Other immoral maxims don't lead to explicit *internal* contradictions like this, and, instead, Kant tries to show how they lead to *external* contradictions. We've seen that external contradictions occur between (1) the proposed universal rule and (2) another inherent rational obligation. For example, it is wrong to waste my talents since it is contrary to my inherent rational obligation to develop my talents. It is wrong to deny charity to others since it is contrary to my inherent rational wish to receive charity when I am in need. For most other immoral actions that Kant does not specifically illustrate, it is easiest to see these as involving external contradictions as well. Stealing is wrong, perhaps, because it is contrary to our rational obligation to live in peace with our neighbors. Murder is wrong, perhaps, because it is contrary to our rational obligation to respect the lives of others. These seem to be genuine enough contradictions to sidestep Mill's criticism.

Anscombe's Criticism: There Is No Procedure for Constructing Maxims

In a famous essay entitled "Modern Moral Philosophy" (1958), contemporary British philosopher **Elizabeth Anscombe** criticizes virtually the entire lineup of traditional moral philosophers. With regard to Kant, she argues that Kant's "rule about universalizable maxims is useless without stipulations as to what shall count as a relevant description of an action with a view to constructing a maxim about it." That is, for any action I pick, I could devise a wide variety of maxims that might represent my action. But how do I know which one is the *correct* maxim? To illustrate Anscombe's criticism, we will use a rather grotesque example that Kant himself discusses. Suppose I yank out one of my healthy teeth and sell it to a dentist, who will then insert it into someone else's mouth. We would expect any adequate moral theory to condemn this action. So, if Kant is correct, universalizing this action should generate a contradiction. But what is the maxim of my action here? It might be that "I should pull out my tooth and sell it to a dentist," or that "I should extract a healthy part of my body and sell it," or that "I should pull out my right upper molar and sell it to a dentist by the name of John Smith." Each of these maxims has entirely different implications, and if I can't figure out exactly which maxim represents my action, then I can't test the action by universalizing it. So, Kant's categorical imperative fails to give us the guidance that we need.

However, Anscombe's criticism misses the point about what a "maxim" is, and Kant really does provide an appropriate way to construct maxims. The key to constructing a maxim is to determine the *intention* behind an action. Kant illustrates the connection between maxims and intentions here:

> Every immoral man has his maxims. . . . May a man, for instance, mutilate his body for profit? May he sell a tooth? May he surrender himself at a price to the highest bidder? . . . What is the intent in these cases? It is to gain material advantage. (*Lectures,* "The Supreme Principle of Morality)

Kant is correct that, if we want to understand the moral worth of someone's action, we must look beyond the specific action and examine the underlying intention. For example, if I hit a pedestrian while driving my car, from a moral standpoint it makes a big difference whether I was hoping to hit or to avoid the pedestrian. Just as it is important to discover one's underlying intention in moral assessments, it is also important in criminal law, especially in determining the severity of punishment. Today, we don't speak about the *maxim* of our actions but prefer to speak simply about our *intention.* Philosophers in Kant's time, though, were comfortable viewing intentions as maxims. Wolff, for example, writes that "man must have certain maxims or general rules according to which he directs his action, even if he himself does not clearly recognize this."

In constructing my maxim, then, I look to my intention. In the case of the extracted tooth, my intention is, in Kant's words, "to gain material advantage."

The more precisely stated maxim is that "I should disfigure myself by extracting my tooth to gain material advantage." In the spirit of Anscombe's criticism, we must acknowledge that it is sometimes difficult to uncover the *exact* intention behind our actions, but that's a problem that plagues morality in general, and not just Kant's theory. In criminal court cases, prosecutors and defense attorneys may battle for days over a defendant's true underlying intention. It may not be any easier for us as individuals when we struggle to discover why we do things. In fact, Kant believes that it is nearly impossible to discover our precise intentions:

> We can never, even by the strictest examination, get completely behind the secret incentives of action; since, when the question is of moral worth, it is not with the actions which we see that we are concerned, but with those inward principles of them which we do not see. (*Foundations,* 2)

Although I may not know what my exact intentions are for a given action, I can make a best guess or even consider a few possible intentions just to cover all the bases. With the categorical imperative, then, I may have to devise a few maxims and see what the outcome of each would be when universalized. This adds extra steps to the categorical imperative, but they are steps that realistically reflect our limited knowledge of our intentions.

The Value of the Categorical Imperative

Kant's theory of the categorical imperative continues to hold an important place in moral philosophy today. Of the various formulations of the categorical imperative, the most popular ones today are the formula of the law of nature and the formula of the end itself. In conclusion, we will consider the merits of each of these.

Traditional Duty Theory and the Formula of the Law of Nature   Kant undoubtedly believed that his theory of the categorical imperative was unique and that he departed from the moral traditions prior to him. Not only did he believe he departed from moral theories that emphasized personal happiness, he also felt that he moved beyond the traditional duty theories that first inspired him. Again, traditional duty theorists such as Pufendorf, Wolff, and Baumgarten argued that the laws of nature mandate a specific set of duties to God, self, and others. In this view, an action is wrong if it violates our specific duties. These philosophers also believed that all of our specific duties flow from a single principle of natural law. In spite of Kant's attempt to depart from traditional duty theory, he may not have moved as far beyond it as he believed. We can see this more clearly if we speculate about how Kant came up with the idea of the categorical imperative. A section of Kant's ethics lectures entitled "The Supreme Principle of Morality" presents an early discussion of the categorical imperative, and by comparing this to the *Foundations,* we can construct a plausible story line for the development of his theory.

The story begins in the ethics lectures, in which Kant expresses dissatisfaction with the single principle of morality proposed by Baumgarten and Wolff. Roughly, for Kant, their principle reduces to the claim that "we must do good and avoid evil." According to Kant, this principle has no actual substance and simply means that we are *morally obliged to be moral.* Kant, then, believed that we need a better first principle. Perhaps around the same time, Kant was struck by a unique feature of deceitful promises. If we say as a general rule that we may make deceitful promises, then we logically contradict the concept of promise keeping itself. Specifically, we make a promise and deny the institution of promise keeping at the same time. This example of deceitful promises appears very prominently in the ethics lectures. Kant apparently looked for other examples of immoral actions that resulted in similar internal contradictions when universalized, but he found none that perfectly matched. Indeed, this seems to be a one-of-a-kind example. The definitive formulation of the categorical imperative does not appear in the ethics lectures, but Kant does refer to the "supreme principle of morality," which clearly is rooted in the example of deceitful promises.

The story continues in the *Foundations,* where the deceitful promise example is the model for Kant's general formulation of the categorical imperative, as well as the step-by-step procedure of the formulation of the law of nature. That is, we take the maxim of an action, consider it as a universalized rule, and see if a contradiction arises. Since the deceitful promise example was the only illustration that fit this step-by-step procedure perfectly, Kant then modified other examples to fit the procedure, such as the examples of committing suicide, wasting one's talents, and being uncharitable. These examples were modified in two ways. First, the contradictions that Kant exposes are not internal but external. For example, wasting one's talents is wrong since it is contrary to a rational obligation to develop one's talents. In more traditional terminology, wasting one's talents is wrong since it is contrary to the *duty* to develop one's talents. The contradiction arises only when we presume the existence of an independent duty. In our discussion of Mill's criticism, we saw that this is probably the best way to see contradictions with most other immoral actions, such as stealing or murder.

The second type of modification involves universalization. With deceitful promises, an internal contradiction arises *only* when the act is considered as a universal rule. However, the process of universalization is not needed to detect external conflicts with our rational obligations or "duties." If *I alone* fail to develop my talents, then I am still acting contrary to my rational obligation to develop my talents. If *I alone* kill myself, then I am still acting contrary to my rational obligation to stay alive. Again, to make them fit the model, Kant modified these examples by universalizing them, even though universalization is not needed in these cases.

Once we modify Kant's examples, what does the formula of the law of nature amount to? Aside from the one-of-a-kind example of deceitful promises, it tells us that an action is wrong if it violates a duty. And this is essentially what we find in the traditional duty theories of Pufendorf, Wolff, and Baumgarten.

The Value of the Formula of the End Itself   Most discussions of Kant's categorical imperative focus on the formula of the law of nature and the quest for a supposed contradiction. But the real contribution of Kant's categorical imperative may rest in his formula of the end itself. This principle tells us that we should always treat people with dignity, recognizing their intrinsic value, and never treat them as mere instruments to manipulate for our own purpose. If we review our various immoral actions, they all seem to involve using people as instruments and not recognizing their intrinsic value. If I commit an act of theft, deception, assault, or murder, I am using my victim as a tool for my own gratification, and I am certainly not respecting that person's dignity. If we think of moral principles as guidelines for our conduct, then the formula of the end itself seems especially accurate. It also preaches a message about how to become better people: Don't think of people as things that we can manipulate. Kant devised this notion only after thinking for years about the importance of human freedom and our ability to make personal and rational choices in the face of authoritarian attempts to restrict us. To be rational humans *means* that we make choices that shape our lives and the world around us. We need to respect that feature within all people, and it is reasonable to make this respect the cornerstone of morality.

If we see that morality mandates respect for our decision-making abilities, it becomes clearer why we shouldn't voluntarily become homeless. If I choose to waste my talents and live on the street, then I'm not exercising the kind of positive freedom that makes me human. It may *seem* as though I'm making a choice when I voluntarily waste my talents. However, this is only a weak and default choice that results from my failing to scope out life's possibilities and act on them. So, by wasting my talents, I'm disrespecting my decision-making abilities and failing to acknowledge my own intrinsic worth. This is probably the best explanation anyone could give for why it is wrong to voluntarily become homeless.

Kant believed that the formula of the end itself was a different version of the categorical imperative—specifically, a variation on the quest-for-contradiction strategy. It takes a great stretch of the imagination, though, to see how they have much in common, and Kant's motive in linking them may again owe to the influence of his predecessors. Natural law theorists from the time of Aquinas believed that natural law dictates a *single* highest principle of morality, and all of our duties are unified in that principle. We saw that Kant proposed his categorical imperative to replace the empty principle suggested by Wolff and Baumgarten. To Kant's way of thinking, everything that we say about our moral obligations must be grounded in a single principle. Kant then labored to show how the different facets of our moral reasoning tie together in a unified system. Fortunately, today, we don't have to follow the systematic plan of morality laid out by the natural law theorists. It is enough simply to acknowledge and appreciate Kant's conception of human dignity and to see that it has important moral implications for how we view ourselves and others. We don't need to continue trying to squeeze this insight into a unified system.

Summary

Influenced by his predecessors in the natural law tradition, Kant offered the categorical imperative as the supreme principle of morality from which all moral duties emerge. The categorical imperative originates from human reason—as opposed to selfish inclinations—and Kant argued that it can be formulated in different ways, emphasizing different components of human reason. The formula of the law of nature suggests that truly moral actions are those that are free from contradiction when universalized. The formula of the end itself suggests that truly moral actions are those that acknowledge and support a person's dignity and inherent value. Schopenhauer argued that the categorical imperative is essentially egoistic since Kant rejects the role of sympathetic feelings. In response, Kant emphasized the importance of inherent human value, which is a generalized sympathy. Mill argued that the categorical imperative is really utilitarianism in disguise. However, the categorical imperative does not appeal to happiness; it exposes genuine contradictions. Anscombe criticized the categorical imperative for failing to tell us how to construct maxims. Maxims are statements of intention behind an action, though, which may be difficult to accurately identify. Finally, the formula of the law of nature does not depart much from traditional duty theory, and the true contribution of the categorical imperative is the formula of the end itself, with its emphasis on human freedom and dignity.

Study Questions

Introduction

1. According to Kant, why would it be wrong for someone to voluntarily be homeless?

Kant's Moral Theory

Influences on Kant's Theory

2. What was Baumgarten's view of duties?
3. What is the fundamental law of nature for Wolff?
4. What is Kant's view about authoritarian moral commands?

Motives That Influence Our Human Will

5. What are the two classes of motives that influence our will?
6. For Kant, what is the only legitimate motive in moral decision making?

The Formula of the Law of Nature

7. What is the step-by-step procedure indicated by the categorical imperative?
8. Explain Kant's formula of the law of nature in terms of the example of deceitfully borrowing money.

The Formula of the End Itself

9. What is the difference between a "means" and an "end"?
10. What are the negative and positive components to the formula of the end itself?

Criticisms of Kant's Theory

Schopenhauer's Criticism: The Categorical Imperative Reduces to Egoism

11. For Schopenhauer, what are the two motivations that guide human conduct?
12. According to Schopenhauer, what is the real step-by-step procedure implicit in Kant's categorical imperative?
13. According to Fieser, how can we rescue Kant from Schopenhauer's criticism?

Mill's Criticism: The Categorical Imperative Reduces to Utilitarianism

14. Explain how, according to Mill, the categorical imperative actually functions as a utilitarian principle.
15. Give examples of both the internal and external contradictions as indicated in Kant's application of the categorical imperative.

Anscombe's Criticism: There Is No Procedure for Constructing Maxims

16. What is a "maxim," and how do we construct one?
17. According to Fieser, how does the notion of a "maxim" rescue Kant from Anscombe's charge?

The Value of the Categorical Imperative

Traditional Duty Theory and the Formula of the Law of Nature

18. According to Fieser, what two modifications did Kant make to his examples regarding the formula of the law of nature?
19. According to Fieser, when we modify Kant's examples, what does the formula of the law of nature tell us?

The Value of the Formula of the End Itself

20. According to Fieser, what is the best explanation we can give for why it is wrong to voluntarily become homeless?

References

The quotation about the Bowery homeless person named David is from The Bowery Mission home page (http://www.bowery.org/).

Statistics on the homeless are based on fact sheets from the National Coalition for the Homeless.

The quotations from Kant without citations are from *Lectures on Ethics,* translated by Louis Infield (London: Methuen, 1930): "The Supreme Principle of Morality," "The Lawgiver," and "Occupation."

The quotations from Kant's *Foundations of the Metaphysics of Morals* are from the translation by H. J. Paton (New York: Harper, 1948). Other translations are by Lewis White Beck (New York: Prentice-Hall, 1959) and James W. Ellington (Indianapolis: Hackett, 1981).

The quotations by Christian Wolff are from *Reasonable Thoughts on Human Action,* in *Moral Philosophy from Montaigne to Kant,* Vol. 1, edited by J. B. Schneewind (Cambridge: Cambridge University Press, 1990).

The quotations by Arthur Schopenhauer are from *The World as Will and Representation,* Vol. 1, translated by E. F. J. Payne (New York: Dover Publications, 1958), appendix.

The quotations by John Stuart Mill are from *Utilitarianism* (1863), which is currently available in several editions.

The quotations by Elizabeth Anscombe are from "Modern Moral Philosophy," *Philosophy,* 1958, Vol. 33, p. 3; this article is reprinted in her *Ethics, Religion and Politics* (Oxford: Blackwell, 1981).

Suggestions for Further Reading

For a classic discussion of Kant's moral views prior to the *Foundations,* see Paul Arthur Schilpp, *Kant's Pre-Ethical Ethics* (Chicago: Northwestern University Press, 1938).

For a detailed discussion of Kant's moral theory as it appears in Kant's various publications, see Roger Sullivan, *Immanuel Kant's Moral Theory* (Cambridge: Cambridge University Press, 1989).

For a readable account of Kant's *Foundation,* see Roger Sullivan, *An Introduction to Kant's Ethics* (Cambridge: Cambridge University Press, 1994).

For a translation of the *Foundations,* along with several influential essays, see Robert Paul Wolff, ed., *Foundations of the Metaphysics of Morals with Critical Essays* (Indianapolis: Bobbs-Merrill, 1969).

For a commentary on Kant's *Foundation,* see Robert Paul Wolff, *The Autonomy of Reason* (New York: Harper, 1973).

11

Utilitarianism

Introduction

On February 3, 1998, 38-year-old Karla Faye Tucker became the first woman executed in the state of Texas in over 130 years. A former drug addict and prostitute, in 1983 Tucker and a friend ended a three-day drug binge by attempting to steal a young man's motorcycle. They broke into the man's apartment and hacked him and a visiting woman friend to death with a pickax. Afterward, Tucker bragged that she got a sexual thrill from the murders. She and her accomplice were caught a month later and ultimately sentenced to death. Because of her unique situation as a woman on death row, her newly found religious conviction, and her paradoxically warm personality, Tucker gained worldwide notoriety as her execution day approached. Pope John Paul II made a public appeal for clemency. Tucker herself believed that her life should be spared since she had reformed to the point that she was no longer part of society's crime problem but part of the cure. In an interview two weeks before her execution, Tucker explained:

> I can witness to people who have been on drugs or into prostitution or into all of that, and they'll listen to me because they know I understand and can relate to them. And I can keep them from going down that road, because I can let them know. I changed. You can too.

Clemency was not granted, and the execution took place as planned.

Tucker argued that her life should be spared since her remaining alive would serve the greater social good. Her reasoning strategy was utilitarian in nature. Most generally, utilitarianism is the moral theory that an action is morally right if it serves the greatest good for the greatest number of people. To determine whether Tucker should have been executed, the utilitarian would have compared the total good resulting from her execution with the total good resulting from her remaining alive. Tucker believed that more good would result if she remained alive. However, defenders of capital punishment also use utilitarian reasoning and argue that the greater social good is served by executing some criminals. After her execution, a relative of one of Tucker's victims said, in utilitarian fashion, "The world's [now] a better place." Presumably, executing criminals such as Tucker sends a strong signal to other would-be criminals and deters them. It also assists in the psychological healing process of victims and their families.

Utilitarians believe that the *sole* factor in determining an action's morality is the balance of social good versus social evil. Appeals to moral intuitions, social traditions, or God's wishes are not relevant. Utilitarianism has a long history, but the most famous versions of the theory emerged in the eighteenth and nineteenth centuries, particularly in the **hedonistic utilitarianism** championed by Jeremy Bentham and John Stuart Mill. **Hedonism** involves pleasure seeking, and hedonistic utilitarians argue that morality is determined according to how much pleasure or pain is produced from a course of action. For example, on the issue of capital punishment, hedonistic utilitarians would argue that this practice is justified only if it produces a greater amount of pleasure than pain. Other nonhedonistic versions of utilitarianism emerged in later years. We will discuss the development of the utilitarian theory here.

The Historical Development of Utilitarianism

Utilitarianism isn't the invention of any single philosopher, and the general theory is as old as ancient Greece. The Greek philosopher **Epicurus** (341–270 BCE) gives a clear statement of the role of pleasure in moral judgments:

> We count pleasure as the originating principle and the goal of the blessed life. For we recognize pleasure as the first and fitting good, for from it proceeds all choice and avoidance, and we return to it as the feeling-standard by which we judge every good. (*Letter to Menoeceus*)

Pleasure is clearly an important motivator in our lives, and most moral philosophers find at least some place for pleasure within their theories. What is distinct about Epicurus's theory of hedonism, though, is that the gaining of pleasure and the avoidance of pain is the *single* standard by which we determine happiness and thereby judge our actions. Ultimately, Epicurus's theory didn't take hold, and in the centuries following Epicurus, moral philosophers emphasized the roles of virtue, natural law, and the will of God. Humanist philosophers of the Renaissance revived Epicurus's theory, and by the eighteenth century, several philosophers were defending the pleasure criterion of morality.

Eighteenth-Century Contributions   Irish philosopher **Francis Hutcheson** (1694–1747) offered this systematic formula linking morality with happiness:

> That action is best, which procures the greatest happiness for the greatest numbers; and that worst, which, in like manner, occasions misery. (*An Inquiry Concerning Moral Good and Evil*, 3.8)

Here and in his other ethical writings, we find most of the key elements of utilitarianism. First, in Hutcheson's words, we are to *compute* the consequences of our actions. Second, Hutcheson identifies the standard of moral evaluation as the greatest amount of happiness or pleasure that results for all people affected. Third, he provides details about the range of consequences that count; long-term, short-term, direct, and indirect consequences all enter into the computation. Finally, he provides details about what counts as happiness or pleasure: Higher intellectual pleasures and lower bodily pleasures are relevant, but with varying degrees of intensity and duration.

Influenced by Hutcheson, **David Hume** (1711–1776) further developed this theory. Hume argues that, when we survey what people commonly consider to be moral conduct, we must conclude that morally right actions are those that produce useful or immediately pleasing consequences for ourselves or others. Two features are unique to Hume's theory. First, as criteria of moral evaluation, the useful longer-term consequences of actions are as important as the immediately pleasing consequences of actions. Sexual chastity, for example, is morally proper primarily because it has useful consequences in holding together the family unit. Hume uses the term *utility* in reference to these useful consequences, and it is from Hume's expression that later commentators coined the term *utilitarianism*. The second unique feature of Hume's theory is that some actions are useful only when followed *as a rule*. Again, with sexual chastity, isolated instances of sexual fidelity won't have the consequence of holding together family units. Hume believes that, to have useful consequences, chastity needs to be followed *as a rule,* even by single women who are past childbearing age. In Hume's words:

> A single act of justice [or chastity], considered in itself, may often by contrary to the public good; and it is only the concurrence of mankind, in a general scheme or system of action, which is advantageous. (*A Treatise of Human Nature,* 3.3.1)

Hume's reasoning here is the foundation of what was later called **rule-utilitarianism.** By the end of the eighteenth century, dozens of prominent moral theorists, influenced by Hume's theory of utility, proposed similar views. The most important of these theorists was British philosopher **Jeremy Bentham** (1748–1832), who acknowledged Hume as his immediate source of inspiration.

Bentham's Utilitarian Calculus   Bentham presents his theory of utility in

his *Introduction to the Principles of Morals and Legislation* (1789), which he wrote as a kind of moral guidebook for legislators as they make public policy. Although the bulk of this work focuses on issues of criminal conduct, the opening chapters systematically describe how utility is the ultimate moral standard for all actions. Bentham states his principle of utility here:

> By the principle of utility is meant that principle which approves or disapproves of every action whatsoever, according to the tendency which it appears to have to augment or diminish the happiness of the party whose interest is in question: or, what is the same thing in other words, to promote or to oppose that happiness. I say of every action whatsoever; and therefore not only of every action of a private individual, but of every measure of government. (*Principles of Morals and Legislation,* 1.2)

Two features of Bentham's theory contribute especially to its uniqueness. First, Bentham offers a bare-bones moral theory consisting of only one factor: the pleasing or painful consequences of actions. Although earlier theorists put forward the basic elements of utilitarianism, they also incorporated nonutilitarian doctrines into their moral theories. Some of these extraneous doctrines are that morality is ultimately founded on the will of God, that sympathy is needed to counterbalance human selfishness, that virtues underlie our moral actions, that we rationally intuit our duty, and that we judge conduct through a moral sense. For Bentham, some of these doctrines are nonsensical, and the rest are irrelevant. His rejection of these more traditional elements of moral theory gave utilitarianism the reputation of being Godless, impersonal, skeptical, and relativistic.

The second and most important feature of Bentham's theory is his method for precisely quantifying pleasures and pains, better known as the **utilitarian calculus.** Bentham argues that the complete range of pleasing and painful consequences of actions can be quantified according to seven criteria: (1) intensity; (2) duration; (3) certainty; (4) remoteness, that is, the immediacy of the pleasure or pain; (5) fecundity, that is, whether similar pleasures or pains will follow; (6) purity, that is, whether the pleasure is mixed with pain; and (7) extent, that is, the number of people affected. In a footnote to a later edition of the *Principles,* Bentham summarizes these criteria in a rhyme, which he says might assist us in "lodging more effectually, in the memory, these points":

Intense, long, certain, speedy, fruitful, pure—
Such marks in pleasures and in pains endure.
Such pleasures seek if private by thy end:
If it be public, wide let them extend.
Such pains avoid, whichever by thy view:
If pains must come, let them extend to few.

(*Principles of Morals and Legislation,* 4.2)

Bentham is very explicit about how the calculus works. For example, if we wanted to determine the morality of executing Karla Faye Tucker, we would first calculate, one at a time, all of the pleasure and pain that she *personally* would receive from the execution. One specific pleasure/pain that she would experience would involve her contemplating her own death. As she sat in her cell and thought about the fact that she would soon die, she undoubtedly had a strong painful experience of dread. According to Bentham's calculus, we need to construct a pleasure/pain chart that takes into account the first four criteria listed previously. We also need to assign numerical values to these factors, perhaps on a scale of 1 to 10. In Tucker's case, we might get these figures:

	Pleasure	Pain
Intensity:	0	10
Duration:	0	2
Certainty:	0	10
Immediacy:	0	10

Concerning the intensity of her pleasure/pain, we may presume that Tucker derived no pleasure from the events immediately surrounding her death, and she experienced very intense emotional pain at the prospect of losing her life. The duration of the emotional pain would have been relatively brief, but also certain and immediate.

After we chart out the first four factors, we then consider the other three factors separately. Bentham's purity factor involves whether an act produces both pain and pleasure. We've already taken this into account in our chart by noting that Tucker experienced only pain and no pleasure. The fecundity factor involves any similar long-term residual pleasures and pains that might result from an action. Since Tucker's execution was carried out successfully, there were no residual pleasures and pains for her. However, if her execution had been botched on its first attempt and she had to go through the process again a month later, then we would need to devise another pleasure/pain chart for the new execution. Our chart quantifies only the psychological anguish that Tucker experienced when contemplating her own death. However, there were other distinct pleasures and pains that she experienced regarding her execution. For example, she would have been distressed at being permanently separated from her family and frustrated with the criminal justice system. For each of these additional pains or pleasures, we need additional pleasure/pain charts.

Finally, Bentham's extent factor involves all the pleasures and pains experienced by other people. So, once we fully account for Tucker's pleasures and pains, we then construct similar pleasure/pain charts for each pleasure and pain experienced by *each person* affected by Tucker's execution. This includes the pleasures experienced by people who wanted Tucker dead, such as the victim's relatives and those who commiserated with the relatives. But it also includes the pains experienced by those who wanted her alive, such as Tucker's own relatives, and even those like the Pope who oppose capital punishment and are pained by another execution. At this stage, thousands and perhaps millions of pleasure/pain charts would be involved. We then take the combined pleasure score from all charts and compare it to the combined pain score from all charts. If the pleasure column has the higher score, then executing Tucker is moral. If the pain column has the higher score, then the execution is immoral.

Limitations of Bentham's Theory   There are two fundamental problems with Bentham's utilitarianism. First, he imposes a precision on a subject that doesn't allow for it. Working through even a single example shows that it is virtually impossible to do a complete utilitarian calculus, and this constitutes the strongest argument against it. When the *Principles* first appeared, two book reviewers attacked Bentham for the excessive detail throughout his entire discussion. The *Analytical Review* charged that "perhaps the love of discrimination has been sometimes carried too far, and been productive of divisions and subdivisions of little use to a legislator." The *Critical Review* commented more strongly that "long and intricate discussions end in trifling conclusions; affected refinement sometimes stands in the place of useful distinctions, and the parade of system is so highly labored as frequently to disgust." Bentham was well aware of this overall problem with the *Principles,* and for that reason he delayed its publication for nine years.

The second problem with Bentham's theory is that every conceivable human action becomes a moral issue that should be submitted to the utilitarian test. Even a simple act such as selecting toothpaste may involve a pleasure/pain calculus of purchasing one toothpaste brand versus another. Also, pushed to its extreme, Bentham's theory would mean that I couldn't justify spending my time on any simple leisure activities, such as watching TV. Instead, I presumably should spend all my free time actively increasing the general pleasure, such as doing volunteer work for Meals on Wheels.

The root of the problem is that Bentham endorses what commentators call **act-utilitarianism,** rather than the rule-utilitarianism hinted at by Hume. The two approaches may be defined this way:

- Act-utilitarianism: In determining morality, we should calculate the pleasurable and painful consequences of our individual *actions.*
- Rule-utilitarianism: In determining morality, we should calculate the pleasurable and painful consequences of the moral *rules* that we adopt.

Act-utilitarianism involves a two-tiered system of moral evaluation: (1) Right actions are determined by appealing to (2) the criterion of general happiness. For example, according to act-utilitarianism, it would be wrong for me to steal my neighbor's car since this act would produce more general unhappiness. Rule-utilitarianism, though, involves an intermediary step and so is a three-tiered system of moral evaluation: (1) Right actions are determined by appealing to (2) moral rules, which are determined by appealing to (3) the criterion of general happiness. For example, according to rule-utilitarianism, it would be wrong to steal my neighbor's car since this act would violate the rule against stealing, and we endorse this rule since it promotes general happiness. Although act-utilitarianism has the problem that every conceivable action becomes a moral issue, this isn't a problem with rule-utilitarianism. For example, we wouldn't be promoting general happiness by making hard-and-fast rules about choosing toothpastes or watching TV. Instead, general happiness would be better served if we endorsed a rule that allows each of us a range of free activity.

In spite of the problems with Bentham's theory, his view of utilitarianism gained a following. By the mid-nineteenth century, Bentham's name was so strongly linked with utilitarianism that one commentator felt compelled to remind people that Bentham didn't *invent* the doctrine. The next great step in the development of utilitarianism came with British philosopher **John Stuart Mill** (1806–1873).

Mill's Utilitarianism

Bentham was John Stuart Mill's godfather and teacher, and the young Mill was strongly influenced by his mentor's account of utilitarianism. In early adulthood, Mill suffered an emotional breakdown, which he attributed to his heavily analytic education. When Bentham died shortly thereafter, Mill felt free to re-evaluate the ideas of his upbringing. Mill's early writings show a growing disenchantment with Bentham's overly technical utilitarian calculus. In his 50s, Mill finally took the opportunity to write a popular defense of utilitarianism to counter the excessively scientific reputation the doctrine had obtained through Bentham. This appeared in three installments in *Fraser's Magazine* in 1861 and was published in book form in 1863 under the title *Utilitarianism*.

Elements of Mill's Theory   Commentators argue that there is little in Mill's theory that is completely original. In fact, we can outline many features of Mill's theory simply by listing their similarities to those in previous theories. First, like Bentham, Mill believes that the sole criterion of morality is general happiness—that is, the maximum pleasures and the minimum pains that a society of people can experience. Second, like Bentham, Mill believes that this criterion can be expressed somewhat scientifically in the form of a single principle:

> Actions are right in proportion as they tend to promote [general] happiness; wrong as they tend to produce the reverse of [general] happiness. (*Utilitarianism,* 2)

Third, like Hutcheson, Mill argues that happiness consists of both higher intellectual pleasures, and lower bodily pleasures. Finally, like Hume, Mill focuses on the good or bad consequences that emerge from *rules* of conduct, and as such, Mill is classified as a rule-utilitarian.

According to Mill, we appeal to the utilitarian principle only to establish moral rules. On rare occasions, though, we may be caught in a moral dilemma between two conflicting rules. Suppose I borrow your gun and promise to return it when you ask for it. The next day, you have a dispute with your boss and, in a fit of rage, ask for the gun back. I am now caught in a dilemma between two conflicting moral rules: I should keep my promises, yet I shouldn't contribute to the harm of others. In such rare cases, I can determine the proper course of action by appealing *directly* to the utilitarian principle to see which rule has priority. Mill explains this point here:

> We must remember that only in these cases of conflict between secondary principles [that is, rules] is it requisite that first principles [of general happiness] should be appealed to. There is no case of moral obligation in which some secondary principle is not involved . . . (*Utilitarianism,* 2)

In this case, I bring about more happiness by following the rule to avoid harming others, and so I should hold onto your gun.

As noted, Bentham presents a bare-bones account of utilitarianism by not incorporating traditional moral concepts such as the will of God, virtues, a moral sense, rational intuition, and sympathetic feelings. Mill also rejects most of these traditional notions, although he does find a place in his theory for socially oriented moral feelings such as sympathy, dutifulness, and solidarity. For Mill, these feelings are necessary to give people the motivation to pursue general happiness. Without such motivation, utilitarianism would be a sterile principle without any practical value.

General Happiness and Higher Pleasures   The distinguishing feature of Mill's utilitarianism is his differentiation between higher intellectual pleasures and lower bodily pleasures. Although Hutcheson made this general distinction, Mill develops the notion and makes it central to his theory. Mill introduces the topic as a response to the specific criticism that utilitarianism is a doctrine worthy only of swine since swine, too, pursue pleasure. Mill responds that the concept of *pleasure* includes intellectual as well as bodily pleasures, and pigs clearly can't experience intellectual pleasures:

> Human beings have faculties more elevated than the animal appetites and, when once made conscious of them, do not regard anything as happiness which does not include their gratification. (*Utilitarianism*, 2)

Lower pleasures traditionally include those from food, sex, self-gratification, and other "base" instincts. By contrast, **higher pleasures** are those derived from music, art, and other "lofty" intellectual accomplishments. According to Mill, higher pleasures are *qualitatively* superior to lower pleasures insofar as they are more highly valued even when limited in number. For Mill, Bentham erred by attempting to determine total happiness by assigning numerical values to pleasures and pains, with no regard for their qualitative differences. An early commentator wrote that Mill's emphasis on higher pleasures established a "new utilitarianism" since higher pleasures are subjective and thus can't lend themselves to objective quantification. For Mill, then, we can't technically have a utilitarian calculus in which we tally numbers that represent differing quantities of pleasures and pains.

Although we can't calculate general happiness in the way that Bentham describes, Mill nevertheless tried to offer some objective standard for ranking the comparative value of differing pleasures. Specifically, Mill presents a test for determining whether one pleasure is qualitatively superior to another. Take, for example, the pleasures that we may experience from visiting an art museum versus attending a monster truck rally. Assume first that an impartial judge is acquainted with both events. The pleasure from the museum visit will be qualitatively superior if (1) the judge prefers the museum visit to the truck rally, (2) the museum visit is accompanied by some pain (such as a two-hour drive), and (3) the truck rally is quantitatively superior (such as a four-night truck-o-rama). Mill believes that an impartial judge will prefer the higher pleasure to the lower because we all have a sense of dignity, at least initially. People sometimes choose the lower pleasure since it is easy to kill our more noble feelings, and we often don't have the opportunity to keep our intellectual tastes alive:

> Men lose their high aspirations as they lose their intellectual tastes, because they have not time or opportunity for indulging them; and they addict themselves to inferior pleasures, not because they deliberately prefer them, but because they are either the only ones to which they have access or the only ones which they are any longer capable of enjoying. (*Utilitarianism*, 2)

In short, according to Mill, higher pleasures are (1) the main ingredients of general happiness, (2) grounded in our intellectual abilities, (3) qualitatively superior to lower pleasures, (4) spawned by our sense of dignity, and (5) vulnerable to neglect.

To summarize, these are the main points of Mill's utilitarianism:

- General happiness is the sole criterion of morality, and "happiness" is defined as pleasure.
- Higher intellectual pleasures are more valuable than lower bodily pleasures.
- We appeal to the principle of greatest happiness only when evaluating *rules* of conduct, and not individual actions.
- We cannot quantifiably calculate which rules produce the greatest pleasure, although we can objectively determine whether one pleasure is higher than another.

Traditional Criticisms of Mill

Because *Utilitarianism* was written in a popular format, one early commentator noted that he expected Mill to follow up with a "longer and more elaborate" book on the subject. But Mill never did. Within a decade, several studies appeared attacking virtually every aspect of Mill's theory, and by the turn of the century, Mill's book became, as one commentator said, "more universally familiar than any other book in the whole literature of English Utilitarianism." Criticisms of Mill's work continue to this day, many of which attempt to refine his theory and bring it in line with our common moral intuitions. We will look at three classic criticisms of Mill's theory.

Bradley's Criticism: Utilitarianism Conflicts with Ordinary Moral Judgments   One of the earlier arguments against Mill, launched by British philosopher **F. H. Bradley** (1846–1924), is that utilitarian moral judgments often conflict with our ordinary conceptions of moral obligation. For example, it is theoretically possible that cheating on one's spouse maximizes general happiness, but we nevertheless believe that adultery is wrong:

> Let us take the precept, Do not commit adultery. How are we to prove that no possible adultery can increase the overplus of pleasurable feeling? (*Ethical Studies*, 3)

According to Bradley, there are morally proper behaviors that "we should choose even if no pleasure came from them."

We can illustrate Bradley's point further by considering cases in which we might exploit someone if doing so would produce general happiness. For example, suppose a town hero is brutally murdered, the police have no suspects, and the city is on the verge of rioting in protest. In response, the police trump up charges against some insignificant individual, knowing full well that this person is innocent. The town is satisfied, and life returns to normal. To use another illustration, suppose a society arbitrarily singles out a handful of people to become their slaves. The slaves surely suffer, but we might argue that the greater good of that society is served through the slaves' services. However, we commonly feel that it is simply wrong to frame an innocent person or enslave someone, in spite of the general good that these actions might produce. According to Bradley's reasoning, then, utilitarianism is an inadequate moral theory since it can be used to justify these kinds of exploitation in the name of general happiness.

Defenders of utilitarianism have gone to great lengths to show how their system won't exploit individuals. First, utilitarians argue that long-term consequences are a factor in the morality of any action. The possibility of exposing police conspiracies or experiencing slave rebellions are long-term negative consequences of our two sample cases. In fact, the long-term negative consequences of slavery in the United States are still unfolding. Utilitarians are correct that attention to long-term consequences will show the disutility of exploiting individuals in some circumstances. However, the problem remains that, with careful planning and an eye to the future, we might successfully exploit individuals without the penalty of long-term negative consequences. For example, if the police are careful to cover up their conspiracy or if slave owners successfully address the problem of slave uprisings, then perhaps their acts won't have long-term negative consequences.

A second line of defense against the problem of potential exploitation is available to proponents of rule-utilitarianism such as Mill. According to rule-utilitarianism, we don't calculate the consequences of each action, such as enslaving Jones in particular; instead, we calculate the consequences of each *rule* we adopt, such as "Slavery ought to be permitted." When we focus on these exploitive rules, it becomes clear that adopting them will produce more unhappiness than happiness. But critics have countered that, although this may block the adoption of many exploitive rules, some carefully worded exploitive rules may *still* produce more happiness than unhappiness. For example, it may serve the general happiness to adopt the rule "We may torture terrorist prisoners to extract terrorist plots from them." But rule-utilitarians have an answer even to this problem. Let's take this rule: "We may never exploit individuals, even for an alleged greater good." Adopting this blanket policy would cover *all* exploitive situations, including both exploitive actions and exploitive rules. Further, utilitarians would argue that adopting this blanket rule would promote more general happiness than if it wasn't adopted. Even if some instances of exploitation (either acts or rules) do serve the general happiness, most exploitation will result in unhappiness. The tendency of exploitation in general, then, is toward unhappiness. So, a rule prohibiting all exploitation will be one that, on balance, serves the general happiness.

Grote's Criticism: Utilitarianism Only Perpetuates the Status Quo

Suppose we wanted to determine whether capital punishment is morally proper. According to Mill, we find this out by looking at how much pleasure and pain result from actually putting people to death. This involves an experiential inspection of the various consequences—an approach that, in essence, grounds morality in our factual observations. In his posthumously published *An Exami-*

nation of the Utilitarian Philosophy (1870), **John Grote** (1813–1866) criticizes this purely experiential approach to determining our moral obligations. For Grote, appeals to experience will only perpetuate the status quo, and it won't include an ideal moral goal toward which we should aim. In Grote's words, Mill bases morality only on what *is* the case, not on what *ought to be* the case. Morality should include guidelines for moral improvement, but we will never get such guidelines by appealing only to what *is* the case. Grote makes this point here:

> Man has improved as he has, because certain portions of his race have had in them the spirit of self-improvement, or, as I have called it, the ideal element; have been unsatisfied with what to them at the time has been the positive, the matter of fact, the immediately utilitarian; have risen above the cares of the day . . . (*An Examination of the Utilitarian Philosophy*, 13)

According to Grote, to obtain ideal guidelines, we need an *intuitive* knowledge of morality, which is beyond mere experience.

Mill has a solution to this problem. The notion of general happiness is very elastic insofar as it includes "many and various pleasures," with "few and transitory pains." In his *Systematic Logic,* Mill argues that the notion of pleasure is broad and includes all pleasing conscious states. Among these various pleasures, there certainly is room for the pleasure we derive from attempts at moral reform and social improvement. In fact, a key theme throughout *Utilitarianism* is that, over time, the status quo of general happiness will improve through education and science. And this prospect is something that we can take pleasure in *right now*. Therefore, although the criterion of general happiness is based on experiential observation, general happiness is elastic enough to include the pleasure of establishing ideal moral goals.

Unfortunately, elasticity in the notion of general happiness has negative as well as positive implications. To illustrate, Italian philosopher Cesare Beccaria (1738–1794) describes a situation in which a cruel government inflicts pain on its citizens to keep them in a state of fear. However, over time, the government will be desensitized to the suffering it inflicts, and the citizens themselves will increase their level of tolerance for the suffering they can endure. So, over time, the government must become *more* cruel and unjust to maintain the same level of fear that was previously achieved with less cruelty. If Beccaria is correct in his description of our ability to adjust to cruelty, then Grote's criticism is revalidated. After all, our perception of happiness at any given moment—either now or in the future—may not be sufficient to either recognize or condemn excessively cruel conduct. An independent standard of ideal morality is required to assure that cruelty is correctly identified and then condemned. From this perspective, the experiential basis of Mill's utilitarianism appears inadequate.

Albee's Criticism: Higher Pleasures Are Inconsistent with Hedonism

We saw that the most distinctive feature of Mill's utilitarianism is his view that happiness consists of both higher and lower pleasures, and that higher pleasures are qualitatively superior to lower pleasures. It is also this aspect of Mill's theory that has generated the most criticism. The problem is that Mill appears to offer two separate standards of general happiness: (1) pleasure and (2) dignity. If we see pleasure as the sole criterion, then we must deemphasize dignity; if we see dignity as the principal criterion, then we must deemphasize pleasure. Critics of Mill, both past and present, see this as a big problem. American philosopher **Ernest Albee** (1865–1929) concisely states the central issue here:

> The inconsistency, in truth, may be expressed in a word: If all good things are good in proportion as they bring pleasure to oneself or others, one cannot add to this statement that pleasure itself, the assumed criterion, is more or less desirable in terms of something else (e.g., human dignity) which is not pleasure. (*A History of English Utilitarianism*, 12)

We can also express this problem in terms of the distinction that Mill draws between quantitative and qualitative pleasures. If the superiority of higher pleasures *is* quantitative, then the higher/lower distinction is unnecessary, and Mill contradicts himself; if the superiority of higher pleasures *is not* quantitative, then Mill's hedonism is compromised.

The problem here is genuine, and Mill simply can't hold up both pleasure and dignity as the principal standard of happiness. We might try to rescue Mill from this problem and side with either one standard or the other. One option is to reject pleasure as the ultimate standard and judge actions based on the dignifying nature of conduct. This, though, is a rather clumsy standard since we don't typically think of morality in terms of dignifying versus undignifying behavior. Also, this standard will produce counterintuitive moral judgments. For example, any number of medical procedures are undignifying, such as pap smears or prostate exams. Or, think of the indignity simply of going to the bathroom—an activity we share with the lowest of animals. In spite of their inherent indignity, however, these activities are certainly not immoral. And, with regard to more dignifying activities, it doesn't make sense to say, for example, that prostate exams are *less* moral than visits to an art museum.

The other option is to set aside the notions of dignity and qualitative superiority, and simply to see pleasure as the standard of happiness. This solution ultimately brings Mill closer to Bentham, since the difference between pleasures would only be quantitative. This even allows for the possibility of a utilitarian calculus of differing quantities of pleasure. However, this option resurrects the problem that Mill hoped to avoid—namely, that utilitarianism is a doctrine worthy only of swine since swine also pursue pleasure. Ultimately, then, dignity and quantitative pleasure each seem to be inadequate standards of morality.

The Continuing Utilitarian Tradition

Bentham and Mill's hedonistic utilitarianism is a mixed bag. On the plus side, by focusing exclusively on the *pleasure* that results from a course of action, morality stands up to experiential and even scientific judgment. Hedonistic utilitarians argue that we can record experiences of pleasure, quantify degrees of pleasure, and use this as the basis of our moral judgments. Moral assessment, then, isn't a matter of personal feelings or intuitions; instead, hedonistic utilitarianism places the issue of morality squarely in the arena of public observation. Even today, many philosophers and social scientists defend hedonistic utilitarianism because of its objectivity. Books in microeconomics routinely include chapters on techniques for numerically measuring utility.

On the minus side, critics point out that pleasure isn't the only thing in life that is morally significant. Religious and political martyrs are vivid illustrations of this. Many people throughout history have felt morally compelled to defend their religious or political ideals knowing full well that they would be tortured and ultimately killed for their actions. Their lives would have been more pleasurable—or at least far less painful—if they had simply conformed to social expectations. It seems, then, that an important part of our moral assessments goes beyond mere pleasure.

Mill himself acknowledged that mere pleasure isn't the only thing that counts, and as we've seen, he addressed this problem with the notion of higher pleasures. Perhaps Mill would say that martyrs experience higher pleasures that counterbalance their pains. To more successfully address this problem, some contemporary defenders of utilitarianism abandon pleasure altogether as the ultimate criterion and propose instead a standard that is broad enough to include cases like religious and political martyrs. The two most popular alternatives are ideal utilitarianism and preference utilitarianism.

Ideal Utilitarianism and Preference Utilitarianism   Ideal utilitarianism is the view that the morally right course of action is the one that brings about the greatest amount of *goodness,* regardless of what we specifically identify as good. Many things in life are intrinsically good, such as aesthetic beauty, integrity, friendship, fulfillment of desires, fairness, and freedom. However, we shouldn't single out any one of these qualities as definitive, which is exactly what Bentham and Mill did by focusing on pleasure. According to British philosopher **G. E. Moore** (1873–1958), it is actually *impossible* for us to pinpoint all of the qualities that constitute absolute goodness:

> It is just possible that the Absolute Good may be entirely composed of qualities which we cannot even imagine. This is possible, because, though we certainly do know a great many things that are good-in-themselves, and good in a high degree, yet what is best does not necessarily contain all the good things there are. (*Principia Ethica,* 6.11)

Rather than focusing on a specific quality, such as pleasure, we should instead recognize that *any* consequence that counts as good needs to be entered into the utilitarian tally. Suppose I live in a repressive country and am considering voicing my unpopular political opinions. I not only tally the pain I will experience from being tortured, which is clearly bad, but also tally the assertion of my freedom and the integrity of my convictions, which are good things. How do we recognize the various things that count as good? Moore argues that we should start by pointing out the flaws in popular standards of goodness that leave out important goods. Moore concludes that the ideal standard we arrive at will emphasize a mixture of aesthetic enjoyments, such as beauty, and admirable mental qualities, such as sociability. Ultimately, we must rely on intuition to recognize the various goods.

Preference utilitarianism is the view that the morally right course of action is the one that maximizes our *preferences*. Again, if I live in a repressive country and am considering expressing my unpopular political opinions, I would tally my preference for free expression in addition to the pain I would experience from being tortured. Preference utilitarianism is most associated with contemporary British philosopher **R. M. Hare.** There are three key aspects to Hare's account. First, to say that I "prefer" something simply means that I would *choose* that thing if the appropriate situation arose. For example, to say, "I prefer that Karla Faye Tucker be executed," means that I would choose in favor of her execution if I had the chance. Second, my preferences include a combination of both immediate and long-term preferences. Among other combinations, it includes (1) what I prefer right now to attain right now, (2) what I prefer right now to attain in the future, and (3) what I will prefer in the future to attain in the future. Third, my preferences are not merely restricted to myself but also include the preferences of other people. That is, some of my preferences must be impartial and universal, and I must imagine what my preferences would be if I were in someone else's shoes. For example, I would *not* prefer that, if I were Tucker, I should be executed. But I *would* prefer that, if I were a relative of the victim, Tucker should be executed. According to Hare, I need to tally my own preferences for myself and weigh them against what I'd prefer if I were other parties involved. If my preferences focused only on myself, then I would be an egoist, and not a utilitarian.

Both ideal utilitarianism and preference utilitarianism allow us to tally a broad range of possible consequences in our utilitarian calculus. Contrary to hedonism, they recognize that pleasure isn't the only thing that counts. However, ideal and preference utilitarians pay a price for being so inclusive— namely, they lose objectivity. As mentioned earlier, according to hedonistic utilitarians, pleasure can be experientially measured. However, ideal goodness and personal preferences *cannot* be experientially measured. These are founded in gut feelings and private intuitions, which don't lend themselves to public inspection. Consequently, many utilitarians stick with the old hedonistic version in spite of its narrowness.

Problems with the Bare-Bones Utilitarian Formula   Utilitarians from Bentham and Mill onward are united in the view that morality is a matter of weighing the positive versus the negative consequences of a course of action. We described this earlier as a *bare-bones* concept of morality, which doesn't involve other considerations such as virtues, God's will, natural law, or natural rights. Utilitarian writers present different claims about the purpose of the bare-bones utilitarian formula. They sometimes see it as (1) a description of how we actually make moral decisions or (2) a description of how we *should* make moral decisions or (3) a quick and easy test to use in making moral decisions. But no version of utilitarianism is successful in any of these claims.

First, utilitarianism doesn't accurately describe how we always make moral decisions, as we can see from the Karla Faye Tucker story. Although both sides of the dispute at some point offered utilitarian reasoning for their views, they also appealed to a variety of nonutilitarian reasons. Tucker herself believed that, as a matter of simple mercy, society should forgive criminals who reform. Her critics argued that she should be executed based on an "eye for an eye" notion of justice. Appeals to simple mercy or to eye-for-an-eye justice don't involve utilitarian tallies of good or bad consequences. Also, utilitarianism involves a type of arithmetic by which we subtract the weight of the negative consequences from the weight of the positive consequences. Those calling for Tucker's execution appear to have simply dismissed the positive consequences of her staying alive. That is, they did not subtract the positive consequences from the negative ones, as a true utilitarian would.

Second, it isn't clear that we *should* adopt the utilitarian formula when making all of our moral decisions. Kant made this point specifically with regard to capital punishment. Although Kant himself defended the death penalty, he argued that, if we execute a criminal because of its positive value for society, such as crime deterrence, then we are using the criminal as a tool for our own purposes. For Kant, it is always bad to use someone as a tool, even if the person in question *is* a criminal. Finally, in many if not most cases, the utilitarian formula is neither a quick nor an easy way of making moral decisions. It is difficult to see how many people might be affected by a given course of action. It is also difficult to know how to assign weight to the various good or bad consequences that emerge. Although hedonistic utilitarians brag that pleasure can be experientially quantified, the fact remains that scientists haven't yet invented a pleasure meter. Assigning weight to pleasures and pains will still involve some level of subjective judgment.

Perhaps the problem with utilitarianism is its bare-bones claim that morality depends *entirely* on calculations of consequences. Philosophers today are drawn to simple formulas and to simple explanations for complex philosophical puzzles. But moral decision making appears to be one area that we can't account for with a simple, unified formula. Our actual moral decision-making process depends on a patchwork of various theories and explanations that can't be reduced to a single theme. At times, we do rely on utilitarian reasoning, and, to that extent it is an important part of moral decision making. Utilitarians merely need to abdicate their claim to sole authority.

Summary

Many philosophers as far back as ancient times believed that pleasure is the standard by which we should judge moral conduct. Philosophers during the 18th century refined this notion, and with Bentham, we find the classic statement of hedonistic utilitarianism. According to Bentham, we determine whether an action is right by calculating all of the pleasure and pain that results from that action. We noted two problems with Bentham's approach. First, the process of calculating consequences is too long and involved to be of practical value. Second, in Bentham's view, even our trivial actions have moral significance since we should be maximizing general happiness. Both of these problems result from Bentham's being an act-utilitarian, insofar as we must calculate the consequences of *each* of our actions. Mill offered a version of rule-utilitarianism holding that we test only the utility of moral rules, not that of each action. Mill also parted company with Bentham by emphasizing the difference between higher and lower pleasures. For Mill, higher pleasures are more important than lower ones and are also incapable of numerical computation.

Bradley criticized that utilitarianism conflicts with common moral values; for example, with utilitarianism, I could justifiably exploit people if doing so maximized the general happiness. In response, utilitarians point out that such exploitation is not justifiable if we consider long-term negative consequences and if we adopt rules against exploitation. Grote criticized that utilitarianism locks us into the morality of the status quo and doesn't account for moral progress. In response, a utilitarian might argue that we can take pleasure now in the possible moral reforms of the future. Albee criticized that Mill inconsistently holds to two standards of moral value: pleasure and dignity. We've seen that this poses a genuine problem for Mill's theory. Contemporary critics argue that hedonistic utilitarianism is misguided since pleasure isn't the only thing of value in life. In response, ideal utilitarians such as Moore recommend that we tally the total good versus bad that results from a course of action. Preference utilitarians such as Hare recommend that we assess our total preferences regarding a course of action. In any case, we should take into account utilitarian considerations, but this should not comprise our entire moral evaluation.

Study Questions

Introduction

1. What was Tucker's utilitarian argument for why she should not have been executed?
2. In its general form, what is the utilitarian moral theory?
3. What is "hedonism," and what is "hedonistic utilitarianism"?

The Historical Development of Utilitarianism

4. What was Epicurus's view about pleasure?

Eighteenth-Century Contributions

5. What are the four key elements of utilitarianism found in Hutcheson's writings?
6. What are Hume's two contributions to utilitarianism?

Bentham's Utilitarian Calculus

7. What are the seven criteria of Bentham's utilitarian calculus?

References

The interview with Karla Faye Tucker is from *Larry King Live*, January 31, 1998.
The quotation by Epicurus is from *Letter to Menoeceus*, translated by Norman Lillegard, in *Metaethics, Normative Ethics, and Applied Ethics*, edited by James Fieser (Belmont, CA: Wadsworth, 2000).

The quotations by Francis Hutcheson are from *Inquiry Concerning Moral Good and Evil* (1725), in *British Moralists,* edited by D. D. Raphael (Indianapolis: Hackett, 1969).

The quotation by David Hume is from *A Treatise of Human Nature* (1739–40), which is available in several modern editions.

The quotations by Jeremy Bentham are from *Introduction to the Principles of Morals and Legislation* (1789), in *The Works of Jeremy Bentham,* edited by John Bowring (London, 1838–43).

The review of Bentham's *Principles* in the *Analytical Review* is from Vol. 5, 1789, pp. 306–310; the review in the *Critical Review* is from Vol. 68, 1789, pp. 333–340.

The early comment about the popularity of Bentham's theory is from Simon Laurie's *On the Philosophy of Ethics* (Edinburgh: Edmonston and Douglas, 1866).

The early comment about Mill establishing a "new utilitarianism" is from Simon Laurie's *Notes Expository and Critical on Certain British Theories of Morals* (Edinburgh: Edmonston and Douglas, 1868), p. 114.

The quotations by Mill are from *Utilitarianism* (London: Parker, Son and Bourn, 1863), which is available in several modern editions.

In *An Examination of the Utilitarian Philosophy* (London: Bell, 1870), p. 9, John Grote writes that he expected Mill to follow up with a longer book.

Ernest Albee describes the universal familiarity of Mill's book in *A History of English Utilitarianism* (New York: Macmillan, 1902), p. 249.

The quotations from F. H. Bradley are from *Ethical Studies* (London: King, 1876), Essay 3, pp. 81, 97.

The quotations by John Grote are from *An Examination of the Utilitarian Philosophy* (London: Bell, 1870), p. 308.

Cesare Beccaria's point about mental adjustment to cruelty appears in Chapter 27 of his *On Crimes and Punishments* (1764), which is available in several recent translations.

The quotation by Ernest Albee is from *In a History of English Utilitarianism* (New York: Macmillan, 1902), p. 252.

G. E. Moore's version of utilitarianism appears in the closing chapter of *Principia Ethica* (Cambridge: Cambridge University Press, 1903). The term "ideal utilitarianism" was coined in reference to Moore's theory by W. D. Ross in *The Right and the Good* (Oxford: Oxford University Press, 1930).

R. M. Hare's version of preference utilitarianism is in his *Moral Thinking* (Oxford: Clarendon Press, 1981).

Kant's discussion of capital punishment is in *The Metaphysical Elements of Justice,* translated by John Ladd (Indianapolis: Bobbs-Merrill, 1965), pp. 99–107.

Suggestions for Further Reading

Eighteenth-century writers who adopt utilitarian-type reasoning include Claude-Adrien Helvetius, *Essays on the Mind* (1758); Cesare Beccaria, *On Crimes and Punishments* (1764); Joseph Priestley, *Essay on the First Principles of Government* (1768); William Paley, *The Principles of Moral and Political Philosophy* (1785); William Godwin, *Enquiry Concerning Political Justice* (1793).

For recent commentaries on Mill's moral theory, see Fred Berger, *Happiness, Justice, and Freedom: The Moral and Political Philosophy of John Stuart Mill* (Berkeley: University of California Press, 1984); Wesley E. Cooper, *New Essays on John Stuart Mill and Utilitarianism* (Guelph, Ontario: Canadian Association for Publishing in Philosophy, 1979); Samuel Gorovitz, *Utilitarianism with Critical Essays* (Indianapolis:

Bobbs-Merrill, 1971); J. B. Schneewind, *Sidgwick's Ethics and Victorian Moral Philosophy* (Oxford: Clarendon Press, 1977).

For contemporary discussions of utilitarianism, see Michael D. Bayles, ed., *Contemporary Utilitarianism* (Garden City, NY: Anchor Books, 1968); Richard B. Brandt, *Morality, Utilitarianism, and Rights* (New York: Cambridge University Press, 1992); Samuel Scheffler, *Consequentialism and Its Critics* (New York: Oxford University Press, 1988); J. J. C. Smart and Bernard Williams, *Utilitarianism: For and Against* (Cambridge: Cambridge University Press, 1973).

12

Evolutionary Ethics

Introduction

For decades, science fiction writers and futurists have put forth bizarre scenarios involving genetic engineering. We might stockpile human clones for spare body parts. With some genetic cutting and pasting, we might create human drones for menial labor and more brainy people for leadership positions. We might also select from a menu of genetic options and design superhumans who are stronger, healthier, smarter, and longer living. Although these scenarios grab our attention, until recently their scientific reality seemed too far-fetched to take seriously. In 1997, though, Scottish scientists at Edinburgh's Roslin Institute announced that they had successfully cloned a sheep from the cell of another sheep's udder. The new sheep, named Dolly, was the first cloned mammal in scientific history, and the announcement of Dolly's creation brought science fiction much closer to reality. This event sparked a wave of heated ethical discussions, and in a knee-jerk reaction, many scientists and politicians around the world declared that cloning humans was immoral and should be banned. Some claimed that the procedure was too risky at the current stages of research and that at best perhaps only one in ten attempted human clones would be viable, with the remaining nine simply treated as human waste. Others argued that, even if the odds of viability were substantially improved, it would still be inherently immoral to clone humans in view of the potential abuses of this technology, such as creating specialized races. Even as these critics voiced their cautionary views, scientists continued to announce the creation of even more cloned and genetically altered animals.

It was only a matter of time before other scientists and politicians put a different spin on the ethics of human cloning. Scientists in Britain held public debates on the issue, and one scientist commented that "I think what we probably want is to stop the wild and irresponsible notion of cloning whole human beings. . . . But we would like the scientific analogues, the procedures that might in five years' time lead to curing of diseases, to continue." More dramatically, a Chicago physicist publicly announced that, in spite of current opposition, he would begin work on cloning a human: "I've said many times that you can't stop science. . . . God made man in his own image. God intended for man to become one with God. . . . Cloning and the reprogramming of DNA is the first serious step in becoming one with God." And in a controversial book, Princeton University biologist Lee M. Silver argued that ethical debates on bioengineering are all but irrelevant. Regardless of the cautious positions taken by some legislators and scientists, research into these areas will continue at full speed. In our human drive for better health, longer life, and even perfection, we won't be hampered by ethical questions.

The genetic engineering debate today attempts to determine the morality of intentionally altering and improving human DNA. In the second half of the nineteenth century, philosophers asked a related ethical question about the *evolutionary* development of humans. Although nineteenth-century philosophers couldn't foresee the possibility of altering human DNA through gene-splicing techniques, they understood the evolutionary forces at work that might more naturally alter our human nature. Evolutionary theorists noted three such mechanisms. First, human biology is the product of millions of years of natural evolutionary development, and we have every reason to believe that human biological evolution will continue. Second, through selective-breeding techniques, we may speed up the natural evolutionary process of human development. Third, evolutionary development doesn't end with biology but also extends to social and ethical behavior; that is, value systems themselves are shaped by human survival.

From an ethical perspective, the first of these evolutionary mechanisms isn't particularly noteworthy since hundreds of thousands of years might pass before evolution by itself could produce noticeable changes in human physiology. The second of these mechanisms—selective breeding—can no longer be viewed as a serious option in view of the effects of forced sterilization policies in the United States, as well as Nazi efforts at creating a master race in World War II Germany. At their best, selective breeding practices might violate reproductive rights of individuals, and, at their worst, they may too easily lead to genocide. The more mainstream evolutionary ethicists of the nineteenth century focused on the third of these evolutionary mechanisms—namely, that human social behavior is an extended development of biological evolution. In this context, **evolutionary ethics** refers to the view that moral behavior is that which tends to aid in human survival.

Nineteenth-Century Theories of Evolutionary Ethics

Theories of evolutionary ethics hinge directly on more general accounts of biological evolution. Biologists of the eighteenth and early nineteenth centuries offered a variety of explanations for how animals evolve over time. However, in his landmark book *On the Origin of Species* (1859), **Charles Darwin** (1809–1882) championed the explanation of evolution that we've come to accept.

Darwin and the Evolution of Moral Faculties

Darwin's account of evolution, which he calls "natural selection," has three main elements. First, living beings undergo random mutations that are passed on to offspring. Second, most creatures are doomed to early death either because there isn't enough food to go around or because other animals eat them. Third, animals that have the most beneficial mutations will survive and pass those attributes on to their offspring. For example, suppose that two animals are born of the same parents, but one of the newborns has longer legs because of a random mutation. The longer legs enable this animal to run faster than its sibling, and so it is better able to run down prey and to escape from predators. The normal sibling, then, dies while the mutated animal survives, reproduces, and passes the attribute of longer legs on to its offspring. Eventually all of the shorter-legged members of the species die out in the struggle for survival, while the longer-legged members live on. In this manner, attributes of a species change slowly over time, and a new species eventually emerges. For Darwin, species are mutable, and each group of organisms represents only the present status of its species. The apparent development of species over time, from less complex to more complex, is completely unguided and shouldn't be attributed to a built-in natural purpose of things.

Darwin's *Origin of Species* focuses only on the evolutionary development of nonhuman animals. Privately, though, Darwin believed that humans were just one more type of animal and thereby subject to the same evolutionary mechanisms as other animals. In his *Descent of Man* (1871), published twelve years after the *Origin,* Darwin openly addresses the issue of human evolution and devotes almost thirty pages to the evolutionary development of morality. His explanation has two parts, one psycho-physiological and the other social.

From the psycho-physiological perspective, our moral faculties develop directly from our social instincts, such as the inclination to care for children and live in groups. Darwin argues that any animal that developed social instincts "would inevitably acquire a moral sense or conscience" as soon as that animal reached a high level of intelligence. In point of fact, though, only humans have attained that level. The social instincts of ordinary animals enable them to sympathize with members of their social units and to respond to praise and blame, as in the case of dogs. Humans, however, move beyond this and are, in Darwin's words, "moral beings." For Darwin, "a moral being is one who is capable of comparing his past and future actions or motives, and of approving or disapproving of them." In this regard, humans developed a moral sense and also a conscience, both of which aid in our survival, just as social instincts aid in the survival of some animals. The job of the moral sense is to tell us what we ought to do, and the job of the conscience is to give us the appropriate motivation to do the right thing.

The second part of Darwin's evolutionary explanation of morality is social. As we move from a primitive to a moderate state of civilization, we adopt moral principles and attitudes that assist in the survival of our small social unit. We put aside individual interests for the good of the group and advocate patriotism, loyalty, obedience, and self-sacrifice. Darwin explains:

> A tribe including many members who, from possessing in a high degree the spirit of patriotism, fidelity, obedience, courage, and sympathy, were always ready to aid one another, and to sacrifice themselves for the common good, would be victorious over most other tribes; and this would be natural selection. At all times throughout the world tribes have supplanted other tribes; and as morality is one important element in their success, the standard of morality and the number of well-endowed men will thus everywhere tend to rise and increase. (*Descent of Man,* 5)

As our societies become larger and more advanced, we can trace the consequences of our actions to broader groups of people, and our sympathies become more diffused to all races. Ironically, once we reach an advanced level of civilization, we adopt many moral rules that are less related to the preservation of our social group. For example, we care for physically weak and mentally impaired people, which, according to Darwin, is "highly injurious to the race of man." We do this mainly as a byproduct of our enlarged moral sympathies. We also harm the human race when we send our strongest young men to fight in wars, thereby leaving procreation to the weaker men who stay behind. Darwin notes as well that the practice of inheriting wealth from our parents is damaging since it makes us "useless drones." However, always looking to our survival, we create other moral rules that restrict the damage done by these practices.

Although Darwin's account of evolutionary ethics is suggestive, it doesn't systematically explore the subject of ethics. Darwin's defenders took on this task, most notably British philosopher **Herbert Spencer** (1820–1903).

Spencer's Evolutionary Ethics In his book *The Data of Ethics* (1879), Spencer offers what is probably the most detailed nineteenth-century account of evolutionary ethics. Like Darwin, Spencer distinguishes between a biological and a sociological component of evolution. In fact, Spencer sees three interrelated areas of evolution in animals: (1) the animal's species, (2) the animal's bodily functions, and (3) the animal's conduct:

> Three [evolutionary] subjects are to be definitely distinguished . . . the subject of conduct lies outside the subject of functions [movement of limbs, bodily actions], if not as far as this lies outside the subject of structures [types of animals, organisms] still far enough to make it substantially different. (*The Data of Ethics,* 2.3)

Ethics involves the third of these three aspects of evolution—namely, the development of the animal's conduct. Spencer argues that more biologically complex organisms have more complex conduct. Insects, for example, have a very low level of biological complexity and thus have comparatively less complex conduct. Humans, by contrast, have the most biological complexity and thus the most complex conduct, and ethics is the final stage in the development of that conduct. Spencer explains this point here:

> Ethics has for its subject-matter, that form which universal conduct assumes during the last stages of its evolution. We have also concluded that these last stages in the evolution of conduct are these displayed by the highest type of

being, when he is forced, by increase of numbers, to live more and more in presence of his fellows. And there has followed the corollary that conduct gains ethical sanction in proportion as the activities, becoming less and less militant and more and more industrial, are such as do not necessitate mutual injury or hindrance, but consist with, and are furthered by, co-operation and mutual aid. (*The Data of Ethics,* 2.7)

During this final stage of behavioral development, our conduct is more complex principally because it involves such a high degree of mutual cooperation. Think of the mutual cooperation involved in making a city run efficiently. Utility companies, factories, truckers, retail stores, workers, consumers—all must carefully cooperate with each other. When enough people fail to cooperate, such as in work strikes or criminal activities, then society breaks down.

So, if we ask Spencer where morality comes from in the larger scheme of things, his answer is that ethics is the highest evolutionary development of human conduct—namely, mutual cooperation. Suppose that we press Spencer further and ask him what is so morally significant about mutual cooperation. His answer would be that mutual cooperation brings about the greatest amount of universal pleasure. Ultimately, then, highly evolved conduct is good because it facilitates universal pleasure. Drawing on both Bentham and Mill, Spencer proposes a version of hedonistic utilitarianism: Ethical conduct is that which maximizes both our selfish and unselfless motivations.

There are several steps to Spencer's theory of hedonism. First, Spencer argues that the pursuit of pleasure and the avoidance of pain motivate all of our actions, and, consequently, moral good must be associated with pleasures. Second, we have both self-regarding and other-regarding impulses, each of which gives us pleasure when fulfilled. Third, the playoff between our selfish and selfless impulses in larger social groups results in a compromise. That is, my other-regarding inclinations prompt me to give up my selfish interests. However, because you also have other-regarding inclinations, you won't let me completely abandon my selfish interests. As a result, proper conduct is that which produces the greatest satisfaction, as regards both others and myself.

Fourth, and finally, to apply this compromise in practice, we devise principles of equity. At our present and early stage of morality, we advocate the principle that "each [person] claims no more than his equitable share." In time, however, we will evolve beyond this. We will be more other-regarding, and our principle of equity will be that "each [person] restrains himself from taking an undue share of altruistic satisfactions." Ultimately, Spencer believes, we will evolve beyond even this and adopt the principle that "each [person] takes care that others shall have their opportunities for altruistic satisfaction." Currently, these altruistic tendencies within us are "occasional and feeble," but with further evolution they will become habitual and strong.

To recap, here are the main points of Spencer's theory:

- Ethical conduct is the most evolutionarily advanced conduct, emerging only in the most developed life form and in the most advanced human societies.

- The most advanced human conduct involves mutual cooperation, which in turn promotes universal pleasure.
- In our present evolutionary condition, the promotion of universal pleasure involves a compromise between self-regarding and other-regarding inclinations.
- As we evolve, ethical standards will become more altruistic.

Moore's Criticism of Spencer

In 1903, British philosopher **G. E. Moore** (1873–1958) published a work entitled *Principia Ethica,* which in many ways set a new direction for ethical theory in the twentieth century. Moore analyzed the most influential ethical theories of his time—including those of Kant, Mill, and Spencer—and noted a fundamental mistake they all make. In each case, they fail because they wrongly equate moral goodness with some natural or metaphysical property. Spencer, for example, identifies moral goodness with advanced evolutionary development. According to Moore, these philosophers commit what he calls the naturalistic fallacy.

The Naturalistic Fallacy   Moore's explanation of the **naturalistic fallacy** appears in the opening chapter of *Principia*. His discussion rests on a distinction between *simple* and *complex* properties. Compare these two statements:

1. The new banana is yellow.
2. The old banana is speckled.

The attribute "speckled" is a complex property since it involves splotches of several colors. By contrast, the attribute "yellow" is a simple property since it can't be broken down into any constituent part. According to Moore, although we can define complex properties such as "speckled" in terms of their constituent parts, we can't define simple properties such as "yellow." Moore argues that the term "good," like the term "yellow," is a simple property, and thus can't be reduced to any constituent parts. Therefore, we can't define "good" as "pleasure," "highly evolved conduct," or any other property. If we try to define "good" by identifying it with another property, then we commit the naturalistic fallacy. To illustrate the naturalistic fallacy, assume that commendable actions such as charity have these attributes: (1) They constitute the most highly evolved conduct, (2) they promote universal pleasure, and (3) they are morally good. We would commit the naturalistic fallacy if we *identified* the third attribute with either of the first two. This would happen, for example, if we claimed that "moral goodness" and "the promotion of universal pleasure" were the same attributes.

The term *naturalistic fallacy* implies that it is a fallacy to define "good" in terms of properties that we find in *nature,* such as pleasure or evolved conduct. According to Moore, if someone "confused 'good' . . . with any natural object whatever, then there is reason for calling that the naturalistic fallacy." However, there is more to the naturalistic fallacy than simply identifying "good" with a natural object. In Chapter 4 of *Principia,* Moore argues further that it is improper to define "good" in reference to any non-natural or metaphysical quality, as well as to any natural quality. For instance, it is also a fallacy to define "goodness" in terms of doing the will of God, which is a non-natural quality. Scholars now suggest that Moore is actually describing a definist fallacy, which has as subsets the naturalistic fallacy and the metaphysical fallacy. Moore defends his notion of the naturalistic fallacy with what has been called the "open-question argument." That is, for any property that we attempt to identify with "goodness," we can ask, "Is that property itself good?" For example, if I claim that universal pleasure is goodness, the question can be asked, "But, is universal pleasure itself good?" The fact that this question makes sense shows that "universal pleasure" and "goodness" are not identical. Moore believes that no proposed natural or metaphysical property can pass the test of the open-question argument.

Even though it is a fallacy to *define* moral goodness, it isn't a fallacy to claim that qualities such as universal pleasure always *accompany* goodness. For example, it is no fallacy to say that, every time I find an action that is "morally good," I also see that the action produces "universal pleasure." I am simply correlating the presence of two qualities, and not identifying them. Moore writes that "it is a fact, that Ethics aims at discovering what are those other properties belonging to all things which are good." Moore himself believes that we can intuitively recognize a group of such accompanying qualities. He argues that they include aesthetic enjoyments, such as beauty, and admirable mental qualities, such as sociability.

To summarize, here are the main points of Moore's notion of the naturalistic fallacy:

- Moral goodness is a simple, indefinable concept.
- Moral goodness cannot be identified with any natural property (e.g., pleasure).
- Moral goodness cannot be identified with any metaphysical property (e.g., God's will).
- We can note properties that always *accompany* moral goodness, although we don't actually identify these as moral goodness.

Identifying "Goodness" with "More Evolved"   Moore believes that Spencer's evolutionary ethics commits the naturalistic fallacy in several respects. In each case, Spencer supposedly identifies moral goodness with some aspect of the evolutionary process. First, in the following passage, Moore accuses Spencer of committing the naturalistic fallacy for identifying "being more evolved" with "gaining ethical sanction":

> All that the evolution-hypothesis tells us is that certain kinds of conduct are more evolved than others; and this is, in fact, all that Mr. Spencer has at-

tempted to prove in the two chapters concerned. Yet he tells us that one of the things he has proved is that *conduct gains ethical sanction* in proportion as it displays certain characteristics. What he has tried to prove is only that in proportion as it displays those characteristics, it is *more* evolved, it is plain, then, that Mr. Spencer *identifies* the gaining of ethical sanction with the being more evolved. (*Principia Ethica*, 2.31)

The phrase "gains ethical sanction" means that some conduct is "ethically commendable." In this sense, Moore complains that Spencer identifies "more evolved" (a natural property) with "ethically commendable" (goodness) and thereby commits the naturalistic fallacy. In response, Moore is attacking a straw man since Spencer has in mind a weaker claim than the identification of "ethically commendable" with "more evolved."

To illustrate, look at these two statements:

1. Ethical commendability is identical to more evolved conduct.
2. Ethical commendability is always accompanied by more evolved conduct.

The first statement clearly commits the naturalistic fallacy, but the second statement doesn't. As we've seen, we commit the naturalistic fallacy when we *identify* some property with goodness, not merely when we note that a property always *accompanies* goodness. Which of these two statements best expresses Spencer's point? The second one. For Spencer, the most evolved form of conduct is mutual cooperation in a society. The result of this conduct is that more pleasure is produced than would be the case if mutual cooperation didn't take place. So, ethical commendability is a feature that always *accompanies* the most evolved conduct, since such conduct produces the most pleasure.

Moore's second criticism is that Spencer equates the natural term "more evolved" with the moral terms "higher" and "better," and thereby commits the naturalistic fallacy again. Moore continues: What a very different thing is being 'more evolved' from being 'higher' or 'better.' . . . But Mr. Spencer does not seem aware that to assent the one is not to assent the other." In fact, Moore is correct that Spencer identifies "more evolved conduct" with "higher conduct." However, we must distinguish Spencer's use of the phrase "higher conduct" from his use of "ethically superior conduct." For Spencer, conduct is *higher* when it is ethically *significant*—that is, when it may be deemed either good or bad. By contrast, conduct is ethically *superior* when it is actually deemed *good*.

Now look at these two statements:

1. More evolved conduct is ethically *significant.*
2. More evolved conduct is ethically *superior.*

Spencer endorses the first statement, but, technically, it doesn't commit the naturalistic fallacy since it doesn't identify more evolved conduct with goodness itself. The second statement does commit the naturalistic fallacy since it specifically identifies more evolved conduct with goodness. However, Spencer nowhere endorses this second statement. Instead, as a utilitarian, he holds as follows:

> 3. Universally pleasing conduct is ethically *superior.*

It is true that this third statement, endorsed by Spencer, commits the naturalistic fallacy. However, this statement in itself is utilitarian, and not evolutionary, in nature. At worst, then, Spencer commits the naturalistic fallacy because he is a utilitarian, and not because he is an evolutionary ethicist.

Identifying "Goodness" with "Universal Pleasure"   Not surprisingly, Moore recognized that Spencer identified "goodness" with "universal pleasure," and he accuses Spencer of committing the naturalistic fallacy for this as well. However, Moore and Spencer have in mind different conceptions of "goodness," and this difference may protect Spencer from committing the naturalistic fallacy. Spencer clarifies his notion of "goodness" here:

> The characters here predicated by the words good and bad, are not intrinsic characters, for apart from human wants, such things have neither merits nor demerits. We call these articles good or bad according as they are well or ill adapted to achieve prescribed ends. (*Data of Ethics,* 3.8)

The difference between these two notions of "goodness" can be expressed in this way:

- *Intrinsic goodness:* Wisdom is good because it contains within itself a foundational property of goodness.
- *Extrinsic goodness:* Wisdom is good because it brings about a specific external consequence (such as pleasure) that we call "good."

Moore holds to a notion of *intrinsic* goodness, which entails that there exists a unique and concrete property of goodness. Similar to the way that the property of yellowness covers a banana, Moore believes that the unique property of goodness permeates good things. Spencer, by contrast, makes no such assumption, but instead merely stipulates that "good" refers to some external or *extrinsic* quality, such as pleasure. We can see this difference in how both Spencer and Moore describe "good" things. Spencer uses phrases such as "acts we *call* good," "we *ascribe* goodness," and "we *apply* them [i.e., 'good' and 'bad']." Moore, by contrast, speaks in terms of something *being* good.

Given their differing notions of "good," we may argue that Spencer doesn't commit the naturalistic fallacy and that for Moore "good" is indefinable only because Moore sees goodness as an intrinsic property. Since Spencer rejects the idea that things are intrinsically good, and instead assumes that the term "good" is by itself an empty placeholder, then it would be no fallacy for Spencer to define "good" in terms of pleasure. The issue is no longer one of fallaciously identifying two properties (i.e., pleasure and intrinsic goodness), but one of denying the notion of intrinsic goodness altogether. The dispute isn't definitional, but metaphysical, and concerns the question of moral realism. Moral realism is the view that goodness is an independent and objective quality of the world—

one that right actions possess intrinsically and that wrong actions lack. Whereas Moore endorses moral realism, Spencer doesn't, arguing instead that there is no objective quality of goodness intrinsic to right actions.

It was not Moore's intention, nor is it in the spirit of Moore, to reduce the issue of the naturalistic fallacy to a mere denial of moral realism. Perhaps, then, we should place some parameters on the naturalistic fallacy to separate it from the moral realism question: We commit the naturalistic fallacy only when (1) we assert intrinsic goodness, and (2) we identify goodness with a second property, such as pleasure, which always accompanies a morally commendable action. Given that Spencer's theory falls outside the first parameter, he can't be accused of committing the naturalistic fallacy.

Evolutionary Ethics Today

The evolutionary ethics of Darwin and Spencer was a short-lived phase in the history of moral philosophy. One reason for its limited appeal was that the most sophisticated accounts of evolutionary ethics, such as Spencer's, were simply versions of hedonistic utilitarianism. The evolutionary component provides an interesting causal explanation for why we value various pleasures, but, in the end, our recommended moral duty is simply to maximize universal pleasure.

Lingering Problems with Evolutionary Ethics   Although we've rescued Spencer's account of evolutionary ethics from Moore's criticism, there remain fundamental problems with such theories that make them untenable. One problem with theories of evolutionary ethics concerns how we distinguish less evolved from more evolved conduct when comparing one society to another. Many evolutionary writers, including Spencer, believed that primal human cultures had less evolved conduct, and industrialized societies more evolved conduct. Presumably, moral development paralleled this social development. Similarly, British anthropologist Edward Tylor (1832–1917) sketched an evolutionary development of religious beliefs from primitive to advanced societies. According to Tylor, the most primitive societies were animistic, believing in spirits that inhabited natural objects. This evolved into polytheistic belief in a multiplicity of deities, which in turn gave rise to monotheistic belief in a single God. Finally, for Tylor, the most advanced societies abandon religious belief entirely, and a metaphysical perspective evolves that explains natural phenomena in terms of science and ethics. The chief problem with this approach is that we lack objective criteria for distinguishing less evolved from more evolved conduct. Little suggests that behavioral interaction in primal cultures is socially less evolved than behavioral interaction in technological societies. Without a clearly defined evolutionary spectrum of social behavior, we cannot draw a correlation between such behavior and varying degrees of moral development.

A second problem with nineteenth-century theories of evolutionary ethics is that they were unjustifiably optimistic about our ultimate moral destiny. Virtually all evolutionary writers believed that, although we are more ethically evolved than primal societies, we've not yet achieved moral perfection. They argued though, that it is simply a matter of time before we get it right. Spencer, for example, maintained that we will become more *altruistic* through further evolutionary development. This optimistic attitude of moral improvement was part of the spirit of the times and carried over into the early twentieth century. Social theorists dubbed World War I "the war to end all wars" since they saw it as the final hurdle to jump in achieving a condition of social harmony. However, this optimism was unfounded, as the brutality of World War I and the succession of devastating wars that followed proved.

Our current vision of our future moral development appears to be mixed, as we can infer from science fiction stories. For example, the *Star Trek* series depicts humans in an advanced state of moral altruism. Personal greed is all but absent, and each battle brings humans a step closer to peace throughout the galaxy. By contrast, the *Alien* movie series shows humanity at its worst. People slaughter each other and place entire civilizations at risk simply to achieve some short-term personal gain. Paradoxically, as viewers, we relate to both the optimistic and pessimistic visions in these science fiction sagas. We can foresee the future as a much more ethical place, yet we can also envision the future as an extension of present human urges at their worst. Our views concerning our future moral evolution are caught in the middle.

Sociobiology and Moral Ambivalence   In recent years, evolutionary ethics has come back with a vengeance, principally through the vehicle of sociobiology. In his groundbreaking book *Sociobiology: The New Synthesis* (1975), Edward O. Wilson argues that questions of morality—and all other questions of human social interaction—are directly linked with evolutionary biology. As such, Wilson believes that issues of ethics are better treated by biologists rather than philosophers:

> Scientists and humanists should consider together the possibility that the time has come for ethics to be removed temporarily from the hands of the philosophers and biologicized. (*Sociobiology*, 27)

The morality of sociobiology is not the optimistic vision of altruism that Spencer describes as our evolutionary fate. Instead, Wilson believes that we carry around conflicting values, which are grounded in different genetic predispositions that have evolved for different survival reasons. Sometimes we are inclined to show loyalty to ourselves, and other times we are inclined to show loyalty to social groups:

> The individual is forced to make imperfect choices based on irreconcilable loyalties—between the "rights" and "duties" of self and those of family, tribe, and other units of selection, each of which evolves its own code of honor. No wonder the human spirit is in constant turmoil. (*Sociobiology*, 5)

In Wilson's words, evolution makes us morally *ambivalent* insofar as we have conflicting moral loyalties.

In response to Wilson's dismal picture of moral ambivalence, we might maintain that some standard of morality lies outside of the evolutionary process. British evolutionary biologist **Thomas Huxley** (1825–1895) made this point most clearly. Near the end of his life, in reconsidering the relation between evolution and morality, Huxley parted company with Darwin and Spencer. According to Huxley, evolutionary forces generate a war of all against all, just as Hobbes described. The only way to rise above our warring tendencies is to rely on ethical intuitions that are distinct from evolution. To make his case, Huxley argues that if we assume that evolution explains the origin of our *social* behavior, then we must also accept that evolution explains the origin of our *antisocial* behavior:

> The thief and the murderer follow nature just as much as the philanthropist. Cosmic evolution may teach us how the good and the evil tendencies of man may have come about; but, in itself, it is incompetent to furnish any better reason why what we call good is preferable to what we call evil than we had before. ("Evolution and Ethics")

Huxley believes that it is a mistake to think that, just because survival of the fittest is the source of our organic development, it is also the source of our ethical standards. The two forces are, in fact, at odds with each other, and there is a point at which the organic process of human evolution is replaced by that of ethical development.

Huxley is correct that there are clear limits to how the notion of survival of the fittest applies to proper behavior. The following quotation is a good illustration of this:

> Were woman of the same sex as man, that is, were she simply another kind of man, she would soon be eliminated from the earth under the operation of the ordinary law of the survival of the fittest. . . . It is self-evident then that any system which looks to a career for women independent of man, such as man pursues, is abnormal, and injurious to her interests. ("On the Material Relations of Sex")

The nineteenth-century author of this passage argues that women shouldn't have independent careers since their evolutionary survival hinged on protection by men. For the sake of argument, let's grant Huxley's initial point—unfounded as it is—that a race of humans constituted like women might have become extinct in the struggle for survival. However, the subsequent inference of a rule against independent careers for women is far from obvious. There is a point at which evolutionary considerations are simply irrelevant, and we base our moral rules about women's careers on other factors.

Using Wilson's terminology, even if humans are genetically predisposed to have ambivalent loyalties, true morality attempts to move beyond this. Although Huxley himself isn't clear about what nonevolutionary factors are relevant for forming our notions of morality, the history of philosophy offers us a variety of possible moral theories from which to choose.

Natural Selection as an Analogy   The more optimistic 19th-century theories of evolutionary ethics, such as Spencer's, are not necessarily false, but they raise questions that are largely unanswerable. Perhaps in time social scientists will find a definitive way of correlating social complexity with moral progress. Perhaps in time we will have the proper vantage from which to say that we are in fact improving ethically. Until then, the jury remains out. However, even if we set aside the notions of biological development and evolutionary progress, natural selection is still an effective analogy for understanding how we endorse specific behaviors. Taken literally, nineteenth-century theories of evolutionary ethics maintained that moral behavior is that which tends to aid in *human* survival. Taken analogically, though, we might say that moral behavior is that behavior which *itself* tends to survive in social environments. People perform a variety of actions, some of which are suitable to current social environments and others of which are not. People who behave unsuitably are denounced, punished, or even executed; ultimately, the unsuitable behavior dies out and the suitable behavior survives. For example, in past social environments, it was unsuitable for women to pursue independent careers, and women who attempted to do so faced virtually insurmountable obstacles. In current social environments, by contrast, it is suitable for women to seek careers, and women who remain homemakers often feel compelled to defend their decision.

We can't deny that there is a kind of social selection that attempts to weed out unacceptable behavior within a given social environment. Today, political correctness is a dominant social factor, and society doesn't tolerate actions that are politically incorrect. Does morality simply reduce to the systematic social selection of acceptable behavior? Certainly not in the short term, but maybe in the long term. The short-term climate that endorsed anti-Semitism in Nazi Germany can only be described as evil. However, if we look at social trends that survive over the long term, after perhaps a hundred or so years of conflict, these trends become more recognizable as "moral." Beneath these changes, then, lurks a deeper behavioral value that is being selected. Surviving trends over the past century include those that denounce sexism and racism. Perhaps the failure of communism in the former Soviet Union after less than a century means that something is inherently wrong with completely eliminating free-market enterprise. Perhaps the long-term tendency toward socialism in all countries, including the United States, means that something is inherently good about distributing part of our wealth based on the needs of others.

Assessing long-term social trends is difficult, especially the most recent ones. The recent disputes about the ethics of bioengineering are uniquely new, and in the future, we can expect various short-term trends in reaction. Some reactions will be cautious, prohibiting the application of cloning and other techniques to humans. Other short-term trends will more aggressively apply bioengineering techniques to humans. The surviving long-term trend, though, is so far off that we can't predict the outcome. In the meantime, we must remain content with scenarios and warnings from science fiction.

Summary

With the appearance of Darwin's *On the Origin of Species,* biologists and philosophers of the nineteenth century attempted to frame morality as an extension of the evolutionary biological process. Darwin argued that there are two evolutionary components to morality. First, there is a psycho-physiological component involving the development of moral faculties. Second, there is a social component insofar as we develop different moral standards as societies become more complex. Building on Darwin's view, Spencer argued that our most evolutionarily advanced human morality involves mutual cooperation, which in turn promotes universal pleasure. In time, according to Spencer, our notions of universal pleasure will become more altruistic.

Moore criticized Spencer for committing the naturalistic fallacy. Moore claimed that we commit the naturalistic fallacy any time we identify moral goodness with some quality, such as pleasure. First, Moore argued that Spencer commits the fallacy by identifying "being more evolved" with "gaining ethical sanction." In response, we've seen that Spencer only claims that ethical commendability is always accompanied by more evolved conduct. Second, Moore argued that Spencer commits the fallacy by identifying "more evolved conduct" with "higher conduct." In response, we've seen that Spencer claims only that more evolved conduct is ethically *significant,* not that it is ethically *superior.* Third, Moore argued that Spencer commits the fallacy by identifying universally pleasing conduct with ethically superior conduct. In response, we've seen that the naturalistic fallacy hinges on the notion of intrinsic goodness, and Spencer has in mind a notion of extrinsic goodness.

In more recent years, Wilson argued from the perspective of sociobiology that evolution spawns a morality of ambivalence, while Huxley claimed that morality lies outside of the evolutionary process. Finally, evolutionary ethics may be a useful analogy for seeing how moral standards develop, insofar as moral standards are those that survive in social environments.

Study Questions

Introduction

1. What are some of the feared abuses of bioengineering?
2. What is Lee Silver's view about ethical discussions concerning bioethics?
3. What are the three mechanisms of evolution noted by nineteenth-century evolutionists?
4. What is the definition of "evolutionary ethics?"

Nineteenth-Century Theories of Evolutionary Ethics

Darwin and the Evolution of Moral Faculties

5. What are the three main elements of Darwin's account of natural selection?
6. According to Darwin, what are the jobs of the moral sense and the conscience, respectively?
7. For Darwin, what is the "social" component of moral evolution?

8. According to Darwin, what are some moral rules that we develop in our higher stages that are *not* related to the preservation of our social group?

Spencer's Evolutionary Ethics

9. According to Spencer, what are the three areas of evolution, and which of these involves morality?
10. Explain the hedonistic element of Spencer's evolutionary ethics.
11. What are the four main points of Spencer's account of evolutionary ethics?

Moore's Criticism of Spencer

The Naturalistic Fallacy

12. What is the difference between a simple property and a complex property?
13. Explain the difference between the "definist fallacy," the "naturalistic fallacy," and the "metaphysical fallacy."
14. Give an example of a statement noting that a property always accompanies moral goodness.

Identifying "Goodness" with "More Evolved"

15. Concerning Moore's first criticism of Spencer, what is wrong with Moore's accusation that Spencer identifies "being more evolved" with "gaining ethical sanction"?

Identifying "Goodness" with "Universal Pleasure"

16. Concerning Moore's second criticism of Spencer, what is wrong with Moore's accusation that Spencer identifies "more evolved conduct" with "higher conduct"?
17. What is the difference between intrinsic goodness and extrinsic goodness, and which do Spencer and Moore hold to, respectively?
18. To avoid having the naturalistic fallacy collapse into a dispute about moral realism, what are the two parameters we may place on the naturalistic fallacy?

Evolutionary Ethics Today

Lingering Problems with Evolutionary Ethics

19. What is the problem with attempts by evolutionary ethicists to correlate moral development with social development?
20. What is the problem with the optimistic view taken by evolutionary ethicists concerning our future attainment of moral perfection?

Sociobiology and Moral Ambivalence

21. What is Wilson's sociobiological view of ethics?
22. What is Huxley's criticism of evolutionary ethics?

Natural Selection as an Analogy

23. Describe the literal and analogical notions of natural selection in evolutionary ethics.
24. Give an example of a social trend that survived over the long term.

References

The public statement by Chicago physicist Richard Seed was made in January 1998.

The public statement by Colin Campbell, British chairman of the Human Genetics Advisory Commission, was made in January 1998.

Lee M. Silver's discussion of the ethics of cloning is in his *Remaking Eden: Cloning and Beyond in a Brave New World* (New York: Avon Books, 1997).

The quotations by Charles Darwin are from *The Descent of Man* (1871), Chapter 5, which is available in several recent editions.

Herbert Spencer's *The Data of Ethics,* originally published in 1895, is available in several editions, including the first volume of his *Principles of Ethics.* The quotations are from *The Data of Ethics* (New York: Appleton, 1895).

The quotations by G. E. Moore are from *Principia Ethica* (London: Cambridge University Press, 1903).

The distinction between the definist fallacy and the naturalistic fallacy is in William Frankena's "The Naturalistic Fallacy," *Mind,* 1939, Vol. 48, pp. 464–477.

For a more detailed discussion of Moore's criticism of Spencer, see James Fieser, "Spencer, Moore, and the Naturalistic Fallacy," *History of Philosophy Quarterly,* 1993, Vol. 10, pp. 271–277.

The quotations by Edward O. Wilson are from *Sociobiology: The New Synthesis* (Cambridge, MA: Harvard University Press, 1975).

Thomas Huxley's book *Evolution and Ethics and Other Essays,* originally delivered in a 1893 lecture series, is available in several editions. The quotation is from *Evolution and Ethics and Other Essays* (New York: AMS Press, 1970; reprint of the 1896 authorized edition), p. 80.

The quotation on women's careers is by E. D. Cope in "On the Material Relations of Sex," *Monist,* 1890, Vol. 1, pp. 39–40.

Suggestions for Further Reading

For discussions of nineteenth-century evolutionary ethics, see Antony Flew, *Evolutionary Ethics* (London: Macmillan, 1967); John C. Greene, *Darwin and the Modern World* (Baton Rouge: Louisiana State University Press, 1961); Henry Sidgwick, *Lectures on the Ethics of T. H. Green, Mr. Herbert Spencer and J. Martinear* (London: Macmillan, 1901).

For discussions of sociobiology and recent approaches to evolutionary ethics, see Frans de Wall, *Good Natured: The Origins of Right and Wrong in Humans and Other Animals* (Cambridge, MA: Harvard University Press, 1996); Matt Ridley, *The Origins of Virtue: Human Instincts and the Evolution of Cooperation* (New York: Viking Penguin, 1997).

For a discussion of G. E. Moore's ethics, see John Hill, *The Ethics of G. E. Moore: A New Interpretation* (Amsterdam: Van Gorcum, 1976).

13

Emotivism and Prescriptivism

Introduction

Some things in life are so obviously immoral that there is nothing about their ethical status to dispute. In World War II, Nazi Germany exterminated 6 million Jews. Shortly after the Vietnam War, Cambodia's Communist leader Pol Pot attempted to turn his country into an agrarian utopia and, in the process, killed more than a million of his people. Many of civilization's worst moral crimes are acts of genocide, in which specific racial/ethnic groups are deliberately eliminated.

Recently, a new atrocity has been added to the list of genocidal acts—namely, the slaughter of almost a million Tutsi people in the African country of Rwanda. Rwanda has two main ethnic groups: (1) the Hutu, which made up 85 percent of the population, and (2) the Tutsi, which made up about 14 percent. The two groups continually competed for political dominance over the country, and the dominant Hutu group feared the possibility of Tutsi control. By 1994, the Rwandan government was weakened because of widespread famine and various rebel attacks. A Hutu rebel force killed the Rwandan president of twenty years, and the new Hutu rulers sought to end their problems by targeting the Tutsi for elimination. During a 100-day period in the summer of 1994, the Hutu succeeded in killing two-thirds of the country's Tutsi people. Hundreds of thousands of Hutu people went from house to house—often in their own neighborhood—raping, robbing, and murdering their ethnic rivals. The killings were mainly done at close range, with machetes, spears, and clubs.

The more horrible the offense, the more resolute we are about our moral assessment, and in the worst cases we describe the offenses as "evil," a term that we reserve for only the most immoral actions. In spite of how vivid and self-evident some immoralities are, there is still a vagueness in our moral judgments that needs clarification. What *exactly* do I mean when I say, "It is wrong to commit genocide"? Most moral philosophers of the past assumed that our moral judgments were simply about the presence or absence of some moral quality. The phrase "It is wrong to commit genocide" could be variously interpreted according to these theories:

Scotus's theory: "Genocide is contrary to God's commands."

Locke's theory: "Genocide violates our natural rights."

Clarke's theory: "Genocide is contrary to eternal moral relations."

And these are only three of many possible interpretations.

In the early twentieth century, however, many philosophers began to question this approach. When I make the statement "It is wrong to commit genocide," I am not making a factual statement about the presence or absence of a moral quality. Instead, I am merely expressing my personal attitudes, feelings, and recommendations about genocide. It makes no difference how obviously immoral or evil the conduct is; the actual meaning of my moral assessment is simply a reflection of my individual attitude. This view was developed in two related theories. According to the theory of **emotivism**, the fundamental meaning of moral utterances is that they express our feelings. According to **prescriptivism**, the fundamental meaning of moral utterances is that they prescribe or prompt others to adopt some specific behavior.

When first proposed, both of these theories were sharply attacked. For critics, it seems that my moral condemnation of genocide, for example, is much more than a reflection of personal emotions and urgings. There is something *factually* wrong about using such weapons. We will look at the emotivist and prescriptivist theories and see if they are as off the mark as critics argue.

Ayer's Theory

One of the founders and staunchest defenders of emotivism and prescriptivism was British philosopher **A. J. Ayer** (1910–1989). Ayer's ethical views are presented in his influential book *Language, Truth and Logic* (1936), a work that defends a controversial philosophical position known as logical positivism. Since Ayer's view of moral judgments is largely an offshoot of logical positivism, we will briefly look at that theory.

Logical Positivism and the Verification Principle   Philosophers for centuries commonly distinguished between two kinds of statements, such as these:

1. All bachelors are unmarried men.

2. The door is brown.

The first statement is true by definition and doesn't rely for its truth on sense perception or observation. If we know that the word "bachelor" by definition includes the notion of a single male, then it is clearly true that "all bachelors are unmarried men." Philosophers commonly call this kind of sentence an *analytic* statement, which also includes mathematical truths such as "3 times 5 is equal to half of 30." By contrast, the truth of the second statement can't be established merely through definitions, but instead relies on sense perception and observation. We must visually *observe* the color of the door to establish that it is brown. Philosophers call sentences of this kind *empirical* statements.

Scottish skeptic **David Hume** (1711–1776) pushed the distinction further and argued that analytic and empirical statements were the *only* legitimate types of knowledge that we have. Commentators refer to this view as "Hume's fork" since, according to Hume, all legitimate quests for knowledge "fork" or divide between these two types of statements. Hume ruthlessly applied this principle to traditional philosophical discussions and rejected any philosophical theory if it involved neither analytic nor empirical truths. Hume dramatically expresses this method of assessment here:

> When we run over libraries, persuaded of these principles [i.e., Hume's fork], what havoc must we make? If we take in our hand any volume of divinity or school metaphysics, for instance, let us ask, "Does it contain any [analytic] abstract reasoning concerning quantity or number?" No. "Does it contain any [empirical] experimental reasoning concerning matter of fact and existence?" No. Commit it then to the flames. For it can contain nothing but sophistry and illusion. (*Enquiry Concerning Human Understanding,* 12.3)

Inspired by Hume, philosophers of the logical positivist movement in the 1930s adopted a similar method of assessing the truth and meaning of knowledge claims. They proposed what they called the "verification principle," and, like Hume, they used it to test the meaning of various assertions.

Ayer's account of logical positivism and the verification principle is perhaps the best known, and he gives his principle here:

> The principle of verification is supposed to furnish a criterion by which it can be determined whether or not a sentence is literally meaningful. A simple way to formulate it would be to say that a sentence had literal meaning if and only if the proposition it expressed was either analytic or empirically verifiable. (*Language, Truth and Logic,* Introduction)

According to Ayer, a statement is meaningful if it is either analytic or empirically verifiable. Ayer took great pains to show precisely what is involved in both analyticity and empirical verifiability. Most simply, a statement is *analytic* if it is either explicitly true by definition or reducible to statements that are true by definition. A statement is *empirically verifiable* if some possible experience will either confirm or disconfirm it. To illustrate Ayer's verifiability principle, consider these statements:

1. Triangles have three angles.
2. The White House is in Washington, DC.
3. There are flowers growing on the planet Neptune.
4. Every two minutes, everything in the universe doubles in size.

The first of these statements is meaningful since it is analytically true by definition that triangles have three angles. Statement 2 is meaningful since we can empirically verify the location of the White House by going to Washington and seeing it. Statement 3 is also meaningful since at least in theory it is possible to construct a spaceship and fly to Neptune to confirm or disconfirm whether flowers are growing there. Finally, Statement 4 is meaningless since it is neither analytically true by definition nor empirically verifiable. Specifically, it isn't empirically verifiable since any theoretical measuring device I might use will *itself* also double in size.

Using the verification principle, Ayer rejects as meaningless various assertions about metaphysics, religion, and ethics. For example, Ayer considers the following metaphysical statement by British idealist philosopher F. H. Bradley: "The Absolute enters into, but is itself incapable of, evolution and progress." For Ayer, this statement is meaningless since it is neither analytically true nor empirically verifiable. Take, now, an ethical statement such as "It is morally wrong to commit genocide." This statement is also meaningless since it, too, is neither analytically true nor empirically verifiable. Although moral utterances are factually "meaningless" in Ayer's strict sense of that term, they are not complete gibberish. That is, they are not on the same level as the nonsensical utterance "The time now is green." When I make moral utterances, people know how to respond appropriately to me in their actions and in their words. Ayer concedes this much and recognizes that moral utterances perform some practical function in our lives, even though they are factually meaningless.

Descriptive Utterances versus Performative Utterances

Descriptive Utterances versus Performative Utterances   To better understand the nonfactual practical function of ethical utterances, we need to distinguish between two types of utterances: (1) factually descriptive utterances and (2) implicitly performative utterances. Although Ayer himself didn't use this precise terminology, he relied on the underlying concepts. Factually **descriptive utterances** are those that pass the test of the verification principle, such as these:

Triangles have three angles.

The door is brown.

Jones claims to have seen Elvis.

Smith's pierced eyebrow is infected.

More generally, each of these utterances is either a true or a false statement about the world. To test, for example, whether "The door is brown" is factually descriptive, we need only to ask, "Is it true or false that 'The door is brown'?" Since this question is intelligible, the statement "The door is brown" is factually descriptive.

By contrast, implicitly **performative utterances** are a special class of statements that technically fail the test of the verification principle and so are not factually descriptive. Examples include these:

Shut the door!

Keep your dog out of my yard!

Oh, my aching back!

Three cheers for Old Glory!

The first two statements are commands, and the second two are expressions of feelings. Although we understand what is being said in each of these utterances, the statements don't literally express truths or falsehoods. Using the test just given, it makes no sense to ask, "Is it true or false that 'Shut the door'?" In addition to being nonfactual, they are implicitly performative in the sense that they verbally accomplish some task. As such, they can be reasonably translated into statements that begin with the phrase "I hereby . . ." For example, I can rephrase each of the prior utterances as follows:

> I hereby ask you to shut the door.
>
> I hereby ask you to keep your dog out of my yard.
>
> I hereby express my feelings concerning my aching back.
>
> I hereby express my feelings for Old Glory.

Now examine this list of moral utterances:

> It is wrong to commit genocide.
> Donating to charity is good.
> Murdering people is wrong.
> Mother Teresa was a good woman.

Are these utterances factually descriptive, or are they implicitly performative? The traditional view of moral utterances is that they are factually descriptive, since it seems intelligible to ask, "Is it true or false that 'Donating to charity is good'?" This traditional view is sometimes called **cognitivism** since it holds that the truth-value of moral utterances can be known or are subject to cognition. A clearer name for this view, though, is **descriptivism** since we are providing factual descriptions in our moral utterances.

Ayer challenges the descriptivist interpretation of moral utterances and argues that, although they may *appear* to be true or false statements about the world, they are not *really* factual descriptions. Instead, they are implicitly performative utterances, which are disguised as factual descriptions. In Ayer's terminology, they are "pseudo-concepts":

> We say [of ethical statements] that the reason why they are unanalysable [or factual] is that they are mere pseudo-concepts. The presence of an ethical symbol in a proposition adds nothing to its factual content. Thus if I say to someone, "You acted wrongly in stealing that money," I am not stating anything more than if I had simply said, "You stole that money." In adding that this action is wrong I am not making any further statement about it. I am simply evincing my moral disapproval of it. It is as if I had said, "You stole that money," in a peculiar tone of horror, or written it with the addition of some special exclamation marks. The tone, or the exclamation marks, adds nothing to the literal meaning of the sentence. It merely serves to show that the expression of it is attended by certain feelings in the speaker. (*Language, Truth and Logic,* 6)

Ayer argues here that the presence of an ethical term in a sentence adds no factual content, but only performs the function of expressing our feelings. This view is sometimes called **noncognitivism** since it holds that the truth-value of moral utterances cannot be known or isn't subject to cognition. We will use the name **performativism** in reference to this view, given its emphasis on performing rather than describing something.

Emotivism and Prescriptivism   According to Ayer, we perform two distinct tasks with our moral utterances. First, moral utterances express our feelings, similar to the way we express our feelings with the statement "Three cheers for Old Glory!" This aspect of Ayer's theory is commonly called **emotivism**. To illustrate, the statement "Mother Teresa was a good woman" simply expresses our approval of her, and it could be reworded more accurately as "Three cheers for Mother Teresa!" Alternatively, we can state it as "I hereby express my feelings of approval for Mother Teresa." In Ayer's interpretation, *expressing* my feelings about Mother Teresa isn't the same thing as *reporting* my feelings about her. Compare these two statements:

1. Three cheers for Mother Teresa!
2. I approve of Mother Teresa.

The first of these statements expresses my feelings of approval of Mother Teresa and isn't factual. However, the second of these reports my feelings and is factual since it is either true or false that "I approve of Mother Teresa."

At an initial glance, the difference between expressing feelings and reporting feelings seems trivial. For Ayer, though, the difference is enormous. When I make moral assessments, my expression of feelings doesn't even rise to the level of a report. When I morally approve of something, I am merely acting like a cheerleader. And when I morally disapprove of something, I am merely acting like a heckler. Ayer doesn't claim to have invented this theory but explains that Hume hinted at it 200 years earlier:

> If we did insist on extracting from Hume a reformulation of our moral statements, we should come nearer the mark by crediting him with the modern "emotive" theory that they serve to express our moral sentiments rather than with the theory that they are statements of fact [that report] about one's own or other people's mental condition. (*Hume*, p. 85)

According to Ayer, the second thing we do with our moral utterances is issue commands, similar to the way we give a command in the statement "Keep your dog out of my yard!" Ayer makes this point here:

> It is worth mentioning that ethical terms do not serve only to express feeling. They are calculated also to arouse feeling, and so to stimulate action. Indeed some of them are used in such a way as to give the sentences in which they occur the effect of commands. (*Language, Truth and Logic*, 6)

This aspect of Ayer's theory is commonly called **prescriptivism**, in the sense that we prescribe, or urge others to adopt specific behavior. For example, the statement "Murdering people is wrong" is primarily a command urging people to not murder. This statement could be more accurately reworded as "Don't murder!" or "I hereby ask you to not murder."

Contemporary British philosopher R. M. Hare helped clarify this prescriptive component of moral utterances. According to Hare, although when I make moral utterances I *intend* for you to do something, technically I don't use moral utterances to *persuade* you to do something. Moral prescriptions are not just another means of inducing someone to act, such as propaganda, bribery, or torture. Instead, prescriptive language presupposes that someone asks us, "What shall I do?" The answer to this question is the prescriptive command "You should do X." This is similar to what is implied by ordinary commands, such as "Shut the door." When I utter this command, I am not *coaxing* you to shut the door. Because I assume that you are already predisposed to respond to my request to do something, I am merely signaling you to respond in that way.

To summarize, here are the main points of Ayer's theory:

- Statements are factually meaningful only if they are either analytically true by definition or empirically verifiable.
- Moral utterances are not factually meaningful, but only implicitly perform something.
- The emotive performance of moral utterances is that they express our personal feelings.
- The prescriptive performance of moral utterances is that they urge others to adopt specific behavior.

Criticisms of Ayer

When Ayer's *Language, Truth and Logic* first appeared, many readers were horrified at his bold attempt to reduce traditional areas of philosophical discourse to meaningless utterances. One such response was this:

> Under the pretence of ultimate wisdom it [Ayer's book] guillotines religion, ethics and aesthetics, self, persons, free will, responsibility and everything worth while. I thank Mr. Ayer for having shown us how modern philosophers can fiddle and play tricks while the world burns.

Ten years after the publication of his book, Ayer noted that his treatment of morality in particular "provoked a fair amount of criticism." We will look at two main criticisms, each of which Ayer responded to.

Ross's Criticism: Performativism Is Based on the Faulty Verification Principle   British philosopher **W. D. Ross** (1877–1971) charged that Ayer's performativist account of moral utterances rests on the verification principle. Since, according to Ross, the verification principle has problems, performative theory inherits those faults. What is wrong with the verification principle? Let's note two commonly mentioned problems. First, logical positivists have difficulties when deriving an acceptable formulation of "empirical verifiability." Suppose I define empirical verifiability in this way:

> A statement is empirically verifiable if it is possible to have some direct experience that will confirm its truth.

Unfortunately, this criterion won't apply to obviously factual statements such as "All humans are mortal." The problem here is that no direct experiences can fully verify universal statements. Although logical positivists continually attempted to refine the notion of "empirical verifiability," no revision appears to be immune from similar counterexamples.

A second problem with the verification principle is that it fails its own test. Suppose I framed the verification principle in this way:

> A statement is factually meaningful only if it is either analytic or empirically verifiable.

My utterance itself is neither analytic nor empirically verifiable, so my statement isn't factually meaningful. On the one hand, if I insist that my utterance *is* factually meaningful, then I must conclude that the verification principle is too restrictive. On the other, if I accept that my statement of the verification principle is factually meaningless, then I don't have a good reason to advise you to accept the verification principle. For these and other reasons, there are genuine problems with the verification principle.

To the extent that Ayer's performative theory of moral utterances is based on the verification principle, then Ross seems correct that Ayer's performativism also has problems. In response to Ross's criticism, Ayer argued that his performative theory of moral utterances is "valid on its own account," irrespective of its initial association with the verification principle. For Ayer, when someone makes a moral utterance, such as "Mother Teresa was a good woman," we are entitled to ask whether that statement is factually descriptive or implicitly performative. Ayer believes that we won't find any descriptive content in it and so must see it as implicitly performative.

However, Ayer's response isn't satisfactory. It doesn't seem possible to brand moral utterances as purely performative without appealing to either the verification principle or a similar principle that is just as restrictive. Here is Ayer's principal argument for performativism:

1. Moral utterances are either factually descriptive or implicitly performative.
2. Moral utterances are not factually descriptive.
3. Hence, moral utterances are implicitly performative.

The key premise is the second one. What reason do we have to maintain that moral utterances are not factually descriptive? Our only answer is to show that they don't live up to a specific standard of factualness. At a minimum, this requires that we consider conservative litmus tests for factualness, such as whether an utterance is true by definition and whether an utterance is empirically verifiable. If we stop at these two litmus tests, then we thereby rely on the verification principle. But suppose we consider additional litmus tests that are more inclusive, such as whether an utterance has practical value in our lives. Even this test, though, will render moral utterances factually descriptive and won't give Ayer the result he wants. So, Ayer's argument locks us into a litmus test that is at least as restrictive as the verification principle, if not actually the verification principle itself.

In short, Ross apparently is correct that Ayer's performativist account of moral utterances fails since it rests on the questionable verification principle.

Moore's Criticism: Performativism Does Not Account for Moral Arguments

ments   According to Ayer, moral utterances are not statements of fact, but are merely performative in the sense that they express our feelings and urge others to adopt our view. This means that if you and I dispute a controversial moral issue, such as abortion or capital punishment, we are not disputing facts. Instead, for Ayer, we are just expressing different opinions. British philosopher **G. E. Moore** (1873–1958) argued that performativism is an inadequate theory of moral utterances since it doesn't recognize that in moral disputes we really are arguing over facts. Stated precisely, Moore's criticism of performativism is this:

1. If performativism is true, then we cannot factually argue about questions of moral value.
2. In point of fact, we *can* engage in genuine factual arguments about questions of moral value.
3. Therefore, performativism is false.

In defense of premise 2, Moore maintains that an important and obvious feature of morality is that we can argue about questions of moral value, and our arguments involve questions of fact:

> When I judge of a given action that it was wrong, and you perhaps of the very same action that it was not, we are not in fact differing in opinion about it at all; any more than we are differing in opinion if I make the judgment "I came from Cambridge to-day" and you make the judgment "*I* did not come from Cambridge to-day." (*Philosophical Studies*, 10)

Moore states here that moral disputes are not merely differing opinions; instead, the disputes are factual in nature. For example, I may argue that abortion is morally permissible, and you may argue that it is morally wrong. We may argue back and forth on the issue, examining factual evidence and drawing factual conclusions. However, if performativism is true, then moral arguments of this sort are not possible. For Ayer, what *appears* to be a moral argument is in reality more like two snakes hissing at each other. Moore, by contrast, thinks that moral disputes are not just hissing matches, but instead have a genuine argumentative component.

Ayer was aware of Moore's criticism, but he wasn't convinced. According to Ayer, if we look closely at moral disputes, we see that we never use arguments to show our opponents that they have the wrong ethical feelings or the wrong value systems. The most we can do in a given case is show that our opponent is mistaken about some facts, such as a person's true motive or the actual consequences of a person's action. If our opponent isn't persuaded by these facts, then we give up reasoning with that individual and start insulting him or her for having an inferior sense of morality. For Ayer, this shows that the central aspect of moral assessment involves not facts or argumentation, but rather presupposed value systems. Again, at this crucial level, so-called moral disputes are just hissing matches.

American philosopher **Charles L. Stevenson** (1908–1979) helps clarify this point. According to Stevenson, when we engage in moral discussions, we principally dispute with each other about our respective *attitudes,* and not about *facts.* To illustrate this difference, if I say, "Bob's car is a Ford," and you say, "Bob's car is a Chevy," then we are disputing facts. But if I say, "Bob's car is cool," and you say, "Bob's car is uncool," then we no longer have a dispute about facts, but instead have a dispute about attitudes. Unlike factual disputes, attitude disputes can't be resolved by simply appealing to facts. For Ayer, then, ethical statements such as "Abortion is morally permissible" involve disputes of attitude.

[handwritten margin note: Dominated by feelings]

Does Ayer's response to Moore succeed? Ayer is correct that we often resort to insults when our quick and ready factual observations fail to win our opponents over to our side. However, resorting to insults doesn't necessarily mean that we've reached a performative level in the discussion in which all reasoning fails. Instead, we may just be displaying our frustration that we don't have enough time to overturn the huge body of beliefs that make up our opponent's value system. Each of our value systems is the result of years of education, indoctrination, and reinforcement. The individual beliefs are woven together into a larger fabric that collectively reinforces each strand. But, with enough new facts and enough time, we can unweave the old fabric and replace it with a new one. For example, after four years of science classes in college, a student might revise or reject his or her literal understanding of the biblical view that God created the world in six days. We resort to insults when we see that we can't duplicate the educational experiences of four years of college within five minutes of conversation.

Descriptive and Performative Elements

These criticisms suggest that Ayer's principal mistake was restricting moral assessments to *only* performative components. There is little doubt that part of our moral assessment involves performative expressions of feelings and commands. However, at least some of the time, our assessment also involves a factually descriptive component. Moral philosophers after Ayer recognized this and offered theories combining the descriptive and performative elements. The two leading contributors to the discussion are Stevenson and Hare, both of whom we mentioned earlier.

Stevenson's and Hare's Theories Near the end of his life, Ayer commented that his account of ethical judgments was "much more adequately developed by the American philosopher Charles Stevenson in his 1944 book *Ethics and Language.*" Here, Stevenson explains how moral utterances involve both performative and descriptive elements. He observes that our use of moral language in everyday life is very vague and that there is no single way to analyze all moral utterances. Sometimes the purpose of my moral assessment is mainly to reflect my personal attitudes; other times I aim to make more objective judgments.

To simplify matters, Stevenson proposes two distinct patterns that cover the various ways in which we naturally make moral judgments. The first pattern for analyzing moral utterances is this:

"This is good" means (1) I approve of this and (2) I want you to do so as well.

This pattern contains both descriptive and performative elements. The first phrase, "I approve of this," literally *describes* my feelings, but it also *expresses* my feelings, particularly when accompanied with specific gestures and tones of voice. The second phrase, "I want you to do so as well," is literally a description of my desire to influence you. However, it too has a performative component and involves my attempt to urge you to change your attitude. In this first pattern, the descriptive parts of my utterances are completely limited to my own attitude.

The second pattern for analyzing moral utterances extends the descriptive element beyond my personal attitude:

"X is good" means (1) X has various morally relevant qualities (e.g., X is universally pleasing), and (2) hooray for X, and (3) you should approve of X as well.

Compared to the first pattern, this second pattern emphasizes more objective descriptive qualities, such as, for example, that a particular action is "universally pleasing." This pattern also downplays the descriptive references to the speaker's attitude—specifically, the speaker's reports of his or her feelings. According to Stevenson, this emphasis on more objective descriptions allows "descriptive references of the ethical terms to become as complicated as any occasion or context may require." However, Stevenson notes, just because this second pattern allows one to include a string of objective qualities, such as universal pleasure, it isn't necessarily any more ethically rich than the first pattern. Any quality that we link with X in this second pattern we can indirectly squeeze into what we say about X in the first pattern, particularly when we offer reasons for approving of something.

In his book *The Language of Morals* (1952), Hare offers a different account of the relation between the descriptive and performative elements of moral utterances. Hare's theory focuses principally on the prescriptive rather than the emotive component of moral assessments. According to Hare, the descriptive component of moral utterances changes from judgment to judgment while the prescriptive component stays the same. Take, for example, the utterance "Genocide is wrong." The descriptive meaning of this may widely vary depending on who makes the utterance and what moral theory that person ascribes to. For example, it can mean "genocide is contrary to God's will," or "genocide violates human rights," or dozens of other things. However, regardless of who makes the utterance and what theory he or she follows, the prescriptive meaning is precisely the same: "Don't commit genocide." Because the prescriptive meaning of moral utterances is constant, Hare concludes that the prescriptive meaning is primary and the descriptive meaning is secondary.

Additional Performative Functions of Moral Statements   We learn from Ayer that moral utterances are performative insofar as they express our emotions and prompt others to behave in certain ways. However, we don't want to follow Ayer's zealousness and say that moral utterances are *only* performative, and *never* descriptive. We learn from Stevenson that there are many types of moral utterances and that we can't impose a single interpretation on them all. Finally, we learn from Hare that the factually descriptive components of moral utterances vary in different contexts. When we include both performative and descriptive elements in our analysis of moral utterances, the usual attacks against emotivism and prescriptivism are no longer appropriate. We have only produced a fuller and more psychologically accurate depiction of moral utterances. For example, when I make the moral assessment that "Genocide is immoral," my assessment may mean all of the following at the same time:

Performative

I hereby express my feelings of disapproval concerning genocide. (emotive)

I hereby urge you to adopt my attitude. (prescriptive)

Descriptive

I disapprove of genocide. (report of feelings)

Acts of genocide contribute to general unhappiness. (natural description)

Acts of genocide violate our human rights. (metaphysical description)

But the analysis of our moral statements shouldn't end here. Moral psychology is very complex, and the odds are that we will continually discover additional nuances of meaning in our moral judgments and add them to the list started by Ayer, Stevenson, and Hare. We will note four additional performative implications of moral statements.

First, the emotive component of moral utterances needs to be split into two parts. When Ayer and Stevenson discuss the emotive element of moral utterances, they principally have in mind the emotional approval or outrage that we express toward a person who performs an action. Suppose, for example, that someone robs your house. According to their theories, when I say that "Robbery is wrong," I am expressing my disapproval of the individual who robbed you. In addition to this emotional reaction against the robber, though, I am also expressing sympathetic sorrow toward you insofar as you are harmed by the robber. We can similarly see two emotive elements to our approval of good conduct. Suppose, for example, that after you are robbed, a generous person replaces your stolen property free of charge. When I say, "Charity is good," I am expressing both my emotional approval of the donor and my sympathetic joy toward you. So, using the example of genocide, if I state that genocide is immoral, my utterance in part means this:

I hereby express my feelings of disapproval of the perpetrators; and

I hereby express my sympathetic sorrow toward the genocide victims.

We may call these, respectively, the *emotively approving/disapproving* and the *emotively sympathetic* functions of moral utterances.

A second meaning of at least some moral utterances is that we are asserting the truth of our moral judgment. This is most evident when we are disputing something with someone and we want to underscore that our moral judgment is true, or perhaps even absolutely and universally true. Explicit examples might include "It is true that genocide is immoral," "It is an absolute truth that we have duties toward our fellow humans," and "It is a universal truth that we forfeit our rights when we violate the rights of others." I can also *implicitly* make truth assertions in moral judgments without using the actual words "it is true that." Suppose you say, "I don't believe that genocide is wrong." In response, I may say, "But genocide *is* wrong." My aim here is to assert that something which you believe to be false is actually true. Asserting truth in our moral judgments is another performative element of moral utterances, and not a descriptive element. We don't add descriptive content to our judgment by underscoring its truth component. Asserting truth is more like adding a special exclamation point to the end of a sentence. As such, if I implicitly or explicitly state, "It is true that genocide is immoral," my utterance means this:

I hereby assert the truth of the statement "Genocide is immoral."

We may call this the *assertive* function of moral statements.

A third performative element included in at least some moral utterances is that we make statements to *remind* ourselves of our previously established moral attitudes. Beginning early in childhood, we adopt various moral standards from our parents, and as we mature, we continually add to the list. It would be nice if we could remember all of these standards all of the time, but, in point of fact, we can't. We can remember the obvious standards, such as that it is wrong to lie, steal, and murder; however, more specific moral standards are easily forgotten. For example, I may forget that it is wrong to make obscene gestures at other motorists on the highway or that I should treat strangers respectfully. Even the issue of genocide is one that might require some memory jogging if the issue comes up only every few years. When we make moral statements and engage in moral debates, at least part of the task is to bring us up to speed on our previously established moral views. So, if I state that genocide is immoral, my utterance in part means this:

I hereby remind myself that I previously disapproved of genocide.

We may call this the *recollective* function of moral utterances.

A fourth and related performative function of moral utterances is that we use them to motivate ourselves to do the morally right thing. Ayer, Stevenson, and Hare each noted that we make moral statements to prescribe or urge *other* people to adopt our views. However, people sometimes makes moral statements to motivate *themselves* to behave morally. Suppose someone leaves a wallet unguarded for a moment and you are tempted to take it. You may say to yourself that stealing is wrong in order to help yourself resist the impulse. You may even give yourself reasons that stealing is wrong, such as that it violates people's rights or that it causes more unhappiness than happiness. Hearing the dialog in your mind or reciting it out loud may sometimes provide the motivation to do the right thing. And, at least some of the time, this is just what we do. So, if I state that genocide is immoral, my utterance in part means this:

> I hereby urge myself to behave consistently with my disapproval of genocide.

We may call this the *self-motivative* function of moral utterances.

Skeptical Implications of Extreme Emotivism and Prescriptivism   The best way to deflect criticisms of emotivism and prescriptivism is to retain the descriptive components of our moral statements and simply supplement this with various performative components. Nevertheless, when philosophers today discuss emotivism and prescriptivism, they typically have in mind the more extreme view that Ayer proposed, which allows no room for descriptive components. The extreme versions of emotivism and prescriptivism are attractive to people who are skeptical about speculations concerning laws of nature, divine commands, and eternal truths. The only thing we know for sure about moral judgments is how they make us feel, and it is best to restrict our moral theories to that. So, when I say, "Murder is wrong," I am really expressing my negative feelings about murder and am imploring you to adopt my attitude. This is not only skeptical but pessimistic since it puts moral judgments on the same level as other expressions of personal preference, such as "The tuna casserole today is horrible, and I suggest that you avoid it."

Two centuries ago, extreme emotivist and prescriptivist theories would have brought down the wrath of religious and political officials for undermining the stability of social values. Philosophy wasn't just armchair speculation for those officials. They believed that the riffraff of society would latch onto any theory that led to anarchy, and that reducing morality to personal preference would invite such chaos. Today, no one sees emotivism, prescriptivism, or any other pessimistic moral theory as a social threat, so proponents are not attacked with the same zeal as were philosophical villains from past centuries.

Even though the extreme theories of emotivism and prescriptivism pose no threat to society, we still should consider whether they adequately capture the meaning of our moral statements. The issue of genocide highlights a big problem with the adequacy of these theories. Genocide is clearly one of the greater moral evils facing human society, and the seriousness of the issue is not fully captured by the emotivist and prescriptivist accounts. In these theories, it seems that the serious nature of the genocide issue simply involves adding the word *extreme* to our utterances:

> I hereby express my *extreme* disapproval concerning genocide.

> I hereby *extremely* urge you to adopt my attitude.

This, though, does not fully capture the urgency of situations such as the systematic slaughtering of nearly a million Rwandans. Suppose that, instead of inserting "extreme" only once, I insert it twice, such that "I hereby express my *extreme, extreme* disapproval concerning genocide." But this also doesn't fully capture the urgency of the issue. How many times, then, must I insert "extreme" before I can adequately express the issue's importance? The fact is that there is only so much extreme disapproval that I am psychologically capable of expressing, and with colossal evils such as genocide, I will psychologically max out long before I begin to capture the issue's true importance.

To fully depict the importance of the genocide issue, then, I have no choice but to bring in *some* descriptive component about the immorality of genocide that extends beyond my limited psychological expressions. Traditional moral theories offer a variety of descriptive elements that better convey greater urgency, such as "Genocide is contrary to God's commands," "Genocide violates our natural rights," or "Genocide is contrary to eternal moral relations." As skeptics point out, though, these statements rest on concepts that have serious philosophical problems, and some of these concepts might simply be gibberish. The safest way to add a descriptive component, though, is to steer clear of metaphysical descriptions and instead make a generic moral statement, such as "Genocide is morally evil." It is true that the skeptic might still dispute the factual nature of "moral evil." However, unlike metaphysical descriptions, the notion of "moral evil" is universally understood and tied to virtually everyone's common life experiences. The less we attempt to clarify the concept of moral evil, the better it serves as a factual description of humanity's most immoral deeds.

Summary

Ayer advanced the logical positivist view that statements are factually meaningful only if they are analytic or empirically verifiable. Thus, for Ayer, moral statements such as "Genocide is wrong" are not factually meaningful since they fail this test. Although moral statements don't factually describe anything, they nevertheless have a performative function, and by making moral statements, we accomplish specific tasks. One task, according to the emotivist theory, is that we express our feelings. Another task, according to the prescriptivist theory, is that we urge others to adopt our views.

Ross rightly criticized Ayer for grounding his view of morality on the faulty theory of logical positivism. Moore rightly argued as well that Ayer's theory fails to take into account genuine disagreements of fact. But the principal fault of Ayer's theory is that it confines the meaning of moral statements to performative elements and completely rejects the descriptive elements. Stevenson developed Ayer's theory by offering two patterns for interpreting moral statements, both of which contain performative and descriptive elements. Hare argued that the performative elements of moral statements take primacy over the descriptive elements since the performative elements are the same for everyone, while the descriptive ones have a variety of meanings.

To the common list of performative elements of moral statements, we added several new functions: the emotively sympathetic, the assertive, the recollective, and the self-motivative. Moral skeptics today sometimes adopt extreme theories of emotivism and prescriptivism, which reject any factually descriptive component of moral statements. But this doesn't adequately depict the importance of major moral tragedies, such as genocide, and we must bring in a factual component, the safest of which rests on the factual notion of moral evil.

Study Questions

Introduction
1. How do differing moral theories interpret the statement "Genocide is wrong"?
2. Define "emotivism" and "prescriptivism."

Ayer's Theory

Logical Positivism and the Verification Principle
3. Give examples of analytic statements and empirical statements.
4. What does Hume recommend that we do with books that do not contain analytic or empirical statements?
5. What is Ayer's verification principle?
6. Based on Ayer's verification principle, why is the following statement meaningless: "Every two minutes, everything in the universe doubles in size."

Descriptive Utterances versus Performative Utterances
7. What is a "factually descriptive statement"?
8. What is an "implicitly performative statement"?
9. Give an example of an implicitly performative statement that is an expression of feelings.

Emotivism and Prescriptivism
10. According to emotivism, how may we reword the statement "Mother Teresa was a good woman"?
11. According to prescriptivism, how may we reword the statement "Mother Teresa was a good woman"?
12. According to Hare, what is the most accurate way of understanding prescriptive commands?

Criticisms of Ayer

Ross's Criticism: Performativism Is Based on the Faulty Verification Principle
13. What is Ross's criticism against Ayer's performativism?
14. What are the two common criticisms against logical positivism?
15. What is Ayer's response to Ross's criticism?

Moore's Criticism: Performativism Does Not Account for Moral Arguments
16. According to Moore, performativism cannot adequately account for moral arguments. What is Moore's main argument?

17. What is Ayer's reply to Moore?
18. What is Stevenson's distinction between disputes of attitude and disputes of fact?

Descriptive and Performative Elements

19. What was Ayer's principal mistake in his moral theory?

Stevenson's and Hare's Theories

20. What was Stevenson's general view about how we should analyze moral utterances?
21. According to Hare, what is a key feature that distinguishes the prescriptive meaning from the descriptive meaning of moral utterances?

Additional Performative Functions of Moral Statements

22. What are some additional performative functions of moral utterances that Fieser notes?

Skeptical Implications of Extreme Emotivism and Prescriptivism

23. According to Fieser, why can't emotivism and prescriptivism adequately capture the meaning of moral statements that condemn genocide?

References

A. J. Ayer's *Language, Truth and Logic* first appeared in 1936, and in 1946 Ayer added a lengthy introduction clarifying and revising some of his points. The text of the 1946 edition is available in a recent facsimile reprint by Dover Publications; the quotations here are from the Dover edition.

Ayer's emotivist interpretation of Hume is in *Hume* (New York: Hill and Wang, 1980).

W. D. Ross's attack on Ayer is in *The Foundations of Ethics* (Oxford: Clarendon Press, 1939), pp. 30–41.

G. E. Moore's attack on Ayer is in *Philosophical Studies* (London: Routledge, 1992), "The Nature of Moral Philosophy."

Ayer's comment about Stevenson is from *Philosophy in the Twentieth Century* (New York: Vintage Books, 1994), p. 139.

The quotations by Charles L. Stevenson are from *The Ethics of Language* (New Haven, CT: Yale University Press, 1944).

R. M. Hare's distinction between descriptive and prescriptive meanings of ethical terms is found in *The Language of Morals* (Oxford: Oxford University Press, 1952) and, more briefly, in his article "Ethics," in *A Concise Encyclopedia of Philosophy,* edited by J. O. Urmson.

Suggestions for Further Reading

R. M. Hare's ethical views are in his three main books: *The Language of Morals* (Oxford: Oxford University Press, 1952); *Essays on the Moral Concepts* (Berkeley: University of California Press, 1972); *Moral Thinking: Its Levels, Method, and Point* (Oxford: Clarendon Press, 1981).

C. L. Stevenson's ethical views are in his two main books: *The Ethics of Language* (New Haven, CT: Yale University Press, 1944) and *Facts and Values* (New Haven, CT: Yale University Press, 1963).

For discussions of emotivism and precriptivism, see Mary Gore Forrester, *Moral Language* (Madison: University of Wisconsin Press, 1982); John Ibberson, *The Language of Decision: An Essay in Prescriptivist Ethical Theory* (Houndmills, England: Macmillan, 1986); Stephen Satris, *Ethical Emotivism* (Boston: Nijhoff, 1987); Ezra Talmor, *Language and Ethics* (New York: Pergamon Press, 1984); J. O. Urmson, *The Emotive Theory of Ethics* (London: Hutchinson, 1968).

14

Best Reasons Morality and the Problem of Abortion

Introduction

An unnamed 14-year-old girl sparked a controversy when, in her twenty-fourth week of pregnancy, she requested an abortion in her home state of Arizona, which prohibits abortions after 20 weeks. With her mother dead and her father in prison, the girl had been in foster care since age 5. Her request for an abortion made its way through the Arizona court system, and ultimately the Arizona Supreme Court was swayed by the fact that she was pregnant from a rape and that she had taken a variety of drugs during her pregnancy. The court decided to assist her in obtaining an abortion in the nearby state of Kansas, in which late-term abortions are permitted. Shortly after the court's decision, an anti-abortion group called Kansans for Life made a concerted effort to locate the girl and provide her with abortion alternatives. The anti-abortion group failed in its efforts, though, and the girl obtained the abortion.

This sad case shows how complex the issue of abortion can get. Even if we have gut feelings about how to judge cases like this, it is often difficult to intelligently organize our thoughts on the subject. There is first the question of the moral status of the fetus. Do human fetuses have the same moral value and rights as adult humans? Pro-life groups such as Kansans for Life believe that they do from the moment of conception and that, except in rare circumstances when a mother's life is at risk, abortion is simply murder since it violates the fetus's right to life. On the other end of the spectrum, many pro-choice advocates believe that unborn fetuses lack the same moral value that you or I have. According to them, it makes no sense to attribute this special value to an unconscious cluster of cells. Instead, a human organism obtains this value only after achieving a specific level of development, and birth is typically seen as the dividing line. In this view, then, abortion is not murder. There are also in-between positions holding that fetuses get their special value sometime between conception and birth—perhaps when a fetus could in theory survive outside of the womb. By limiting abortions to the first five months of pregnancy, the Arizona legislature implicitly took this compromise position.

For the sake of argument, let's suppose that the pro-life side wins this debate, and we accept in principle that fetuses have strong moral value from the moment of conception. Nevertheless, a second question arises about when a fetus's right to live may be overridden by stronger considerations. For example, most pro-life advocates recognize that a mother's right to life is stronger than that of her fetus's right to life. So, if the mother's life is at risk because of a pregnancy, then it is morally justifiable to kill the fetus to save the mother's life. On the other end of the spectrum, pro-choice advocates list a variety of additional factors that take precedence over the fetus's alleged right to life. One is the mother's right to control her own body; another is the burden that unwanted children place on society. A recent controversial sociological study suggests that, following legalization, the sharp increase in abortions during the 1970s prevented the existence of many potential criminals in the 1990s. Pregnant women most likely to have abortions are young, single, and poor; and this is the type of home environment from which criminals often emerge. Although the social benefit of abortions may not by itself override a fetus's right to life, it is one factor that some people may consider when forming their views on abortion.

Few traditional moral theories are equipped to handle controversies as complex as the abortion issue. Consequently, few people debating abortion will discuss the issue from the standpoint of promoting moral virtues, observing moral duties, or maximizing human happiness. Traditional theories may be very good at explaining why murder *in general* is wrong, but they don't help determine whether we commit murder when aborting a fetus. We determine the morality of abortion and other controversial actions by sifting through competing arguments for and against a particular course of action. Frustrated by the limitations of traditional theories, several moral philosophers have offered an alternative that better reflects our actual process of moral reasoning. Their proposal is that the morally right course of action is simply the one that is supported by the best reasons. We will examine the abortion issue here by following the best reasons approach.

The Process of Moral Reasoning

The leading proponents of the best reasons approach are Stephen Toulmin and Kurt Baier. We will look at how both of these philosophers contributed to the theory.

Toulmin's View of Moral Reasoning   The **best reasons theory** of morality emerged at a time when moral philosophers were highly critical of rationalistic approaches to morality. Influenced by the emotivist theory, many moral philosophers were inclined to see moral judgments as expressions of emotions rather than as rational decisions. According to emotivists, if I say, "Abortion is wrong," then I am principally expressing my negative feelings about abortion and recommending that other people adopt my attitude. In his book *An*

Examination of the Place of Reason in Ethics (1950), contemporary British philosopher **Stephen Toulmin** argues that the emotivist interpretation neglects the most important element in making ethical judgments—namely, the logic of moral reasoning.

In explaining the logic of moral reasoning, Toulmin first argues that moral reasoning is different from scientific reasoning. Suppose, for example, a scientist argues that light rays bend in outer space. The point of the scientist's argument is to alter our *expectations* about physical reality—in this case, our expectations about the nature of light rays. By contrast, when someone argues that abortion is wrong, the point of the argument is to alter our *feelings* and *behavior*. Although scientific experiments certainly are relevant to shaping our expectations about physical reality, they may not be relevant to altering our feelings and behavior about moral issues like abortion.

According to Toulmin, the principal job of the moral reasoning process is to answer the question "Is this the right thing to do?" and I determine this by seeing whether my action conforms to the accepted rules of moral obligation. Often this kind of reasoning is simple. For example, I can easily figure out that it is wrong for me to steal my neighbor's lawnmower since I would be going against accepted rules that prohibit stealing. However, the reasoning process sometimes is more complex, as when I must consider several conflicting rules. For example, to determine if having an abortion is the right thing to do, I may consider a variety of moral, legal, and religious rules that conflict with one another. As Toulmin notes, the issues become so complex that there is no simple rule to follow in resolving the question:

> Moral reasoning is so complex, and has to cover such a variety of types of situations, that no one logical test (such as "appeal to an accepted principle") can be expected to meet every case. (*Reason in Ethics*, 11.4)

To resolve such complex issues, Toulmin believes that we must wear several hats for different jobs. We must wear the hat of a psychologist to know how people feel in different circumstances. We must wear the hat of an engineer to handle all of the factors in life's practical situations. We must wear the hat of the artist to be sensitive to when one established rule overrides another. And in special cases, we must even wear the hat of the economist to tackle complex social issues like hunger, unemployment, and homelessness.

Baier's View of Moral Reasoning

Toulmin offers a glimpse at the complex process of moral reasoning, but he doesn't provide a step-by-step procedure for making moral judgments. In his book *The Moral Point of View* (1958), contemporary philosopher **Kurt Baier** gives us these details. Like Toulmin, Baier believes that the job of moral reasoning is to answer the question "What should I do?" According to Baier, to answer this question, we employ two distinct reasoning processes: (1) We *survey* the facts, and (2) we *weigh* the facts. In surveying the facts, we are looking for all of the relevant considerations that might impact on performing a particular action. Suppose, for example, that a stranger offers to sell me a new TV for half the price that it would cost me in an appliance store. One fact relevant to my decision is that I'd be saving a lot of money if I bought the TV, and saving money is typically a good reason for performing an action. At the same time, in view of the price the stranger is offering me, the odds are fairly good that the TV is stolen merchandise, and I'd be breaking the law if I knowingly bought stolen merchandise. So, a second relevant fact to my decision is that I'd likely be breaking the law if I bought the TV, and breaking the law is typically a good reason for *not* performing an action.

Once we line up the relevant facts, we then weigh these facts. To weigh the facts, though, we need some guiding principles that will tell us when one fact is more important than another. Suppose, for example, that I use the principle of selfishness to weigh the facts just given pertaining to my purchasing the TV. Saving money may be more conducive to selfishness than is obeying the law. So, when weighing the facts using the principle of selfishness, the best thing for me to do is buy the TV. However, selfishness is only one of many principles. Here is a short list of relevant principles that Baier mentions:

- We should pursue short-range self-interest.
- We should pursue long-range self-interest.
- We should obey the law.
- We should pursue religious interests.
- We should not lie.
- We should not steal.

According to Baier, the principles toward the bottom of this list are more important than those at the top. So, although buying the TV would indeed help me attain some short-range self-interest, it would not be conducive to most of the other principles on the list.

The most important of these principles are the ones at the very bottom of the list, which are distinctively moral. Baier believes that these principles are for the good of everyone alike and constitute a *moral,* as opposed to a *selfish* or *religious,* point of view. Baier gives two reasons that the moral principles are superior to those higher on the list. First, since moral principles involve the good of everyone, they will be less harmful than other principles—specifically, the selfish principles. Second, even from our individual selfish standpoint, we sometimes further our own self-interest when we pursue the good of everyone. Suppose, for example, that everyone in my neighborhood is at war with everyone else. According to Baier, it will be in my best interests to participate in a general truce so long as my neighbors also abide by the truce. The truce will certainly serve the larger interests of the neighborhood, but it will also serve *my* interests since I can then leave my house without being attacked.

Toulmin and Baier both believe that morality involves assessing the best reasons for a particular course of action. Although they differ in what they emphasize, we may summarize their shared strategy as follows:

- The morally correct action is that which is supported by the best reasons, without regard to our emotions.

- We begin by accurately collecting the relevant facts for and against a course of action.
- We then assess the comparative strength of these facts using various principles.
- The best principles to use are those that constitute a moral point of view.

Best Reasons and Applied Ethics   In recent decades, a special branch of moral philosophy called **applied ethics** has become popular. The aim of this subdiscipline is to resolve a wide range of moral controversies in different areas of human activity. Discussions in medical ethics address the problems of abortion, euthanasia, patient confidentiality, bioengineering, and any new medical situation that has moral implications. Discussions in environmental ethics address the problems of animal testing, animal rights, and species extinction. Other moral controversies include pornography, homosexuality, computer privacy, the social responsibility of businesses, capital punishment, and nuclear war.

The best reasons theory of morality was devised to address the failures of traditional moral theories in resolving complex problems such as these. In fact, many moral philosophers today who write on applied ethics issues follow the best reasons approach. The best reasons strategy is a very natural approach to the moral reasoning process, and perhaps one of the better ways of tackling complex moral problems, such as abortion. To better illustrate the best reasons approach—and also to uncover its limitations—we will look at the abortion issue in more detail.

The Fetus's Moral Status

We noted earlier that the abortion controversy rests on two distinct issues: (1) determining the moral status of a fetus and (2) balancing a fetus's interests against the interests of others. We will begin with the first of these issues and follow the reasoning procedure sketched by Toulmin and Baier.

Gathering the Facts   Imagine that an alien spaceship lands in your backyard and two bizarre-looking creatures step out. Watching them through your window, you conclude from their behavior that they come in peace. You therefore decide that it is more appropriate to invite them to stay in your guest bedroom and less appropriate to shoot them and cook their carcasses on your grill. In short, specific facts about the aliens imply that they have a moral status similar to that of humans. Because of their moral status, we will recognize that the aliens have specific moral rights and that we have moral duties to respect those rights. In the abortion debate, we are looking for similar facts about a fetus that tell us whether that fetus has the same moral status as an adult human. If its moral status is sufficiently strong, then it will have the same right to life as an adult human, and its strong moral status would be a good argument against abortion. But if its moral status is sufficiently weak, then it will have a weaker claim to life than an adult human, and its weak moral status would be a good argument in support of abortion.

To illustrate, suppose a woman is 1 month pregnant and is considering having an abortion. Following Baier, we need to list all of the facts about that 1-month-old fetus that are relevant to the woman's decision. First, there are facts that speak against the moral status of a fetus and thus support a decision to have an abortion. Pro-choice advocates point to a variety of features that a 1-month-old fetus lacks, which we may encapsulate in these two facts:

1. The fetus does not actually have higher mental qualities, such as advanced rationality, sociability, the ability to conceive of oneself as existing in time, and the ability to appreciate life's value.

2. The fetus does not actually have lower mental qualities, such as consciousness of one's surroundings and the ability to experience pleasure and pain.

Fact 1 specifies the obvious point that a 1-month-old fetus does not have the higher mental abilities that we find in adult humans. It does not have the advanced rationality needed to play chess, do mathematical calculations, or speak in an advanced language. It does not have the social abilities to develop bonding and loving relationships. It does not have a conception of itself as a living thing with a past and a future. It also does not have the ability to appreciate the value of life's various opportunities. Concerning fact 2, a 1-month-old fetus does not even have the lower mental abilities that we find in some animal life. Animals such as chickens and mice appear to be aware of their environment and to have conscious experiences of pleasure and pain. But a 1-month-old fetus's brain isn't developed enough to allow for these kinds of experiences. These features are the qualities that we would look for in assessing the moral status of *any* organism, whether it be an alien, an animal, a human adult, or a human fetus. The upshot of these two facts is that a 1-month-old fetus, in its actual state, lacks all the features connected with an organism having a strong moral status. These facts, then, support a woman's choice to have an abortion.

After we list the facts that count *against* the moral status of a 1-month-old fetus, our next task is to list facts that speak *for* its moral status. Two principal facts emerge that are parallel to those listed previously:

3. The fetus belongs to a species whose members typically have higher mental qualities (listed in item 1), and thus the fetus has the potential to have those qualities.

4. The fetus belongs to a species whose members typically have lower mental qualities (listed in item 2), and thus the fetus has the potential to have those qualities.

Although a 1-month-old fetus does not *actually* possess higher and lower mental qualities, it has the *potential* to develop these features. This potential, then, is a fact that supports the moral status of a 1-month-old fetus and counts against a woman's choice to have an abortion.

The Extreme Pro-Choice Potentiality Principle

Once we list all of the facts relevant to the moral status of the 1-month-old fetus, our next task is to see which list of facts is weightier. According to Baier, we use relevant moral principles to weigh the merits of competing facts. Which moral principles are relevant to weighing our four facts? All four facts concern the merits of potentiality versus actuality. To weigh the competing facts against each other, then, we need a guiding moral principle that addresses the central issue of potentiality versus actuality. Hopefully, the principle that we use will be acceptable to all parties in the dispute; otherwise, the process of weighing the facts might be biased in favor of one side of the dispute.

To begin our search for the appropriate moral principle, let's first consider a principle that an extreme pro-choice advocate might offer:

- *Extreme pro-choice potentiality principle:* Only an organism's actual qualities are relevant to its moral status, and its potential qualities are not important at all to its moral status.

This principle gives weight only to facts 1 and 2, which deal with the fetus's *actual* qualities. Facts 3 and 4 are deemed irrelevant since they deal only with the fetus's *potential* qualities. Using this principle, then, the relevant facts support the view that a 1-month-old fetus does not have a strong moral status.

What reason might someone have for holding the extreme pro-choice principle and thus rejecting the relevance of potential qualities? Joel Feinberg gives an argument here:

> In 1930, when he was six years old, Jimmy Carter didn't know it, but he was a potential president of the United States. That gave him no claim *then,* not even a very weak claim, to give commands to the U.S. Army and Navy [which only an actual U.S. president can do]. ("Abortion," Sect. 4)

According to Feinberg, just as someone must be an *actual* U.S. president to command the U.S. military, an organism must *actually* have qualities such as higher rationality to have a strong moral status. This analogy suggests that, as a rule, a thing's potential qualities are irrelevant to claims that must instead be based on actual qualities. However, Feinberg's analogy is not successful. If we wanted, we could rewrite the U.S. Constitution to give potential presidents all of the rights that actual presidents have. This might also require that we devise a way of recognizing potential presidents when they are 6 years old. In any event, we can write laws to say almost anything that we want about the relevance—or lack of relevance—of potential qualities. Instead of looking at legal examples for guidance, we should look at moral examples that more closely parallel the facts about a fetus. Unfortunately, there aren't any real-life examples that perfectly parallel the facts about a fetus, so we must invent an example.

Imagine that genetic engineers created a breed of superearthworms. For the first year of their lives, these worms would look and behave just like normal earthworms, and they would also have the same minimal nervous system capacities as normal earthworms. That is, they could respond to external stimuli but would have neither higher nor lower mental qualities. They clearly wouldn't have the ability to do mathematics and wouldn't even be conscious of their surroundings. However, after its first year of life, the superworm would quickly sprout arms, legs, and a head, and would acquire higher mental abilities that matched those of an adult human. During this later stage of the superworm's life, we certainly would treat the superworm differently than normal earthworms since it would have all of the qualities needed to have a strong moral status. In fact, we *should* treat the superworm the same as we would an adult human.

But what about the early stages of a superworm's life when it is mentally and physically indistinguishable from a normal earthworm? Would it be acceptable to use it as bait for fishing? At a minimum, we must say that the potential mental abilities of a superearthworm are to some degree relevant to its early-stage moral status. People would refuse to buy earthworms from their fishing supply store unless assured that they were buying only normal earthworms, and not early-stage superworms. This does not necessarily mean that early-stage superworms have a strong right to life, for it may not necessarily be wrong to humanely euthanize them. It would be wrong, though, to kill them in this somewhat heartless fashion at the end of a fishing hook, and this does imply that its early-stage moral status would be stronger than the moral status of a normal earthworm. If we accept this intuition, then we must reject the extreme pro-choice principle, since an organism's potential is at least somewhat relevant to its moral status.

The Extreme Pro-Life and Moderate Potentiality Principles

Having rejected the extreme pro-choice principle, let's now consider a principle that an extreme pro-life advocate might offer:

- *Extreme pro-life potentiality principle:* An organism's potential qualities are as important to its moral status as are its actual qualities.

This principle gives as much weight to an organism's potential qualities (facts 3 and 4) as it does to an organism's actual qualities (facts 1 and 2). Using this principle, then, facts 3 and 4 support the view that a 1-month-old fetus in fact has a strong moral status. However, using our superworm example, we can see that we must also reject this principle. We've granted that early-stage superworms have a higher moral status than normal earthworms. But this does not necessarily mean that the moral status of early-stage superworms is as high as that of late-stage superworms. Just as with humans, we should see that late-stage superworms deserve to be educated, loved, and given emotional support. However, early-stage superworms would not deserve these specific things since they don't have the capacity to benefit from them. Although *we* might feel better by attempting to educate, love, or emotionally support them, our efforts are misdirected from the standpoint of the early-stage superworm's capacities. In fact, if we run through the list of universal human rights endorsed by the United

Nations, very few would be appropriate to an early-stage superworm's capacities, such as rights to political asylum and peaceful assembly.

By analogy, the potential qualities of a 1-month-old fetus are not as important to its moral status as are its actual qualities. Rejecting both the extreme pro-life and pro-choice principles, we are left with a principle that is somewhere in between the two extremes:

* *Moderate potentiality principle:* An organism's potential qualities are relevant to its moral status, although not as relevant as its actual qualities.

This, then, is the principle that we must use when weighing facts 1 and 2 against 3 and 4. The crucial question finally emerges: Are a 1-month-old fetus's potential qualities (facts 3 and 4) relevant to establishing a strong or only a weak moral status? Again, if its moral status is sufficiently strong, then it will have the same right to life as an adult human; if its moral status is sufficiently weak, then it will have a weaker claim to life than an adult human. We can attempt to answer this question by looking again at the superworm analogy.

We noted that it would be wrong to heartlessly use early-stage superworms as fishing bait. But how would we feel about killing early-stage superworms in a more humane fashion, such as by lethal injection? We would likely be appalled by this practice, too. If your local community actually discovered early-stage superworms slithering through people's backyards, community leaders would set up programs to gather them up and resettle them in controlled areas. Trained superworm spotters would patrol neighborhoods night and day with worm detection equipment. The controlled areas would be free from birds and other natural predators, and they would be protected with the same zeal that naturalists apply to protect endangered species. In short, we would recognize that they had *some* right to life, although it would not be as strong as a fully developed superworm's right to life. All other things being equal, if we had to choose between the life of an early-stage superworm and the life of a fully developed superworm, we would choose the latter.

By analogy, a 1-month-old human fetus has *some* right to life, although it would not be as strong as an adult human's right to life. So, when applying the moderate potentiality principle to the facts, we conclude that a 1-month-old fetus's potential qualities are sufficient to establish a mid-level moral status with a mid-level right to life. In the absence of overriding factors, then, the best reasons show that it would be wrong to abort a 1-month-old fetus. The reasoning here is restricted to the facts about a 1-month-old fetus. To test our intuitions about abortion at other stages of development, we might devise other analogies. For example, to determine the moral status of a 1-day-old zygote, we might think about how we would treat an early-stage superamoeba. For a 7-month-old fetus, we might think about an early-stage superchicken. Judging from the results of our discussion so far, we'd most likely conclude that a 1-day-old zygote has only a low-level right to life, and a 7-month-old fetus has a high-level right to life, perhaps as strong as that of an adult human.

The Fetus's Interests versus Others' Interests

Determining the moral status of the fetus is just the first issue to address in the abortion controversy. The next issue involves balancing the fetus's interests against competing interests of others. As with the previous issue, we want to first gather the facts and then weigh those facts.

Gathering and Weighing the Facts   Pro-choice advocates list a variety of extenuating circumstances about a pregnancy that are good reasons for having an abortion. What if a pregnancy is life-threatening to the mother? What if it resulted from rape and wasn't a matter of the mother's choice? We can encapsulate these and other considerations in two main facts:

1. Sometimes pregnancies cause great harm to a mother.
2. Sometimes pregnancies are not completely a matter of choice.

Both of these facts draw on the notion of *autonomy*, that is, self-rule. A mother's right to autonomy implies that she should be able to stop pregnancies that cause her harm and obstruct her free choices.

On the opposing side of the controversy, pro-life advocates list one simple but crucial fact:

3. A fetus has a specific moral status, and thus has a specific right to life.

The mere fact that a fetus has a specific right to life is a good reason for not having an abortion. Extreme pro-life advocates believe that all fetuses have a strong right to life. However, our previous discussion suggests that a fetus's right to life varies from weak to strong based on a consideration of both its actual and potential mental qualities. The best interpretation of fact 3, then, is to stipulate the specific level of a fetus's right to life based on its qualities. To make our discussion more interesting to pro-life advocates, let's stipulate that we are considering aborting an 8-month-old fetus whose mental qualities are sufficient to give it a strong right to life. Let's stipulate even further that the fetus's right to life is as strong as that of an adult human.

Having gathered our facts, we again need to find a principle by which we can weigh the merits of facts 1 and 2 against fact 3. The central question involves when issues of autonomy outweigh the fetus's right to life. Following the example of our prior discussion, there are three contending principles for consideration, two extreme and one moderate:

- *Extreme pro-choice autonomy principle:* Issues of autonomy always outweigh a fetus's right to life.
- *Extreme pro-life autonomy principle:* Issues of autonomy never outweigh a fetus's right to life.
- *Moderate autonomy principle:* Issues of autonomy sometimes outweigh a fetus's right to life.

As we will see, it is best to follow the moderate principle, which acknowledges that issues of a woman's autonomy at least sometimes outweigh a fetus's right to life. In applying this principle to the facts, we again need to invent an example that will serve as a guide. Let's set aside thought experiments about super-worms—which had only a mid-level right to life—and try another that is more appropriate to an 8-month-old fetus's strong right to life.

Imagine that much of the world has been destroyed by a nuclear war and that all of the surviving people are sterile due to radiation. To keep the human race from going extinct, some genetic scientists discover a way of cloning humans in their laboratory. Unfortunately, the cloning process is imperfect, and it produces only 18-year-olds who for nine months are very weak and not alert enough to speak or communicate in other ways. During these nine months, each clone requires continuous monitoring from a single caregiver. Quickly adapting to its caregiver's unique biorhythms, the clone will in fact die if its caregiver breaks contact for even a moment. The scientists are able to produce the clones in such abundance that anyone can voluntarily become a caregiver. But, to assure that caregivers take their jobs seriously and establish a strong bond, the scientists require that the caregivers be handcuffed to their assigned clones throughout the nine-month period. Caregivers then push the handcuffed clones around in wheelchairs. Although it seems cumbersome at first, the caregivers soon adjust and go about much of their normal business.

Although the scientists expect caregivers and clones to remain handcuffed throughout the entire nine months, the scientists are not unreasonable and under extenuating circumstances will remove the handcuffs. However, the reasons must be very good in view of the fact that the clones will die if the cuffs are removed. By looking at some extenuating circumstances, we can see which reasons would justify removing the handcuffs.

Some Extenuating Circumstances   Imagine that you live in the world just described, and you voluntarily become a caregiver to an assigned clone. In your case, though, something goes wrong. As the clone adapts to your biorhythms, it drains you of your energy to the point that your own life is at risk. If you remain handcuffed to your clone, then you will both die; however, if the handcuffs are removed, then you will live but your clone will die. Would this be a satisfactory reason for the scientists to remove your handcuffs? When the lives of both the caregiver and clone are at risk, it seems appropriate to remove the handcuffs and at least save the life of the caregiver. Suppose, though, that your life becomes at risk in the final weeks of your caregiver task, and the odds are good that the clone could survive even if you died. In this case, the scientists must choose between your life and the life of the clone. To persuade the scientists to choose your life, you make this argument: "When I signed up for this task, I recognized that my life would be restricted in many ways. However, I didn't completely give up my right to control my destiny, especially the most important part of my destiny that is my very life." Reflecting on this and the fact that the clone is not alert to what's going on, the scientists could reasonably decide to remove the handcuffs and save your life.

Suppose now that, as a caregiver, you are not technically at risk of dying, but the mental stress and inconvenience of your task have become more than you can manage. You say to the scientists, "My initial decision to become a caregiver wasn't well thought out, and the burden of my task is far more trying than I ever imagined. Every component of my life is now oppressive, and more than anything else I want to regain control of my life." The scientists express their sympathies but turn down your request. "Although your task is overwhelming right now," they say, "it is nevertheless only a temporary burden, and at some point you will regain control of your life. It is just not reasonable to kill your clone in exchange for your short-term emotional relief."

Suppose next that someone maliciously mugs and beats you. Just for fun, your attacker forces you at gunpoint to go to the cloning institute and be handcuffed to a clone. Your attacker gets his laughs and then runs off. The clone immediately adapts to your biorhythms and can't now be detached without dying. You then approach the scientists: "I am cuffed to this clone against my will. I didn't want anything to do with this, but it was brutally forced on me. Now I would like to undo as much of this tragedy as I can, so please uncuff me and let me put my life back together." The scientists express sorrow but urge you to embrace the caregiver task in spite of your tragic circumstances. "The life of the clone is now at issue," they say, "and you must try to look beyond how this came about." You reply, "But the life of the clone is not my responsibility. It is not my fault that there aren't better safeguards at your institute to prevent situations like mine from occurring. And now, by denying my request, you compound and prolong this invasive violation against me." "Nevertheless," the scientists say, "the final decision comes down to weighing your short-term emotional relief against the life of the clone. The life of the clone is simply weightier."

Suppose next that the scientists occasionally produce more clones than there are volunteer caregivers. To address the problem, the scientists construct a world-class amusement park and stipulate that each evening one out of every hundred visitors will be randomly cuffed to take on a clone. Everyone who enters the park is made aware of the rules and thus understands the risks. In spite of the risks, the plan is a success, and the amusement park quickly becomes a favorite pastime for many people. Suppose that, when walking by the park, you become intrigued by the amusements inside. You don't really want to risk being cuffed to a clone, but the rides are so enticing that you throw caution to the wind and go inside. As you leave for the parking lot at closing time, the scientists jump out and cuff you to a clone. You then protest, "I admit that I know the rules of the park. However, I'm here not so much as a matter of rational choice but because of an irresistible lure." The scientists respond, "Indeed, the purpose of the amusement park is to give people that extra nudge to become caregivers. This nudge, though, is certainly not irresistible. Our park isn't the only form of entertainment available to you, and if the urge to enter the park is so strong, you should simply have stayed away from this part of town."

Imagine finally that many townspeople would like to visit the amusement park but don't want to risk being selected as a clone caregiver. Sympathetic to the desires of these people, the scientists sell visitors' cards that exempt patrons from caregiver selection. The downside to the cards is that they require continual updating and restrict cardholders from riding some of the best rides. Nevertheless, the visitors' cards become popular, and now almost everyone in town visits the park on a regular basis. Cardholders soon realize that the magnetic strips on the back of their cards sometimes malfunction and incorrectly register the card as invalid. The consequence is that out of every 30,000 cardholders who enter the park, one is cuffed to a clone. The scientists are aware of this problem and promise to fix it in the future, but for the time being the glitch poses a risk to the cardholders. Suppose that you are an unlucky cardholder and the scientists cuff you to a clone. You quickly object that your magnetic strip must have malfunctioned. The scientists respond, "You have to understand that we get that excuse all the time. Maybe your card is valid, maybe it's not; but once a magnetic strip malfunctions, there's no way that we can tell. You were aware of this risk when you entered the park, and like non-cardholders, you assume responsibility when you take on that risk."

Other Extenuating Circumstances   These five scenarios attempt to address questions about abortion in some extenuating circumstances. These circumstances involve (1) when a pregnancy places a woman's life at risk, (2) when a pregnancy becomes a serious emotional burden for a woman, (3) when pregnancy results from rape, (4) when a pregnancy results from the lure of the moment, and (5) when a pregnancy results from contraception failure. In each case, the moral status of the clone closely parallels the best-case scenario for the moral status of an 8-month-old fetus possessing a strong right to life. That is, we are presuming that the clone has the same rights to life as an adult human, but that it is not currently alert to its situation and can't communicate its preferences. In only the first of these examples—a life-threatening pregnancy—is it clear that a woman's interests override an 8-month-old fetus's strong right to life.

We must note, though, that our judgment is likely to be much different for earlier stages, when fetuses have a weaker moral status. To tap our intuitions in these cases, we need to alter the experiment to reflect the fetus's weaker statuses. So, instead of being cuffed to a human clone for nine months, we should think about being cuffed first to an early-stage superamoeba for a few weeks, then to an early-stage superworm for a few months, then to an early-stage superchicken for a few more months, and finally to a human clone for the remainder. If we assessed all four of these fetal stages according to the five extenuating circumstances discussed so far, we would have to construct twenty different scenarios. This would take a considerable amount of time and still would not exhaust all of the possibilities. For example, we've yet to consider problem pregnancies in which a fetus is deformed or harmed by a woman's drug use. We've not considered pregnancies that result from incest or cases in which a mother is in her early teens. We've also not considered pregnancies that cause great social harm, such as when continued population growth threatens to bring on wide-scale starvation. Some pregnancies even involve more than one extenuating circumstance. For example, the 14-year-old girl from Arizona was pregnant from rape, was exceptionally young, and had taken drugs during her pregnancy.

When we consider all of the factors, it becomes clear that the abortion controversy isn't about a single issue; rather, it is about a collection of perhaps a hundred issues. Legislators and judges should think hard about as many of these as possible before establishing legal policies on abortion. You and I, though, might wish only to think through the most representative cases. Here are some hints about how some representative cases might turn out.

One case involves what is sometimes called the "morning-after pill." If a woman takes the pill shortly after conception, then the zygote will be flushed from her body. At this stage, the zygote's moral status would be on a par with that of an early-stage superamoeba. The zygote's right to life is so weak that it may be overridden by even the weakest interests of a woman, such as considerations about being overwhelmed by the passion of the moment. A second case involves abortions at 2 months, which is the time at which physicians commonly recommend the procedure. At this stage, the fetus is not capable of perceiving its surroundings, and its moral status would be similar to that of an early-stage superworm. As we've seen, early-stage superworms have a mid-level right to life. Considerations about being accidentally caught in the passion of the moment may not be enough to override this mid-level right, although considerations of severe emotional distress may be adequate. A third case involves abortions at 5 months, a time when fetuses acquire lower mental qualities, such as perception. With a moral status similar to that of early-stage superchickens, considerations of emotional distress may not be enough to override the fetus's right to life, although considerations of rape may be adequate. We've already considered the case of abortions at 8 months, when fetuses have a moral status on par with that of adult humans. Here, only life-threatening pregnancies are sufficient to override the fetus's strong right to life.

Limitations of the Best Reasons Approach

The abortion controversy illustrates the chief benefit of the best reasons theory of morality. It is an effective tool for tackling the most complex controversies, and it allows us to enter into as much or as little detail as we want. It also allows us to draw on a variety of intuitive moral concepts such as autonomy, personal interest, public interest, and the right to life. Traditional moral theories are not this generous and don't let us select so widely from among differing moral principles. Although the abortion controversy illustrates the benefits of the best reasons theory, it also illustrates its limitations.

The first problem with the best reasons approach is that its step-by-step procedure is too mechanical and does not reflect the actual process by which we investigate moral issues. The procedure first tells us to lay out all the relevant facts for and against a course of action. But we often don't uncover all of the facts until much later in the reasoning process. For example, until we start actually arguing the pros and cons related to the moral status of a fetus, we may not even think about the fact that 5-month-old fetuses are capable of perception. The procedure next tells us to lay out relevant rules by which we balance the pros and cons. The problem here is that even the best rules are too general to offer us exact guidance. For example, the moderate autonomy principle states, "Issues of autonomy sometimes outweigh a fetus's right to life." On face value, this doesn't tell us, for example, whether a raped woman's autonomy outweighs a 5-month-old fetus's right to life. This only becomes clear when we actually begin weighing the competing arguments. The general rules, then, are useless, and if we devise particular rules, these will emerge only at the end of our reasoning process and so will also be useless. In spite of these procedural problems, though, the spirit behind the best reasons approach—namely, the process of weighing competing arguments—remains valid.

A second potential problem with the best reasons approach is that it relies on a person's private intuitions in the process of selecting relevant principles and in weighing competing arguments. This problem is highlighted when someone simply disagrees with our intuitions, such as, for example, the intuitions in the various abortion thought experiments. Baier attempts to address this problem by having the person adopt the stance of an objective judge or impartial spectator while we tap our intuitions in various situations. However, it may be an illusion to think that—on a moment's notice—we can psychologically step outside of our private intuitions and adopt a truly impartial perspective. Even if we could quickly adopt a slightly more impartial stance, that stance might reflect only the views of popular culture that we are exposed to in talk shows and news commentaries—and these may not be any better than our own private intuitions. So, the possibility of conflicting moral intuitions seems to present a genuine challenge for the best reasons approach. However, this problem is inherent in the nature of morality itself and will surface within all moral theory. Every moral theory that we consider rests on some foundational intuition about what kinds of actions or lifestyles are good. We continually dispute with moral philosophers about their underlying intuitions, and we reject moral theories that don't match our own intuitions. Like it or not, morality is grounded in our intuitions, and these often conflict.

There is a third and more serious problem with the best reasons approach. Although this approach closely captures how philosophers and lawyers think about moral problems, it does not represent the way most of us face real-life moral controversies. We sometimes simply follow the traditions in which we were raised, with moral reasoning playing no part. We don't think about balancing competing reasons, and we may not even care whether the authorities within our traditions ever went through this reasoning process. Toulmin and Baier would dismiss such blind appeals to tradition as irrational. However, it is wrongly elitist simply to dismiss appeals to tradition. Humans aren't designed to be rational calculating machines all day. We lock onto various traditions and let inertia carry us along for much of the time. This includes moral traditions from which none of us can fully escape—not even the advocates of the best reasons approach.

Summary

As articulated by Toulmin and Baier, the best reasons theory of morality tells us that an action is morally correct if it is supported by the best reasons. We first collect all the facts that constitute good reasons for and against an action. We then look for moral principles that are relevant to the facts. Finally, using these moral principles, we balance the "pro" facts against the "con" facts. This procedure allows us to tackle complex moral controversies that involve a wide range of facts and a wide range of interests.

Applying this procedure to the abortion controversy, we first addressed the issue of the fetus's moral status. The crucial facts involved (1) facts about a fetus's actual mental qualities, which support an abortion decision, and (2) facts about its potential mental qualities, which go against an abortion decision. The central moral principle related to these facts is that an organism's potential qualities are relevant to its moral status, although not as relevant as its actual qualities. When weighing the facts with this principle, we concluded that an early-stage fetus has a weak moral status and a later-stage fetus has a strong moral status.

We next looked at situations in which the fetus's right to life could be set aside in favor of more compelling interests of the mother. The crucial facts here involved (1) facts about a woman's autonomy interests and (2) facts about a fetus's right to life. The central moral principle relevant to these facts is that issues of autonomy sometimes outweigh a fetus's right to life. When balancing the facts with this principle, we concluded that, in the early stage of pregnancy, most considerations of autonomy will outweigh a fetus's right to life. However, in the last stage of pregnancy, only life-threatening situations outweigh a fetus's right to life.

Study Questions

Introduction

   1. What are the principal issues involved in the abortion controversy?

The Process of Moral Reasoning

   Toulmin's View of Moral Reasoning

   2. What is the difference between scientific reasoning and moral reasoning?

   3. What are some of the different hats that we have to wear in moral reasoning?

   Baier's View of Moral Reasoning

   4. What are the two distinct reasoning processes that we use in moral reasoning?

   5. What are the different points of view that we might adopt as we select principles?

   6. According to Baier, why is the moral point of view superior to others?

Best Reasons and Applied Ethics

7. What is the aim of applied ethics?

The Fetus's Moral Status

Gathering the Facts

8. Briefly, what are the four facts relevant to the moral status of a fetus?

Extreme Pro-Choice Potentiality Principle

9. According to Fieser, what is wrong with Feinberg's analogy regarding potential U.S. presidents?
10. According to Fieser, what is wrong with the extreme pro-choice potentiality principle?
11. What age fetus does the early-stage superworm represent?

Extreme Pro-Life and Moderate Potentiality Principles

12. Why does Fieser reject the extreme pro-life potentiality principle?
13. What age fetus does the early-stage superchicken represent?

The Fetus's Interests Versus Others' Interests

Gathering and Weighing the Facts

14. Briefly, what are the three facts relevant to balancing the fetus's interests against the interests of others?
15. What age fetus do the handcuffed clones represent?

Some Extenuating Circumstances

16. What situation regarding the clones represents pregnancies when the mother's life is at risk?
17. What situation regarding the clones represents pregnancies that result from rape?

Other Extenuating Circumstances

18. According to Fieser, what is the only scenario in which the mother's interests overrides an 8-month-old fetus's strong right to life?
19. What does Fieser conclude about the morning-after pill?

Limitations of the Best Reasons Approach

20. What are the three limitations of the best reasons approach?

References

The theory linking increased abortions to decreased crime is discussed in Abraham McLaughlin's "A Jarring Theory for Drop in US Crime," *The Christian Science Monitor,* September 12, 1999.

The central part of Stephen Toulmin's moral theory is in Part III of *An Examination of the Place of Reason in Ethics* (Cambridge: Cambridge University Press, 1950).

The central part of Kurt Baier's theory appears in Chapter 3 of *The Moral Point of View* (Ithaca, NY: Cornell University Press, 1958).

The quotation by Joel Feinberg is from "Abortion," in *Matters of Life and Death,* 2nd ed., edited by Tom Regan (Englewood Cliffs, NJ: Prentice-Hall, 1986).

Suggestions for Further Reading

For a discussion of Toulmin's view of ethics, see Tore Nilstun, *Moral Reasoning: A Study in the Moral Philosophy of S. E. Toulmin* (Lund, Sweden: Studentlitteratur, 1979).

For a discussion of Baier's ethical views, see J. B. Schneewind and Gerard Gaul, *Reason, Ethic, and Society: Themes from Kurt Baier, with His Responses* (Chicago: Open Court, 1996).

James Rachels discusses and adopts the best reasons approach to morality in Chapter 1 of *The Elements of Moral Philosophy*, 3rd ed. (New York: McGraw-Hill, 1999).

For philosophical discussions of the abortion issue, see Charles P. Cozic and Stacey L. Tripp, eds., *Abortion: Opposing Viewpoints* (San Diego: Greenhaven Press, 1991); Joel Feinberg, *The Problem of Abortion* (Belmont, CA: Wadsworth, 1984); Don Marquis, "An Argument That Abortion Is Wrong," in Hugh LaFollette, ed., *Ethics and Practice: An Anthology* (Oxford: Blackwell, 1996); Michael Tooley, *Abortion and Infanticide* (London: Oxford University Press, 1983); Mary Anne Warren, "Abortion," in Peter Singer, ed., *A Companion to Ethics* (Oxford: Blackwell, 1991).

15

The Interrelation between Different Ethical Theories

Introduction

In 1999, a 30-year-old man named Ronald L. Shanabarger suffocated his 7-month-old son in an act of revenge against his wife. Although the coroner initially ruled that the child had died of Sudden Infant Death Syndrome, Shanabarger later confessed to the murder and explained his motive. Three years earlier, when Shanabarger's father had died, Shanabarger's girlfriend—later to become his wife—had refused to come home early from a vacation cruise to comfort him. He had then schemed his revenge and fathered the child solely for the purpose of killing him to spite his wife. On the tragic evening, he put plastic wrap around his son's face and left the room to wash his hands and brush his teeth. Returning later, he removed the wrap and placed his son face down in his crib. Shanabarger confessed his crime to the police since he was haunted by the visual image of his son's flattened and purple face. When confessing, he begged the police to shoot him.

This story stands out in several ways. It is an example of an action that is indisputably immoral. It involves a single, simple act with clear intention and precise planning. The consequences of Shanabarger's action are also horrifying. Although these points of the story are evident, moral philosophers go a step further and try to explain exactly why actions like this count as immoral. There are scores of philosophical theories about the nature of morality and our specific obligations, and from different theories, we might get different explanations about the immorality of Shanabarger's action. He failed to acquire the proper virtues of benevolence and temperance. He neglected his basic duties as a father. He violated his son's rights. He created an enormous amount of pain for his wife and other relatives. Philosophers might also say that he violated age-old cultural traditions, or the will of God, or the codes of moral decency that bind our society together. Which of these descriptions is the best explanation for Shanabarger's immoral action?

Moral philosophers today typically emphasize a single approach to understanding morality; familiar names of such approaches are utilitarianism, virtue theory, duty theory, divine command theory, and social contract theory. Proponents of these theories sometimes attempt to connect their specific theory to central features of other theories; other times they go out of their way to reject rival theories. Because of this tension between theories, we learn different moral theories in isolation from each other and assume that if we accept one moral theory then we must reject the other theories. This approach also puts us on a quest to uncover the single *true* theory that captures the notion of morality better than all other theories.

This isolationist approach to moral theories is a comparatively recent phenomenon. Until perhaps the nineteenth century, moral philosophers were very eclectic. They tried to incorporate as many components of differing theories as they could, and as a new theory came along, they would find some way to squeeze that theory into their overall system. They still disputed with other moral philosophers—and sometimes vehemently—but the disputes largely consisted of emphasizing one feature of a theory more than another.

Some moral philosophers today are discontent with the current isolationist approach to moral theories. They believe that no single theory will adequately capture the nature of morality and that we need many theories to do the trick. Some philosophers assimilate two or three theories; others suggest that we sporadically draw from the complete range of moral theories as our specific moral situations require. We will explore two ways of interrelating various moral theories. First, we will follow the model of earlier moral philosophers and try to systematically integrate as many as we can into a single coherent package; that is, we will present an **ethical supertheory**. Second, we will see more informally how each ethical theory can have value in our common moral lives by helping us visualize our moral obligations.

An Ethical Supertheory

To begin the task of integrating different moral theories, we may follow the lead of eighteenth-century moral sense theorists, particularly Francis Hutcheson (1694–1747) and David Hume (1711–1776). Hutcheson and Hume differentiated between three psychologically distinct players in moral assessment: the agent, the receiver, and the spectator. Using the chapter-opening case as an illustration, Shanabarger is the agent who willfully performed an action—specifically, the act of killing his 7-month-old son. His son, wife, and other family members are the receivers of the action, and we are the spectators who observe what is going on and pass judgment on Shanabarger. So, the agent performs an action, which impacts the receiver and triggers a response in the spectator. In normal situations, these three roles are continually shifting. For example, Shanabarger eventually realized that he, too, was negatively impacted by killing his son, so he was both the agent, and one of the receivers. Similarly, he assumed the role of spectator when he finally passed negative judgment on himself and asked to be killed. Although we slide from one role to another and sometimes assume more than one role at the same time, for ease of explanation, we will think of the three roles as being held by three different people. We will consider the key elements of all three roles.

The Duties and Virtues of the Agent   We first want to consider the role of the moral **agent** who performs an initial action. In the most ideal situation, an agent has moral intuitions about a wide range of moral duties. At a given time, an agent will have intuitions about lying, stealing, cheating on a spouse, and hundreds of other acts. Many of these intuitions are very specific, such as what he should do if he finds someone's wallet on the street. In the most ideal situation, as the agent reflects and acts on his various duties, he will develop good habits, or virtues, that have him consistently and automatically performing his duties. For example, insofar as the agent has a duty to help others in need, he will develop the virtue of charity.

Corresponding to each duty, then, there is some specific virtue that the agent will ideally acquire. We can categorize the agent's various duties and virtues into different groups. It is important to note, though, that any grouping of duties will only be a tool of convenience, and the agent himself may not necessarily consider categorizing his duties in any way at all. One convenient scheme of duties is this (the names of corresponding virtues are in parentheses):

> Duties to others—correlate with the receiver's demands on others
>> Equity
>>> Don't harm others (nonharmfulness)
>>> Don't interfere with the liberties of others (tolerance)
>> Benevolence
>>> Help those in need (charity)
>>> Improve the world (public spirit)
>
> Duties to oneself—same as the receiver's demands on him- or herself
>> Survival—as concerns one's bodily well-being
>>> Stay healthy (health-consciousness)
>>> Avoid risky behavior (safety-consciousness)
>> Happiness—as concerns one's mental well-being
>>> Seek various pleasures (temperance)
>>> Improve self-image (self-respect)

According to this scheme, we may divide duties between those that an agent has toward *others* and those that he has toward *himself*. This was a common way of distinguishing between duties during the seventeenth and eighteenth centuries, which we find first systematically articulated by Samuel von Pufendorf (1632–1694).

Borrowing terminology from Samuel Clarke (1675–1729), duties to others divide into two key groups: (1) duties of *equity* and (2) duties of *benevolence*. Duties of equity largely involve leaving people alone and not mistreating them. Duties of benevolence go a step further and require that we take an active roll in improving people's lives. Immanuel Kant (1724–1804) encapsulated all of our equity and benevolence duties into a single principle: We should treat people as an end, and never as a means to an end. According to Kant's reasoning, when I am inequitable—that is, harmful or unjustifiably interfering—I am in fact manipulating people for my own satisfaction and using them as a means. When I fail to be benevolent—that is, not helping those in need or failing to improve the world—I am ignoring the intrinsic value of people and not treating them as an end. Both our equity and benevolence duties emerge in response to demands that receivers place on an agent. For example, insofar as the local grocery store owner places a demand on the agent not to steal, the agent intuitively recognizes that he has an equity duty not to steal from the grocery store. Similarly, insofar as an injured person places a demand on us to help him, then the agent intuitively recognizes that he has a benevolence duty to assist the injured person.

As the outline shows, our equity duties are of two types. The first is to avoid harming others, which includes not killing, assaulting, harassing, cheating, or stealing from others. There are countless types of harms that an agent can do to a receiver; some involve physical violence, and others are nonviolent and principally involve violations of trust, such as lying, committing fraud, or breaking agreements. The basic virtue associated with all of our duties to avoid harming others is nonharmfulness. The second type of equity duty is to avoid interfering with the liberties of others. Unless someone is harming us, we have a basic duty to let people say what they want, do what they want, and go where they want. The basic virtue associated with our duties to avoid interfering with others is tolerance. Turning to the agent's duties of benevolence, these also fall into two main categories. The first involves helping others in need, such as people who are injured, starving, or otherwise destitute. The duty associated with this is charity. The second type of benevolence duty involves improving the world, such as through education, medical improvements, or cultural development. The virtue associated with this is public spirit.

Continuing with the outline, in addition to duties to others, moral agents also have duties to themselves, which emerge from demands that they place on themselves. Pufendorf split these duties into two groups insofar as some duties concern our physical body and others concern our mind, or mental well-being. Bodily duties to ourselves are essentially survival duties, and they involve staying healthy and free from injury. Ordinarily, this means avoiding lifestyle choices that would shorten our lives or drive us to suicide. The virtues associated with survival duties are health-consciousness and cautiousness. Duties pertaining to our mental well-being involve our happiness. Part of our happiness hinges on various pleasures that we experience in life, such as romance, friendship, food, and entertainment. The general virtue associated with these is temperance, or restraint. Part of our happiness also hinges on our self-image and on seeing ourselves as valuable people; the virtue here is self-respect. This has various subcomponents based on common ways that we develop our self-image. A central subcomponent here is to develop our talents through our vocation, which involves the virtue of proper ambition.

This division of duties rests on how an agent would intuitively see his duties in the most ideal situation. Our actual moral intuitions, though, are not fixed but are continually adjusted through reflection. There are two main ways that the agent uses moral reflection. The first involves adapting moral intuitions to unique situations. Ideally, our intuitions give us various common conceptions of moral duties, and we each reflect on these and mold these to fit our unique circumstances. Aristotle (384–322 BCE) argued that the reflective process in our individual situations often involves developing habits of moderation. So, with charity, for example, if I help too little I will be stingy, and if I help too much I will be overgenerous and wasteful.

Sometimes our reflective process is consistent with the underlying thrust of our moral intuitions. For example, suppose that I find someone's laptop computer on a park bench. Even though I may not have any immediately clear intuitions about what I should do, I can reflect on my more evident duties and determine that I should try to find the owner. At other times, though, our reflective process might actually pull us away from our initial moral intuitions and make us bad people. Shanabarger is a good illustration of this. After his girlfriend failed to cut short her vacation, he reflected on what he believed was justly owed him, and he resolved to even the score through his horrible plan. We can accept that Shanabarger was justly disappointed by his girlfriend's vacation decision. His reflection on this, though, fell far short of his initial and more general moral intuitions. His notions of duty became twisted, and the corresponding habits that he developed became vices rather than virtues.

A second aspect of moral reflection involves the fact that our ideal common moral intuitions give us only a list of *tentative* duties, which W. D. Ross (1877–1971) dubbed "prima facie." Sometimes our ideal moral duties conflict. Suppose, for example, that a man is running from a gang of thugs and I see him slip into a nearby warehouse. The thugs then ask me if I know where the man went. On the one hand, I have a tentative duty to tell people the truth and not mislead them; on the other, I have a tentative duty to avoid contributing to physical violence. So, I'm trapped between two competing duties. However, through moral reflection, I come to see that one of the duties is stronger than the other. In this case, my duty to avoid violence is clearly weightier than my duty to tell the truth.

This notion of tentative duties helps explain another long-time riddle about moral duties. Some duties, such as benevolence, are what Pufendorf calls "imperfect" insofar as they don't require precise behavior on our part. Even though I should help people in need, I can't reasonably help everyone in need whom I see. It seems, then, that I need to pick out some needy people to help and ignore others. The problem is that I am not physically or financially capable of helping everyone. For each case of charity that I consider, my tentative duty to help others may be overridden by my duty of making myself happy. Once again, it is a matter of moral reflection to balance the competing duties. Hopefully, I'll find some cases in which being charitable will be consistent with my duty of providing happiness to myself.

Rights, Virtues, and Consequences Regarding the Receiver   A second role in the moral assessment process is filled by the **receiver**, who makes demands on moral agents. In the Shanabarger case, the main receivers were Shanabarger's son, wife, and relatives. They all demanded certain moral behavior from Shanabarger, and they were all adversely affected by Shanabarger's moral failure. In the most ideal situation, the list of receiver's demands is a mirror image of the agent's duties; these demands are outlined here:

> Demands on others—correlate with the agent's duties to others
>> Negative rights to be left alone
>>> Freedom from various harms (proper assertiveness)
>>> Freedom to perform various liberties (considerateness)
>> Positive rights to improve one's welfare
>>> To be helped when in need (gratitude)
>>> To have a better future (patience)
>
> Demands that we make of ourselves—same as the agent's duties to him- or herself
>> Survival—as concerns one's bodily well-being
>>> Stay healthy (health-consciousness)
>>> Avoid risky behavior (safety-consciousness)
>> Happiness—as concerns one's mental well-being
>>> Seek various pleasures (temperance)
>>> Improve oneself (proper ambition)

Given the parallels between this list and the previous one, we don't need to go through it point by point. Some items, though, need clarification. First, as receivers, the demands that we make on others are called "moral rights." However, the term "rights" does not make sense when we think of the demands that receivers place on themselves. For example, I don't say that I (as a receiver) have a *right* to avoid risky behavior, which I (as an agent) have a duty to follow. Instead, it makes more sense to say that I (as a receiver) place a special demand on myself, which I (as an agent) have a duty to follow.

A second point of clarification involves the virtues associated with a receiver's demands. For every ideal demand that we make on others or ourselves, there is a virtuous habit that consistently guides that demand. First, when I demand my right to be free from various harms, the virtue is proper assertiveness. If I am not assertive enough, then an agent may not respect my demand; if I am too assertive, then the agent may find me obnoxious. Second, when I demand my right to be free to perform various liberties, the virtue is considerateness. Suppose, for example, that a receiver asserts his liberty-based right to smoke, and he thereby demands that the agent has a duty to let him smoke. The receiver needs to be sensitive to when he should assert this right. For example, it would be insensitive to assert this right around someone with emphysema or during a church service. Third, when I demand my right to be helped, such as when I've been in a car accident, the virtue is gratitude. Fourth, when I demand my right to a better future as provided by publicly spirited people, I need to apply the virtue of patience and not expect social improvements immediately.

A third point of clarification involves the connection between rights and duties. Specifically, rights theorists debate about the extent to which there is an *exact* parallel between duties and rights. In many cases, the correlation between the two is indeed clear. For example, if I owe you $10, then you (as a receiver) can rightfully demand that I (as an agent) pay you, and I clearly have a duty to pay you. In other cases, though, the correlation isn't as clear. If you are starving, then it doesn't seem that you (as a receiver) can rightfully demand that I *specifically* (as an agent) should help you. Many dilemmas involving duties and rights can be resolved by thinking of duties and rights as being only *tentative*. For example, you may have a tentative right to demand help from me, but upon reflection, this may be overridden by my tentative right to be happy.

The scenario that we've painted so far involves an ideal posture between the agent and receiver. It represents a slice of time just prior to when an agent actually performs an action that affects the receiver. In real life, though, time does not freeze: The agent carries out the act, and this has consequences on the receiver. If the agent acts according to his ideal duties, then the consequences will typically be good ones; if he acts against his ideal duties, then the consequences will typically be bad ones. For example, in Shanabarger's story, Shanabarger as the agent acted contrary to his ideal duties, and the action had tragic consequences. His son was one receiver, and for him, his final moments involved being suffocated. His wife was another receiver, and for her, Shanabarger's act undoubtedly psychologically scarred her for life. The range of negative consequences in this story varies greatly and includes physical pain, emotional anguish, frustration, and perhaps every other negative emotion one could experience. Jeremy Bentham (1748–1832) attempted to explain all of these consequences as types of pleasure and pain. R. M. Hare attempted to explain these in terms of preferences that we have for or against something. Both of these explanations, though, are too limiting. In Hare's case, it seems to trivialize some experiences, such as physical torture, reducing them simply to psychological preferences against something. The safest route is to refer to consequences in terms of their goodness versus badness, or perhaps in terms of their positive versus negative outcomes.

The Spectator's Spontaneous and Reflective Assessments   Once an agent performs an action that negatively affects a receiver, the role of the **spectator** is to make a pronouncement about the morality of the agent's conduct. In many cases, this is a two-part process. The first part involves a spontaneous assessment. As soon as the spectator is presented with the basic facts of the situation, she will spontaneously react with a moral assessment from the vantage of her basic moral intuitions. For example, when presented with Shanabarger's story, a spectator would likely express emotional outrage at Shanabarger's action and pronounce it grossly immoral. This assessment is a knee-jerk reaction to two essential facts of the story: (1) Shanabarger violated his basic duties, and (2) this produced very bad consequences. Both of these facts are central to the spectator's initial spontaneous response, which we can illustrate with two counter-examples. Suppose that Shanabarger attempted to kill his son, but his wife came home and rescued the boy just in time. In this situation, the first fact would remain the same—Shanabarger violated his duties—but the bad consequences would not be as severe. We would then expect the spectator's spontaneous reaction to be less severe. Or suppose, alternatively, that Shanabarger was actually a morally upright person and that he killed his son as a result of a drug that accidentally turned him into a homicidal maniac. In this situation, the facts are at least somewhat different regarding whether he intentionally violated his basic duties, yet the consequences were still just as bad. Again, we would expect the spectator's spontaneous reaction to be less severe.

So, a spectator's spontaneous assessment will be in reaction to facts regarding both the agent's duties and the consequences of the agent's conduct. The spectator's spontaneous assessment might be emotionally charged. In spontaneously assessing Shanabarger's action, the spectator may experience outrage at Shanabarger, which would result from cognitive dissonance between the facts of the situation and the spectator's common moral intuitions. The spectator may also experience sorrow in sympathetic reaction to the victimized receivers—namely, Shanabarger's son and wife. When making her spontaneous assessment, the spectator implicitly or explicitly asserts that "Shanabarger is morally wrong." With this statement, the spectator expresses her feelings of outrage toward the agent and her feelings of sorrow toward the receivers. Also, with this statement, the spectator puts forth as fact that Shanabarger's act runs contrary to the spectator's common moral intuitions.

The second part of the spectator's assessment process is a delayed reflective assessment. After the spectator issues her spontaneous assessment, there is an opportunity for closer moral reflection on the two basic facts of the story. The spectator can try to uncover the precise duties that Shanabarger violated, and she can also consider more carefully the negative consequences that resulted from Shanabarger's action. Advocates of the best reasons approach, such as Kurt Baier, maintain that this kind of assessment involves (1) surveying all of the relevant facts and (2) assessing them with sound principles. This may also involve an inspection and reevaluation of the spectator's initial moral intuitions.

The primary virtue that underlies the spectator's process of reflective assessment is *impartiality,* which involves eliminating personal bias regarding either the agent or the receiver. Once the spectator has finished her reflections, she may make another—and perhaps differing—assessment of the agent's action. Regarding Shanabarger's action, suppose that the spectator's reflective assessment is the same as her initial spontaneous assessment. That is, upon reflection, she again implicitly or explicitly states that "Shanabarger is morally wrong." With this statement, the spectator may again express her feelings of outrage toward Shanabarger and her feelings of sorrow toward the victims. This statement also reaffirms the fact that Shanabarger's act runs contrary to the spectator's common moral intuitions. In her reflective assessment, though, the spectator may have some additional meanings behind her statement. She may be urging other spectators to adopt her negative assessment of Shanabarger, and she may also be motivating herself to follow her basic moral intuitions and not go down the path that Shanabarger did.

Moral Reflection and the Source of Moral Intuitions   The account of morality just described involves moral intuitions in three ways. First, the agent intuitively understands that he has various duties. Second, the receivers intuitively understand that they place justified demands on other people and themselves. Third, from a survey of the agent's duties and the harm caused to receivers, the spectator intuitively approves or disapproves of the agent's action. It is no coincidence that the intuitions of agent, receiver, and spectator parallel each other in their moral content. When I play each of these roles at various times, I am in fact drawing from the same underlying source of intuitions within me, and so, in the most ideal situation, my specific intuitions in each of these roles will be the same.

We've seen, though, that moral intuitions for agent, receiver, and spectator are not fixed, and we continually alter these through reflection. Sometimes we alter them to the point that our intuitions as agents, receivers, and spectators no longer line up. For example, Shanabarger seriously altered his agent intuitions concerning his duties to others, yet he appears to have kept intact his receiver intuitions about the scope of his own rights. The **Golden Rule** is a principle of moral reflection that helps us keep our agent intuitions and receiver intuitions in sync. The Golden Rule tells me to act toward others in ways that I would want others to act toward me. That is, I should keep my duties to others parallel to my rights that I demand of others. In addition to the Golden Rule, we may find other rules of thumb that help guide the process of moral reflection. For example, the simple rule "Be impartial" is a guide for the delayed reflective assessment process of spectators. Philosophers have described the general process of moral reflection with various names; Aristotle calls it practical wisdom; John Rawls calls it reflective equilibrium. Hopefully, we will exercise our moral reflection properly, and when we do this consistently, we have the virtue of good sense.

Having listed our general moral intuitions, we now need to ask where our ideal moral intuitions come from. The answer is that they arise through a complex relation between natural inclinations and social tradition. At their most foundational level, our moral intuitions rest on an array of natural inclinations that we all have. Thomas Aquinas (1225–1274) and most moral philosophers after him listed what they believed were morally relevant natural inclinations: to seek pleasure, to avoid pain, to preserve our lives, to procreate, to educate our offspring, and to live in social units. These inclinations by themselves, though, won't give us meaningful moral intuitions. For example, the inclination to procreate in and of itself might prompt us simply to be sexually active, and not incline us to be responsible parents. Further, sociobiologists of recent years, such as Edward O. Wilson, argue that the process of evolutionary biology has produced conflicting inclinations, such as loyalties to ourselves versus loyalties to groups.

Natural inclinations, then, only take us so far in the formation of our ideal moral intuitions. Social contract theorists such as Thomas Hobbes (1588–1679) explain how basic social agreements bring us a step further in our conceptions of morality. For Hobbes, natural inclinations by themselves will put us in brutal conflict with others. To preserve our lives and live in peace, we mutually agree to set aside basic hostilities. Contrary to Hobbes, though, we should not see this as a literal "agreement" or "contract." Instead, it is more like a situation of social reciprocity that we are content to perpetuate. That is, I behave civilly, and in exchange for this, I receive protection from the governing body that my society establishes. This contentment with social reciprocity provides us with some basic moral intuitions, particularly an agent's duties of equity, which keep us from harming others and interfering with one another's liberties. This also forms the basis of the receiver's negative rights insofar as the receiver can justifiably demand to be free from various harms and free to perform various liberties.

However, social reciprocity alone can't explain the basis of our remaining moral intuitions. Social traditions further shape our intuitions about what constitutes harm and what constitutes a justifiable liberty. Traditions also shape our intuitions about helping others in need and about making the world a better place. Ethnic groups, religions, political organizations, and family clans typically develop conceptions of what the good life is and what we need to do to become happy. As anthropologists point out, many of these notions vary from culture to culture and involve specialized rules about sexual activity, mating rituals, death rituals, and many other activities. In addition to social traditions, our own individual preferences contribute to shaping at least some of our moral intuitions, particularly regarding our duties to ourselves and the corresponding demands that we place on ourselves.

Many traditional philosophers felt that natural inclination and social tradition alone can't adequately account for our moral intuitions. Plato (428–348 BCE), for example, believed that moral standards are grounded in a higher objective level of reality, one that is spiritual in nature. Similarly, John Duns Scotus (c. 1266–1308) believed that moral standards are rooted in God's creative will. Theories about higher levels of morality and God's will present enormous metaphysical problems, and so it may be best to set these speculations aside and base morality on the observable phenomena around us—namely, natural inclinations and social traditions. However, people who insist on incorporating these metaphysical elements might follow the example of natural law philosophers, who maintain that God implants objective moral standards into our natural inclinations and social traditions.

That, in a nutshell, is where our moral intuitions come from. Many of our moral intuitions are likely to stay fixed from one culture to another and over time, especially those that are foundational to social reciprocity and the establishment of social peace. However, as our social traditions shift over time, so too will at least some of our moral intuitions. Our moral attitudes about slavery and the social status of women are cases in point. Not only have some specific moral intuitions shifted over time, but even our general way of articulating our moral intuitions has shifted. Today, we describe the moral agent's role mainly in terms of duties, and the receiver's role in terms of rights. However, 1000 years ago, philosophers expressed the agent's role in terms of sins that the agent should avoid. And 3000 years ago, sages expressed the agent's role in terms of what a "wise person" or a "dutiful son" would do.

Isolationist Ethical Theories versus an Ethical Supertheory

It isn't particularly important whether we conceive of our moral intuitions in terms of duties, sins, or wise people. What is important is that the concepts we use capture the full range of morally relevant life experiences in our various roles as moral agents, moral receivers, and moral spectators. The downfall of many **isolationist ethical theories** is that they don't capture the full range of experiences in our three roles. Utilitarians, for example, have accurately depicted the significance of consequences regarding the spectator's moral assessments. However, utilitarianism is a clumsy and counterintuitive way to explain the agent's various obligations, the receiver's rights, and the underlying source of morality. Other isolationist approaches to moral philosophy will similarly fail, including virtue theory, rights theory, sociobiology, social contract theory, and cultural relativism. Given the complexity of our moral notions today—both in common life and in our theoretical discussions—we need an ethical supertheory that does justice to the various moral roles of agent, receiver, and spectator. The ethical supertheory presented here is one way of integrating our diverse moral notions. Although this may not be the only possible ethical supertheory, it is a natural arrangement of component theories. This is principally because it follows the general scheme of eclectic philosophers from the past and places the component theories precisely where these philosophers originally intended them to go. For example, proto-utilitarian philosophers such as Hutcheson and Hume placed the consequentialist component of morality precisely where we inserted it here. That is, they believed that part of the spectator's assessment involved a reaction to the consequences of the agent's action on the receiver.

To summarize, here are the main points of the ethical supertheory:

- The agent has moral intuitions about his duties to others (equity and benevolence) and to himself (survival and happiness).
- The receiver has moral intuitions about the rights she demands from others (negative and positive) and the demands that she places on herself (survival and happiness).
- The spectator intuitively makes both a spontaneous and a reflective assessment of the agent's action based on facts about the agent's duties and the consequences of the agent's actions on various receivers.
- All of our moral intuitions are subject to change through moral reflection.
- There are virtues or good habits that correspond with our various roles as agents, receivers, and spectators.
- Moral intuitions arise from a complex interrelation between natural inclination, social reciprocity, social tradition, and personal preferences.

Moral Images

Our ethical supertheory attempts to fit together many pieces of a complex puzzle. And this is typically what we expect a philosophical theory to do. From the standpoint of our common-life moral experiences, though, we don't think about the moral assessment process in such a detailed way. In fact, in our common-life moral activities, we may not even think of morality as involving a division of labor between an agent, a receiver, and a spectator—particularly because our roles are continually shifting, which blurs the role we are playing at any given time. In view of this disparity between philosophy and common life, we may want to know whether philosophical moral theories have any real value for our common-life conceptions of morality. We will trace how traditional moral theories may have practical value in terms of moral images that they present.

The Function of Moral Images in Common Life   A moral image is a concept that helps us visualize the nature of morality, such as the image of a happy society or the image of a God who creates morality. We often think visually about the moral relationships we have with each other, and the more visual we can make our moral theories, the more helpful they will be. We can see the value of images in Shanabarger's story. What finally made him personalize the evil nature of his action was the visual image of his son's flattened and purple face after rigor mortis had set in. If he had fixed on this image beforehand, it might have enlivened his sense of moral obligation to his son, and he might have set aside his horrible scheme. Moral theories can't anticipate images as vivid as this one, but perhaps the images that they do offer can take hold of most of us. Indeed, the entire range of traditional moral images is potentially relevant for understanding the nature and content of our common-life moral obligations. These may be most helpful when they are like movie images that contain some plot and character development. We might also see them as moral fables that help symbolize or personify the hidden nature of morality.

In the spirit of our ethical supertheory, *all* traditional moral images are potentially relevant to understanding morality in our common-life situations. Although it is possible that a single image might illuminate everything we need to know about morality, it seems that we don't yet have the perfect moral image that satisfactorily answers all of our moral questions. So, we will gain a more complete understanding of morality when we entertain a range of traditional moral images. We noted that isolationist moral theories often are set up as rivals to each other. For example, if morality is ultimately founded on the consequences of actions, then it can't be ultimately founded on intuitive duties. Again, though, in the spirit of our ethical supertheory, such blatant inconsistencies don't arise when we interpret moral theories as moral images. The image relating to an action's consequences may illuminate one aspect of morality, and the image relating to moral duties may illuminate another. These differing moral images don't immediately conflict with each other any more than the differing lessons from two fables might conflict. For example, in one children's fable, I may learn that I should plan for the future; in another, I may learn that I should be spontaneous. Both fables, though, may still teach valuable practical lessons.

We will look at the role of moral images in several traditional moral theories. Moral theories are largely of two types, normative and metaethical, so we will consider both kinds in turn.

The Normative Image of the Golden Rule

The Normative Image of the Golden Rule   Normative ethical theories aim at giving us practical moral guidance. Our behavior is morally good when we follow that guidance, and our behavior is morally wrong when we act contrary to it. Philosophers have offered scores of normative theories over the years, and each of these have moral images embedded in them. The most famous of all normative guidelines is the Golden Rule, which tells me to act toward others in ways that I would want others to act toward me. For example, I should not steal from other people since I would not want others to steal from me. Although Europeans and Americans are most familiar with the Golden Rule as Jesus expressed it in the New Testament, the Golden Rule appears in the classic literature of most ancient civilizations:

> Hinduism: "This is the sum of duty: do nothing to others which would cause you pain if done to you." (*Mahabharata* 5:1517)
>
> Buddhism: "Do not hurt others in ways that you yourself would find hurtful." (*Udana-Varga* 5:18)
>
> Confucianism: "Tzu-kung asked, saying, 'Is there one word that may serve as a rule of practice for all one's life?' The Master [Confucius] said, 'Is not reciprocity such a word? What you do not want done to yourself, do not do to others.'" (*Analects*, 15:23)
>
> Taoism: "Regard your neighbor's gain as your own gain, and your neighbor's loss as your own loss." (*T'ai Shang Kan Ying P'ien*)
>
> Zoroastrianism: "That nature alone is good which refrains from doing to another whatever is not good for itself." (*Dadistan-i-dinik*, 94:5)
>
> Judaism: "What is hateful to you, do not do to your fellow man. That is the entire Law; all the rest is commentary." (*Talmud*, Shabbat 31a)
>
> Christianity: "Always treat others as you would like them to treat you: that is the law and the prophets." (*Matthew* 7:12)
>
> Islam: "No one of you is a believer until he desires for his brother that which he desires for himself." (*Sunnah*)

The appearance of the Golden Rule in so many cultures shows that it expresses a widespread mode of moral thinking. Even if we don't consciously apply this general principle to specific actions in our daily lives, we often follow it spontaneously. For example, I may spontaneously hold open a door for someone carrying a heavy package. When I look at the person, I might immediately recognize how difficult it would be for me if I were carrying a heavy package. I then help out in a way that I imagine I'd like to be helped. A similar quick intuition might prompt me to avoid lying, stealing, or killing.

Although it is a valuable indicator of moral conduct, there are limitations to the Golden Rule when we attempt to apply it as a universal guideline. Early Christian philosopher Augustine (354–430) exposes a problem when we consider the morality of wife swapping:

> What if someone's lust is so great that he offers his wife to another and willingly allows him to commit adultery with her, and is eager to enjoy the same freedom with the other man's wife? (*On Free Choice of the Will*, 3)

In this case, if I am willing to let someone sleep with my wife, then, based on the Golden Rule, it would be okay for me to sleep with that man's wife. The problem with the Golden Rule is that it requires me to know beforehand what is right and wrong. That is, I must know beforehand that it is wrong for someone to steal from me or to sleep with my wife; only then can I reverse the situation and conclude that it is wrong for me to steal from someone else or to sleep with someone else's wife. This is a problem because, if I know beforehand what is right and wrong, I don't really need to consult the Golden Rule to tell me what is right and wrong.

We find value in the Golden Rule, not so much as a mechanical guide for discovering morality, but because of a concrete image that it gives us, which helps us personify our moral obligations. The specific image is *me in someone else's shoes*. When I am considering the morality of a particular action, my decision might be properly guided when I think of this image. The image may remind me of what I should do, or it may give me the proper motivation to carry out what I already know I should do. It may not work in all cases—as with Augustine's wife-swapping example—but it may work in enough cases to be worth remembering and at least occasionally consulting. If the image fails to take hold, we may turn to other normative images, and the more images we have, the more likely we will find an image that does take hold.

Philosophical Normative Images   When we turn to normative theories offered by the great philosophers of our European and American tradition, we will likely see that they parallel the features of the Golden Rule. That is, many famous normative theories express a common mode of moral thinking that we find in other cultures around the world. Also, these traditional normative theories can't serve as universal guidelines unless we know beforehand what is right and wrong. So, as with the Golden Rule, traditional normative theories are not particularly valuable as mechanical rules for *discovering* morality; instead, their value rests in their normative images, which *remind* us of our obligations and *motivate* us to act properly. It isn't immediately clear how we initially gained our knowledge of morality, which we later recollect and personalize through moral images. However, we most likely first gained moral knowledge early in life—long before we ever heard of normative principles such as the Golden Rule. It is the job of developmental psychologists to give us these details, although the explanation would probably involve a complex web of human instinct and social acclimation. It is the job of moral philosophers to give normative guidelines that remind us of our obligations and motivate us to perform them. We may briefly sketch here some of the images embedded in leading normative theories.

One image is that of what we may call the "moral saint," namely, the person who has mastered the art of ethical behavior and so achieved perfection. The moral saint knows precisely what it takes to be moral and, more importantly, will always act in the proper manner. One of the oldest illustrations of the moral saint is in the Book of Proverbs from the Hebrew Bible. Several proverbs focus on the admirable attributes of the "wise person" in contrast to the reprehensible behavior of the "foolish person." For example, "The wise store up knowledge; when a fool speaks, ruin is imminent" (Proverbs 10:14). The great Chinese philosopher Confucius takes a similar approach by describing the features of the superior person, who is unbiased, honest, consistent, cautious, humble, respectful, kind, studious, and righteous. Aristotle also takes this approach in his *Nicomachean Ethics,* which analyzes twelve principal virtues that the perfectly virtuous person should have. The hallmark of Aristotle's virtuous person is the ability to acquire moderate habits of behavior. For example, if we are habitually temperate in what we eat, then we will avoid the extremes of both gluttony and undereating. Some contemporary feminist ethicists depict the image of the moral saint as a nurturing, caring woman. The more we read the writings of Confucius, Aristotle, or feminist ethicists, the more complete a picture we get of the moral saint, which will then serve as a model for what we should become.

A second image is that of a peaceful society, particularly that presented in Thomas Hobbes's social contract theory and similarly by Chinese philosopher Mo-tzu (480–390 BCE). Hobbes in fact paints two images, one bad and one good. The bad image is a state of war in which selfish people brutally compete with each other to acquire life's necessities. The good image is that of a peaceful society in which people mutually agree to give up some of their freedom in exchange for the cooperation of others and protection from the government. For Hobbes, then, we should picture our moral obligations in terms of preserving a peaceful society through mutual agreements.

A third image is that of a codebook of moral law. We all understand how political laws are mandated by governments and how we incur stiff penalties if we violate those laws. Parallel to this, we can picture morality as a collection of laws that are mandated by God or nature, which also provide penalties if we violate them. This is one of the more common normative images presented worldwide, and it is especially prominent in religious texts, such as the Ten Commandments in the Hebrew Bible. The most philosophically sophisticated versions of this approach are the duty theories of Samuel von Pufendorf through W. D. Ross. According to these philosophers, we should picture immoral actions as crimes that violate our various duties to God, ourselves, or others; moral actions, by contrast, follow our required duties. The specific moral image behind this theory is a codebook of moral law that we should all abide by. A fourth and often related image is that of our territories of freedom, which we find in rights theories beginning with John Locke. For Locke, my rights to life, health, liberty, and possessions involve an area of freedom that surrounds me, and within this area I can exercise my rights as I see fit. When people violate my rights, they encroach on my territory and restrict my freedom. Morality, then, primarily involves not encroaching on someone's territory of freedom.

A fifth image is that of my future happiness. According to ethical egoists, my moral conduct should be directed by whatever will serve my long-term best interests. When acting, then, I should focus on the image of my future happiness and reject the kinds of actions that hinder my achieving this goal. Related to this is a sixth image involving a happy society. Utilitarians such as John Stuart Mill maintain that the best course of action is that which tends to produce the greatest happiness for the greatest number of people, and so the goal of our actions is to create the happiest society that we can. I should then reject the kinds of actions that go against the image of a happy society.

A seventh image, suggested by Immanuel Kant, is that of the dignified person. For Kant, humans are special because of our ability to make free choices and shape the world around us. This ability gives us dignity, and even the worst criminals among us are valuable because of this dignity. When acting, then, we should keep in mind the image of everyone as dignified individuals and treat people respectfully. An eighth image is that of the moral judge, who listens to the best arguments for and against a course of action and then determines which is most reasonable. This is the approach taken by Kurt Baier and other advocates of the best reasons ethical theory. When acting, we should keep in mind the image of a rational judge and make sure that the action we choose can be backed by the best reasons.

All eight of these images serve the same purpose—namely, to remind us of our moral obligations and to motivate us to carry them out. Based on these images, then, why is it wrong to steal? For eight reasons: (1) because a moral saint wouldn't steal, (2) because stealing threatens the existence of a peaceful society, (3) because stealing goes against the codebook of moral law, (4) because stealing encroaches on someone else's territory of freedom, (5) because stealing is not conducive to your future happiness, (6) because stealing is not conducive to a happy society, (7) because stealing does not respect the dignity of the person from whom you are stealing, and (8) because a moral judge would decide that stealing is not supported by the best reasons.

Common-Life Normative Images   In addition to the normative images that philosophers give us in their theories, there are other normative images that we draw on more informally in common life. Although less sophisticated than philosophical normative images, people probably think about these images in their moral conduct more often than they do philosophical images. One image is that of a supernatural moral spectator—that is, a person that watches us and approves or disapproves of our actions. Suppose I am considering stealing a car. I might believe that a supernatural being is literally monitoring my behavior and that this being will be disappointed with me if I choose to steal. Not wanting to disappoint my supernatural spectator, I decide not to steal. The supernatural spectator may be God, a saint, or a deceased family member. Many cultures show special reverence for their ancestors and view the spirits of the dead as extensions of their living families. In their spiritual state, the ancestors see what goes on among their living descendants, and the living are continually reminded to not offend the ancestors through immoral behavior. In addition to literal supernatural spectators, we might also think more figuratively and simply imagine what loved ones would think of our behavior. For example, what would my mother think if I stole a car? I may similarly look at a family photo and think about how my spouse and children would feel if I did something immoral. The key to the image of the moral spectator isn't so much the fear of punishment by the spectator as the guilt that we might experience simply by disappointing the spectator.

A second common image is that of supernatural moral punishment, whereby we are penalized for our immoral deeds in a realm beyond that of our ordinary lives. In this view, although some of our immoral actions may escape detection and punishment by people on earth, there are larger cosmic forces that keep an accurate tally of our conduct. Many Eastern religions hold to the doctrine of karma, which holds that we will suffer for our immoral actions in a reincarnated life. Thus, for example, if we are bad enough in this life, then in our next life we may be born with bad health or into a poor family with no prospect of financial success. To ensure that my next life is at least as favorable as my present life, I need to be on my morally best behavior. Western religions present the image of hell, a place of torment that God sends us to when we don't meet God's expectations. The Roman Catholic image of purgatory tells us that, before we can get to heaven, God will send us to a transitional spiritual location in which we must counterbalance all of our evil actions with good actions. In addition to images of punishment in an afterlife, there is a similar view that larger forces of fate are at work to make sure that, even in this life, what comes around goes around. Perhaps I shouldn't steal because fate may punish me by having someone burglarize my house.

Philosophers see many of these common-life normative images as superstitious, and for that reason, they have little interest in refining them. In fact, says Hume, the job of philosophy is to provide an "antidote [to] superstition and false religion." So, according to Hume's reasoning, philosophers should reject these images and offer more scientifically grounded moral theories. However, just as we don't want to take philosophical normative images literally—such as conceptions of a happy society—we may not wish to take these common-life images literally either. When I think about how my mother would react if she saw me steal a car, I clearly don't literally believe that she *can* see me. This is merely an image that captures my imagination. Similarly, even if I don't believe in ancestral spirits, reincarnation, hell, purgatory, or cosmic fate, these images may be intriguing enough to capture my imagination and guide my conduct.

Metaethical Images   We've seen that the job of normative theories is to offer moral guidance for our actions. The second main area of moral theory is **metaethics**. Metaethical theories don't attempt to give moral guidance; instead, they explain where morality comes from and what we are really doing when we make ethical judgments. There are a wide range of metaethical theories, and as with normative theories, we can find practical value in terms of the images that they offer. Metaethical images help us visualize the underlying nature of morality, which might similarly motivate us to do the right thing.

One metaethical image is that of a morally relative society—that is, a society that creates its own traditions and moral values. Protagoras (485–420 BCE) and Sextus Empiricus (fl. 200 CE) believed that different societies create different moral standards and that social approval within those societies is the complete justification for all these standards. If we interpret this theory literally—as a factual claim about the nature of morality—it would quickly conflict with rival metaethical claims. If we hope to move beyond metaethical disputes, we must set aside its literal claim and search for the larger concerns of cultural relativists that prompt them to advance their theory. We can uncover the relativists' concerns by considering what they are mainly reacting against. A major concern of cultural relativists is that we are often unfairly biased against moral views that are different from our own. I may look at the customs of people in China and reject them simply because they are different from my own customs. By entertaining the image of a morally relative society, we may be less biased against the customs of other cultures.

A second metaethical image is that of a higher moral reality—that is, a spiritual realm that houses moral truths. Plato argued that there is an unchanging, spiritlike realm of the forms beyond the changing physical world around us, and within that higher realm we find perfect moral forms. Inspired by Plato, Ralph Cudworth (1617–1688) argued that moral principles are eternal truths that exist in a higher spiritual realm. Plato and those he inspired are concerned that we might see morality as merely a feature of the changing and inferior world around us. Morality is a quest for perfection, and the image of higher moral reality conveys this vision.

A third image is that of a rationally ordered universe in which everything—including morality—follows a logical order and has a rational purpose. From Aquinas onward, natural law theorists believed that human nature reflects the rational plan of the universe, and we discover morality through human reason. Natural law theorists are concerned that we might be irrational or arbitrary in our assessment of morality. Instead, there is a uniformity in what morality demands of us all, and we can see this in the image of a rationally ordered universe.

A fourth image is that of divinely commanded morality, which involves a picture of a supremely powerful creator who authors moral standards and commands all people to follow them. We find this view in the divine command theories of Scotus and Pufendorf. These philosophers were partly motivated by strong religious convictions and the desire to preserve as much of God's authority as possible. However, they also had a specifically moral concern that people might lose sight of the urgency of their moral obligations. That is, even if I acknowledge the correct set of moral obligations, I may not think that they are very important. Divine command theorists expressed the urgency of moral obligation in the most authoritative means available, which we find in the image of divinely commanded morality.

A fifth image is that of an evolving society, which progressively places greater emphasis on the well-being of others and less emphasis on personal interest. According to Herbert Spencer's (1820–1903) conception of evolutionary ethics, we are presently at a highly evolved state of moral development, although not quite as developed as we should be. Spencer is concerned that we might restrict our view of morality to our present stage of social development, which needs improvement. The image of an evolving society emphasizes the hope that we will rise above our current moral limitations.

A sixth and final image is that of people expressing their feelings, which depicts people shouting "Hooray!" for conduct that they approve of and "Boo!" for conduct that they disapprove of. The nature of morality, then, is largely an issue of human emotional responses, and not an issue about facts such as personal or social happiness. In their emotivist theories, A. J. Ayer (1910–1989) and Charles Stevenson (1908–1979) are concerned that we might be misled by unfounded factual claims about the nature of morality, and the image of people expressing their feelings emphasizes the nonfactual components of morality.

Again, these six theories might conflict with one another if we understand them as literal descriptions about the nature of reality; but they don't conflict if we understand them only as images that convey various concerns about the true but hidden nature of morality. In that light, we can benefit from considering the complete range of metaethical images that traditional philosophers offer.

To summarize, here are the main points of the view regarding the moral images that we've discussed:

- Moral images are concepts that help us visualize the nature of morality, and the more traditional images we entertain, the more complete our understanding of morality will be.

- Various normative images remind us of our moral obligation and motivate us to act properly.

- Various metaethical images help us visualize different concerns about the hidden nature of morality.

- From a nonphilosophical common-life perspective, the primary value of traditional moral theories rests in the variety of moral images that they offer.

Study Questions

Introduction

1. What does Fieser mean by an "isolationist approach" to moral theories?
2. In what way were moral theories of the past eclectic?
3. What does Fieser mean by an "ethical supertheory"?

An Ethical Supertheory

    4. Describe the differing psychological roles of agent, receiver, and spectator.

The Duties and Virtues of the Agent

    5. What are virtues, and what is their function regarding our various duties?

    6. How does Kant encapsulate our duties of equity and duties of benevolence?

    7. What is the first way in which the agent uses moral reflection?

    8. In what way are our various duties tentative?

Rights, Virtues, and Consequences Regarding the Receiver

    9. Why doesn't the term "rights" make sense when we think of the demands that a receiver places on him- or herself?

  10. What is involved in the virtue of proper assertiveness?

  11. Why does Fieser think that it is too limiting to explain the consequences of an act in terms of the pleasure or preferences of a receiver?

The Spectator's Spontaneous and Reflective Assessments

  12. Explain the difference between the spectator's spontaneous assessment and delayed assessment.

  13. What are the two sets of facts that are relevant to the spectator's assessment of an agent's conduct?

  14. What is involved in the virtue of impartiality?

Moral Reflection and the Source of Moral Intuitions

  15. What are the three ways that moral intuitions are involved in morality?

  16. How do natural inclinations form our moral intuitions?

  17. What is the role of social reciprocity in forming our moral intuitions?

  18. What role does social tradition play in forming our moral intuitions?

Isolationist Ethical Theories versus an Ethical Supertheory

  19. What is the downfall of many isolationist moral theories?

Moral Images

The Function of Moral Images in Common Life

  20. What is a moral image?

The Normative Image of the Golden Rule

  21. What is Augustine's criticism of the Golden Rule?

  22. What image is conveyed by the Golden Rule?

Philosophical Normative Images

  23. Briefly list the eight philosophical normative images.

Common-Life Normative Images

  24. What are some of the traditional conceptions of the image of supernatural moral punishment?

Metaethical Images

  25. Briefly list the six metaethical images.

References

The earlier chapters in this book discuss the component parts of the ethical supertheory and the theories behind the various normative images.

The various quotations of the Golden Rule are adapted from *The World's Great Scriptures*, edited by Lewis Browne (New York: Macmillan, 1946), p. xv.

The quotation by Augustine is from *On Free Choice of the Will*, translated by Anna S. Benjamin and L. H. Hackstaff (Indianapolis: Bobbs-Merrill, 1964), Book 3.

The quotation by Hume is from "Of Suicide," included in *Essays: Moral, Political, and Literary*, which is available in several recent editions.

Glossary

absolute power, argument from Voluntarist argument that, insofar as God has absolute power, God has the ability to create moral standards.

Academy Ancient Greek school founded by Plato that became skeptical a few generations after Plato's death.

act-utilitarianism A version of utilitarianism associated with Bentham that advocates tallying the positive and negative consequences of each act performed; this is in contrast to rule-utilitarianism.

agent (moral) The psychological role that a person plays when performing an action that affects a moral receiver; this notion is associated with the moral receiver and moral spectator.

Albee, Ernest (1865–1929) American philosopher who criticizes Mill's utilitarianism insofar as higher pleasures are inconsistent with hedonism.

Anscombe, Elizabeth Contemporary British philosopher who criticizes modern moral theories for inconsistently developing the notion of moral rules.

applied ethics A branch of moral philosophy that attempts to resolve a wide range of moral controversies in different areas of human activity, such as abortion, suicide, capital punishment, and homosexuality.

Aquinas, Thomas (1225–1274) Medieval philosopher who developed the definitive medieval account of natural law theory.

Aristotle (384–322 BCE) Ancient Greek philosopher who argued that morality involves the development of virtues.

Ayer, A. J. (1910–1989) British philosopher who advocated logical positivism and the moral theories of emotivism and prescriptivism.

Baier, Kurt Contemporary philosopher who advocates the best reasons approach to moral philosophy—namely, that the morally right course of action is simply the one that is supported by the best reasons.

Balfour, James (1705–1795) Scottish philosopher who criticized the theory of cultural relativism.

Bentham, Jeremy (1748–1832) British political philosopher whose classic statement of utilitarianism involves calculating units of pleasure from each of our actions.

best reasons ethics A moral theory associated with Stephen Toulmin and Kurt Baier that the morally right course of action is simply the one that is supported by the best reasons.

Bradley, F. H. (1846–1924) British idealist philosopher who criticized utilitarianism for conflicting with ordinary moral judgments.

Burke, Edmund (1729–1797) Irish philosopher who opposed natural rights theory for being too abstract.

Calvin, John (1509–1564) French Protestant reformer who advocated the voluntarist view that God creates moral standards.

Cambridge Platonists A seventeenth-century British philosophical movement at Emmanuel College, Cambridge, that repudiated Calvinistic voluntarism.

cardinal virtues The four primary virtues in Plato's theory—namely, wisdom, courage, temperance, and justice.

categorical imperative A central principle in Kant's moral theory—namely, "Act only on that maxim by which you can at the same time will that it should become a universal law."

Cicero (106–43 BCE) Eclectic Roman philosopher who discusses moral duties and provides an early account of natural law.

Clarke, Samuel (1675–1729) British moral philosopher of the natural law tradition who argued that moral laws are grounded in eternal moral relations.

cognitivism The theory that moral utterances are factually descriptive.

Cooper, Anthony Ashley (the Earl of Shaftesbury) (1671–1713) British moral philosopher who advocated that humans have a moral sense that perceives right and wrong conduct in others.

Cudworth, Ralph (1617–1688) British Cambridge Platonist philosopher who argued that morality is grounded in unchanging eternal truths.

cultural relativism The theory that moral obligations are grounded in the approval of social cultures.

Darwin, Charles (1809–1882) British biologist who argued that through human evolution we acquired moral faculties and through social evolution we develop moral standards.

descriptive utterances Utterances that are factually descriptive and are either true or false; this is in contrast to performative utterances.

descriptivism See *cognitivism*.

direct duties A term in duty theory referring to a moral obligation toward someone who has a claim against us; direct duties are contrasted with indirect duties.

divine command theory The moral theory, also known as voluntarism, that moral standards are completely created by God's will.

duty theory (traditional) A moral theory originally arising out of the natural law tradition according to which we judge moral conduct in reference to an intuitive list of duties, typically to God, ourselves, and others.

emotivism The theory that moral utterances are principally performative and express our feelings; this theory is associated with prescriptivism.

Epicurus (341–270 BCE) Ancient Greek philosopher and founder of the Epicurean school that emphasized achieving happiness by minimizing pain and pursuing pleasure.

Euthyphro puzzle A problem articulated by Plato as to whether the gods create moral standards or whether they abide by moral standards external to them.

evolutionary ethics A nineteenth-century theory of ethics associated with Darwin and Spencer that explains morality in terms of biological and social evolutionary forces.

feminine ethics A feminist approach to ethics maintaining that moral theory should be modeled after women's experiences and focus on appropriately caring for others in each unique circumstance.

forms, theory of Plato's theory that the reality of things is located in a spirit realm containing the archetypes of objects and concepts, including moral concepts.

formula of the end itself A version of the categorical imperative in Kant's theory maintaining that we should treat people as an end in itself, and never as a means to an end.

formula of the law of nature A version of the categorical imperative in Kant's theory—namely, "Act as if the maxim of your action were to become through your will a universal law of nature."

Golden Rule A general moral principle that we should act toward others in ways that we would want others to act toward us.

Good, the In Plato's philosophy, the highest form and the ultimate source of moral perfection.

Grote, John (1813–1866) British moral philosopher who criticized Mill's utilitarianism insofar as it perpetuates the morality of the status quo.

Grotius, Hugo (1583–1645) Dutch natural law philosopher who developed a system of international law.

Hare, R. M. Contemporary British moral philosopher associated with the notions of prescriptivism and ideal utilitarianism.

hedonism A moral theory associated with Epicurus and utilitarians that humans are pleasure seeking and that pleasure is the criterion of moral goodness.

hedonistic utilitarianism The utilitarian theory associated with Bentham and Mill that we should maximize total pleasure; this is in contrast to ideal and preference utilitarianism.

higher pleasures A notion associated with Mill's utilitarian theory that higher intellectual pleasures are qualitatively superior to lower bodily pleasures.

Hobbes, Thomas (1588–1679) British philosopher who presented the most complete early account of social contract theory.

human rights A term in rights theory referring to moral rights that we have universally by virtue of being human.

Hume, David (1711–1776) Scottish skeptical philosopher who argued that morality is a matter of feeling and not rational judgment.

Hutcheson, Francis (1694–1747) Irish/Scottish moral philosopher who advocated that humans have a moral sense that perceives right and wrong conduct in others.

Huxley, Thomas (1825–1895) British evolutionary biologist who argued against evolutionary ethics.

Hyde, Edward (1609–1674) British politician who criticized Hobbes for denying the eternal and immutable status of morality.

hypothetical imperatives In Kant's theory, the obligations that are of the form "If you want *some thing,* then you must do *some act*"; this is in contrast to the categorical imperative.

ideal utilitarianism The utilitarian theory associated with G. E. Moore that we should maximize total good as we intuitively perceive good; this is in contrast to hedonistic and preference utilitarianism.

imperfect duties A term in duty theory referring to duties such as charity that do not require precise behavior and that are not justifiably backed by punishment; imperfect duties are contrasted with perfect duties.

indirect duties A term in duty theory referring to a moral obligation toward someone because of a claim that a third person has against us; indirect duties are contrasted with direct duties.

individual relativism The theory that moral obligations are grounded in each person's own approval.

intellectualism The moral theory that moral standards exist independently of God's will and that God endorses them only through his reason; this view stands in contrast to voluntarism.

intuitionism A nineteenth-century term for duty theory, especially insofar as moral duties are grounded in foundational commonsense intuitions.

***is/ought* problem** A problem pointed out by Hume that many moral theories attempt to derive *ought* from *is;* for Hume, no collection of facts will ever entail a judgment of value.

isolationist ethical theories Theoretical approaches to ethics, largely since the nineteenth-century, that emphasize one dominant theoretical notion, such as rights or consequences, and reject other notions as rivals.

Kant, Immanuel (1724–1804) German philosopher who argued that morality consists in following a supreme rule of reason—namely, the categorical imperative.

legal rights A term in rights theory referring to rights that are creations of governments and do not apply universally to all humans. Legal rights are associated with positive rights and civil rights; they are also in contrast to natural, human, and moral rights.

Locke, John (1632–1704) British philosopher who argued that, in the state of nature, we have natural rights to life, health, liberty, and possessions.

Luther, Martin (1483–1546) German Protestant reformer who advocated the voluntarist view that God creates moral standards.

MacIntyre, Alasdair Contemporary virtue theorist who stresses the importance of grounding virtues in social traditions.

Mackie, John L. (1917–1981) Australian philosopher who defended cultural relativism and moral skepticism.

Marx, Karl (1818–1883) German political philosopher and founder of communism who criticized rights theory for failing to be community oriented.

mean, doctrine of Aristotle's view that virtues lie at a mean between two more extreme vices.

metaethics Ethical theories that investigate where our moral principles come from and what they mean.

Mill, John Stuart (1806–1873) British philosopher who advocated utilitarianism and emphasized the difference between higher and lower pleasures.

mind-body problem Philosophical issue involving how mental events connect with bodily acts.

Montaigne, Michel Eyquem de (1533–1592) French philosopher influenced by the Pyrrhonian skeptical tradition, who defended cultural relativism.

Moore, G. E. (1873–1958) British philosopher associated with the concepts of the naturalistic fallacy and ideal utilitarianism.

moral nihilism The theory that there are no binding moral values at all.

moral objectivism The theory that morality has an objective foundation that is independent of human approval; this theory is in opposition to moral relativism.

moral relativism The general moral theory that moral values are *human* inventions; this theory includes both individual relativism and cultural relativism.

moral rights A term in rights theory referring to rights that apply universally to all humans and that are not creations of governments; moral rights are in contrast with legal rights.

moral sense theory A moral theory associated with Shaftesbury and Hutcheson that we have a sixth moral sense that perceives right and wrong conduct in others.

moral skepticism The theory that there are no objective moral values.

natural law theory The theory that God endorses specific moral standards and fixes them in human nature; we discover these standards through rational intuition.

natural rights A term in rights theory referring to moral rights that we have universally as are naturally conferred on us.

naturalistic fallacy A moral concept advocated by G. E. Moore that we commit a fallacy when we identify moral goodness with some quality, such as pleasure.

negative rights Rights to be left alone, which include the freedom to perform various liberties and the freedom from various harms; this is in contrast to positive rights.

noncognitivism The theory that moral utterances are principally performative and not factually descriptive.

normative ethics Ethical theories that arrive at moral standards that regulate right and wrong conduct.

Ockham, William of (c. 1285–1349) Medieval English philosopher who advocated the voluntarist view that God creates moral standards.

original position A notion in John Rawls's moral theory according to which people impartially devise rules of justice.

Paley, William (1743–1805) British moral philosopher who presented a theistic version of the theory of utility— namely, we should maximize utility since God would want us to be happy.

perfect duties A term in duty theory referring to duties such as keeping contracts that require precise behavior and that are justifiably backed by punishment; perfect duties are contrasted with imperfect duties.

performative utterances Utterances that are not factually descriptive but that accomplish some task with the implied injunction "I hereby . . ."

performativism See *noncognitivism.*

Plato (428–348 BCE) Ancient Greek philosopher who argued that truth is grounded in a higher spiritual level of reality—namely, the realm of the forms.

positive rights Rights to receive help from other people, also called welfare rights; this is in contrast to negative rights.

practical wisdom A rational ability in Aristotle's virtue theory that helps us find the virtuous mean.

preference utilitarianism The utilitarian theory associated with R. M. Hare that we should maximize our preferences; this is in contrast to hedonistic and ideal utilitarianism.

prescriptivism The theory that moral utterances are principally performative and prescribe behavior; this theory is associated with emotivism.

prima facie duty A term introduced in the duty theory of W. D. Ross that refers to duties that are tentatively binding until they are outweighed by a stronger duty.

prisoner's dilemma A notion in social contract theory that explains the warring condition of the state of nature by paralleling it to a prisoner who turns in an accomplice to receive a lighter sentence.

Protagoras (485–420 BCE) Ancient Greek Sophist who is famous for the individual relativist position statement that "Man is the measure of all things."

Pufendorf, Samuel von (1632–1694) German natural law philosopher who presents a systematic theory of moral duties to God, oneself, and others.

Pyrrho (c. 365–275 BCE) Ancient Greek moral philosopher who argued that nothing is truly good or bad and that we must suspend judgment about moral matters.

Rachels, James Contemporary American moral philosopher who opposes cultural relativism.

Rawls, John Contemporary American moral philosopher who, inspired by social contract theory, establishes rules of justice in a hypothetical original position.

receiver (moral) The psychological role that a person plays when being affected by an agent's conduct; this notion is associated with the moral agent and moral spectator.

Reid, Thomas (1710–1796) Scottish philosopher of the commonsense tradition who opposed Hume's view that moral approval is only a feeling.

relations, moral A notion in the moral theory of Samuel Clarke that moral laws are grounded in eternal moral relations; similar to mathematical relations.

revoking previously established moral laws, argument from Voluntarist argument that, insofar as religious texts depict God as revoking previously established moral laws, God has creative power over these moral laws.

rights theory A moral theory arising out of the natural law tradition according to which we have basic rights that are not creations of governments; related to this theory are natural, human, and moral rights.

Ross, W. D. (1877–1971) British philosopher who defended intuitionist duty theory.

Rousseau, Jean-Jacques (1712–1778) French philosopher who argued that the state of nature is a condition of creativity.

rule-utilitarianism A version of utilitarianism that advocates acting according to rules insofar as the adoption of such rules benefits the greater good; this is in contrast to act utilitarianism.

Schopenhauer, Arthur (1788–1860) German idealist philosopher who argued that Kant's categorical imperative reduces to egoism.

Scotus, John Duns (c. 1266–1308) Medieval Scottish philosopher who advocated the voluntarist view that God creates moral standards.

Sextus Empiricus (fl. 200 CE) Greek philosopher of the Pyrrhonian skeptical tradition who defended cultural relativism.

Shaftesbury, the Earl of (Anthony Ashley Cooper) (1671–1713) British moral philosopher who advocated that humans have a moral sense that perceives right and wrong conduct in others.

Sidgwick, Henry (1838–1900) British moral philosopher who defended utilitarianism.

social contract theory The moral theory first developed by Thomas Hobbes that, to preserve our lives, we mutually agree to set aside our hostilities and live in peace.

social diversity, argument from The argument that cultural relativism is a better explanation of social diversity than is moral objectivism.

Socrates (469–399 BCE) Ancient Greek moral philosopher and teacher of Plato.

Sophists Ancient Greek philosophers who taught rhetoric and often had skeptical views about morality.

spectator (moral) The psychological role that a person plays when approving or disapproving of an agent's conduct; this notion is associated with the moral receiver and moral agent.

Spencer, Herbert (1820–1903) British evolutionary philosopher who argued that mutual cooperation is our most evolutionarily advanced conduct, which produces universal pleasure.

state of nature A prepolitical environment described by Hobbes and other social contract theorists, which fosters conflicts and inclines us to form a contract to live in peace.

Stevenson, Charles L. (1908–1979) American philosopher associated with the moral theory of emotivism.

Suarez, Francisco (1548–1617) Spanish monastic philosopher who developed Aquinas's theory of natural law.

Sumner, William Graham (1840–1910) American sociologist who defended cultural relativism.

supertheory, ethical An ethical theory that systematically incorporates together the key elements of traditional moral theories; this is in contrast to isolationist ethical theories.

synderesis Greek term for "innate moral consciousness," which is a central part of medieval moral theories.

tacit consent The notion in social contract theories, such as Locke's, that we silently consent to the authority of governments when we receive benefit from governments.

theological virtues Three virtues noted in the New Testament—namely, faith, hope, and charity.

Thomas Aquinas (1225–1274) Medieval philosopher who developed the definitive medieval account of natural law theory.

Toulmin, Stephen Contemporary British philosopher who advocates the best reasons approach to moral philosophy—namely, that the morally right course of action is simply the one that is supported by the best reasons.

Universal Declaration of Human Rights Document adopted by the United Nations in 1948 that advocates a long list of human rights that apply to all people.

utilitarian calculus A notion associated with Bentham's utilitarianism that we can quantitatively calculate units of pleasure that result from our actions.

utility, theory of Moral theory associated with David Hume and William Paley that good actions are those that maximize utility; this theory was the immediate forerunner to utilitarianism.

veil of ignorance A notion in John Rawls's moral theory according to which we become ignorant of our social status while devising rules of justice in the original position.

virtue, moral A good character trait that regulates emotions and urges.

virtue theory The theory that the foundation of morality is the development of good character traits, or virtues.

voluntarism The moral theory, also known as divine command theory, that moral standards are completely created by God's will; this view is in contrast to intellectualism.

William of Ockham (1285–1349) Medieval English philosopher who advocated the voluntarist view that God creates moral standards.

Wilson, Edward O. Contemporary sociobiologist who argues that humans acquired conflicting senses of loyalty though evolution.

Xenophanes (570–475 BCE) Ancient Greek philosopher who defended cultural relativism with respect to religious beliefs.

Zeno of Citium (334–262 BCE) Ancient Greek philosopher and founder of the Stoic school that emphasized resigning oneself to fate.

Index